THIS DISTRACTED AND
ANARCHICAL PEOPLE

THE NORTH'S CIVIL WAR

Paul A. Cimbala, series editor

This Distracted and Anarchical People

*New Answers for Old
Questions about the
Civil War–Era North*

Edited by
Andrew L. Slap and
Michael Thomas Smith

FORDHAM UNIVERSITY PRESS
NEW YORK   2013

Fordham University Press has no responsibility for the persistence or accuracy of URLs for external or third-party Internet websites referred to in this publication and does not guarantee that any content on such websites is, or will remain, accurate or appropriate.

Fordham University Press also publishes its books in a variety of electronic formats. Some content that appears in print may not be available in electronic books.

Library of Congress Cataloging-in-Publication Data

This distracted and anarchical people : new answers for old questions about the Civil War–era North / edited by Andrew L. Slap and Michael Thomas Smith.
  p. cm. — (North's Civil War)
 Includes bibliographical references and index.
 ISBN 978-0-8232-4568-0 (cloth : alk. paper) — ISBN 978-0-8232-4569-7 (pbk. : alk. paper)
  1. United States—History—Civil War, 1861–1865. 2. United States—Politics and government—1861–1865. I. Slap, Andrew L. II. Smith, Michael Thomas, 1970–
 E468.9.T457 2013
 973.7—dc23

                2012023505

Printed in the United States of America

15 14 13 5 4 3 2 1

First edition

For our mentor,
Mark E. Neely Jr.

Contents

Foreword

Some forty years ago, I was a member of Mark Neely's PhD dissertation committee at Yale University and sat in on his defense of that thesis. It may surprise the contributors of essays to this volume on his behalf that the subject of that dissertation, if I remember it correctly—organic theories of society in antebellum America—had virtually nothing to do with the subjects about which he has subsequently written so perceptively and prolifically: Abraham Lincoln, the Civil War, and nineteenth-century politics and political culture. Neely's scholarship has consistently been characterized by certain virtues. The most basic concern his research. Not only has he been an indefatigable miner of often difficult-to-find-and-use primary sources strewn across the United States, but on occasion—here *The Boundaries of American Political Culture in the Civil War Era* comes to mind—he has also been extraordinarily imaginative in identifying surprisingly useful and revealing sources. Second, virtually all his published scholarship in essays as well as books displays a contrarian penchant for challenging the conventional, or at least the current, wisdom about the topics he addresses. These challenges, moreover, have frequently contained stunningly original insights. Probably the two best-known examples of his revisionist bent are the Pulitzer Prize–winning *Fate of Liberty: Abraham Lincoln and Civil Liberties*, in which he dramatically ratchets downward the number of so-called arbitrary arrests of civilians by the Lincoln administration during the Civil War; and *The Union Divided: Party Conflict in the Civil War North*, in which he sharply disputes the argument that two-party conflict was beneficial to the Union's war effort. Third, as a concomitant of the second, Neely leaves no doubt in readers' minds about his thorough command of the historiography relevant to the topic he is exploring. His fellow historians have not always agreed with him, but they have long known they must pay close attention to what he says.

Although not all eleven essays in this volume build directly on Neely's own lines of research, collectively they embody many of Neely's own strengths. All of them, for example, display a thorough command of the secondary literature relevant to their topics, and almost all rely on extensive research in primary sources. Several of them, moreover, do in fact provide additional verification of arguments first advanced by Neely himself. In "'A Press That Speaks Its Opinions

Frankly and Openly and Fearlessly': The Contentious Relationship between the Democratic Press and the Party in the Antebellum North," for example, Matthew Isham embraces Neely's point that much can be learned by paying close attention to nineteenth-century newspapers. Here Isham questions the fealty of the ostensibly partisan press. He shows that local Democratic newspapers often put government-aided development of local economies ahead of the official party line against any positive state aid to economic growth.

The essays by Robert M. Sandow and Matthew Warshauer examining Copperheadism in Pennsylvania and Connecticut confirm Neely's argument that the continuation of two-party competition during the war harmed rather than benefited the North's war effort. The very title of Warshauer's essay says it all: "Copperheads in Connecticut: A Peace Movement That Imperiled the Union." A significant subtheme of these essays, aside from the importance of Copperheadism outside the Midwest, is that Democratic resistance to the Union war effort was local in origin and organization rather than part of some nationally orchestrated conspiracy.

The essays by Jonathan W. White and Timothy J. Orr also echo Neely's concerns in *The Union Divided*. White's "'For My Part I Dont Care Who Is Elected President': The Union Army and the Elections of 1864" challenges the conventional wisdom that the Civil War converted most Union soldiers into supporters of Lincoln in 1864 and the Republican Party after the war. He focuses on soldiers who had no interest in voting for anyone and Democrats who loathed Lincoln but were often deterred from voting for George B. McClellan by either officers' pressure or their own distaste for the Democrats' peace platform and McClellan's running mate, George H. Pendleton. Whatever the reason, he maintains, Lincoln's four-fifths of the separate vote cast by soldiers in the field exaggerates the Republican Party's popularity among the troops. Democratic soldiers are in a sense the victims of White's story. In Orr's fascinating study, "'All Manner of Schemes and Rascalities': The Politics of Promotion in the Union Army," in contrast, Democrats are the villains. Relying imaginatively on extant records of state adjutant generals in northern states, who were responsible for recommending company and regimental promotions to their governors, Orr demonstrates how officers with Democratic proclivities both in the field and back in state capitals systematically blocked promotions of deserving soldiers with Republican loyalties. Here was another way, in short, where the continuation of two-party conflict in the North demonstrably hamstrung the Union war effort.

Whether the Civil War was the first "modern" or "total" war is another topic that attracted Mark Neely's attention, and it is clearly the pivot around which

Michael J. Bennett's contribution revolves. "The Black Flag and Confederate Soldiers: Total War from the Bottom Up?" argues that historians investigating the totality of the Civil War have focused too much on top-down strategies of so-called hard war against enemy civilians, and not enough on ground-up surveys of how soldiers on the battlefield treated wounded or captured foes. He does not attempt to compare how Union and Confederate soldiers acted in these situations, but his unflinching portrayal of Confederate savagery against helpless boys in blue is hair-raising. "How Confederates treated Yankee soldiers when they were not armed," he concludes, "spoke volumes about where the war was in terms of its totality, violence, and the breakdown of the values its participants endured."

The subject that first attracted Mark Neely's attention once he left graduate school was Abraham Lincoln. Michael Thomas Smith's interesting essay, "Abraham Lincoln, Manhood, and Nineteenth-Century American Political Culture," suggests that closer attention to matters of gender yields a better understanding of both Lincoln and his critics. "The role of masculinity in shaping both political discourse and political reality," he maintains, "remains underappreciated." During the war, he argues, all of Lincoln's critics, whether Republicans or Democrats, faulted Lincoln for lacking "forceful masculine qualities." Conversely, according to Smith, "it was at root gendered, masculine qualities that earned" Lincoln the "respect" of his supporters.

I have not read every word Mark Neely has written, but gender analysis does not strike me as something that has been on his front burner. Nor do I associate the topics of the remaining essays by Christian B. Keller, Karen Fisher Younger, Barbara A. Gannon, and Andrew L. Slap with anything in the work of Neely with which I am familiar. The essays on Liberia and Aunt Lucy Nichols, indeed, strike me as sui generis, for they are not as directly shaped by existing historiography as most of the other pieces collected here. The same is not true of Slap's piece on the marital patterns of black Union Army veterans after the Civil War. I must note here that Slap is the only author in this collection whom I personally know; I served as the outside reader of his PhD dissertation at Penn State several years ago. If Mark Neely has ever mentioned a word about southern freedmen's postwar marriages, I have never read or heard it. But Slap's intriguing essay reminds me of Neely's scholarship in two other ways. First, Slap has imaginatively located a primary source that is central to his investigation yet seems surprising to me. These are the petitions from and testimony by widows of black army veterans for federal pensions decades after the Civil War had ended. In short, it was precisely the military service of the black men involved in Slap's story that accounts for the recorded sources he could use to study it—rather like the federal records of civilian arrests Neely famously plumbed in *The Fate of Liberty*. Second, Slap here directly and convincingly challenges the conventional wisdom that black couples that had lived together in slavery immediately after the war sought to marry formally and legally. Instead, prewar patters of black cohabitation often continued for decades after 1865. Here is a fresh and important conclusion.

But one could make the same comment about this collection of essays as a whole. It is a fitting tribute to one of our most inventive and important historians of the Civil War era.

Michael F. Holt
University of Virginia

Acknowledgments

We, the editors and contributors, organized this volume to honor Mark E. Neely Jr., a historian whose scholarship speaks for itself. He has authored eight books, and coauthored another six, as of 2012, including the Pulitzer Prize–winning *Fate of Liberty: Abraham Lincoln and Civil Liberties*. Among his numerous articles is "Was the Civil War a Total War?" selected in 2004 as one of the three most influential articles in fifty years of *Civil War History*. Mark Neely's scholarship, grounded in primary sources and careful analysis, has consistently challenged established orthodoxies. For instance, he tackled the decades-old belief that the two-party system helped the North during the Civil War in *The Union Divided: Party Conflict in the Civil War North*, and contested an increasing acceptance of the harshness of the conflict in *The Civil War and the Limits of Destruction*. While not everyone has agreed with his conclusions, every historian of the era has had to contend with his arguments. He has profoundly shaped a number of important discussions in Civil War history, ranging from Lincoln's record on civil liberties to the effects of the northern political system to whether the Civil War was a total war.

Mark's prodigious and influential scholarship is even more impressive considering his career path. He got his PhD from Yale in 1973 with a dissertation on "The Organic Theory of the State in America," just after the academic job market in history collapsed. Mark spent twenty years as director of the Lincoln Museum in Fort Wayne, Indiana, doing his research and writing at night and on weekends. Mark did not get his first tenured position until 1992, the same year he won the Pulitzer Prize. After six years as the John Francis Bannon Professor of History and American Studies at Saint Louis University, Mark became the McCabe-Greer Professor of Civil War History at the Pennsylvania State University in 1998. It was as students at Saint Louis and Penn State that the contributors to this collection came to work with Mark.

The reason we wish to honor Mark is not his academic work, but what he has meant to us as a mentor. Mark taught us the same rigorous scholarship that he practiced himself, emphasizing the importance of following primary sources and carefully analyzing arguments. In many ways he fundamentally changed how we both think and process information. Mark demanded excellence, even if it meant draft after draft of a chapter or countless trips to the library and archives. Of course, he also inspired us, as we saw him spend hour after hour cranking microfilm in the dimly lit microforms room. He was generous with his time as well, spending hours talking with us in his office, returning a dissertation chapter within twenty-four hours of getting it so we could meet a deadline, or writing countless letters of recommendation. Many of us occasionally felt guilty about what he could have been accomplishing without spending his time trying to make us historians. But Mark did spend the time and energy, and for that we owe him our careers.

We were also fortunate to get to know Mark as a person. We discussed such different topics as tennis and Japanese woodblocks. We enjoyed the hospitality of Mark and his wife, Sylvia, when they invited us to their home. It says something about him that years after getting our degrees most of us remain in regular contact with Mark.

We would be remiss not to also acknowledge others who directly contributed to this book's creation. Paul Cimbala has published several of our books in his series at Fordham University Press and was an enthusiastic supporter of this project from the start. It has been a pleasure to work with Fredric Nachbaur, director of the Press, who made numerous suggestions to improve the volume. The readers for the Press, Michael Green and Brian Miller, both made constructive critiques of the essays and the volume as a whole. At an early stage, Gary Gallagher and Ken Noe both offered support and advice about editing essay collections.

Most important, though, we dedicate this book to our mentor, Mark E. Neely Jr., to whom we owe so much. Thank you.

THIS DISTRACTED AND
ANARCHICAL PEOPLE

Introduction

New Answers for Old Questions
about the Civil War–Era North

Andrew L. Slap and
Michael Thomas Smith

"Revising interpretations of the past is intrinsic to the study of history."
So begins Eric Foner's grand 1988 synthesis, *Reconstruction: America's Unfinished Revolution, 1863–1877*. Unlike most previous works on Reconstruction, Foner's starts in the middle of the Civil War with emancipation because first and foremost his theme is "the centrality of the black experience." According to Foner, "From the enforcement of the rights of citizens to the stubborn problems of economic and racial justice, the issues central to Reconstruction are as old as the American republic, and as contemporary as the inequalities that still affect our society." While the black experience is not central to James McPherson's Pulitzer Prize–winning *Battle Cry of Freedom: The Civil War Era*, also published in 1988, the preface makes clear the title is no accident. McPherson declares, "The multiple meanings of slavery and freedom, and how they dissolved and re-formed into new patterns in the crucible of war, constitute a central theme of this book." Acknowledging that at first the North did not fight to end slavery, McPherson insists that by late 1863, "the North was fighting for a 'new birth of freedom' to transform the Constitution . . . into a charter of emancipation." Foner's and McPherson's works have been the most important and influential books on the Civil War era in the last quarter century. In addition to their magnum opuses in 1988, both men have written many other books, trained dozens of leading historians, published some of the best-selling textbooks for U.S. history and Civil War courses, and in countless other ways shaped the study of the Civil War–era decades.[1]

Foner and McPherson, particularly in their master works, synthesized many other historians' original scholarship to become the most prominent leaders of an interpretation that might be called the Freedom School, which emphasizes emancipation as a major northern war aim and the most important result of the Civil War. Almost as important as emancipation to the Freedom School was the very transformation of the nation, which was often connected to emancipation. In a section titled "The World the War Made," Foner writes of Republicans, "In their unprecedented expansion of federal power and their efforts to impose organization upon a decentralized economy and fragmented polity, these measures reflected what might be called the birth of the modern American state." McPherson, meanwhile, insists that a "crucible fused the several states bound loosely in a federal *Union* under a weak central government into a new *Nation* forged by the fires of a war." The Freedom School has produced excellent scholarship and welcome changes from previous interpretations. It is vital never to forget the centrality of slavery as a cause of the conflict, the importance of the African American perspective, or the changes wrought by the Civil War era. Still, the now orthodox focus on the Civil War as a struggle for freedom and its transformative nature have obscured aspects of this important era, such as divisions within the North and continuity in the nineteenth century. The Civil War's sesquicentennial is an appropriate time to question interpretations of the conflict that have already predominated for a generation.[2]

The Freedom School was a needed reaction to previous generations of scholarship, which considered slavery and race to be secondary issues in the Civil War. Horrified by the bloodshed of World War I, many historians in the 1920s began arguing that the Civil War was a "needless war," caused by a blundering generation's inability to compromise, a conflict in which no substantive issues were at stake. Some historians, most notably Arthur M. Schlesinger Jr. in widely read article published in 1949, insisted that these revisionists were wrong and that the slavery was a moral issue on which there could be no compromise. Schlesinger's position, however, was overshadowed by a concurrent wave of nationalist historians who emerged in the years following World War II. Led by Allan Nevins, they saw the war as a costly but positive step toward the emergence of the United States as a stronger, more centralized nation and subsequently as a force for good in the world. This interpretation, though, still tended to overlook the critical importance of slavery and emancipation to the conflict. In the wake of the civil rights movement in the 1960s, historians rediscovered the centrality of slavery and race to the breaking and reforging of the Union, providing a valuable corrective to the arguments of scholars in the early and mid-twentieth century and contributing to the creation of the currently dominant paradigm.[3]

While Foner and McPherson have been two of the most prominent historians challenging previous interpretations of the Civil War era, the Freedom School has been a broad-based reinterpretation of the period. Some of the new scholarship naturally came from their many PhD students. For instance, Foner student

Melinda Lawson's nuanced study of nationalism in the Civil War North contends that the war revealed the fragility of the American idea as a basis of national unity and inspired many northerners to adopt European methods of nation building to "forge a new American national identity and patriotism." According to Lawson, "The war had profound centralizing effects on the nation's politics and economics: it gave rise, in effect, to the modern American nation state." In addition, Lawson argues that the war changed conceptions of American national identity and relationship with issues of race, insisting that "the Civil Rights Act of 1868 began the process of codifying some of those changes." Protégés of Foner and McPherson alone, however, would not have enabled Lawson to state properly that "most historians of the Civil War agree: the war, they argued, fostered a metamorphosis in American national identity." In fact, most historians of the Civil War era in the last generation have actively supported and espoused the central tenets of the Freedom School.[4]

Chandra Manning, for example, actually went beyond the standard interpretation of the Freedom School to argue that the Civil War can best be understood as an ideological crusade for American liberty in her provocative book *What This Cruel War Was Over: Soldiers, Slavery, and the Civil War*. Most Civil War historians in the last two decades have thought most Union soldiers initially opposed emancipation and only gradually became antislavery. In the standard work on why soldiers fought, McPherson argues, "By the summer of 1862, antislavery pragmatism and principle fused into a growing commitment to emancipation as both a means and goal of Union victory" and "that prevalence increased after the low point of early 1863 as a good many anti-emancipation soldiers changed their minds." Drawing heavily on previously little used regimental newspapers from the Union Army, Manning argues that Union soldiers early in the war overwhelmingly embraced the goal of ending slavery, making the war a genuinely revolutionary experience. The desire to punish the South for secession, the overwhelming urgency of the war effort, the good impression made by the determination and effectiveness of African American troops, and the desire to do what they increasingly conceived of as the will of God, all combined to produce a powerful commitment among Union soldiers to making the war one of liberation for the slaves. While conceding "backsliding" on the equal rights issue following the conflict, she stoutly insists that at the conclusion of the war, this emancipationist sentiment overwhelmingly held sway.[5]

David Blight focused on what happened to this supposedly dominant emancipationist sentiment in his 2001 prizewinning *Race and Reunion: The Civil War in American Memory*. According to Blight, three visions of Civil War memory have

collided and combined over time: the reconciliationist vision, the white suprem-
acist vision, and the emancipationist vision, the latter of which was "embodied in
African Americans' complex remembrance of their own freedom, in the politics
of radical Reconstruction, and in the conceptions of the war as the reinvention of
the republic and the liberation of blacks to citizenship and Constitutional equality." Not surprisingly for a scholar who states in the prologue that he has "in every
chapter . . . kept [his] eye on race as the central problem in how Americans made
choices to remember and forget their Civil War," Blight concludes, "In the end
this is a story of how the forces of reconciliation overwhelmed the emancipationist vision in the national culture, how the inexorable drive for reunion both used
and trumped race."[6]

Heather Cox Richardson cuts to the chase in the first sentence of *The Greatest
Nation on Earth: Republican Economic Policies during the Civil War*, the standard
work on northern economic policy since its publication in 1997. Richardson simply declares, "During the Civil War, Republicans transformed the United States."
She then expertly analyzes how the ideology of the Republican Party influenced
the huge and wide-ranging legislation that Congress passed during the war, con-
tending that "beginning in July 1861, when party members passed novel revenue
and confiscation laws, through the passage of the Thirteenth Amendment in
1865, the Republicans tailored fundamentally important national legislation in
accordance with their economic beliefs. As they did so, they articulated a new
national policy that altered the course of the nation."[7]

Michael Vorenberg, who was a graduate student at Harvard with Richardson,
also agrees that the Civil War transformed the nation. His book *Final Freedom:
The Civil War, the Abolition of Slavery, and the Thirteenth Amendment* argues that
the process of amending the Constitution to end slavery led Americans to believe
that they were in fact empowered to change the Constitution. While Vorenberg
nicely navigates the competing arguments over whether the Constitution did
more to shape the Civil War or the Civil War to shape the Constitution, he ultimately insists that "the amendment helped redirect Americans' attention to the
concept of a living Constitution and set the stage for the drama of constitutional
revision during the next seven decades."[8]

The books mentioned in the last few paragraphs are just a few of a multi-
tude published in recent decades that might be considered part of the Freedom
School. Even more books are being published for the Civil War sesquicentennial,
but many seem to be variations on the current interpretation as seen in some of
the most prominent works published in the first year of the war's anniversary. For

instance, David Blight revisits the connection between race and Civil War memory in *American Oracle: The Civil War in the Civil Rights Era*. David Goldfield clearly states his thesis in the title of his new book, *America Aflame: How the Civil War Created a Nation*. While emphasizing the often-neglected role of religion, Goldfield contends, "The Civil War was both the completion of the American Revolution and the beginning of a modern nation." Adam Goodheart insists in *1861: The Civil War Awakening* that slavery was not only the cause of this transformative conflict, but that "men and women at the time, on both sides of the conflict, did understand it as a war against slavery, even before it began." According to Goodheart, "Many white northerners and even some white Southerners were ready to say *Enough*. Enough compromise of principles; enough betrayal of people and ideals; enough cruelty; enough gradual surrender of what had been won in 1776." It is clear that the Freedom School remains the dominant academic interpretation of the Civil War.[9]

In recent years, though, some historians have begun to challenge aspects of the Freedom School. Unquestionably, slavery caused the Civil War, African Americans must remain key actors in the drama, and the conflict was a major event in U.S. history. Without denying the fine scholarship of the Freedom School, these historians have questioned whether this interpretation might require some qualifications—a slight adjustment, at least, to the prism through which we look at and try to understand the most massive trauma in American history. Edward L. Ayers, a former professor of history and dean at the University of Virginia before becoming president of the University of Richmond, directly challenged James McPherson and his historiographical allies in the 2003 prizewinning *In the Presence of Mine Enemies: The Civil War in the Heart of America, 1859–1863*. Many Americans looking to understand the Civil War, according to Ayers, "usually look close to the surface, seeing the North as a modern society in obvious conflict with an archaic South, the future in conflict with the doomed past." Singling out McPherson's *Battle Cry of Freedom* as the example of this interpretation, he contends that "these works of national affirmation, so beautifully rendered, emphasize the national redemption brought by the war's trial and sacrifice. . . . Nations need, and crave, such encouraging histories, films, and novels. But nations also need other kinds of stories if they are to use history wisely, if they are to learn all they can from their past." Ayers has since called for a "new revisionism" in Civil War scholarship, which he hoped would "place more distance between nineteenth-century Americans and us," in order to more accurately understand the conflict on its own terms. "Slavery and freedom," he asserted, "remain the keys to understanding the war, but they are the place to begin our questions, not to end them." Further, he hoped that this new wave would allow us to "recognize that the Civil War did not represent the apotheosis of American ideals."[10]

Gary Gallagher, a former colleague of Ayers at the University of Virginia, has long been a leader in challenging the orthodoxies of the Civil War era. Gallagher's prizewinning 1999 *The Confederate War* attacked the then prevailing interpretation that internal dissent was responsible for the Confederacy's defeat, emphasizing the persistence of popular will and nationalism within the Confederacy through four years of hard war. Gallagher's interpretation of the Confederacy was influential, and not just through his scholarship. Like Foner and McPherson, Gallagher has influenced the profession in a number of ways, including training dozens of PhDs and editing the prominent Civil War list at the University of North Carolina. Over a decade after *The Confederate War* Gallagher turned his revisionist lens northward in his 2011 volume *The Union War*. He argues that a desire to protect and preserve the Union's republican government drove the northern war effort, and not any particular desire to transform the nation. Northerners ultimately embraced the destruction of slavery as a means to this end, much more than as an end in itself. "The profound prejudice that existed in the United States between 1860 and 1880" was too powerful a limiting factor to allow for any really transformative social changes other than those necessitated by wartime demands. "The wartime generation maintained continuity regarding their principal goals in the war," namely, "to reunite the nation." Gallagher specifically took issue with Chandra Manning's contention that Union soldiers were strongly antislavery from early in the war, asserting that her source evidence was insufficient to merit this claim. The "Union war" was an ideological crusade for freedom, as Gallagher saw it, but its primary goal was the preservation of the country's somewhat exclusionary republican government and not the transformation of the nation.[11]

The response to *The Union War* demonstrates that a fierce debate is brewing over how to interpret the Civil War. Gallagher directly criticized Melinda Lawson in the book for not including soldiers and the military in her discussion of wartime nationalism in the North. Reviewing *The Union War* for the *New York Times*, Eric Foner spent an entire paragraph specifically taking Gallagher to task for criticizing Lawson. In an almost entirely negative review, Foner insists that Gallagher's "theme of continuity seems inadequate to encompass the vast changes Americans experienced during the Civil War." Passions may be rising among Civil War historians because the field is in flux, with scholars increasingly dissatisfied with interpretations that have dominated for decades but not certain about the future. In a state of the field article that Gallagher protégé William Blair commissioned for the *Journal of the Civil War Era* in 2011, Frank Towers considers Foner and McPherson central figures in a modernization interpretation of the Civil War that he thinks has guided scholarship about the cause of the conflict for the last half century. The modernization research agenda, according to Towers, "foregrounded slavery as the war's cause, situated within a global process of modernization." Significantly, though, he contends, "In the past decade, the modernization agenda has shown signs of collapse," citing a combination of synthesis and critique points in the recent literature similar to that which presaged the fall of previous interpretive paradigms about the Civil War. Finding that "the most striking thing about current research is its diversity and openness," Towers suggests that, "as in earlier transitions between research agendas, the present moment is one of possibilities. All students of the Civil War's causes would do well to take advantage."[12]

We mean to take advantage of the current ferment in the field, which is becoming profound enough that many scholars are beginning to notice. The contributors organized this volume a couple of years ago because they saw these growing debates about the very nature and meaning of the Civil War—which seem to occur every generation—as an opportunity to explore paradigms that have stood for decades. A pervasive acceptance of interpretations of complex issues can stifle learning and understanding. The contributors to this collection think that there is much to value in the scholarship and interpretations of the Freedom School and other long-standing paradigms—but that there is also much to gain in questioning the accepted wisdom. Interestingly and importantly, the contributors sometimes agree with certain interpretations of the Freedom School, or the modernization agenda, while disagreeing with others, and at times they even argue among themselves. The phrase "this distracted and anarchical people," used by William Tecumseh Sherman in reference to the difficulty of mobilizing and governing the North during the Civil War, could refer just as much to historians of the era.[13]

The first two essays explore ways in which existing paradigms have obscured important aspects of the Civil War era. Interpreting the Civil War as the genesis of modern America, as the Freedom School does, tends to suggest that the Republicans were the forces of modernism and anyone who opposed them was thus against "progress," including southerners and antiwar Democrats. Matthew Isham examines the Democratic press in the antebellum North and finds that these papers, which were pledged to promote party principles, often undermined those principles and generated intra-party factionalism by embracing the emerging market economy and economic legislation usually only associated with the Republican Party. While Isham complicates our understanding of Democrats and questions of modernization, Michael Smith injects issues of gender and masculinity into the study of Civil War politics. He argues that historians' emphasis on topics like race and economic modernization limited our understanding of the importance of gender and masculinity in the mid-nineteenth century. Building on the work of historians like Amy Greenberg, Smith contends that Abraham Lincoln combined two aspects of idealized manhood—aggressive masculinity and restrained manliness—to navigate the currents of Civil War–era politics.

Robert Sandow's and Matthew Warshauer's dueling essays on the nature of Democratic opposition to the war demonstrate both the vibrancy of debates over interpreting the Civil War and this volume's agnosticism. Jennifer Weber, a James McPherson protégé, has argued in *Copperheads: The Rise and Fall of Lincoln's Opponents in the North*, the current standard work on the subject, that Democratic opposition was a real threat to the Republican war effort. During the conflict Republicans called Democrats who opposed the war Copperheads after the snake, to signify that they were both secretive and dangerous, and the pejorative has remained with them ever since. Sandow insists that the pejorative name is unfair and Weber has taken Republican wartime propaganda at face value. Focusing on the Pennsylvanian Appalachians, one of the centers of wartime opposition in the North, Sandow acknowledges that Democrats did organize and resort to extralegal resistance, but contends that such dissent was largely grassroots and uncoordinated, posing no significant threat to the war effort. He argues that wartime opposition is normal throughout American history, and the extreme partisanship of the Civil War era's two-party system magnified this typical and legitimate dissent into an exaggerated danger for political purposes. Warshauer, meanwhile, comes to a completely different conclusion. He argues that the two-party system so inflamed partisanship that wartime politics in Connecticut provide ample evidence to support Weber's position. Warshauer insists that the Democrats' fierce and sometimes violent opposition posed a real and direct threat to the Union war effort.

While Sandow and Warshauer study how the two-party system affected the war effort on the home front, Timothy Orr explores the impact of the two-party system on the Union Army itself. He directly challenges the long-standing paradigm that a two-party system helped the North by channeling dissent into legitimate forms, thus dissipating its danger. Orr finds that partisan politics influenced military promotions, allowing less capable officers to take charge and causing friction within units. Thus Orr contends that the partisanship of the two-party system directly hurt the military capabilities of the Union Army, something that victory has long disguised. Also focusing on politics within the army, Jonathan White takes issue with McPherson's assertion that the large number of Union soldiers who voted for Lincoln in 1864 demonstrated the army's emancipationist sentiment. White uses letters to show that many soldiers voted for Lincoln as the lesser of two evils and that a significant number decided not to vote at all. White's analysis of letters and voting records therefore suggests that the importance of the overwhelming majority of soldiers voting for Lincoln is overstated and cannot be construed as representing broad support for emancipation. Christian Keller likewise has issues with McPherson's portrayal of the Union Army, albeit from a different perspective. Keller argues that while McPherson may be one of only a few "celebrity" Civil War historians who have utilized ethnicity as an interpretive lens (in his case, in *Battle Cry of Freedom*), he still spent only one paragraph on ethnic soldiers in *For Cause and Comrades*. Analyzing the extant literature on the Germans and Irish in the war, Keller contends that the importance of ethnicity in understanding the Civil War North has been neglected, and he discusses how some new work in the field could substantially change our interpretations of the conflict.

Michael Bennet contends that there are inconsistencies in the Freedom School's interpretation of the Civil War as simultaneously a redemptive national conflict and the first modern total war. Examining Confederate atrocities against Union soldiers, Bennet argues that white southerners so passionately hated the North that they frequently disregarded the rules of war. He thinks that historians have avoided accounts of atrocities because they represent everything that the war was not supposed to be about: treachery, brutality, and killing without meaning. For Bennet, the unreasoning savagery made the conflict a total war, stripping the Civil War of its ideological and redemptive power.

The last three essays engage issues of race, but in different ways and with different results than the Freedom School. While Foner has long considered larger global dimensions of emancipation, many of the Freedom School, like Mc-Pherson, concentrate on emancipation as a story of national redemption for the United States. Karen Younger complicates this account by placing emancipation and issues of race in an international context. She examines the interaction between African Americans in the United States and Liberia to deepen our understanding of racial issues during the Civil War and beyond. One issue of race that historians have considered long settled was the effect of emancipation on African American marriage practices. For decades historians have thought that African American slaves quickly adopted legal and formal marriages after emancipation. Andrew Slap shows that many African Americans maintained traditional marriage practices for decades after the Civil War, suggesting that we should question to what extent the Civil War suddenly changed society and made the United States a "modern" nation. Barbara Gannon, meanwhile, investigates how the case of Lucy Nichols shows the complicated interactions of gender, race, and Civil War memory. Directly challenging David Blight's assertion that Union veterans abandoned the emancipationist vision of the war, Gannon argues that the Twenty-Third Indiana Volunteer Infantry's acceptance of Nichols as a member of their community proves that veterans long maintained a commitment to emancipation as a vital component of the war and its memory.

Ultimately, history is an argument. The sparks and spaces between competing arguments often provide the greatest insight into the past. Although an absolutely complete understanding of the Civil War will never be possible, we must take first steps first, however tentative. This book is meant to be tentative and suggestive. We mean mostly to replace pat answers with questions and to stimulate debate.

"A Press That Speaks Its Opinions Frankly and Openly and Fearlessly"

The Contentious Relationship between the Democratic Press and the Party in the Antebellum North

Matthew Isham

In 1851, Joseph Edward Gray, the successful owner–editor of the largest Democratic newspaper in Cleveland, Ohio, reflected on the virtues of the flourishing American press. Though the majority of American newspapers were partisan sheets dependent on subscriptions from voters and occasional patronage from party leaders, Gray described the press as a fiercely independent institution that served the public above all. He celebrated "a Press that speaks its opinions frankly and openly and fearlessly, that looks into and criticizes the action of the 'powers that be' and devotes itself—with a few exceptions—to the good of the mass—*the mass* by whom it is sustained."[1] This image of a stalwart, independent press belied reality, however. Partisan newspapers were not wholly independent, of course, and their editors never were able to express their own opinions as fearlessly as Gray maintained, particularly if they clashed with those of party leaders. Indeed, in the antebellum era, newspapers' political content was the subject of frequent and sometimes fierce clashes between editors and elements within their own parties. These intra-party conflicts spawned factional divisions that seriously weakened the Democratic organization in the North prior to the Civil War and exposed organizational fissures that would lead to the demise of the partisan newspaper network itself after the war.

Though partisan newspapers were vital instruments for recruiting party members and mobilizing voters, they also were a source of constant irritation to party leaders, who struggled to control their political content. Mark Wahlgren Summers has noted that party presses "were not easily kept in tune." Thomas C. Leonard went even further and argued that irresponsible reporting "outside the control of canny party operatives" seriously destabilized party politics in the antebellum period.[2] To try to keep them in tune, party leaders favored newspapers with inflated printing contracts for official party and government business. Though most editors did not rely on the party's largesse to keep the businesses solvent, Summers has argued that this patronage corrupted those who received it, effectively purchasing positive coverage of the party and its leaders. On the other hand, editors who failed to win these lucrative contracts recklessly and vindictively assailed the party that had spurned them. In the main, partisan editors were neither the greedy tools nor the vengeful mavericks portrayed by Summers. They sought patronage largely as recognition of their hard work and to enhance their status within both the party and their community. Consequently, editors' relationships with party leaders were marked by conflict, negotiation, and compromise, as they sought to serve the organization while also preserving a large measure of independence.

This essay examines the complicated relationship between Democratic editors and party leaders in the North during what was arguably the party's greatest period of success: the expansionist years of the Polk administration. Yonatan Eyal recently demonstrated that the project of continental expansion in the 1840s modernized the Democratic Party's economic outlook and dramatically altered its character, particularly in the North.[3] Expansion generated heated contests between party leaders, newspapers, and voters over the mission and future of their party. The annexation of Texas and the subsequent acquisition of Mexico's northern territories during the U.S.–Mexican War left the United States in possession of approximately 750,000 square miles of new land by 1848.[4] This tremendous accession of land inspired robust debates in the partisan press over how best to integrate the new territory into the United States, particularly concerning the related issues of internal improvements (to link the West and East together) and the potential westward expansion of slavery.

Seduced by visions of a gathering flood of commerce from the newest members of the Union, many Democratic editors in urban markets called for local and regional infrastructure developments that would allow communities throughout the North to tap into the burgeoning national market and transform national expansion into local wealth. Many also promoted liberal corporate charters, particularly for railroads, to attract private investment in such projects. This editorial boosterism was at odds with many of the North's rural Democrats, who lived far from urban market networks and had been impoverished by the depression caused by the Panic of 1837. According to Jonathan Earle, these Democrats clung to a radical egalitarianism that condemned slavery and unfettered (urban) capitalism as twin oppressors of the laboring masses. To illuminate these dual conflicts and illustrate their consequences for the party's northern wing, this essay will examine the chief Democratic journals in the cities of Portland, Maine, Albany, New York, and Cleveland, Ohio, all of which sought to tap into evolving national and international market networks that emerged in the wake of the country's continental conquests.[5]

The growth of newspapers and the establishment of political parties in the antebellum United States were intimately intertwined. As suffrage expanded among white men in the early nineteenth century, political news became a valuable commodity. Further, federal postal laws sharply discounted the cost of transporting newspapers through the mail, allowing editors to reach a large audience and to subscribe to a variety of newspapers themselves.[6] Democrats and Whigs further subsidized this ever-growing network of newspapers throughout the country, which gave them a national reach as well as a local presence in virtually every town of consequence. Their support practically guaranteed that many towns would have at least two newspapers, and often more, providing opposing political views. In an apt analogy, the editor of an antebellum political temperance journal likened the role of a party newspaper to the circulatory system in the human body: "It is the press that, like the heart, must send forth its constant, healthful, and invigorating pulsations, and keep the various parts of our organization in a condition for efficient action."[7] Parties benefited immensely from newspaper networks that expounded party creeds and helped turn out voters at the polls. Therefore, despite intermittent and sometimes debilitating conflict between editors and the parties, both groups needed each other.

The owner–editors of these journals were sincere in their party affiliation and their belief in their party's core principles, but they did not consider themselves or their newspapers mere party tools. Most editors personally compiled the eclectic content for their journals and typically penned each editorial themselves. Though readers would find similar themes in all Democratic papers, each newspaper remained unmistakably the individual creation of its editor, and these men were determined to preserve their freedom to conduct their journals as they saw fit. Glenn Altschuler and Stuart Blumin have argued that editors were responding to the tastes of their readers "when they wrote pieces boosting the local community in a nonpartisan fashion, and when they piously objected to the insertion of party into institutions and events that ought to remain 'above' politics."[8] Yet partisan editors were not merely playing it safe when they downplayed partisan messages in their newspapers. Rather, they were exercising their editorial freedom and demonstrating that they served their community and their readers ahead of their party.

In many ways, the individual character of these newspapers was an asset for parties reaching out to heterogeneous communities of voters. The frequency of publication (most antebellum partisan journals published at least three times per week) and the constant appearance of predictable political themes schooled readers in a vernacular language that identified them as Democrats and provided a common ground for communicating with fellow party members. Indeed, many Americans did not read newspapers individually, but rather in communal gatherings at the post office, the dry goods store, at court days, or other public venues. Whether in public or private, the reading of partisan newspapers was a repetitive ritual in which, as communications theorist James Carey succinctly described it, imparting information was of secondary importance to portraying and confirming "a particular view of the world."[9] This practice made newspapers ideal for building party identity. Jean Harvey Baker aptly noted that Democrats did not embrace a unitary ideology, but rather imbibed a set of shared attitudes that "served more as movable fences than as solid fences" in distinguishing them from their political opponents. Though she did not single them out, Democratic journals played a signal role in erecting those movable fences, shaping Democratic attitudes to fit the outlook of their readers in different communities.[10]

Democrats and Whigs initially had coalesced around rival economic programs, the former sharply opposed to government intervention in the economy and the latter animated by a desire to employ government wealth and power to shape and develop that economy. Whigs developed the grandiose American System, consisting of a national bank to manage the country's currency supply, a high tariff on imported goods to protect American manufacturing, and a program of internal improvements to link regional markets into a national web, funded with credit from the bank and proceeds from the tariff. Sean Wilentz has painstakingly demonstrated that Democrats did not necessarily oppose the dizzying growth of the market. Instead, they fought against "a commercial system run wholly by and foremost for capitalists" under the American System.[11] Yet Democratic editors in urban, commercial centers gradually abandoned this outlook as they became increasingly comfortable with a commercial system dominated by capitalists. This attitudinal shift brought bullish Democratic editors into collision with stalwart radicals, who castigated editorial deviations from the party's economic message.

This was particularly true in Maine where Democratic leaders immediately sought to translate the Polk administration's program of continental expansion into concrete benefits for the state. Democratic Governor John W. Dana noted that the new territory gave the country "an extent of coast on the Pacific almost equal to that on the Atlantic with a practical line of communication between the two oceans. Thus situated between Europe and Asia, we become the central point, and command the commerce of the world."[12] With Portland's spacious, protected deepwater harbor and the state's close sailing proximity to Europe, Maine figured to reap the benefits of transcontinental trade bound for overseas shipment.

In pursuit of that goal, the state's Democratic leaders vigorously supported the development of a railroad link between Portland and Montreal, Canada. Such a road would allow Portland to tap into the Great Lakes trade that coursed through Montreal and also attract English trade bound for Canada. Moreover, it would allow Portland to emerge from the shadow of Boston, whose railroad networks dominated New England and brought most regional trade to its own bustling harbor. Democratic legislators spearheaded the chartering of the Atlantic and St. Lawrence Railroad Corporation in Maine in February 1845, just before the outbreak of the Mexican War.[13]

William Pitt Preble, one of the founders of Maine's Democratic Party, worked tirelessly to solicit investment in this signal improvement project. He joined prominent Whigs in lobbying the state legislature to pass a bill authorizing the city of Portland to issue $1.5 million in city scrip to the railroad.[14] This broke with recent Democratic opposition to public investment in internal improvements, following the bankruptcy of many such projects in the North during the Panic of 1837. In response to that crisis, radical Jacksonian leaders placed sharp limits on states' abilities to pledge the public credit to so-called mixed corporations charged with executing public works. Indeed, the *Belfast Republican Journal*, situated in the state's rural mid-coast region, insinuated that railroad corporations requested public aid only to save themselves from crippling debt. Alarmed by the resumption of pledging public credit to corporations, its editor insisted that the state was not "established to stand in the position of the endorser of the credit of men or corporations when such men or corporations find that a foolish speculation or a gross miscalculation has periled their property."[15]

The *Republican Journal* gave voice to the concerns of party members in Maine's rural hinterlands who were wary of the Atlantic and St. Lawrence Railroad's desire to reconfigure the state's market networks. The railroad assumed considerable latitude to determine how other railroads would connect to its own line and the Portland market. The editors of the *Republican Journal* feared that the corporation sought to monopolize the rail traffic throughout much of the state, and their fears were soon confirmed by the behavior of the road's corporate board. The board chose a wide gauge for the railroad, in part to carry heavy freight but also to prevent smaller, narrow-gauge railroads from connecting with it. The board also rejected efforts by the directors of the Kennebec and Portland Railroad, which served central Maine and the mid-coast region, to negotiate a connection between the two roads that would have given the latter access to Portland. On another front, Charles Holden, editor of the state's largest Democratic daily, the *Portland Eastern Argus*, lobbied the legislature to forbid the chartering of parallel roads in close proximity to the Atlantic and St. Lawrence's lines. Together, these initiatives enabled the Atlantic and St. Lawrence to propose its own subsidiary rail links into the central Maine hinterlands, while enjoying protection from the competition of smaller, local roads like the Kennebec and Portland.[16]

This represented a dramatic break with radical Democratic attitudes toward exclusive charter rights and monopoly practices. Democratic antipathy for monopoly practices had been cemented in the landmark Supreme Court decision in the case of *Charles River Bridge v. Warren Bridge*. In that 1837 decision, Chief Justice Roger Taney argued that states could rescind exclusive privileges in the charters they granted for public works if the public need demanded it. He further decided that wherever a charter was vague in the rights it conveyed, the state legislature was free to interpret the charter to serve the best interests of the public.[17] This decision encouraged Democrats to equate exclusive corporate charters with monopoly practice.

Less than a decade removed from that decision, however, Holden glibly maintained, "as odious and dangerous as *monopolies* are considered, we never knew an instance of any corporation in the United States having a monopoly of anything." Discomfited by the party's broad interpretation of the Atlantic and St. Lawrence's charter rights, radical Democrats attempted to safeguard the public credit by introducing a bill into the legislature that required individual liability for all corporate stockholders. The *Eastern Argus* warned that the bill would scare off potential investors, and Holden rallied pro-development Democrats to defeat it with Whig help. The stupefied editor of the *Bangor Whig and Courier*, the leading Whig journal in eastern Maine, marveled that Maine's Democrats "are now eloquent in their praises of corporations—have forgotten they were once monopolies, and now out-whig the Whig party in supporting them."[18] Indeed, the *Eastern Argus* sanctioned the Atlantic and St. Lawrence Railroad's blatant and largely successful efforts to monopolize rail traffic throughout much of central and southern Maine.[19]

Decades later, John Poor, the man who first conceived of the Portland-to-Montreal rail link, asserted that certain Democrats had "made no secret of their design to throw party overboard on the railway question, and, if need be, break down their party in the State on it, rather than longer forego the advantages of railroads."[20] Holden and the *Argus* were in the vanguard of this controversial effort. Poor exaggerated these men's willingness to break up their party, but the railroad issue did divide Maine's Democrats sharply, and there was a pronounced drop in the Democratic vote in the state canvass in 1845, the year that the legislature incorporated the railroad. Temporarily weakened by this friction, the party nonetheless held together.[21]

Holden was not simply serving Democratic leaders like Preble and Dana when he promoted the railroad project and fended off the criticism of radical Democrats, however. Instead, he primarily was serving his fellow entrepreneurs. Though he was only a modestly successful businessman, Holden identified closely with the wealthy entrepreneurs who funded and directed the railroad's operations. The editor could not match these men's capital investment in the railroad, but his promotion of the project in the pages of his widely circulated newspaper made him indispensable to the railroad's success, and it elevated his social status, allowing him to claim an intimate association with the state's wealthiest and most dynamic businessmen.

Building on his association with these entrepreneurs, his paper consistently supported the interests of the company's largest investors ahead of the interests of the numerous small stockholders in Portland who had invested in the road at the paper's urging. In 1849, as the railroad was under construction, its board of directors announced that it would auction off all shares that were $35 or more in arrears (individual shares had been offered at $50 and sold with as little as $5 down). Auctioning off delinquent shares threatened to wipe out widespread public ownership of the road, which small investors had regarded as a "project of the people."[22] As chairman of the Democratic Central Committee and editor of the *Argus*, Charles Holden could have opposed the auction and redeemed the democratic pretensions of the Atlantic and St. Lawrence project. Instead, his paper urged the auction's swift completion in order to raise short-term capital to fund the road's construction to the Quebec border.[23] In his service to the corporate board, Holden did not hesitate to overhaul the party's economic principles to meet their needs, regardless of the outraged opposition of the railroad's dispossessed small investors or the party's radical core.

One might presume that Holden's dramatic makeover of the Democratic Party in Maine was a unique case. His and like-minded editors' zeal to modernize transportation networks and bridge the gap between the expanding local and national market systems, however, influenced them to supplant political principle with pragmatism and expedience. Even in those northern communities already well integrated into the market web, Democratic editors bucked tradition and challenged the authority of party leaders who were reluctant to embrace public investment in improvements. In upstate New York, for instance, Edwin Croswell of the Albany *Argus*, Isaac Butts of the Rochester *Republican*, and Henry Utley of the Rome *Sentinel* led a faction of so-called conservative, or pro-development, Democrats in challenging radicals for control of the state party.

In 1823 future President Martin Van Buren's vaunted Albany Regency, a group of politicians that controlled the New York Democratic Party, had tabbed the young Croswell to edit the *Albany Argus*, the party's mouthpiece. He initially distinguished himself for his loyalty and ferocity in pressing the Democratic cause, but he became increasingly disenchanted with the Regency's intensifying radicalism after the Panic of 1837. Like many other northern states, New York found itself nearly bankrupted by mounting debt on unfinished canal projects after the financial panic. State bonds had lost roughly 25 percent of their value, and in 1842 the legislature hastily passed the so-called Stop and Tax Law, which halted canal construction and mandated offsetting taxes for future improvement projects. This fiscal belt-tightening preserved the state's credit and shepherded it through the financial crisis, but Croswell feared that the Stop and Tax Law would prevent further improvements to the state's nonpareil canal system and stifle efforts to broaden and enhance its transportation network, namely through railroad construction.[24]

Specifically, Croswell worried that a recent railroad-building spree by Boston capitalists would siphon trade away from the Erie Canal and drastically reduce New York's commercial windfall. The editor repeatedly urged New York City capitalists to invest in a network of upstate railroads that would erect a "system of commercial defence against the rivalry of Boston" and preserve New York City's position as the nation's premier commercial emporium. The Rome *Sentinel* and several other small Democratic papers in communities that stood to benefit from railroad links echoed Croswell's call for increased investment in improvements. Beyond the immediate desire to preserve New York's commerce against poaching from other states, railroad building fulfilled the editor's notion of his public service. He intoned, "The rail-way is becoming a marked element in the progress of civilization throughout the world," and he was determined to remove political and legal obstacles to this engine of progress.[25]

Of course, Croswell's motives were not simply, or even primarily, altruistic. Enriched by his widely read newspaper and state printing contracts that amounted to $25,000 per year, the editor became one of Albany's leading entrepreneurs. He urged continuous development and refurbishment of internal improvements that would preserve the state's commercial wealth and potentially benefit his own investments in several banks, railroads, and manufacturing concerns. As early as 1836, his editorials voiced the outlook of the state's speculative entrepreneurs. Indeed, he repeatedly called for the repeal of laws prohibiting debt financing of internal improvements and consistently criticized the Regency's radical economic policy in the pages of the very journal that was supposed to promote them.[26]

The Regency subsequently withdrew its support from Croswell in 1844 and established a rival paper, the *Albany Atlas*, to promote the party's official dogma. Though Democratic leaders sustained the new paper with the printing contracts that formerly had gone to Croswell, the *Atlas* never attained the circulation or impact of the more established *Argus*. Croswell was relatively unaffected by his loss of patronage, and when the state assembly later divided state printing contracts by department and mandated a competitive bid process, he won the contract to print public notices with a bid of $0. The editor claimed that his bid was a magnanimous gesture to the citizens of New York that would save the government up to $37,000 in printing costs.[27] In reality, the crafty and vindictive Croswell submitted his unbeatable bid solely to deny much-needed patronage to his struggling rival, the *Atlas*.

Unlike in Maine, where radical and progressive Democrats distrusted each other but remained relatively united, New York Democrats became sharply and violently divided as each faction fought for control of the party and the lucrative state patronage that it entailed.[28] Radicals derisively branded the apostate Croswell and like-minded Democrats as Hunkers, a corruption of a Dutch term, signifying officeholder. The term connoted scheming politicians who abandoned Democratic principles in their selfish desire for the spoils of office. Hunkers in turn dismissed radicals as Barnburners, myopic ideologues who would destroy the party itself in their zealous desire to purge it of anyone who did not hew strictly to radical principles.[29]

Hunkers and Barnburners battled for control of municipal and county central committees, which exercised considerable power over the choice of delegates to party conventions and candidates for political office. The ferocity of the struggle to dominate these committees was illustrated vividly at the Albany County Democratic Party convention in April 1846. The election of convention delegates in the city of Albany was rife with fraud, and the city's Hunkers contested several seats that had been awarded to their Barnburner rivals. State Attorney General John Van Buren, son of the former president and leader of the Barnburner faction, feared that Hunker delegates from the countryside would invalidate the contested seats and seize control of the convention. To forestall this possibility, Van Buren and *Atlas* owner James French employed hired bullies from Albany to disrupt the convention. Several Hunker delegates were beaten, one was stabbed, and the convention splintered into two bodies, each nominating competing slates of candidates for the upcoming state elections. Though Albany County's Hunkers and Barnburners eventually compromised on a new slate of candidates, Democratic divisions enabled Whigs to capture the governor's chair and the state house of representatives, while Democrats retained a nearly two-to-one advantage in the senate in that year's elections.[30]

The roiling conflict between Barnburners and Hunkers came to a head at the state convention in Syracuse in 1847. For weeks prior to the convention, the Rome *Sentinel* and other pro-improvement Democratic journals in the state repeatedly criticized the performance of Azariah Flagg, the state's longtime comptroller and loyal lieutenant of the elder Van Buren. As a radical, Flagg practiced strict fiscal economy, refusing to risk state funds to consummate improvements to the canal system that had been left unfinished since the Panic of 1837. While the state party's radical leaders planned to renominate Flagg to his post, Croswell, Henry T. Utley of the *Sentinel*, and other maverick Democratic editors lobbied Hunker delegates to the state convention to oppose his nomination. Indeed, the prominent rallying cry in these newspapers leading up to the convention was "new men!"[31]

Hunkers held a slim majority of delegates when the convention opened, and the atmosphere in the meeting hall was contentious from the beginning. Hunkers hoped to craft a party platform that would encourage the resumption of large-scale internal improvements, while Barnburners countered the improvement mania with an intensified focus on antislavery. In 1846, Congressman David Wilmot, a Democrat from Pennsylvania, had introduced an amendment to a $2 million appropriations bill to fund the country's ongoing war against Mexico. The amendment expressly prohibited slavery in any territories gained from Mexico. The appropriations bill failed to pass both houses of Congress with the amendment intact, and the measure's supporters failed to attach it to subsequent appropriations. Still, the amendment lived on as the Wilmot Proviso, a potent symbol of northern opposition to the seemingly outsized political power of the slave states.[32] Still bitter over pro-slavery Democrats' leading role in denying Martin Van Buren's renomination for president in 1844, New York Barnburners embraced the Proviso as a means of challenging what they saw as an increasingly aggressive slave power. At the Syracuse convention, Barnburners sought to write the principles of the Proviso into the state party platform.

These radical Democrats saw the Proviso as a test of party loyalty, separating "true," radical Democrats from mere "doughfaces," conservatives who meekly tolerated pro-slavery Democrats for the sake of party unity. Arthur Schlesinger Jr.

and Sean Wilentz both hailed the Barnburners' principled commitment to antislavery as the purest expression of their egalitarian principles. When the prevaricating Hunkers who led the Syracuse convention obstructed the adoption of the Proviso, Barnburners walked out in righteous anger. They assembled several weeks later in Herkimer in a rump convention, pledged themselves to the principles of "Free Trade, Free Labor, Free Soil, Free Speech, and Free Men," and thereby gave birth to the Free Soil political movement.[33]

This hagiographic interpretation suggested that New York Democrats principally split over the issue of slavery, forcing Barnburners to inaugurate a third party movement in order to purify the sordid, doughface politics of the North. A closer examination of the Syracuse convention, however, belies this tidy narrative. The timing of the Barnburners' walkout revealed a more cynical cause of their precipitate decision to bolt the convention. Hunkers held tenuous control of the convention committees, but both factions compromised and concurred in the initial nominations for state cabinet positions. When Hunkers united to block Flagg's renomination, however, Barnburners suddenly moved to suspend the nominating process and proceed to the consideration of the platform. They immediately brought up the Wilmot Proviso for debate. Fearing that Barnburners would try to shore up support for Flagg while the Proviso was under consideration, Hunkers maneuvered to table the motion and resume the nomination process.

The defeat of the Proviso was not the cause of the convention's rupture, but merely the pretext. It provided cover for a radical faction smarting from the loss of Flagg's influential cabinet position. Though the Herkimer convention laid the groundwork for the eventual birth of the Free Soil Party the following year, at its inception it simply focused on regaining control of the New York Democratic Party. The first ten resolutions passed by the Herkimer gathering put forth the tried-and-true economic issues that had brought the party to power after the Panic of 1837: free trade, fiscal retrenchment, and preservation of the Stop and Tax Law. Not until the eleventh resolution did the convention celebrate the "dignity and rights of free labor" and decree that all future territory must be kept free of slavery.[34] Barnburners were not insincere in their free soil beliefs, but those beliefs did not take on political urgency until Hunkers had wrested control of the party from them.

The rupture of the Syracuse convention suggests that the newspaper campaign against Flagg did not merely exacerbate existing factional divisions in the party, but directly caused the party's outright split. Croswell, Utley, and others' relentless challenges to the Regency caused besieged Barnburners to abandon the Democracy, as the Democratic Party was popularly known, and launch a third-party movement to preserve their political clout. With this movement they hoped to chastise their Hunker rivals and purify the Democratic Party. The initial result of the third-party movement, however, was that the Whigs crushed both groups in the state elections in 1847, piling up majorities of between twenty-three thousand and thirty-eight thousand votes as they swept the races for executive branch offices, including the much sought after comptroller position. The successful newspaper campaign to dump Flagg thus had the unintended consequence of prostrating the entire party. Triumphant Whigs prepared to steer state printing contracts toward their own presses (despite the competitive bid mandate, the legislature still had ways of disqualifying certain presses from the process), but this had little impact on Croswell. His strong base of subscribers and his foray into banking had provided him with sufficient income and credit to make up for the loss of patronage. Indeed, these sources of cash and credit effectively had subsidized his rebellion against New York's Democratic leaders.

Though the Free Soil revolt initially was born out of factional conflicts that were particular to New York, it soon became the primary means by which the North's radical Democrats tried to reassert control over their party's direction and message. Like their progressive colleagues, Free Soilers also employed newspapers to broadcast their message to the voting masses. In some cases, they even wrestled progressive Democrats for control of the latter's journals. In Portland, Maine, Charles Holden took on O. L. Sanborn as a publishing partner in 1845.[35] Sanborn and Holden's political views largely were consonant, but the former was far more sympathetic to the Free Soil cause than was Holden. In 1850, the Democratic caucus in the state legislature nominated two candidates to fill Cumberland County's seats in the state senate. Holden dutifully supported these nominations, but the county's Free Soil Democrats hastily organized a convention to replace one of the candidates with a man of more pronounced antislavery principles. Holden condemned this irregular maneuver in the *Eastern Argus*, but Sanborn then penned an article in the paper announcing that he disagreed with the paper's principal editor on this issue, and that he would support the new candidate's bid for the senate seat.[36] The cordially conflicting editorials in support of rival candidates imparted a schizophrenic character to the journal. Both editors seemed unwilling to compromise, but their willingness to tolerate this impasse suggested their business partnership was more important to them than was party solidarity.

While the North's old radicals used the Free Soil movement to discipline a Democratic Party that they thought had lost its way, the Polk administration worked to head off Free Soil defections and admonish Democrats to toe the party line. In 1847, Joseph Gray's *Cleveland Plain Dealer*, one of the leading papers in Ohio's Western Reserve, took up the Wilmot Proviso. Though Gray supported the Polk administration, the editor also did not hesitate to employ the Proviso as a criticism of the president's seemingly pro-southern policies. Western Democrats like Gray lobbied the president unsuccessfully to sign bills to improve harbors on the Great Lakes, hoping that it would increase the flow of commerce from new western territories through the Great Lakes and on to the East. While westerners were frustrated in their commercial hopes, southern slaveholders anticipated a windfall of new slave territory from the costly war against Mexico. Gray spoke for a number of western Democrats who believed that the Polk administration ignored their needs, and he used the Proviso to admonish the president that he "shall not purchase territory with *our* money" only to open it to slavery.[37]

This was not the first time Gray had bucked the leadership of his party. When Ohio's radical Democratic leaders picked David Tod to represent the party in the governor's race for a second time in 1846 (Tod had lost the 1844 election), the disappointed editor refused to stump for the candidate. He registered his dissent by prominently publishing the resolutions of two counties in northern Ohio that explicitly rejected the state party platform prior to the election.[38] Gray objected to a radical anti-bank plank in the party's platform, believing it only would serve to alienate voters in the growing commercial center of Cleveland. Much like his editorial colleagues in Albany and Portland, he desired reforms that would unleash credit for the commercial development of his community.

Gray's refusal to support Tod's candidacy had put him at odds with the leaders of his state party, but his support for the Proviso elicited the ire of the Polk administration and cost the editor lucrative federal patronage. In the summer of 1847, a rival Democratic newspaper in Cleveland, the *Times*, won the contract to advertise the U.S. Post Office's lists of unclaimed letters and mail lettings for Cleveland and its surroundings. The *Times* had been founded with the assistance of Ohio's radical Democratic leaders to punish Gray for his abandonment of the Tod campaign. According to federal law, postal contracts were supposed to go to the newspapers of largest circulation in each American city, and the fledgling *Times*'s anemic subscriptions lagged well behind the *Plain Dealer*'s. In January 1848, Gray traveled to Washington to present a petition in favor of internal improvements from the Great Lakes states. While there, he also met with Postmas-

ter General Cave Johnson to state his case for the Post Office contract based on
the superior reach of his newspaper. According to Gray, Johnson responded that
the newspaper's circulation was of no concern to him, for a "Proviso paper" was
unworthy of the Polk administration's support.[39]

Johnson's presumptuousness in criticizing the political content of the *Plain
Dealer* predictably outraged Gray. In the pages of his newspaper, the editor protested, "Cave Johnson is entrusted with no such charge as regulating the political
opinion in the North, on this or any other subject." The postmaster had proscribed Gray's newspaper simply "for persevering in its right to freely discuss one
of the most momentous subjects that ever engaged the thoughts of freemen, one
that hangs like a portentous cloud over the destiny of our common country."[40]
The editor resented Johnson's challenge to his editorial freedom and its inher-
ent critique of Gray's management of his business. In his mind, his loyal service
to the Polk administration, particularly his support for the Mexican War and
Oregon treaty, warranted a patronage reward, regardless of his opinions on the
Proviso and his strained relations with the leaders of the Ohio Democracy.

Financial need did not animate Gray's desire for the Post Office contract. The
success of his newspaper and a steady stream of private printing jobs allowed him
to move his growing press operations into a new building in 1848, constructed
with his own funds. By 1851, the *Plain Dealer* was operating five presses, including a modern, steam-powered cylinder press, to manage the increasing volume
of printing jobs. Regardless of his financial success, Gray craved the recognition
and enhanced political influence that federal patronage entailed. His strained
relations with Ohio's radical Democratic leaders threatened to marginalize him
within the state party, but federal patronage could shield him from this possible
fate and sustain his upstart challenge to radicals' authority in the Buckeye State.
Though he had failed in his bid for the U.S. Post Office contract during Polk's
tenure, Gray eventually earned appointment as Cleveland's postmaster during
Franklin Pierce's Democratic administration. More useful than a simple advertising contract, the postmaster's position came with the authority to hire employees, allowing the editor to build a cadre of loyalists in the Cleveland post
office who would carry on his opposition to radical Democrats on the Western
Reserve.[41]

In 1848, however, an admonished Gray attempted to forge a compromise with
the Polk administration that would allow him to save face and maintain at least
a pose of editorial freedom. His *Plain Dealer* shifted course and sought to de-
emphasize the Proviso by arguing that Congress lacked the jurisdiction to impose the measure on the territories.[42] This position had been floated by a hand-

ful of politicians hoping to sidestep the divisive slavery issue altogether prior to the 1848 federal elections. One of those was Senator Lewis Cass of Michigan, campaigning to succeed President Polk (who did not seek a second term) as the Democratic Party's presidential nominee for 1848. Gray believed that Cass would better represent the interests of the West in Washington, both in the dispensation of patronage and the funding of badly needed improvements to spur western commerce. The editor became an early booster of the senator's presidential aspirations and a convert to his concept of federal nonintervention in the territories. Cass proposed granting territorial residents popular sovereignty (labeled squatter sovereignty by its critics) to establish their own laws regarding slavery, ostensibly to preserve those residents' right of self-determination.

The senator had crafted his notion of popular sovereignty as an alternative to the Wilmot Proviso and the Free Soil movement it had spawned. Not surprisingly, supporters of the Proviso and Free Soil roundly rejected Cass's solution to the divisive issue of slavery in the territories. None of this dissuaded Gray, however, from trying to marry the principles of Free Soil to Cass's campaign for the presidential nomination of the Democratic Party. Despite obvious evidence to the contrary, the editor argued in the columns of the *Plain Dealer* that popular sovereignty actually preserved, rather than rejected, the principles and the aims of the Proviso, and the editor swallowed whole Cass's argument that denial of territorial settlers' right of self-determination would be unconstitutional.[43]

The editor stubbornly clung to his Free Soil sympathies while promoting the political fortunes of a man who disdained that movement. When Cass won the Democratic nomination at the national convention in Baltimore in May 1848, the *Plain Dealer* likely was the only journal in the country to jubilantly declare, "Free Trade, Free Labor, and Free Soil! Forever! Hurrah for Gen. Cass!!!"[44] Only when antislavery Democrats joined antislavery Whigs to launch the Free Soil Party in August 1848 did Gray finally abandon the movement. Until that moment, however, the editor blithely assumed vast creative license to portray Cass's campaign to conform to Gray's vision of what the party's principles should be. His incongruous promotion of both Cass and Free Soil demonstrated a curious effort at compromise with party leaders. While he gave up the specific issue of the Proviso ostensibly to placate the Polk administration, he nevertheless clung to Free Soil as long as possible to keep the larger antislavery issue alive.

The Free Soil movement's third-party insurgency in 1848 highlighted partisan newspapers' potential to disrupt the functioning of the party system itself. Edwin Croswell's campaign against Flagg and the party's economic platform literally cleaved the party in two in the Empire State and provided the bulk of converts to the Free Soil Party. Charles Holden's rejection of the party's Jacksonian principles exasperated Maine Democrats' radical minority, which later retaliated with their own Free Soil insurgency. In Ohio it was Gray himself who utilized the movement to chastise the pro-slavery elements in the Polk administration and outflank the radical leaders of the Ohio Democrats.

In all three states, the Free Soil uprising led to the resurgence of Whig fortunes. In New York, Whigs held the governor's chair from 1847 through 1852, and they dominated the state legislature from 1847 to 1849 and again in 1851, during which time they elected William Henry Seward and Hamilton Fish to the U.S. Senate. In Maine, Free Soilers sharply reduced the Democratic Party's majority in the state legislature in 1846 and 1848, and though the party rebounded after each of these setbacks, the combination of political antislavery and temperance ultimately would topple Maine's Democrats in the 1850s.[45] In Ohio, Free Soilers ended up holding the balance of power in the legislature between the evenly matched Democrats and Whigs. Though the movement ultimately was short-lived, in the short term it significantly hampered Democrats' ability to compete with Whigs at the local and state level in several northern states.

Many of the Free Soil movement's Democratic converts, having registered their dissent over the direction of the party, soon returned to the fold in exchange for certain concessions. New York Democrats and Free Soilers fitfully reunited in 1849 and 1850. A lasting Democratic reunion resumed only after Croswell agreed to step down as editor of the *Argus* in 1855.[46] By that point the Free Soil Party was dead, and Democrats faced a new foe, the nascent Republican Party. With Croswell on the sideline, the *Argus* merged with its radical rival, the *Atlas*, under the joint management of Croswell's nephew, Sherman, and *Atlas* proprietor James French. Appropriately enough, a crippling party split that had been occasioned by a factious newspaper war subsequently was healed through the merger of these rival papers.

The short-lived Free Soil insurgency had laid bare the persistent conflicts between partisan editors and party leaders. Due to their decentralized organization, national and state political parties were able to influence but not control the editorial content of the partisan newspapers that supported them. Party organizations could withhold patronage from recalcitrant editors like Gray, or support the establishment of rival papers, as in the case of both Gray and Croswell. Neither measure substantially cut into these editors' base of loyal subscribers or seriously challenged their newspapers' standing in their communities. Instead, well-established editors like Holden and Gray might experience the deprivation of patronage most acutely as a loss of status or a lost opportunity to build a sustainable opposition to their own party's leadership. Editors typically were modest businessmen, but party and government patronage imparted to them a degree of political clout and social influence they otherwise would not have enjoyed. Holden captured editors' desire for the status and recognition that official printing contracts conferred when he complained, "If any class of men have peculiar claims to official honors, it is the editorial fraternity. No movement can succeed without them. In political machinery they constitute the main wheels—yet, when victory is attained, they are thrust aside like drift wood."[47] While the promise of patronage and the prestige it conferred could influence editors to conform their political commentary to the desires of party leaders, the effectiveness of this tool of coercion proved rather limited.

Despite the conflicts that it generated, partisan editors' efforts to preserve their editorial freedom from party dictates had some benefits for the parties. The frequency of newspaper publication allowed great flexibility in refashioning party principles and goals to apply to local exigencies and shifting political concerns. It also allowed partisan editors considerable leeway in refurbishing seemingly outdated party positions to meet the dynamic, changing needs of their community. Specifically, editors like Holden, Croswell, and Gray led the charge to unshackle the Democratic Party from the increasingly anachronistic economic outlook of radical party leaders, who resolutely opposed government promotion of economic development. In this manner they aided immensely in moderating Democratic radicalism and modernizing the party's outlook, making it more palatable to their urban readers. Ironically, in doing so they also weakened their party's position in relation to their political opponents in the North prior to the Civil War.

Despite their sincere attachment to party, editors simply did not make obedient foot soldiers. Their identification with the entrepreneurial class that was transforming their cities buffered urban editors somewhat from the embarrassment of losing favor with party leaders. And it was those entrepreneurs, not party leaders, whom partisan editors emulated most. When Samuel Morse's telegraph first went into operation in May 1844, its first practical application was to transmit news from the Democratic national convention in Baltimore to an audience of congressmen in Washington DC. When the telegraph was extended to Cleveland three years later, Joseph Gray believed its most practical application was to transmit business, not political, news. He urged "merchants and businessmen of the West" to "take a CLEVELAND PAPER, with reports of the New York Market smoking hot."[48] Gray's appeal to the businessmen of the West exposed his and many of his colleagues' desire to cut loose from reliance on the party and seek the support of the prospering urban business class, a development that would not occur until after the Civil War.

Despite his own conflicts with the Polk administration, when Gray surveyed the state of the American press in 1851, he was optimistic. He contrasted the liberty of the press favorably with its English counterpart, which published at the pleasure of the monarchy and Parliament. He asserted that the American press "could furnish them much profitable instruction in all that give dignity to the newspaper—liberty of speech, prompt exposure of wrong, and an abiding affection in the hearts of the million."[49] This was a highly idealized vision of the press, of course. Editors' liberty of speech and their willingness to expose wrong were hotly contested, as the editorial careers of Gray and Holden clearly demonstrated. This was especially galling for a class of men who saw themselves as independent entrepreneurs on the same footing with the most respected businessmen of their communities. To preserve this image of themselves, editors alternately negotiated, clashed, and compromised with party leaders over the political content of their papers, striving to retain as much editorial freedom as possible. Party leaders similarly were exasperated by editors' combative independent streak, their seeming lack of concern with the divisions their newspapers spawned within the party organization, and the party's own inability to keep these papers reliably in tune. In some ways, then, the challenges that the Democratic Party faced from its own intractable media in the antebellum North rivaled the challenges they faced from other parties.

Abraham Lincoln, Manhood, and Nineteenth-Century American Political Culture

Michael Thomas Smith

The struggle over interpreting Abraham Lincoln's image and character during his long political career reveals much about the contested terrain of appropriate male behavior in mid-nineteenth-century America. Lincoln impressed many observers as being quite masculine, with his physical size, strength, and endurance, combined with his image as a rugged "rail-splitter," playing a pivotal and underappreciated role in his popularity. He further won acclaim as a steady leader with outstanding integrity, in keeping with the Victorian conception of manliness being fundamentally defined by morality and restraint. By combining elements of both these aspects of idealized manhood—aggressive masculinity and restrained manliness—Lincoln broadened his appeal to reach Americans of different social classes and political ideologies. Being able to lay claim to the qualities of both of these forms of manhood was essential to political success in the Civil War era.[1]

Reflecting the centrality of these concepts of manhood to the era's political culture, Lincoln's critics also attacked him along gendered lines. His wartime radical detractors saw him as weak, hesitant, and vacillating, despite his good intentions; in short, they contended that he lacked the appropriate degree of masculine force of character that the crisis necessitated. Democratic critics charged that he lacked the basic rudiments of gentlemanly character, portraying him as crude and animalistic. The Kentucky-born Lincoln could be characterized by various detractors as either a westerner or a southerner, regions that in the minds of some produced men deficient in both manners and self-command. As a result of his lack of a gentleman's character and moral power, he supposedly shrank from his appropriate duties, enabling sinister advisers to control his party and administration. The evil outcome—tyranny and profligacy—thus stemmed from his unmanliness. The common view of Lincoln as a paternal figure further exacerbated the conflict over his image; his supporters saw him as a wise, kind father figure, while his critics saw him as an unfit, henpecked patriarch whose weakness threatened the stability of the family/nation.

The world of formal American politics in the nineteenth was an all-male club, with men possessing a privileged monopoly on voting and officeholding, a fact that while generally well-known, has profound implications for the era's political culture that remain ill understood. Historians of the Civil War era have greatly enriched our understanding of the role of nationalism, race, economics, and republicanism in the era's political culture. The role of masculinity in shaping both political discourse and political reality, however, remains underappreciated. A closer look at Lincoln's image as portrayed by both his supporters and detractors helps illuminate the formative role of concepts of manhood in this political culture.

Opponents charged that Lincoln lacked the manly force of will to force his subordinates to behave ethically and appropriately—to do his duty as president, in other words. Democratic Congressman William Richardson of Illinois alleged on the House floor in 1861 that "Lincoln—and I have known him from boyhood's hour till now— . . . has not the will to stand up against the wily politicians who surround him and knead him to their purposes." Being a weak man, this critic alleged, even if Lincoln were personally honest, he could still not impose appropriate and necessary order on his underlings. "He has no ability or will to achieve great and elevated things," another Democratic editor agreed. A New York Copperhead bitterly charged that the nation's liberties would truly be threatened by the administration, but for the fact that Lincoln "is too weak and foolish a man to carry forward and consummate his crimes." But since he was "the tool of men of still worse passions than himself," the nation still had much to fear.[2]

Some Republicans expressed the same basic fear that Lincoln lacked the masculine force needed to impose his will on others. An Illinois Republican wrote Senator Lyman Trumbull, "I have felt and do feel that he lacks much of the firmness, decision, and sternness with which God so usefully blessed Andrew Jackson," the paragon of forceful presidential leadership whose quashing of the South Carolina nullification movement worried northerners hoped, but doubted, Lincoln would imitate with equal determination and effectiveness during and after the secession crisis. Lincoln's attorney general Edward Bates told the artist Francis Carpenter that while his chief "comes very near being a perfect man, according to my ideal of manhood," he did possess one important deficiency. "He lacks but one thing . . . the element of *will*," which the stern old Missourian believed prevented him from making difficult but necessary decisions at times (such as upholding the execution of deserters). All these critics, friendly or otherwise,

Democrat or Republican, perceived Lincoln's failing in specifically gendered terms, suggesting the power of concept of idealized manhood in the era's political culture. To truly be an effective leader, one needed basic masculine qualities, both outer and inner.[3]

Given these fears that Lincoln lacked masculine force of character or will, it made sense that concerns emerged during the war that Lincoln was controlled by some sinister figure or figures behind the scenes. One Democratic paper suggested in 1864 that "Mr. Lincoln . . . has been the mere plastic tool of such men as [Senator Zachariah] Chandler" and other radical Republicans. A more often-cited culprit was Secretary of State William H. Seward, the original front-runner for the Republican presidential nomination in 1860 and a politician of vast skill, experience, and personal charm. It was widely believed that Seward had exerted great and not altogether positive influence over the presidential administration of Zachary Taylor and the presidential campaign of Winfield Scott. As Lincoln, like those two generals, lacked much experience on the national political scene, it would make sense for the longtime head of the party to play the leading role in running the administration. Seward himself rather expected this to be the case, in fact, thinking that he would be "the premier" of the administration, though Lincoln swiftly disabused the New Yorker of this idea.[4]

But the idea continued to linger that, as one abolitionist put it, "Seward is *really* President, Lincoln only nominally so," and that the "heartless villain" Seward was responsible for delays in adopting emancipation other radical policies. The widespread belief that Seward exerted a "controlling influence upon the mind of the President" (as the influential Senator William P. Fessenden put it) helped drive the notorious cabinet crisis of 1862, in which Lincoln had to allay the fears of Republican senators that he had lost control of the administration to his subordinate. Lincoln later joked about their apparent belief "that when he had in him any good purposes, Mr. S contrived *to suck them out of him unperceived*." But the political crisis was a real one, though skillfully defused by the president, who managed through his characteristic combination of tact and determination to keep his cabinet as well as his party together without giving in to this attempted infringement by legislators on the internal workings of the White House.[5]

Although the fears that Lincoln was dominated by his secretary of state (or Seward's longtime mentor and friend, Albany Republican boss Thurlow Weed) abated, they did not disappear. In 1863 the radical Boston *Commonwealth* worried that Seward, "a man of a terrible and indomitable will," continued to hold Lincoln in his "clutches." Later the same year famed abolitionist William Lloyd Garrison fumed in the *Liberator* that "if in any month of Mr. Seward's administration, he had chosen strenuously to urge upon Abraham Lincoln the abolition of slavery throughout the country . . . the war would have ended in our victory six months thereafter." Given Lincoln's domination by his nominal underling, Garrison worried "whether a vote for old Abe will not choose Seward to be again acting President." A Democratic paper charged in 1864 that the administration's major policies had been "mapped out and perfected . . . [in] the New York home of Thurlow Weed." The New York Copperhead Chauncey Burr charged in his bitterly antiadministration paper that "Mr. Seward . . . entered the Cabinet, as Lucifer entered Paradise, only for evil," determined to gain revenge against Lincoln for wresting the party's presidential nomination away from him. "He has drawn Lincoln into acts that his very weakness would have shrunk from with fear, unless pushed on by a superior strength. He is the fiend of the administration," and "Mr. Lincoln has been an easy tool of Mr. Seward's revenge." Through superior wiles and talent, the secretary of state had supposedly imposed his will on the lesser man who held the position to which he had himself aspired. Nearly a decade after the close of the war, wartime cabinet member and devoted Lincoln admirer Gideon Welles was so annoyed by the persistence of this idea (as reflected, for example, in a eulogy for the recently deceased New Yorker delivered by his friend Charles Francis Adams) that he wrote a book explicitly denying that Seward "was the master mind" of the administration and dominated Lincoln through his "superior intellectual power." The insider Welles knew who the man in charge of the cabinet actually was, but many outsiders did not.[6]

Other critics of Lincoln similarly saw him as too weak to manage his undoubtedly sometimes unruly and dissension-plagued cabinet, but saw other forces at play behind the scenes manipulating him. Postmaster General Montgomery Blair and his powerful family (including his father, Francis Preston Blair Sr., a veteran editor and close associate and adviser of Andrew Jackson, and brother Frank Blair, Missouri's leading Republican, a congressman, and a Union Army general) drew considerable suspicion along these lines. A New York Republican charged that "Mr. Lincoln has virtually put himself into the power of the Blair family," which this writer particularly deplored given the ongoing feud between the conservative Blairs and more radical Secretary of the Treasury Salmon P. Chase. An Iowa Republican likewise wrote that although Lincoln was "a great and good man," he had fallen under the sway of these influential conservatives, who had destroyed his potential usefulness. "Had the president avoided the Blair influence," it might have been otherwise. These critics might have been somewhat mollified when Lincoln asked for Blair's resignation from the cabinet in September 1864, apparently as part of a deal with radicals to win their support for his presidential candidacy. At least one Republican editor feared that Montgomery Blair's malign influence would continue, however, if he "remain[ed] . . . an influential member of the [informal] Kitchen-Cabinet," as his father had been in the Jackson administration.[7]

Secretary of War Edwin M. Stanton was also widely suspected of exerting undue influence over the supposedly weaker-willed Lincoln. The gruff, overbearing, hard-driving Stanton—of whom Frederick Douglass (who knew Stanton personally owing to his work assisting in the recruitment of African American troops) wittily said, "Politeness was not one of his weaknesses"—certainly represented a strikingly different personality type from the affable Lincoln. An Ohio Democrat in 1863 snidely charged that "Mr. Stanton . . . is virtually President." Ulysses Grant in his memoirs commented that "it was generally supposed that . . . the Secretary was required to prevent the President's being imposed on," as Lincoln lacked the firmness to do so himself. Grant asserted that this was "not a correct view," and that "in matters of public duty" Lincoln "had what he wished, but in the least offensive way . . . Mr. Lincoln did not require a guardian to aid him in the fulfillment of a public trust." As Grant realized, though, this was exactly what many worried observers believed, owing to their skepticism as to the power of Lincoln's masculine force of will.[8]

Other cabinet members and prominent politicians were also suspected of being the power behind Lincoln's throne. Some feared that shadowy "shoddy" government contractors controlled Lincoln, especially after a series of scandals early in the war that ultimately cost Stanton's predecessor as secretary of war—the incompetent, corrupt Simon Cameron—his job. Pittsburgh's Democratic editor charged that "President Lincoln has served Mr. Cameron's purposes most effectually," owing to "a weakness which is . . . disastrous. An honest man when used and abused by a political sharper, damages his country quite as much as if he were a sharper himself." Prominent War Democrat Daniel S. Dickinson of New York, a supporter of the administration's conduct of the war, privately considered Lincoln "honest and sincere," but regretted that he was "managed by office-holders and contractors." While not accusing "Honest Abe" of personal corruption, these critics instead suggested that he lacked sufficient manly force of character to stand up to the corruptionists whose greed threatened the maintenance of the republic.[9]

Lincoln expressed amusement at the well-intentioned advice of a longtime ally from Illinois who suggested early in his administration that he needed a stronger, wiser man behind the scenes "to run you," as this friend believed Thurlow Weed "ran" William H. Seward. The ever-tolerant, good-humored Lincoln could afford to laugh at this suggestion (as did Seward), knowing that he called the shots when it mattered, in implementing policies like emancipation or in the appointment and dismissal of key political and military personnel. Despite what we can now see as its fundamental untruth, however, the idea that the wartime president was not a strong enough man to dominate his own administration profoundly troubled many northerners.[10]

For much of 1864, radical Republicans discontented with Lincoln's leadership attempted to win public support for one of several possible rival candidates, particularly Salmon P. Chase, John C. Frémont, and Benjamin F. Butler. While these three former Democrats turned Republicans were generally associated with more radical policies than was the moderate Lincoln, the most visceral argument that their advocates made on their behalf was that they represented more forceful masculine qualities than did the cautious president. Chase himself hinted at this in a somewhat coy letter to his son-in-law: "I think that a man of different qualities from those the President has will be needed for the next four years. I am not anxious to be regarded as that man; but I am quite willing to refer that question to the decision of those who agree in thinking that some such man should be had." What was most fundamentally needed, more than new policies—and indeed, Chase would have found it difficult to disassociate himself from Lincoln's policies, given that he was a senior member of the administration—was a new, better man. The stately, imposing Chase, whom Lincoln himself praised during their early association as "about one hundred and fifty to any other man's hundred," seemed to many hopeful radicals, and especially to himself, to personify this quality. Chase overplayed his hand by challenging the president from within the administration, as the patient Lincoln realized he likely would, and withdrew from the presidential race in March. Lincoln's critics would have to look elsewhere for a superior man.[11]

Union General John C. Frémont, famed as "the Pathfinder" for his prewar western explorations, was actually nominated to run against Lincoln by an incongruous assortment of disaffected radicals and Democrats, who hoped that "a positive man in the White House, a radical," would prove superior to the "weak person, of average ability," who currently occupied it. His candidacy generated little popular support and Lincoln apparently negotiated privately with radical leaders to get Frémont to withdraw from the campaign, in exchange for the ouster of his enemy Montgomery Blair from the cabinet. Lincoln professed himself little surprised at Frémont's ineffectuality. When John Hay told him he thought the Pathfinder "would be dangerous if he had more ability and energy," Lincoln was reminded of an amusing story he shared at his rival's expense. Frémont, he thought, was "like Jim Jett's brother. Jim used to say that his brother was the damndest scoundrel that ever lived, but in the infinite mercy of Providence he was also the damndest fool." It would take more a more industrious and talented man than that to unseat the Illinois rail-splitter.[12]

Many northerners thought they could potentially find such a man in another Union general, Benjamin F. Butler of Massachusetts, who they believed represented the best possible replacement for Lincoln. While somewhat notorious for his alleged corruption and controversial "woman order," which threatened to legally treat the ladies of occupied New Orleans as prostitutes if they showed disrespect to Union soldiers, Butler was widely popular in the North. His aggressive persona (assisted by his talent for self-promotion) struck many observers as just what the perilous times demanded. As the New England radical Franklin Sanborn put it in an 1863 speech, he had concluded that "men of action" like Butler were "the only men fit to govern" the nation during wartime. The country's salvation depended on "men who can carry great draughts of power." Butler himself rather agreed. He had informed his wife in 1862 that "it is coming—a military dictator. God grant the man may be one of power and administrative capacity." With utterly uncharacteristic modesty, he did not name himself as this coming man, but others were willing to do so. Radical Congressman George Boutwell of Massachusetts argued in 1864 that "if Butler were nominated for Presidency and elected, the rebels would at once give up . . . Such is the feeling and conviction of all the best men." This extremely optimistic assertion overestimated Confederate respect for the "Beast" Butler, but does suggest what a high estimation some northerners had for the powerful masculine force they associated with the general. Butler himself declined to cooperate with the radicals plotting against Lincoln, and the president minimized the political threat the general presented by keeping him on active duty in the largely backwater Department of Virginia and North Carolina until he could be safely relieved of command after the election had passed. Lincoln's opponents might have believed that a better man should be nominated and elected in 1864; the public, however, ultimately thought otherwise.[13]

Other criticisms of Lincoln were made in gendered terms as well. A Republican editor from Boston in December 1862 mocked Lincoln for stating in his recent annual message to Congress, "We cannot escape history. The fiery trial through which we pass will light us down with honor or dishonor to the latest generation." Lincoln would be remembered for his deficiencies as a man, this editor asserted. "History must inexorably assign him a place in the rear, along with many weak and inadequate men of the time." A Chicago radical alleged in an 1864 speech that "Abraham Lincoln was the weakest and worst man that ever filled the Presidential chair." A New York Democrat, also in 1864, similarly charged that "of all the men who have filled the President's office, he is the least capable, manly, practical or consistent." The Democratic *Brooklyn Eagle* the same year ridiculed the "obscure lawyer of Springfield, Illinois," under whose leadership "so impotently had the strength of the nation been directed . . . Mr. Lincoln is a very ordinary man . . . A man with a great head and heart might have secured this country from its troubles had he been placed where Mr. Lincoln is." Further, "Mr. Lincoln is as emaciated, loose-jointed, awkward-built a man as ever shuffled along the streets of Washington . . . in physical strength McClellan is as much superior to Mr. Lincoln as he is morally and intellectually." The Democratic candidate supposedly outclassed Lincoln in all the varied qualities, physical and otherwise, that together constituted manhood. Beyond differences over policies, strategy, or appointments, this was the most primal charge that Lincoln's political opponents leveled. The struggles of the Union cause could ultimately be blamed on the president's inadequacies as a man.[14]

Critics even seized on one of the odder episodes of Lincoln's presidency and tried to use it to embarrass him in specifically gendered terms. Following the death of their son Willie, the distraught Mary Todd Lincoln turned to Spiritualism for solace. She participated in several séances in the White House in an attempt to communicate with her deceased son, and a skeptical Abraham attended one. Spiritualism as a movement was near its zenith in the 1860s, but still it raised eyebrows to have such unconventional practices taking place in the president's home. Nor did the Spiritualist Church's official endorsement of his reelection in 1864 at their national convention in Chicago help Lincoln get past this embarrassing episode. The Democratic *Chicago Times* repeatedly attacked Lincoln for being "an unbelieving Spiritualist," but interestingly tended to ridicule what this association suggested about Lincoln's manhood more than his also controversial religious views. The editor sneered that "it was eminently fit and proper that the strong minded women and weak minded men—the females in trousers and the males in petticoats . . . should declare for Old Abe. Old Abe belongs to the sect . . . [of] he-women and she-men." Both by allowing his wife to indulge in Spiritualism, and by associating with a movement with a strong female leadership presence and commitment to women's rights, Lincoln had thus proven himself wanting as a man. In essence, this association proved that the rail-splitter was in fact what one much later Republican leader would have referred to as a "girly man." Gendered concepts lurked very close to the surface of political and social issues that might at first glance seem unrelated. His opponents realized the political value of idealized manhood, and Lincoln's was constantly contested.[15]

Lincoln and his allies, however, were able to counter these charges of deficient manhood most effectively. During Lincoln's 1860 presidential campaign, his supporters famously portrayed him as the rail-splitter candidate, feeling that his already well-known nicknames "Old Abe" and "Honest Abe" lacked the fire and verve that would be most appealing and effective. Beyond presenting their candidate as a humble "self-made man," emphasizing how he symbolized the possibilities of their party's free labor ideology, Republicans also took pains to emphasize the powerful masculinity of their candidate. He made himself into a man—and what a man! This was the primal idea underlying the politically masterful rail-splitter concept. At the Illinois state Republican convention that nominated him, his supporters displayed two fence rails (provided by his cousin John Hanks) that Lincoln had supposedly split himself as a young man. Subsequent campaign prints framed Lincoln and vice presidential candidate Hannibal Hamlin with similar rails, helping to cement the association. His young admirer Grace Bedell wrote Lincoln, in the letter in which she successfully lobbied him to grow a beard, that "the rail fence around your picture makes it look very pretty." Presumably "pretty" was not the association that the Republican national committee was striving to create with the image, nor the first word that would have sprung into most people's heads upon seeing the candidate's craggy, masculine features.[16]

Lincoln's campaign biographer (and later American literary giant) William Dean Howells heavily emphasized the rail-splitter association, and the candidate's physical strength and prowess generally. As a youngster, Howells wrote, Lincoln "with his axe did manful service . . . indeed, with that implement he literally hewed out his path to manhood." Though Lincoln actually despised physical labor, his biographer presented it as being essential to true manhood, and certainly it was central to the free labor ideology of the new party of which Lincoln was now being cast as both the actual leader and imagined symbol. Howells also noted Lincoln's skill at wrestling, particularly his famed match with Jack Armstrong soon after his arrival in New Salem, which, despite its indecisive outcome, helped him win the friendship and eventually the political support of Armstrong and his brawling friends, the "Clary's Grove Boys." Howells asserted that "this seems to have been one of the most significant incidents of his early life," which was probably true in terms of paving the way for his political career. And the author clearly believed that it could still be "significant" in winning admirers for his new, far more ambitious campaign in 1860. Howells also noted that Lincoln's talent for wrestling greatly endeared him to the company he commanded during the Black Hawk War: "In those wrestlings he was never thrown but once, and then by a man of superior science who has not his equal in strength." (Tellingly the author here prefers to highlight Lincoln's brute physical power over his skill and technique as a wrestler, which he is more willing to concede to another man.) "These [along with his good nature] were qualities which commended him to the people" in his early political campaigns. Raw masculine force, demonstrated publicly time and again, thus provided an essential basis for his public career.[17]

Interestingly though, Howells's biography, which Lincoln personally amended and approved, while dealing at some length with his amateur wrestling bouts, did not mention his well-known near duel with Illinois Democrat James Shields in 1842. Lincoln's choice of broadswords "of the largest size" as weapons helped resolve the dispute with the much smaller Shields without actual violence, as did Lincoln's willingness to offer a conciliatory explanation for his motives in supposedly writing the letters that had offended the other man. Though observers often characterized participation in honor conflicts in nineteenth-century America as evidence of masculine courage and pride, Lincoln's embarrassment about this incident and preference not to publicize it suggests that he rather agreed with the Whig editor who criticized him for displaying a lack of manly character by engaging in a barbaric, un-Christian ritual.[18]

Like Howells, other admirers of Lincoln noted his physical size, power, and endurance. In 1861 a Republican editor from Pennsylvania wrote that Lincoln "is powerfully built, 6 feet 4 inches in height, and is not so slender as generally represented," suggesting that already perceptions of Lincoln's physique had become contested. Likewise, an observer at his first public reception as president praised Lincoln's "towering figure and commanding presence," which enabled him to "stand like a hero" in the face of swarming multitudes of office seekers and other curious onlookers. A White House visitor in 1864 wrote admiringly of the president's "Atlantian shoulders . . . fit to bear the weight of [the] mightiest" burdens. The often sharp-tongued Pennsylvania Republican Thaddeus Stevens hyperbolically described Lincoln in an 1864 speech as "a modern Hercules . . . who could throw" his diminutive opponent in that year's presidential campaign, George B. McClellan, "as far as an Indian could shoot an arrow."[19]

Though he generally expressed himself in more modest terms, Lincoln prided himself on his strength as well. When visiting the army in Virginia in 1865, a surgeon worried that Lincoln must be exhausted after hours of handshaking while visiting wounded soldiers. Lincoln instead mildly remarked that he had "strong muscles," and then put on a remarkable exhibition backing up that assertion. First he picked up a heavy axe and "chopped away vigorously" for several minutes. After this, grasping the axe one-handed by the end of the handle, he extended it horizontally, and held it perfectly steady. Following his departure, several "strong soldiers" tried to imitate this accomplishment, but none could. The rail-splitter continued to win admiration for the very public feats of strength and endurance that his masculine body could perform.[20]

Supporters also praised Lincoln for his moral power. This inner strength manifested itself perhaps most obviously in his well-known honesty and integrity. This quality also was fundamentally gendered, as these Victorian Americans saw it, since it outwardly displayed his inner manly character and self-command for all to see. Thus Nathaniel Hawthorne could in 1862 praise Lincoln in the *Atlantic Monthly* as "the man of men," particularly because "he is evidently a man . . . of powerful character. As to his integrity, the people have that intuition of it which is never deceived." Lincoln's generally perceived rectitude demonstrated his inner worth. The *Albany Evening Journal* quoted a New York correspondent who attributed the president's popularity to "his manly common sense, and his unquestionable integrity . . . amid the false pretense and double-dealing of three-fourths of the public men with whom he has been brought into contract." His manly force of character seemed proof against the corrupting influence of politics, to which only weaker men fell prey. Lydia Maria Child, an abolitionist often critical of Lincoln and his policies, was impressed by this quality as well. She thus wrote in 1864 to Lincoln's friend Senator Charles Sumner, "I wish him to be re-elected. Amid the prevailing corruption, it is no small thing to be able to trust in a man's *honesty*." A New York Republican writing the same summer agreed that "the popular regard for Mr. Lincoln is due, in great part, to his personal character, to his sincerity and honesty." As a result of the public perception of Lincoln's manly self-command, this writer thought, no other candidate was likely to successfully challenge "so strong a man as the candidate of the Republican party." Lincoln's inner manly qualities, being rightly perceived and appreciated by the public, thus translated into further masculine dominance over the administration and his potential foes. Such was the actual political power of Lincoln's self-disciplined manhood and integrity.[21]

Even more critically for his success in governing, but building on their appreciation for his personal physical strength and moral integrity, his admirers insisted that Lincoln possessed the masculine force of will and determination to impose discipline and obedience on others when necessary. This essential quality of manhood was often characterized in descriptions of Lincoln as "firmness," a phrase suggestive of physical qualities but primarily referring to a moral or mental trait, which some of his critics had specifically used as well when listing his supposed deficiencies. Two Republican papers from Boston both expressed their admiration for Lincoln using this term. In December 1863 the radical *Commonwealth* professed pleasure at the president's recently delivered annual message to Congress, although the editor had ridiculed the previous year's message, asserting that history would remember Lincoln as a weak, inadequate man. Another year's acquaintance and reflection, however, had altered the paper's editorial stance on the quality of the president's manhood. The editor most specifically praised the message for its emphasis on Lincoln's continuing commitment to emancipation as a war aim. But this policy, the editor asserted, revealed something fundamental about Lincoln's masculine qualities. "We know that he is a firm and honest man, and that he is master of the situation, President of the United States and not controlled by Cabinet or clique," as suspicious critics had so often charged. Lincoln's characteristic determination to stick to a policy once he had settled on it, and what this perceptive writer now understood as Lincoln's mastery over his strong but sometimes discordant cabinet, was good enough for him. "It is all that we need ask," in fact.

The more moderate *Advertiser* agreed the next month that it had taken "a tenacious hold upon a matured purpose, to carry the president through" the stormy period that had befallen the nation. "Some critics," the writer conceded, "regard him as wanting in firmness, because, under representative institutions, he has not thought it wise to refuse to public opinion and the popular will any part in forming his official judgments." Far from lacking in firmness of will, this writer insisted, Lincoln in fact possessed sufficient reserves of this essential manly quality to do his duty as the head of the republic, despite constant criticism. Lincoln was man enough to ignore his critics, who at times seemed to be legion, and pursue the course that he believed to be right and that the people as well as posterity would ultimately approve. As another New England editor had earlier presciently predicted in a letter praising Lincoln for the Emancipation Proclamation, "Your firmness . . . will win you the blessing of our country & the world, now & evermore."[22]

Indeed, Lincoln's political success was possible largely due to his skill in demonstrating to peers and the public that he could assert the mastery over other men, and consequently his power over the course of events that were essential to nineteenth-century political leadership and claims to public authority. His perceptive secretary John Hay wrote of the "old man" he came to admire so much through daily association in the White House as a "backwoods Jupiter" running the "machinery" of government "with a hand equally steady & equally firm." Elsewhere he wrote glowingly, "There is no man in the country, so wise, so gentle, and so firm. I believe the hand of God placed him where he is." Hay was not alone in seeing this possibly divinely granted quality of "firmness," which due to his vantage point he could appreciate better that most, as being essential to Lincoln's greatness. Even an often critical London paper had to concede belatedly following Lincoln's murder that the "gigantic . . . rail-splitter from Illinois" had ultimately "won for himself . . . by firmness, and by a certain progressive and expanding power," the respect and admiration of all. Lincoln's masculine physical stature and power, under the control and direction of his manly will and determination, according to these admirers, were the essential tools that enabled him to succeed in his great tasks as the savior of the Union and the emancipator of American slaves. It was at root gendered, masculine qualities that earned the respect of these supporters and, as they perceived it, enabled him to succeed. "The Lincoln image" that made him so admired, respected, and, ultimately, beloved, was fundamentally a masculine one.[23]

My analysis of Lincoln's image suggests that the two contrasting, contested ideals of aggressive masculinity and prototypically Victorian manliness as self-restraint coexisted throughout the Civil War era, and both played vital roles in the nation's political culture. If anything, the importance of establishing a reputation for masculine power in the creation of political credibility and popularity has been greatly underestimated. Both the long sectional political conflict over slavery and the Civil War itself confirmed long-standing public associations between masculine force and effective political leadership, although the restrictions of Victorian manhood had to be met at least minimally as well. Lincoln's masculine rail-splitter image came first and was most central to his political rise. Only later did he develop the unique image for manly kindness, mercy, and restraint that ultimately distinguished him.

Damnable Treason
or Party Organs?

*Democratic Secret Societies
in Pennsylvania*

Robert M. Sandow

In 1964, intellectual historian Richard Hofstadter coined the phrase "paranoid style" to signify the "heated exaggeration, suspiciousness, and conspiratorial fantasy" that has characterized American partisan politics. He attributed the defect to "confrontation of opposed interests" and noted that party rancor increased during "historical catastrophes or frustrations." To Hofstadter, practitioners of the style were seldom pragmatic or compromising, and "through distorting lenses" imagined their own high principles under assault by sinister forces.[1] The political quarreling of the Civil War exemplified this phenomenon and scholars have written at length about the extent and nature of wartime partisanship. At the core of Republican Party rhetoric was the assertion that Democratic opposition was "disloyalty" undermining the war effort through treasonous speech and armed resistance to government authority.

Perhaps because of the moral weightiness of dissent in war, interpretations of antiwar Democrats, or Copperheads, often range from condemnation to apologetics. The most recent broad study, Jennifer L. Weber's *Copperheads: The Rise and Fall of Lincoln's Opponents in the North*, reasserted the Republican paradigm of Democratic disloyalty. A principal contention of *Copperheads* was to validate Republican accusations that opposition was widespread, conspiratorial, militant, and damaging to Union forces and thus worthy of the scorn heaped on them by Union soldiers.[2] Weber's vigorous narrative is national in scope, but evidence presented from community study offers alternative interpretive models. Despite the heavy emphasis in scholarship on midwestern opposition, *Copperheads* acknowledged that the Pennsylvania Appalachians contained "the most serious resistance in the country."[3] Scrutiny of military evidence suggests otherwise, however, and this study demonstrates the value and need for more community studies of the Civil War era. Democrats there did organize and resort to extralegal resistance, but such dissent was largely grassroots and uncoordinated rather than the imagined large-scale national conspiracies forming a staple of Republican discourse. Moreover, a politics of fear and the partisan language of "disloyalty" exaggerated the extent and nature of opposition. Lastly, opponents of the war, like Confederate ideologues, frequently justified resistance as a political act modeled on the memory of the Revolution as an armed struggle of the people against tyranny. Recovering this "libertarian" perspective is part of a larger understanding of how partisan rhetoric shaped the issue of resistance.

Wars are periods of national crisis during which issues of dissent and "loyalty" become highly charged. The question of whether a loyal opposition is legitimate becomes even more complicated during civil wars that threaten the existence of a nation and the fabric of a society. A key question for a democracy in war is how to balance individual civil rights and liberties against the needs of the nation and the sovereignty of the state. The limits of wartime dissent and the boundaries of acceptable words and behavior are often contested in a public discourse on "loyalty" or "patriotism." This question becomes more difficult in a protracted conflict accompanied by the onset of war weariness. The operation of two-party politics intensifies debate in reaction to partisan interpretations of the war's policy and events. Historians had once argued that the operation of a two-party system mitigated extremism and was an advantage to the northern war effort.[4] Mark E. Neely Jr. challenged this stale "two-party-system theory," illustrating how partisan opposition maintained voter fears at fever pitch. Neely suggested that the main theme of Republican "paranoid style" was to replace fears of the "Slave Power" with fears of "sedition."[5]

Partisan rhetoric and the national crisis of war had two results. For Republicans, partisanship generated fears of widespread conspiracy and armed resistance. Leaders warned that the republic was under threat from external and internal foes and instituted a number of measures to suppress dissent in the name of loyalty. For opposition Democrats, party heads heightened the fears of rank-and-file members that the government and its founding principles were being subverted by Republican war measures. They likewise depicted the "Union as it was" under assault, drawing on a Revolutionary language of "tyranny" and "despotism." The language of this rhetorical duel was largely generated by party elite and intended for partisan effect to galvanize voters. It had serious consequences at the grassroots level, contributing to community divisions and generating significant levels of alarm, tension, and sometimes violence. Republicans fearful of Jacobin plots pleaded with the government to enforce order using the military. Democrats saw conscription, suspension of civil liberties, and emancipation as proofs of government corruption. In their minds, these actions nullified the authority of the Lincoln administration and justified armed resistance to its war measures.

To a large degree, wartime perspectives have continued to frame historiographical debate, but viewpoints frequently reflect contemporary circumstances or attitudes. The interpretation of antiwar Democrats has shifted considerably over the last 150 years. Wartime Republicans fashioned the most enduring icon — the paradigm of disloyal "Copperheads." The reproachful term relied on the central metaphor of the venomous snake but carried with it a number of component parts. Peace Democrats were selfishly partisan, reckless southern sympathizers, and traitors to the imperiled nation. This "fire in the rear" (as Lincoln phrased it) was also charged with the creation of armed "secret societies" intent on resisting federal authority and undermining the northern war effort.[6] Republican dialogue stoked voter fears over a shadowy organization dubbed the "Knights of the Golden Circle," purported to exist throughout the North. Apprehension existed that the KGC or its subsidiary groups would enact secession in the Midwest and carry out acts of sabotage behind the lines.

Maintained by postwar "bloody shirt" politics, the Copperhead discourse remained fixed well into the period of reconciliation. For those who experienced the war, the term Copperhead required no explanation. It was often used as an epithet generally synonymous with the Democratic Party, even by those aware of distinctions between advocates of war and peace. The broad application of the term has left scholars with a significant problem of definition. More sensitive studies distinguish core issues that divided Democrats and challenge the utility of simple categorization into war and peace factions.[7] Wartime Republicans maintained and benefited from oversimplification. General John A. Logan's *The Great Conspiracy: Its Origins and History* (1886) typified the scornful attitudes held by Union veterans. Peace Democrats were malignant agitators who "endeavored to conceal their treacherous designs under a veneer of gushing lip-loyalty" while they "'fired upon the rear' of our hard-pressed Armies." Though once an Illinois Democrat, Logan became a radical Republican and an organizing figure in the Grand Army of the Republic. The GAR was instrumental in the creation of a national Memorial Day and pushed for the adoption of a schoolchildren's "pledge of allegiance."[8] For those unfamiliar with the term "Copperhead," late-century reference works preserved its wartime flavor. One deliciously partisan example defined it as "a venomous biped, of Northern birth and Southern tendencies; a term applied in the late civil war to Northern sympathizers with the Confederates; a disloyal person."[9]

The first generation of professional historians said little on the subject of wartime Democrats and did little to challenge the prevailing view. The dominant mode of inquiry focused on the extent and legitimacy of dissent and whether the Lincoln administration was justified in stretching constitutional limits to preserve authority. Such works generally avoided discussion of the motivation for dissent and tended to defend Lincoln's actions as necessary.[10] The "nationalist" historian James Ford Rhodes is an oft-cited example. Without denying the utility of an opposition party, Rhodes asserted that Peace Democrats had a civic obligation to support the war "when the Ship of State is in distress." To Rhodes, draft resistance was a moral failure.[11]

The outbreak of World War I revealed how contemporary wartime loyalty debates shaped historical interpretations. William A. Dunning paralleled the plight of Lincoln and Woodrow Wilson, vindicating both for the suppression of civil liberties against "disloyalty." "'Pacifists' and 'pro-Germans,'" wrote Dunning, "caused as much distress to agitated patriots as did Copperheads and Southern sympathizers, and produced no less astonishing exhibitions of what is now called 'war psychology.'"[12] The historian Robert Abzug asserted that Dunning "fell victim to the same wartime fears which transformed sauerkraut into victory cabbage."[13] Postwar disillusionment, however, led "revisionist" historians such as Avery O. Craven to reassess Democrats in a more positive light. In the face of a "needless war," Democrats were a salutary balance against abolitionist extremism. Revisionists distrusted hawkish manipulations of patriotism and subversion of civil rights.[14]

The pendulum swung again with the outbreak of World War II, during which two studies appeared that revived elements of the Republican Copperhead discourse. The wartime atmosphere is clearly seen in George Fort Milton's unscholarly *Abraham Lincoln and the Fifth Column*, a work whose transparent title revealed the workings of a twentieth-century viewpoint.[15] A protégé of Avery Craven named Wood Gray wrote a more significant study titled *The Hidden Civil War: The Story of the Copperheads*. Looking most closely at the Midwest, Gray accepted Democratic secret societies as genuine and detailed a purported failed plot of the "Sons of Liberty" to remove the Old Northwest from the Union. He distinguished blame, though, condemning the manipulative party leaders rather than their misled, impoverished masses. In a lengthy defense of military arrests and suspension of habeas corpus, Lincoln wrote likewise in 1863, "Must I shoot a simple-minded soldier boy who deserts, while I must not touch a hair of a wiley agitator who induces him to desert?"[16] Gray warned that their type—partisan and opportunistic—was "dangerous in a democracy . . . [and] necessitate a constant vigilance in any period that they may be identified and combated."[17] Gray deserves some credit, nonetheless, for providing a context to Democratic opposition and for describing organized resistance as a reaction to Republican suppression. The onset of the Cold War and the fear it engendered of subversives in American society gave resonance to Gray's dire caution. In 1959, Allan Nevins, a dean of Civil War scholarship, praised his work as "one of solid thoroughness by a university historian, with a full analysis of forces."[18]

The reputation of Peace Democrats languished until the publication in 1960 of *The Copperheads in the Middle West* by iconoclast Frank L. Klement. Rejecting stereotype and the dominant debate over "loyalty," Klement sought to understand the socioeconomic cause for Democratic opposition. He presented them as "conservative" civil libertarians frustrated and disadvantaged by their wartime role as opponents of the Lincoln administration. Klement pointed to the poorer regions of the lower Midwest where market connections faced both South and East. The "Butternuts" were Negrophobic and their western identity made them resentful of domination by eastern elites. Klement also examined how war opponents were united in their denunciation of Republican war policies, notably emancipation, conscription, and military arrests. His work dismissed the charges of Democratic secret societies as Republican propaganda exploited for political gain.

Klement was not without his critics. To be fair, *The Copperheads in the Middle West* was not the first comprehensive reappraisal of the motives for resistance. His research built on a growing body of state and regional studies, predominantly of the Midwest, that sought to explain Copperheads on their own terms. While appearing after the turn of the century, such work took off in the 1930s.[19] Because Klement's work did not acknowledge a historiographical context, Robert Abzug criticized the book for not offering a new perspective on the peace movement.[20] Scholar Richard O. Curry questioned to what degree explanations of soil fertility, southern origins, and midwestern sectionalism illuminate the underpinnings of Copperheadism more broadly. Quantitative scrutiny of midwestern data did not always fit this general mold, and it held less analytic power in other border and eastern states. This led Curry to question the midwestern model and ask whether the "sound and fury" of dissent there has obscured the strength and importance of "conservative Unionism" in other states of the Union.[21] Klement's contribution is undeniable, and a comprehensive bibliography tallied sixty-eight books, chapters, and articles as proof of his vigorous pen and zeal to dispel slanderous mythologies concerning the Copperheads.[22] Of this corpus, Mark E. Neely Jr.

summed, "The shrewd and painstaking work of historian Frank L. Klement over the last thirty years has proved, beyond any reasonable doubt, that no systematic, organized disloyal opposition to the war existed in the North."[23]

Since Klement, a great deal of fruitful inquiry has appeared to help reevaluate the wartime Democratic Party and the significance of resistance. The "new political history" movement of the 1970s and 1980s brought attention to issues of ordinary voters, political culture, and social values. Joel Silbey's *A Respectable Minority* and Jean Baker's *Affairs of Party* exemplified this approach.[24] Other studies outside this movement, including Mark Neely's *The Union Divided*, looked specifically at how vigorous party competition shaped the conflict and attitudes toward dissent. Additionally, studies of Copperheadism outside the Midwest offered parallels and challenges to previous findings.[25]

In this context, Jennifer Weber's recent study emerged as a repudiation of Copperhead revisionism. Her work, *Copperheads*, rightfully emphasized the pervasiveness of Democratic dissent and its divisiveness at the community level. In an otherwise contemptuous portrait, Weber conceded that "most Copperheads were not traitors." Much like Wood Gray, she judged them reckless obstructionists, naive, anachronistic, and partisan opportunists. *Copperheads* largely ignored the historiography of the subject, targeting Klement as an apologist. Neither did the author dwell at length on motivations for Copperheadism. She offered a bland mélange of southern origins, western sectionalism, racism, and conservative political ideology—a homogenization that echoed the midwestern model.[26]

Most significantly, Weber repeated Republican assertions that opposition "damaged the army's ability to prosecute the conflict efficiently" by resisting the draft, encouraging desertion, and diverting soldiers to the home front. She argued further that "clandestine organizations such as the KGC" were proven by the sheer volume of references to them found in primary sources of the period. Weber did not distinguish, however, between uncoordinated grassroots resistance and allegations of mass, party-led societies. Her statements more accurately attest to the power of partisan rhetoric to fuel voter anxieties.[27] *Copperheads* illustrated a prophetic warning by the historian Jean Baker more than twenty-five years earlier: "Because the copperhead myth has provided a useful image of how Americans should not behave during war, it will resist even the most determined efforts at excision, and students of the Civil War era may expect to meet it, in various guises, for many years to come."[28]

One problem facing historians today is the intellectual baggage of a paradigm of patriotism solidified in the Civil War era. Partisanship and the exigencies of war encouraged Republicans to stress a conception of nationalism that emphasized "unconditional loyalty" to the federal state and the abandonment of political parties. As German émigré and Republican intellectual Francis Lieber intoned in his influential "No Party Now" speech, "We declare that this is no question of politics, but one of patriotism."[29] This emergent nationalism defined criticism of the administration and opposition to its conduct of the war as treasonous dissent. Civilians brought before military tribunals could be charged with the following crime: "The commission of acts of disloyalty against the Government of the United States, and uttering disloyal sentiments and opinions, with the object of defeating and weakening the power of the Government in its efforts to suppress the unlawful rebellion now existing in the United States."[30] This call for universal patriotism was predicated on a "doctrine of necessity," in which the peril of the Union required the unwavering support of all its citizens. The minister Henry Bellows, influential in the formation of the United States Sanitary Commission and the Union League Club of New York, put it plainly: "To rally round the President—without question or dispute—is the first and most sacred duty of loyal citizens, when he announces, not that the Constitution merely, but that the National life and existence are in peril."[31]

To educate northerners about this new conception of patriotism, wealthy Republicans founded Union Leagues, with their most powerful centers in Philadelphia, New York, and Boston. Their Loyal Publication Societies deluged the North with this core message, and offshoot Union Leagues appeared in northern communities.[32] Scholars have described the rhetoric of unconditional loyalty as a manifestation of "modern" nationalism and the coercive power of the state.[33] This internalized paradigm works in powerful ways against sympathetic portrayals of Copperheads. Times of national crisis magnify the effect, whether it be the World War II publication of Wood Gray's *The Hidden Civil War* or the September 11 backdrop of Jennifer Weber's *Copperheads*.[34] The historian Robert Churchill described the impact of such trauma as a "moral panic" afflicting the nation, in which fears drive a people to identify enemies and take action to control "subversives."[35]

Flummoxed Democrats were at a hopeless disadvantage against the Republican rhetoric of loyalty and unable to effectively counter the reconfigured patriotism. "Theirs was often a bewildered world of powerless frustration," wrote Mark Neely, "and their vision of society a bleak phantasmagoria induced by a political reality substantially unalterable for years."[36] They attempted a feeble symbolic inversion of the Copperhead moniker, fashioning pins or medallions out of copper Liberty Head coins. Historians have rightfully identified this "doctrine of loyalty," in the words of the intellectual historian George M. Fredrickson, as a Republican partisan tactic, but the gravitation of the concept continues to pull some scholars toward it.[37] Even while denouncing the partisan ploy, most Copperhead studies feel obliged to absolve Peace Democrats of the disloyal label.[38]

Democrats offered their own conceptualization of loyalty and patriotism but it failed to blunt the assault on their character. They defined loyalty as a defense of the Constitution, "the Union as it was," and government for whites. Within this framework, Democrats claimed for themselves the role of a "loyal opposition."[39] They denied the doctrine of necessity and held the administration as distinct from government embodied in the laws and the Constitution. The Democratic editor of the *Clearfield Republican*, in Clearfield County, Pennsylvania, thus wrote, "'Old Abe' said, when on his way to the white house, 'that he intended to run the machine as he found it.' Now this, Tho' a very homely expression, and a very indefinite definition of Government, is yet sufficiently illustrative of the distinction. The Machine 'Old Abe' spoke of is the Government, and the running of the Machine is the Administration; so that men may differ greatly as to the best way of running it, and yet find no fault with the Machine."[40] Melinda Lawson's work suggested that Democratic ideas of loyalty were widely held in the antebellum period. Before the war, nationalism was a "contractual" loyalty predicated on weak national government and "suspicions of concentrated power." Moreover, in that era of "contentious party culture," Lawson observed, "definitions of loyalty and national identity during the Civil War revolved around party."[41]

Scholars need to examine the meaning and impact of dissent more fully, but two Pennsylvania regional test cases, in Clearfield and Columbia Counties, allow us to scrutinize the issue at the grassroots level. In both areas, Republican civilian and military authorities became convinced of widespread, armed resistance to the draft. Such fears justified military expeditions in the final months of 1864 aimed at arresting deserters and overawing militant dissent. Purported secret societies were a major inquiry of the military tribunals that followed. These military courts preserved verbatim transcripts of trials as well as a large volume of paperwork. The two counties are significant because they were deemed at the time to constitute the most serious resistance in Pennsylvania. Weber and other scholars have concurred based on initial federal reports published in the Official Records.[42] Close examination of government records, however, does not bear out the charges of armed subversion and large-scale conspiracy.

In the summer of 1864, officials of the Provost Marshal General's Bureau in Pennsylvania grew alarmed over urgent reports of widespread draft resistance. Letters and meetings with citizens furnished sketchy outlines of regional networks of community opposition. Though the problem existed to some degree in nearly every congressional district, Richard I. Dodge, the Provost Marshal for Western Pennsylvania, became worried about two problematic areas: northern Columbia County, in north–central Pennsylvania, and Clearfield County in the densely wooded Appalachian Plateau of the northwest. Both were staunchly Democratic counties and the disaffected regions were disproportionately poor and rural. Clearfield offered additional problems in that the rugged geography of its vast, sparsely populated wilderness offered tremendous potential to hide deserters and draft evaders.

The military tallied a long list of defiant actions in both locations that included harassment and assault of bureau employees, violence that included the mortal shooting of arresting officers, alleged secret societies to oppose the draft, and hundreds of men who had failed to report when drafted. Local Republicans described a climate of fear and made reports on supposed armed groups and weapons caches. Federal officials passed these impressions on to superiors in Washington to sanction military force against "malcontents." Provost Marshal Dodge estimated organized resistance in northern Columbia County at roughly five hundred men. Such opposition appeared most serious in the mountains of Clearfield. At the beginning of November 1864, Dodge sent ominous news to Provost Marshal General James B. Fry: "I am reliably informed that there are at this time from 1,200 to 1,800 deserters, delinquent drafted men, and disloyal citizens, armed and organized, engaged in lumbering on Clearfield River, in Clearfield and Cambria Counties."[43]

The impression that foes of the government were "armed and organized" was a staple of Republican rhetoric, but military expeditions failed to uncover large-scale treason. Dodge noted "a constantly increasing boldness and defiant spirit on the part of the opposers of the Administration, and a growing despondency and indisposition to exert themselves on the part of its friends." In a plan reminiscent of President Washington's 1794 suppression of the Whiskey Rebellion, Dodge ordered Union forces "to enter one county with a force sufficiently strong not only to put down but to overawe resistance."[44] In Columbia County, Dodge employed a mixed force made up of members from the Veteran Reserve Corps as well as other troops belonging to the Department of the Susquehanna. From August through October, soldiers operated in the region arresting deserters and draft evaders and attempting to uncover evidence of an armed conspiracy dubbed the "Fishing Creek Confederacy."[45] The Clearfield expedition came afterward and portions of the 16th Regiment Veteran Reserve Corps arriving in December endured harsh winter service. While officials pronounced the raids a success, they did not validate the reports of organized mass resistance.[46]

Reports of military officials, expeditions, and tribunals offered ample evidence of widespread, uncoordinated resistance at the grassroots level. Pennsylvania thus illustrates a broader phenomenon of deep communal cleavages wrought by the war. The conflict politicized everyday life considerably and became the center of discussion in northern streets, homes, shops, churches, and workplaces. This conforms to interpretations that stress the diversity of northern experiences.[47] Resistance in this "inner civil war" came in a variety of forms, both legal and illegal. Opposition to Republican war measures brought intimidation, destruction of property, and acts of individual and group violence. Targets of violence included civilians, soldiers, and government officials, especially those of the Provost Marshal General's Bureau. Much of the extralegal resistance was a reaction to the draft. Enrollment officers routinely faced threats, assault, and deception, and in mountainous Clearfield a high percentage of them quit their jobs. Men were sometimes discouraged from enlisting, and large numbers of drafted men refused to report. Bureau officers delivering notices or arresting deserters and drafted men were obstructed and attacked—and in both Clearfield and Columbia County men were murdered undertaking such work. The collusion of family and community was one of the most prominent aspects of resistance. Federal officials made note of the many women who lied, assaulted officers, or otherwise aided kinfolk or neighbors.[48]

Conscription was the primary cause for much of this resistance. Criticism of the draft stemmed from different sources of complaint beyond its violations of traditional volunteerism. Reflecting on the provisions of commutation and substitution, a Democratic Club in a farming district of Columbia County denounced the law as "unjust, in that it favors the rich . . . while it consigns the poor man to the hardships and dangers of the battlefield." Protest resolutions also echoed constitutional arguments that the draft "tramples upon the rights of the States, disregards the civil laws and places whole courts under despotic military rule."[49] Other protests were more mundane, such as complaints that federal officials had not properly credited enlistees from the community or that quotas had been calculated erroneously. Poorer regions felt victimized as potential volunteers were lured by the higher bounties in wealthier districts and towns. The Pennsylvania Appalachians also had a large number of roving workers, many of whom were captured on initial enrollment lists. More permanent residents argued that such transients bloated the estimates of available men and artificially raised quotas.

In many ways, resistance was an expression of community desire for local autonomy more than advocacy of "peace."[50] After a former soldier was shot and mortally wounded arresting deserters in Columbia County, an anonymous Democrat summed up community feeling in a letter to the Bloomsburg paper: "We wish it distinctly understood that we seek no harm and shall commit no uncivil acts, unless driven to it. All we ask is to be let alone that we may peaceably pursue our various vocations. We would have it understood, also, that the people do not intend to suffer themselves to be draged [*sic*] from their homes by force to fight for the 'Abolition [of] Slavery.'"[51] The idea that the war had become an emancipation struggle permeated Democratic rhetoric. "THIS WAR IS FOR THE ABOLITION [OF] SLAVERY," proclaimed editor Levi Tate of the *Columbia Democrat*, "not for the Union as it was, not for the Constitution as it is; not for the purpose originally avowed, but for a different and an unconstitutional purpose, *a Nigger war*."[52] Such ranting proved influential given the pervasive racism and fears of the social and economic consequences of black migration.

Some northerners joined together to defy the draft out of a sense of its illegitimacy. In both Columbia and Clearfield Counties, as well as others across the state, unknown numbers of men eligible for the draft formed "mutual protection societies." Such organizations were repeated across the North and pledged members to assist one another if drafted. The manner of assistance could be financial, pooling money or raising subscriptions for commutation, bounties, or substitution. Others relied on promises of group intimidation or violence against understaffed marshals. Republicans reported that such organizations were secret and armed and that they acted as a paramilitary, establishing fortified safe havens and conducting military drills. Frank Klement argued that mutual protection societies were reactions to Republican attacks and the formation of Union Leagues, which he maligned as "the secret and militant arm of the Republican party." Klement saw the Democratic groups of the Midwest as a defense against mob violence and arbitrary arrest as well as the draft. There is little evidence to suggest that party leaders suggested or supported these organizations.[53] It is demonstrable that mutual protection societies did exist and that crowd confrontations with federal officials prohibited arrests or freed prisoners. In Clearfield County during December 1864, two marshals were forced to release two men from custody and ride for their lives in the face of an armed crowd. Military courts convicted five men for the incident. A majority of the defendants and accomplices were recent German migrants into the county. While their defense lawyers made nothing of this fact, their ethnicity offers clues to explain their alienation from the draft.[54]

Defendants in military tribunals claimed that such clubs were inherently political or that the resort to violence was unintended. In defining criminal behavior, Congress had outlawed "entering into, confederating and assisting in forming combinations" against the draft, as well the actions of "harboring, concealing and secreting deserters, and counseling and advising drafted men to absent themselves and evade their duty as soldiers."[55] Defending the military courts as constitutional, Lincoln made the following statement: "He who dissuades one man from volunteering, or induces one soldier to desert, weakens the Union cause as much as he who kills a union soldier in battle. Yet this dissuasion, or inducement, may be so conducted as to be no defined crime of which any civil court would take cognizance."[56] Military authorities took Republican accusations of armed and organized resistance seriously. Federal agents sought to root out alleged secret societies and probed deeply into two seemingly connected institutions: mutual protection societies and communal Democratic Clubs.

Democratic Clubs spread across the state in the spring of 1862, predominantly as a reaction to the formation of Union Leagues. The highly decentralized clubs differed significantly because they lacked the financial and intellectual resources of the urban leagues. They could not shape public discourse as effectively as did the mass publications of their rivals. The *Columbia Democrat* urged on readers "the propriety of at once organizing clubs and establishing reading rooms throughout the county." Editor Tate reminded pointedly, "On the results of the next election in Pennsylvania hang the most important results."[57] While Tate stressed voter organization, Republicans argued that the Democratic Clubs were a front for extralegal resistance.

Democrats were to blame for a significant level of confusion about the clubs. A number of them incorporated elements of fraternal organizations including secret oaths, rituals, passwords and signs of recognition. One defensive postwar reflection considered the clubs a foolish adaptation of common forms used by groups such as the Know-Nothings. According to the author, the clubs "were very modest, unpretending, innocent and unproscriptive, as compared with the Loyal Leagues. The signs were harmless, the oath patriotic, the secrecy slight and the purpose of the association entirely proper if not laudable." "Secrecy is a source of enthusiasm," he continued, explaining the psychology at work, which "was calculated to captivate the unreflecting" and influence elections.[58] To some degree, the Union Leagues and Democratic Clubs were not just about solidifying the political base of the party but contesting for uncommitted voters. The clubs were premature as campaign tools, and many meetings were abandoned with the onset of summer. Democratic Clubs in some areas persisted into 1864, but Lincoln's reelection obviated their usefulness.

It would be misleading, nonetheless, to assert that the clubs had no connections to illegal resistance. When military expeditions arrived in 1864, those accused of attending the Democratic Club meetings were placed on the same lists as those who were observed to obstruct the draft or counsel resistance. The testimony of Peter Kase of Benton Township, Columbia County, typifies how meetings were described. Attendees gathered in homes, schoolhouses, and barns throughout rural areas. Kase recounted the various signs, passwords, and rituals as well as an oath to support the Constitution, but argued that "there was nothing said about resisting the draft."[59] Kase's circumspection may have been accurate for the earliest meetings of these clubs, but he likely left out incriminating details.

In other cases, Democratic Clubs clearly did become the foundation for mutual protection societies. In Clearfield County, the Democrat Club styled themselves the "Democratic Castle," and "lodges" were copied in a number of townships. Here was the closest thing to a grand organized conspiracy, but upon closer inspection it fell considerably short. The Democratic Castle appears to have been founded in August 1864 in the wake of a county-wide organizational meeting for the fall elections. The meeting in Clearfield featured key state leaders, former governor William Bigler, and state senator and rising star William Wallace. Neither man was behind the organization of the "Castle," but local politicians wanted to capitalize on their angry denunciations of the "usurper and tyrant" Lincoln.[60]

The group spread through individual contact and a number of organizational meetings. A founding constitution governed lodge structure and offered its guiding political principles. Members were given an oath, along with secret passwords, grips, and signs of identification. The bland written document, seized as evidence of treason, was no more incendiary than the resolutions of regional Democrat Clubs printed publicly in 1863. An official in the Judge Advocate's office described the organization as "an unformed and crude secret fraternity."[61] It was not overly complex because it was intended for an unsophisticated audience. A farmer from Brady Township was asked to explain the principles of the group. "At the time they were read, I did not understand them very well," he recalled. "I am a very poor scholar." The only core value that witnesses repeated with accuracy was that "we were to stick together and help each other." Military prosecutors sought to clarify the expectations placed on group initiates. One exchange in the trial of an organizing figure was revealing:

Question. What did he say?
Answer. He instructed us, and gave us the signs grips and passwords. He gave us the signs so that in case a drafted man was taken by the Provost Marshals, he, the drafted man, could give the signs, and that the other members could take the man away.

Question. Were all the members bound to assist in his release if called upon?

Answer. As far as I understand it, they were.

Question. Was or was not anything said about calling upon the club, if two or three men could not release a drafted man.

Answer. Yes sir.

Question. What was said?

Answer. It was talked that if two or three could not release the man, we were to notify the club, and get sufficient men to do it.[62]

While the Democratic Castle was defended as purely political, it led to grassroots acts of resistance. The editor of the Clearfield Democratic paper denied any goal to resist conscription: "What others may have interpolated into it, we know not. But if they added any oath, or resistance to any law, it thereby ceased to be consistent with the Constitution upon which it claimed to be founded, and likewise ceased to be 'the Democratic Castle.'"[63] Nevertheless, evidence from military tribunals proved that Castle members resisted the draft and freed prisoners from the custody of marshals. Federal authorities had justified their military expedition in part because of the Democratic Castle. Military courts convicted some of the members but the investigations could not implicate higher political leaders. There is no evidence that the organization spread outside Clearfield County.[64]

Fear of indictment or attack led a number of leaders and newspapers to counsel law and order. Unrestrained newspaper editors faced possible arrest or crowd violence. In May 1863, the Democratic Standing Committee of Columbia County passed the following communication to area citizens, advising the formation of Democratic Clubs: "We recommend to the Democracy of Columbia County the preservation of order, support and obedience to the law and the Constitution; knowing that there is a sovereign remedy for all ills at the ballot box."[65]

As the results of military courts show, generally rank-and-file Democrats rather than political leaders paid the price for resistance through fines and jail. Without doubt, the rhetoric of Democratic leaders raised fears over a Republican "revolution" to alter the nation and its government. Such fears increased the resort to armed resistance, though party leaders were careful to guard their speeches against intemperate calls to arms. The August "monster meeting" of the Democratic Party in Clearfield offered examples. Bigler declared his fidelity to the Union and the government, but "he would not contribute one man, nor one farthing, to prosecute the war for the unlawful purposes set forth by Mr. Lincoln." Wallace referred to the upcoming elections, saying that "it was the duty of all who loved our institutions, to unite for the overthrow of this corrupt and lawless Administration."[66] Pennsylvania Republican leaders were disappointed that military investigations failed to link Bigler and Wallace to acts of resistance.[67]

While Bigler and Wallace no longer made overt calls for militant resistance, they continued to use the memory and language of the Revolution in a way that nurtured it. The diatribes against Lincoln's "tyranny" and "usurpation" were meant to delegitimize his authority. Wallace, for instance, instructed listeners that the Constitution had bound the presidency within "defined and limited powers," and that it was clearly the "duty of the citizen to yield obedience to him." He argued, however, that this "government of law" and all its blessings were subverted by "a prostitution of the powers of the Federal Government, of an interference with the rights of the people, and an attempted control of the powers that were exclusively under the rights of the States." The speaker drove his point home when he told the crowd, "In thus placing himself above the law, Mr. Lincoln had forfeited all right to our respect; that, as a condition precedent to our respect and obedience, he must yield obedience to the law, and that it was the right and the duty of the citizen to denounce him for his breach of duty, and to impeach him and his aiders and abettors before the tribunal of the people for the utter disregard of law."[68] To historians that study wartime rhetoric, Wallace's remarks typify Democratic critiques of the Lincoln administration. It should be acknowledged that the language of this "paranoid style" complicated notions of civic loyalty.

The scholar Robert Churchill has referred to this conception as the "libertarian memory of the Revolution." The radical legacy held several tenets: that government was legitimate in the exercise of authority only when it upheld the rights of citizens and operated within the confines of the Constitution; that the mass of the people had the right and duty to judge for themselves if government had acted accordingly; and that when government violated its sacred trust, its unjust laws were void and the people were justified in the use of armed resistance against them. Proponents of this view stressed "popular nullification," requiring local communities to identify and judge such corruptions and urging unity of action. The legacy also idealized communal "militia" organization as a proper "mode of opposition." Churchill characterized this memory as "a struggle to defend liberty against a corrupt and abusive state . . . by enforcing inviolable constitutional restraints on the power of the state."[69]

Rural Pennsylvanians in disaffected regions understood the historical comparison and the intent of this language. Democratic editor Charles Chauncey Burr articulated this view in an 1865 speech he delivered at a Columbia County Democratic meeting. "Whenever governments attempt to make themselves above the institutions of society," spoke Burr, "it becomes the duty of every patriot to uplift his hand against the government, and to strangle it, and to re-establish again the government as it was before the traitorous revolution commenced."[70] Reverend Burr was a fascinating national figure who published and edited *The Old Guard, a Monthly Journal, Devoted to the Principles of 1776 and 1787*. Denounced by Wood Gray as a "specialist in extremism," Burr's invocation of treason and patriotism stood at odds with his political opponents. His was the only monthly journal consistently expressing the Copperhead perspective.[71] Republicans denied the legitimacy of political violence against the state and discredited the mechanisms of popular nullification and extralegal militias. They further denounced the libertarian memory of the Revolution as dangerous radicalism.[72]

People regularly imagine things that do not exist, and in this case Republicans at all levels perceived these disorganized acts of local resistance as a large-scale armed treason. As Mark Neely pointed out, some historians have interpreted cynically Republican accusations of "sedition" as a partisan trick. He cautioned readers that a great many believed the charges to be true.[73] Numerous Republicans reported threats, vandalism, and attacks against them by Copperheads in their communities. Officials described this as a "reign of terror" justifying the use of military force. When the military expedition to Columbia County arrived in Bloomsburg, a delegation sent Governor Andrew Curtin a telegram. "Can loyal citizens here be furnished two hundred (200) guns?" they asked. "We are surrounded by armed traitors who threaten [to] burn our town."[74] Even if Democratic speeches did not overtly counsel violence, Republican newspapers read between the lines. The *Pittston Gazette* summarized Democratic Fourth of July speeches heard in Benton, Columbia County, in 1863. The "speakers at a Copperhead meeting . . . openly and avowedly . . . counseled their hearers to resist the draft and they would back them in it." The editor blamed these admonitions for the many acts of resistance and violence against officers, and stressed the need to "get up Union Leagues." Evangelizing the "no party" movement, editor G. M. Richart continued, "Join men of different parties who are throwing away old political creeds."[75]

The military men who enforced the draft held the most unenviable position in this struggle. Partisan rhetoric had magnified the imagined threat on both sides. Republican political leaders had great expectations that the military would unmask the conspiracies and defang the Copperheads. The expeditions in Columbia and Clearfield failed to provide significant evidence. Colonel Charles Stewart, who led the expedition into Columbia County, expressed a common viewpoint: "The drafted men I am informed have all gone off and are concentrating in the mountain at the upper end of the County to make a stand if we are not too strong for them."[76] Believing that large-scale resistance was assured, officers had no other choice but to assume that the traitors had escaped. Though considerable numbers of draft evaders were arrested (along with army deserters to a lesser degree), there was almost no organized resistance to soldiers and no signs of the military havens.[77] In February 1865, the editor of the Clearfield Republican wrote an editorial titled "Was Not the Sending of Soldiers to Clearfield a Fraud upon the Government?" In it he wrote, "That some Democrats have been indiscreet, and allowed themselves to commit acts, or use expressions, that are in violation of recent laws, we do not doubt. But the criminal *intention*—always necessary to be proven before conviction—is wanting."[78]

Despite allegations, there is no credible evidence that Pennsylvania contained Democratic secret societies that were part of a national conspiracy. Some federal officials averred otherwise. The infamous October 1864 report by Judge Advocate General Joseph Holt implicated Pennsylvania within the network of the Knights of the Golden Circle.[79] A number of Pennsylvania Republicans likewise repeated contentions like the one printed in the *Brookville Republican* of Jefferson County, that "the Copperheads are in sympathy with, and many of them actually belong to the Knights of the Golden Circle."[80] Arnold Shankman, in his authoritative *The Pennsylvania Antiwar Movement, 1861–1865*, doubts the existence of any such chapters, however.[81] James M. McPherson concurred that the "supposed legions" of the Democratic secret societies across the North "existed more in the fevered imaginations of Republicans than in fact."[82]

Historians have shown uncertainty as to what judgment or lessons should be drawn from this pervasive, extralegal, grassroots opposition. Democrats themselves were divided over appropriate responses to what they perceived as "tyrannical" and "despotic" wartime measures. A great many supported legal remedies rather than illegal ones, emphasizing the weapon of the ballot box and political speech. What encouraged that unknowable proportion to sanction or participate in illegal resistance and armed violence? Given the scant primary sources that might shed light on these motivations, historians have inferred various possibilities. Some highlight, as Republicans did, the influence of bad leadership and partisan speech. Democratic leaders certainly shared guilt in amplifying paranoia with their unceasing attacks on the constitutionality of Republican war policies. Republicans were not blameless in the use of their rhetoric of "loyalty" that criminalized dissenting speech and increased anxieties within communities. Less charitable works have suggested some defect of the people, stemming from ignorance, poverty, or racism. Some Copperheads were undoubtedly despicable characters, but recent scholarship has suggested ways in which localism, ethnicity, regional political issues, and wartime events helped shape patterns of protest as well.

In conclusion, scholarship should focus more on the meaning and impact of dissent during the war, especially through the prism of community studies, rather than on the extent of Democratic "disloyalty." The assumption that resistance undermined the war is accepted with little reflection, and Weber's restatement is only a recent example of its resiliency. Historians addressing the issue of morale in war frequently work, though, from a "modern" assumption that all of a society's resources must support the conflict to achieve victory. Writing on Civil War–era "loyalty and dissent," Jorg Nagler began, "Without the home front, loyal and committed to a cause, politicians in a democratic state hesitate to support a war, and ultimately the battle front collapses."[83] This view holds unconditional support as the ideal type and characterizes dissent as damaging to an ill-defined national psychology. Wood Gray wrapped Copperhead opposition in the twentieth-century term "defeatism," which he saw as afflicting the Lincoln administration like a cancer. Unquestioned national unity, however, was not the political culture of the mid-nineteenth century. Scholars of the era would do well to remember that dissent in war is the norm of American democracy rather than the aberration.

Copperheads in Connecticut

A Peace Movement That Imperiled the Union

Matthew Warshauer

In the immediate aftermath of the Union's loss at Bull Run, many in Connecticut expressed dire concerns over the fate of their little New England state. The worry was not any impending Confederate invasion, but the very real belief that a concerted Democratic secession movement existed. A. A. Pettingill, the editor of the *Bridgeport Republican*, wrote to Governor William A. Buckingham on August 24, 1861, "I am becoming alarmed at the condition of things in this part of the State. Rebels—& very active ones—can be found without going south of the Mason & Dixon line. In other words we have *open traitors* at home." Pettingill insisted, "We are now threatened with a *Peace party* & a formidable one. There are towns in this Co. in which these men now have a decided majority—towns in which a War Tax could not be collected without the aid of military force." He warned further, "There are secret organizations—one in this city—the members of which have *armed themselves for some purpose*—not a patriotic one."[1] Not long after this warning Bridgeport erupted in violence when Democrats held a peace meeting to oppose the war. Intent on breaking up the gathering, P. T. Barnum, the erstwhile showman and a staunch Union supporter, rallied citizens and former Union soldiers (the three-month veterans who had just returned from Bull Run). They chased Democrats off, sang "The Star-Spangled Banner," then turned their sites on the Democratic *Bridgeport Farmer*. The press was destroyed and the editor, Nathan Morse, escaped only by fleeing across the rooftops. This was not the only incidence of violence in Connecticut, nor was it a singular manifestation of Democratic, antiwar sentiment.

Historians have long known that opposition to the Civil War existed in the North. The degree of that opposition, where it existed, and the extent to which it reflected the views of those in a given community, however, has remained a point of contention. Tied to such issues is the question of whether the two-party system was a benefit or hindrance to the Union war effort. A study of Civil War

Connecticut sheds light on such historiographical disputes by demonstrating the very real existence of a Democratic peace movement and the threat it posed to the North's ability to fight for Union.

The earliest studies of the Copperhead movement, as it was called, were those by Wood Gray, George Fort Milton, and Frank L. Klement. All three concentrated on the Democratic peace movement in what is today the Midwest, with Gray and Milton attempting in 1942 to determine whether the Copperheads truly threatened an overthrow of local or state government. Klement insisted in 1960 and later that the movement was, in reality, insignificant and merely the machinations of conspiracy-minded Republicans.[2]

More recently, in 2008, Jennifer L. Weber argued that the Copperheads were not a fringe group or "peripheral issue" dreamed up by Republicans. Rather, the Democratic peace movement was broad based, existed throughout the North (not just in the Midwest), divided neighborhoods, and threatened Lincoln's ability to fight the war. In essence, the Copperheads created a formidable faction that affected both the northern home front and the Union military effort. These latter points intersect directly with the issue of whether two-party competition in the North was an advantage to the Union, for the Copperhead movement most certainly constituted a significant challenge to Republicans intent on stopping southern secession. Weber insisted that Democrats mounted their most serious challenge during the 1864 presidential contest. Many Republicans feared Lincoln would lose, which may have presaged the end of the Union.[3]

The question of beneficial two-party competition was most conspicuously challenged in 2002 by Mark E. Neely Jr., who expressed doubts about what historians had concluded concerning the efficacy of two parties vying for political control, and reminded readers of the "astonishing political conflicts that emerged within the North during the war." Few were advantageous to the Union war effort. Neely insisted that he was raising questions and attempting to stimulate debate on the subject. In 2006, Adam I. P. Smith embraced the topic, largely agreeing with Neely by concluding that partisanship amid the war created serious divisions that often revolved around issues of party legitimacy and nationalism.[4]

Interestingly, Weber's work rightly brought together these two strains of thought, the threatening reality of the Copperhead movement and its impact on party politics. So formidable was the Democratic movement, argued Weber, that it weakened the Union war effort by causing dissent, established a level of animosity that threatened local communities, affected recruiting and the draft, and politicized soldiers on the front who read in letters and newspapers about what was happening at home. None of this was good for the war effort. Like ear-

lier historians, Weber noted in particular that areas of the lower Midwest were
especially wracked by discontent and threatened open conflict. Yet Weber also
noted some incidences of Copperhead activity in other parts of the nation, even
in New England.

Connecticut provides ample evidence of Weber's assertions. From the outset of the war, the state was wracked by internal, sometimes violent dissent that
manifested itself in individual and mob violence; competing Democratic peace
rallies versus Republican pro-war meetings; party newspaper combat in which
each side hurled insults and conspiratorial accusations at the other; Democratic
opposition to the draft; intense racism and criticism of Lincoln's Emancipation
Proclamation; and a dire gubernatorial political contest that revealed a remarkable connection between the home front and Connecticut soldiers serving in the
field. The extent of this conflict leaves no doubt concerning the reality or seriousness of Democratic war opposition, or its negative impact on the Union war effort.

Connecticut's experiences also address related questions posed by historians,
some of which are raised in Robert Sandow's essay in this volume. To what extent, for example, were local peace movements initiated by a state or nationally
directed Democratic "conspiracy"? Was local antiwar activity a function of "top-
down" Democratic political initiatives or grassroots efforts? The answer lay in the
symbiotic relationship between the "people" and their party leaders. The rhetoric
espoused by party leaders inspired citizens on the grassroots level to engage in
dissent, sometimes of a violent nature. Yet the reverse was also true. Rather than
the matter being a "conspiracy" among state or national Democratic leaders to
ignite fervor among the party faithful, the people themselves acted out against
the war and in doing so gave fodder to the party leadership for a more sustained
action. It was fuel to the growing Democratic fire in the rear. Indeed, the party
rhetoric and heat that led to the secession crisis—in the North no less than the
South—was so fully entrenched in the political culture that it is impossible to
separate the actions of the common citizens from their party leaders. All spoke
the same language and acted on it.

Historians have also engaged the extent to which Democratic opposition is
labeled as "conspiratorial" or treasonous, rather than a Republican articulation of
the Copperhead movement. Sandow rightly notes that many historians, including Weber, have concluded that all Democrats opposed to the war were, in essence, traitors. It would seem that one of the keys in fine-tuning our understanding of Democratic war opposition is to make a clear distinction between political
dissent and actual conspiracy in the forms of secret societies like the Knights

of the Golden Circle, an organization that was not significantly, if at all, active in Connecticut. Moreover, the very nature of Democratic dissent needs to be further outlined, perhaps removing the question of disloyalty as it relates to the Union and Constitution, versus disloyalty to the Republican Party and Lincoln's attempts (some of them patently unconstitutional) to save the nation.

Although historians' conclusions on such ideological questions are intriguing, the conflicting answers do not necessarily confirm or deny the existence of a very real, potent Democratic peace movement or the extent to which it hampered the war effort. What the focus on Democratic and Republican ideological arguments does reveal, however, is the extent to which such viewpoints were used for partisan combat, with each party claiming orthodoxy to the Constitution and Union and charging that the other side was the real transgressor. This is where the question of conspiracy takes on the most salience, as both parties attempted to galvanize their base and stir up discontent with the opposition. The effect was a disruption of community on the most basic level, with neighbor against neighbor. Again, Connecticut amply reveals the rhetoric and reality.

Finally, the extent of a "real," quantifiable Democratic conspiracy and the extent to which it measurably affected the Union war effort is a virtually impossible equation. Beyond the issue of defining the meaning of "conspiracy," as outlined above, historians must not forget the lesson that Bernard Bailyn taught us many years ago when studying the American Revolution: the perception of conspiracy is just as powerful a motivator as real conspiracy.

Historians of Connecticut have long known of Democratic dissent during the war. Almost immediately after the conflict's end, William A. Croffut and John M. Morris wrote a lengthy history of the state's involvement and the problems faced by those on the home front, including the sometimes-violent confrontations in communities and the political animosity bred by partisan disagreements. Historians John E. Tallmadge and Joanna Cowden, in 1964 and 1983, respectively, furthered our understanding of the Connecticut peace movement.[5]

Dissent over secession was immediate and virulent. Many in Connecticut believed in states' rights, and there existed rampant antiblack racism. William Lloyd Garrison had once referred to the state as the "Georgia of New England," following the ouster of abolitionist Prudence Crandall. The corresponding criticism of abolition and Lincoln's Emancipation Proclamation were mainstays of Copperhead arguments. From the outset of the war, "peace flags" appeared throughout the state and, as Weber noted, arguments over the Union's future became a "neighbors' war."

What is particularly remarkable is how quickly dissent surfaced, subsided, and surfaced again in the wake of Union military failures. Moreover, it readily made its way into the existing party structure of the state. Indeed, the battle between Democrats and Republicans was intense even in the 1860 gubernatorial contest, with war looming, and many believed that the victory of Republican incumbent William A. Buckingham saved the state for Lincoln in the subsequent presidential election. This tense political competition continued after the fall of Fort Sumter, subsided somewhat, and resurfaced early in 1863, when Union war morale languished at a particularly low ebb. Unlike Weber's conclusions regarding the 1864 presidential campaign representing the high-water mark of the Copperhead threat, it was Connecticut's annual gubernatorial contest in 1863 that most threatened the state. Democrats never fully recovered from their defeat in that election, and in the following year they chose what they hoped was a more palatable War Democrat. Finally, the 1863 election reflected what Weber noted about the politicization of soldiers. The partisan Republican *Hartford Courant* and Democratic *Hartford Times* printed letter after letter from soldiers who wrote regarding the political happenings at home and implored their neighbors to vote one way or the other.

Connecticut had always been a hotly contested state. Throughout the Jacksonian period, Democrats and Whigs battled for supremacy and often traded state political control year after year. When the Whig Party ultimately collapsed, the Know-Nothing and Republican Parties sprang from the ashes of the failed party system.[6] When Republicans finally gained victory in 1858 with the election of Governor Buckingham, they focused intently on maintaining that control in anticipation of the 1860 presidential contest. Connecticut held its state election on the first Monday of April, giving it the second-earliest election cycle in the nation and making it something of a bellwether for the wider national election.[7] If Democrats could reassert control in Connecticut, it might have helped turn the tide in New England and elsewhere in the North. Thus for Republicans, winning the state, and perhaps the nation, required keeping Buckingham in office. All eyes were on Connecticut. The *New Haven Register* declared, "A nation is waiting in almost breathless suspense to hear the results."[8] Understanding the fierce party battle in the 1860 election also reveals the level of political combat that existed in the state and the very real power of the Democratic opposition.

Democrats nominated Thomas H. Seymour, the popular former governor, who had served from 1850 to 1853. Seymour had won lasting fame as a major in the Mexican War and led a famous charge at the Battle of Chapultepec, earning

promotion to colonel for his heroism. After serving as Connecticut's chief executive, Seymour was appointed minister to Russia by President Franklin Pierce and
served from 1853 to 1857.[9] He steadfastly argued throughout the 1850s that the
North was constitutionally bound to support the compromises that had created
the nation, including slavery. Democrats charged that a vote for Buckingham
was tantamount to abolitionism and, further, would destroy the state's important
commerce with the South.

Fearing Buckingham would lose to Seymour, the Republican Party went so
far as to request Abraham Lincoln to divert his travels in New York and New
Hampshire so that the newly prominent Republican spokesman could attempt to
work his common-talk magic on Connecticut. "You have a *special call there*, & a
duty to perform," wrote James Briggs to Lincoln.[10] The future president made five
speeches in the state, at Hartford, New Haven, Meriden, Norwich, and Bridgeport. He received a rousing reception from the state's Republicans, who packed
meeting halls and organized torchlight processions. It was at one such parade
that a new political assemblage was formed, the Wide Awakes, who dressed in
military-like garb, with caps, capes, and torches; they marched in unison and
captured the imagination and admiration of the public. It was a smart, effective
campaign strategy that caught on in other northern states.[11] Lincoln was suit-
ably impressed and recognized the state's importance, writing to Illinois Senator
Lyman Trumbull (originally from Connecticut), "They are having a desperate
struggle in Connecticut; and it would both please, and help our friends there, if
you could be with them in the last days of the fight. Having been there, I know
they are proud of you as a son of their own soil, and would be moved to greater
exertion by your presence among them. Can you not go? Telegraph them, and go
right along. The fiendish attempt now being made upon Connecticut, must not
be allowed to succeed."[12]

The Republican push worked, though barely. Buckingham won reelection by a
mere 541 votes, receiving 44,458 to Seymour's 43,917, with some 10,000 more votes
cast than in the previous year's election. Republicans insisted that the victory
should have been larger, charging that Democrats had imported ineligible voters from New York, and that New York's mayor, Fernando Wood, had organized
and paid for the fraud. James Babcock of New Haven wrote to Lincoln immediately after the election, "The Republicans have come out of their terrible conflict
safely," adding that Lincoln's speeches had been instrumental to the success and
his name was repeatedly mentioned as the party's next presidential nominee.[13]
There is no indication that Lincoln's appearance within the state clinched support

for his nomination at the 1860 Chicago convention. The Connecticut delegation, headed by Gideon Welles, were divided in their views, with only two of the thirteen supporting Lincoln at the outset.[14]

Shortly after reelection, Governor Buckingham delivered his annual message to the General Assembly, devoting the entirety of the last section to the nation's troubles. "The settlement of questions appertaining to the powers of the General Government over slavery," he began, "has hitherto baffled the efforts of our wisest patriots and ablest statesmen." Then, engaging in a brief exposition on the nation's foundations, the governor insisted that the Constitution was "scrupulously guarded from the use of the words 'slave,' or 'slavery,'" and that "testimony is abundant that this compact was made with the idea that slavery was an evil to be tolerated." "But now," he continued, "it is openly declared that slavery, as a system, is just and benevolent; that it is the normal condition of society. . . . Slavery thus becomes a national system, to be defended and protected by statute law." Buckingham expressed alarm that disunion was openly threatened in the halls of Congress: "It has been declared that the election of a President, representing opinions in opposition to the policy just referred to . . . will of itself be a sufficient cause for secession, or for a dissolution of the Union." He proclaimed that "it is hardly necessary to say that the freemen of Connecticut emphatically repudiate such dangerous and revolutionary sentiments, and all action so utterly inconsistent with the first principles of Constitutional liberty."[15]

Many Democrats disagreed with the governor's views. The *Hartford Times* announced that if the South departed from the Union, "it will be useless to attempt any coercive measures to keep them. . . . We can never force sovereign States to remain in the Union when they desire to go out, without bringing upon our country the shocking evils of civil war."[16] When the war ultimately began after the firing on Fort Sumter, the Democratic *New Haven Register* blamed abolitionists for the conflict and insisted that the "Constitution recognized the right of slaveholding," lamenting "that the true policy of the 'friends of the Constitution and Union' should be to instigate a servile insurrection . . . a war of extermination, in which the 'olive branch' is unknown—a war of race against race—black against white."[17] The *Register* denounced the war as a conspiracy, an "Abolition humbug," opining, "If Abolitionist anticipations are realized—what then? Sell them? Ough! Give them liberty—an injury to themselves and a burden to the community? Well, we don't know; but it is evident this subject is destined to give us a good deal of trouble for some time to come."[18]

At the same time that the *Register* blasted the start of war, a white peace flag appeared in Ridgefield, where two men were shot while attempting to tear it down. Other peace flags were raised in Avon, New Milford, New Preston, West Hartford, and Windsor.[19] Upon hearing reports of these flags, the popular Democrat, Thomas Seymour, then serving in the General Assembly, announced that there existed "a growing sentiment among the people for a peaceful settlement— and honorable peace." He insisted that the South could not be forced back into the Union: "There seems to be a radical mistake on the part of many people. They appear to think the South can be conquered. Sir, this is impossible. You may destroy their habitations, devastate their fields and shed the blood of their people, but you cannot conquer them." Seymour also tried to substitute war resolutions for a "fair and honorable termination of the present troubles."[20] The relationship between the previous months of political battle, the actions of citizens, and the words of prominent Democrats like Seymour intersected to create schisms that continued to appear in community after community.

Toward the end of June, tempers flared in Goshen, when Andrew Palmer raised a secession flag on several occasions. The Republican *Litchfield Enquirer* reported that when he was asked to take it down by a committee of "prominent citizens," his remarks "were neither those of a gentleman nor a patriot."[21] By afternoon a crowd of hundreds assembled on the town green, and some 159 men armed with muskets and a cannon marched to Palmer's home, where they demanded the flag and threatened violence. Ultimately, one of Palmer's men was shot in the leg, the flag was "received with hisses and trampled in the dust," and the Stars and Stripes was nailed to the house. To other traitors in the area, the newspaper announced ominously "BEWARE!" and proclaimed, "Those brave young men who have gone forth from us shall never be insulted by the traitor's standard, waving in sight of their own loved homes. Woe to the Traitor, Woe!"[22] The division of Connecticut communities was readily apparent and only beginning.

Following the Union rout at Bull Run, Democrats became even more emboldened, as did patriotic resistance to the movement. Stephen Raymond of Darien fired a cannon in celebration of the rebel victory, and he was quickly met by citizens who confiscated the cannon and threw it in a river. After cheering the Confederate victory, a man in Ridgefield was drenched at the town pump and forced to swear a patriotic oath under the American flag. A group of Democratic women in Danbury led a brass band down Main Street, revealing their support for the rebel victory. Peace and Confederate flags appeared in Cornwall, Easton, Madison, New Britain, New London, North Guilford, Podunk, and Prospect, though they were all promptly torn down. A meeting at Cornwall Bridge passed resolutions calling for "peaceful separation" and declared that "the American Union is forever destroyed." Similar meetings occurred in Bloomfield, Canaan, Danbury,

Monroe, New Fairfield, Redding, Saybrook, and Sharon. The geographic location of these many towns reveals that this was a statewide occurrence, not isolated pockets of discontent. Fights broke out, weapons were brandished, and rocks thrown. The *Hartford Times* announced, "We are opposed to this war. . . . It is crushing the life-blood of New England."[23]

Nathan Morse, editor of the Democratic *Bridgeport Farmer and Advertiser*, displayed true venom, mocking the "grand army" that "ran back" from Bull Run, and jeering that "the heart of the Abolitionists heaved with sorrow at the blasted prospects of their fanaticism, and the diminished hope of a speedy gratification of their bloody will."[24] In part due to Morse's rabid newspaper attacks, tempers in Bridgeport continued to flare and confrontations grew bolder. This is when A. A. Pettingill, the editor of the *Bridgeport Republican*, wrote to Governor Buckingham about the alarming conditions, quoted at the outset of this essay. His concerns were that "Rebels—& very active ones" and "secret organizations" existed. He added that "a Peace Meeting (so called) is held at *Stepney*, some nine miles from here, *this afternoon*. A flag is to be raised & word has been sent here that the thing is to be defended by armed men, 60 or 80 young men." Though he hoped that no violence would ensue, Pettingill recognized that "this state of things cannot continue long without leading to *bloodshed*."[25] Union men, under the direction of P. T. Barnum, tore down the peace banner, chased peace advocates into a nearby cornfield, then regrouped and sang "The Star-Spangled Banner." When they returned to Bridgeport, the crowd swelled to several thousand and marched to the offices of Morse's *Farmer*, where they battered down the door and destroyed everything in sight. As noted, Morse escaped by fleeing across the rooftops.[26]

There is no indication that these meetings or actions were organized by state or national henchmen, or that, as Pettingill reported, secret organizations existed. More likely, these were spontaneous responses to a war that had been brewing for years. Nonetheless, the disturbances of late summer were so widespread and serious that Mark Howard, one of the leaders of the state's Republican Party, wrote to Connecticut-born Secretary of the Navy Gideon Welles, "In no part of the free States is treason more malignant, defiant and insidious than in Conn., and Hartford is the seat of its influence. The feeling here is becoming intense on both sides—many of the traitors now go around armed, and the loyal portion of our community will have to do so, in self-defense. And but a spark is now necessary to kindle a flame that can only be extinguished in blood."[27] George A. Oviate, a Congregational minister from Somers, Connecticut, issued similar warnings to Governor Buckingham: "In Conn. there are many who favor the South, and such men, in the rural districts talk secession openly and do much in demoralizing the people." He insisted that the *Hartford Times* was largely responsible, noting, "Those who read this paper so exclusively are emboldened in their sympathy with the seceders. If this state of things continues, what is before us?" Oviate advocated shutting the *Times* down and implored the governor, "I hope in order to avoid bloodshed an [*sic*] Civil War, . . . [by] your Constitutional authority you would by Proclamation or otherwise would forbid the raising of peace Flags, and also peace gatherings in our area."[28]

There is no indication that Buckingham seriously considered shutting down the *Times*, but he did respond quickly to the issue of peace flags and the potential of violence connected to them. On September 1, 1861, the governor issued a proclamation commenting on "the public exhibition of *peace-flags* falsely so called." Although acknowledging that "the Constitution guarantees liberty of speech and that of the press," he insisted that "the very exercise of our government, the future prosperity of this entire nation, and the hopes of universal freedom, demand that these outrages be suppressed." He continued, "I call upon the officers of the law to be active, diligent, and fearless in arresting, and instituting legal proceedings for the punishment of, those who disturb the public peace, or those who are guilty of sedition and treason, and of those who are embraced in combinations to obstruct the execution of the laws."[29] U.S. Marshal David Carr subsequently announced that traitors would "be summarily dealt with."[30] Arrests ensued, and prisoners were transported to Fort Lafayette in New York.[31] Barnum wrote to Lincoln that these actions "have rendered secessionists *so scarce*, I cannot find one for exhibition in my museum."[32] The back of the peace movement was broken, at least temporarily. Things in Connecticut remained fairly quiet for the next several months, though many residents remained shocked that Democratic sympathies for the South were so strident and that wholesale violent collision had threatened the state so quickly.

Republican legislators who controlled the state's General Assembly vented some of their anger over such matters when the Senate voted to remove from the walls of its chamber the portraits of former Democratic governors Isaac Toucey and Thomas Seymour, because of their opposition to the war and the belief that they had encouraged the peace movement. The portraits were cut out of their frames, which were left empty on the wall for half a day before they, too, were removed.[33]

Lincoln's announcement of the Preliminary Emancipation Proclamation in September 1862 reinvigorated Connecticut's Copperhead resistance to the war. Even War Democrats who had previously tried to work with the Republican administration turned their backs, outraged over abolition and what they believed was a clear avowal that the war was no longer just about saving the Union. Emancipation, violations of habeas corpus, suppression of newspapers, the conscription of soldiers—all these acts, argued Democrats, pointed to Lincoln's despotism as the true source of the nation's destruction. The Emancipation Proclamation, more than any other act, served as the catalyst that revived the Democratic Party within the state and unleashed the most formidable challenge to Republican control during the war.

Combating this Democratic resurgence proved as important as any military aspect of the war. The spring 1863 Connecticut gubernatorial election was pivotal. With outrage over the Emancipation Proclamation and the Union's poor military showing, Democrats targeted the April election as a way to end the state's support of the war. They once again pitted the formidable Thomas H. Seymour against Governor Buckingham. Much like in 1860, all eyes were on Connecticut as an indicator of the Republican Party's potential fate in later elections. This time, however, not everyone was at home and able to vote. Connecticut's 1818 constitution specifically stated that electors had to meet in their respective towns, and when Governor Buckingham asked the state's Supreme Court justices to consider the constitutionality of a law allowing soldiers to vote in the field, he was told without qualification that it would be unconstitutional. The General Assembly passed an amendment in 1864 that allowed soldiers to vote, but this did nothing for them during the contested and very important 1863 campaign.[34]

The concerns and opinions of soldiers ultimately became a primary focus of the news coverage and revealed the extent to which they had become politicized by the happenings at home. In addition to reporting on the parties' nominating conventions, the two principal state papers, the *Hartford Courant* and the *Hartford Times*, devoted page after page to letters from soldiers, with each paper claiming that the men were on its party's side. As the date of the election crept closer, the *Courant* devoted itself to the battle by filling lengthy columns with numerous letters. The ensuing struggle was the most concentrated, sustained political effort of the war, both at home and in the field. The many letters and resolutions sent to the papers by various regiments revealed that many in and from Connecticut were consumed by the possibility of Republican defeat.[35]

The Republicans held their party convention on January 21 in New Haven, where Governor Buckingham easily received the nomination. Yet only a portion of the delegates who might have attended were present, and this made many believe in the party's further vulnerability. Three weeks later the state party's Central Committee published a lengthy appeal, declaring, "A State Election is soon to take place more important than any which has occurred since the foundation of our Government. Connecticut is to declare on the first Monday in April, whether she is in favor of a *dishonorable peace—submission to the demands of armed traitors*, and a *dissolution of the Union*, or whether she is determined at every hazard, to defend the honor of our National Flag and the Union of these States."[36]

The state's Democrats gathered at Touro Hall in Hartford on February 17, with the actual convention to be held the next day. Thomas Seymour, the party's stalwart, uncompromising opponent of the war, received the nomination. At the convention, speakers like William H. Eaton of Hartford, a representative in the General Assembly, regaled the audience with heartfelt denunciations of the war and President Lincoln: "Is any man so low as to be loyal to any man—to Abraham Lincoln, the accidental President? The Democrats of Connecticut will not sustain war waged for the destruction of the Union. We will tell Lincoln that he cannot come into Connecticut, and take men from their homes; that he cannot come into Connecticut and compel men to serve in the army."[37] Another speaker, Henry H. Barbour, revealed the very real danger for Republicans should Seymour win the election: "*We are against the War*. The elections of other States have not been understood by the President. *There have been too many War Democrats chosen*. When Thomas H. Seymour is elected, *the President will understand what that means*."[38] The threat was no further Connecticut support of the war; the connection between party competition and its potentially negative impact on the war effort is clear.

These and other arguments caused Republicans to seethe with indignation. The *Courant* proclaimed that prominent men of the Democratic Party spoke for hours and "not one solitary word or sentence was uttered in condemnation of the rebellion, or of the crimes of its leaders. . . . Such is the shameful position of the Democratic party of Connecticut."[39] In a stroke of propaganda genius, Republicans tainted the meeting with the notorious epithet "Hartford Convention." The Republican *Hartford Evening Press* charged that the Copperheads "have put themselves squarely against the war, and picked out as their candidate about the only public man in New England who has been from the first openly and notoriously *with* the South and *against* the North in this struggle. It is not possible to show that he occupies any different ground than Jeff Davis, except in daring." The paper asked, "What Do 'Peace Men' Want?" and provided the answer: "It would seem that their great desire is to humble the North, to permit its conquest in this war, to strike down democracy and erect on its ruins the aristocratic rule of slaveholders."[40]

The first of the soldiers' letters home appeared on January 20, when the *Times* published an article titled "The Soldiers and Their Feelings," which included an anonymous letter stating, "The feeling here is that the Rebs can never be con-quered by fighting—the soldiers are disheartened." The *Courant* responded on February 9, in "What Some of the Soldiers Say," offering two letters. The first came from an officer of the 15th Connecticut Volunteer Infantry (CVI), "formerly an active Democrat from New Haven," who wrote, "The feeling of the North, which we hear is growing more and more strong against the war, is doing an incalcu-lable amount of injury in this army, and I hope it may soon give way to a feeling of sincere patriotism. Remember and do your duty in voting for Buckingham for Governor." Another soldier wrote, "I was once in favor of compromise, concilia-tion, concession, but that was before the hellish act of firing on our country's flag had been consummated; but now I stand up unbroken and unbent, and my voice is for War! War!! War!!!" Eleven days later, the *Times* published a letter from a Republican soldier, which read in part, "I think it full time this war was over; there have been money and lives enough lost, and we are no better off than we were a year ago; and all for the cussed nigger. We have lost sight of the real object we all commenced the fight for, the Constitution and the Union."[41]

By March, the political competition utilizing soldiers' letters was going strong. There existed a clear propaganda component to the newspaper coverage—one so large that it strains the ability of the reader to separate fact from fiction. It is here that a coordinated effort by party editors most certainly influenced the people. Even if the sentiment espoused in the many letters was somewhat exaggerated, soldier's concerns over politics at home left them conflicted and concerned. To-gether, the *Times* and the *Courant* printed more than forty letters that month, with the majority appearing in the Republican newspaper, which also published eight sets of resolutions sent in by various Connecticut regiments, all of which were in favor of fighting the war and in support of Buckingham.[42] The 20th CVI sent in one such set of resolutions, announcing, "We are amazed to find that, in opposition to us, while here before the foe, and in hostility to the measures which have been adopted for the preservation of our liberties, there are at home men who attempt to conceal their sympathies with the rebellion by a cowardly clamor for peace." The soldiers warned, "When we have crushed the foe in front, we will ourselves, if necessity requires, take care of the more cowardly ones in the rear, who are heaping contempt upon our cause and insult our efforts." Another sol-dier threatened, "How would you and you [*sic*] loving wife or sister like a bloody war in Connecticut in consequence thereof [of a Seymour victory]?"[43]

An officer from the 15th CVI wrote, "I am astonished beyond measure that the democrats of Connecticut should be so bold in their disloyalty. . . . I cannot believe that you will allow them to do it. It would be a burning disgrace to the

State, and a source of sorrow and mortification to the whole loyal country." Another soldier wrote, "You have and can have no idea of the feeling that the bare possibility of the election of such a man [as Seymour] has upon the soldiers. . . . I hope the people of Connecticut have not so far degenerated, as to allow the election of an arch traitor." Other soldiers expressed the same sentiments: "Nothing in all our trials has given us such a *chill*, as the late Copperhead movement in Connecticut. . . . I tell you, the Seymour platform is loudly denounced, by Democrats as well as Republicans." The letter continued, "We say to the Copperheads of Connecticut, if you cannot come down here and shoulder your muskets with us, in defence of your Government, for God's sake and the sake of your country, don't arrange your batteries on the side of Jeff. Davis." Soldiers from the 19th CVI, later the 2nd Heavy Artillery, implored those at home, "We pray you not to crush our resolution, and palsy our arms, by electing for your Governor, *and ours*, a man who hopes for our defeat and humiliation!"[44] One soldier of the 27th sounded the same note: "I hope, in all favor, that our friends will not allow Tom Seymour to be elected Governor of Connecticut. Don't Do It For mercy's sake, don't let him be Governor." A man in the 22nd continued the barrage, expressing amazement at his state's apparent disloyalty: "Do not elect T. H. Seymour, for I do not want to come home to Connecticut and have such a man as that holding the position that those anti-war Democrats—those slimy copperheads—do to a State which ought to be loyal. For Heaven's sake, what is Connecticut coming to?"[45]

One of the most significant resolutions was a statement from the 9th Army Corps, comprising eight different Connecticut regiments, all then stationed in the Louisiana area: "You sent us here (did you not?) to bear onward the stainless folds of Connecticut's flag, side by side with the glorious Stars and Stripes, until perjured Secession shall be ground to powder beneath the iron heel of war. And we will do it; but do not place us between two fires. To-day treason is more dangerous in Connecticut than in Louisiana."[46] The totality of these many sentiments leave little question that political division within Connecticut created a very real concern among soldiers in the field and potentially threatened the war's outcome.

Democrats, too, sent letters to the press, often charging that the *Courant* fabricated the true sentiments of soldiers and that many were coerced into adopting regimental resolutions. A soldier from the 22nd insisted, "Almost to a man, rank and file, heartily endorse the nomination of Gov. Seymour, and daily wish and pray that he may be elected. I never saw in my life a set of men so unanimous for Seymour." He noted that a group of state Republican Party leaders had suddenly appeared in camp to talk about the election, and he was writing "to unmask this vile Niggerhead plot, with its underground work arrangements . . . to make it appear that the soldiers endorse niggerism." He concluded that the regiment's resolutions are "a willful, DELIBERATE LIE." Another soldier from the same regiment stated that the men had held an informal ballot, with Seymour the victor.[47] In reaction, the *Courant* peppered its columns with soldiers' letters denying such statements about the 22nd, and announcing that a regimental ballot had been conducted, with 607 soldiers participating and the vast majority, 431, voting for Buckingham—while only 176 voted for Seymour.[48] Other soldiers' letters countering Democratic claims followed, with one Democratic soldier insisting, "I have not turned Black Republican or nigger worshiper—nothing of the kind—far from it; but Jeff. Davis and his cursed followers want fight, and they shall have it as long as I can play a 30-pound shell at them."[49]

Similar sentiments regarding the 1863 election and concerns over patriotism at home appeared in the personal writings of several Connecticut soldiers. Samuel Fiske, a minister from Madison who wrote under the pseudonym Dunn Browne, bristled at the conduct of Connecticut Democrats, writing, "Give me a 'Hartford *Times*,' or some other appropriate receptacle, for I am nauseated; I am sick, poisoned; have taken something, that, most emphatically, doesn't agree with me; have swallowed the vile and traitorous resolutions of the recent Democratic Convention at Hartford." He continued, "If the dear old State doesn't spew out of her mouth this ill-savoring Tom Seymour Democracy at the coming April election, we of the army will march North, instead of South, to get at the heart of the Rebellion. Talk about demoralization of the army!"[50]

Fred Lucas, of the 19th CVI, wrote more than one hundred letters to his mother. The only time the correspondence shows even a hint of animosity or anger is when it touches on traitors at home. Lucas revealed a grudging respect for southern rebels, but he had no patience for disloyalty in Connecticut:

> Would to God, we in the field could return but to deposit our votes at the coming election and if possible prevent the election of the *traitor Tom Seymour*. His election will inspire the Confederacy with fresh hope and courage. Shame, shame, that Conn. should ever permit such an outrage and insult to her soldiers. But mind you the soldiers, some of them, will return. And they will not forget that while absent from home and unable to protest their rights there, by their own presence and their own votes, there were men so depraved, so vile, so treasonable as to make use of the opportunity thus afforded, to injure, abuse, and insult them, by advocating such measures and endorsed by the Tom Seymour party of Conn.

Lucas promised "*just retribution*," and remarked, "We can have some little respect for an armed traitor in the enemy's ranks but for those who sympathise with treason at home we can have *none* but for them we have the greatest and deepest disgust. It is owing in great measure to their efforts that the war continues."[51]

The Democrats' point of view also appeared in private letters. Sergeant Benjamin Hirst of the 14th wrote to his wife, "They are having a high old time in Conn about Politics, but I think Tom Seymour will be the next governor if they do call him a Copperhead. They got up some Humbug Resolution in our Regiment the other day in which they try to make it appear that the 14th are to a man in favour of Buckingham but I think if they will Vote the Regiment by Ballot they will find it a little differant [*sic*] to what they expect."[52]

Soldiers' sentiments were not the only political weapon in the party arsenals. In late March, as the election grew closer, Democrats held another mass gathering at Touro Hall, again denouncing abolitionism and violations of the Constitution. The *Times* followed with more charges that Republicans "prostitute the war into an Abolition raid."[53] Republicans countered with the unorthodox use of a female political speaker, a Quaker from Pennsylvania named Anna Dickinson, who arrived in Connecticut on March 24 and traveled the state for twelve days, appearing every night before audiences that were both supportive and hostile. Dickinson was a mesmerizing orator who, apparently, withstood the attacks of hecklers easily and playfully. The *Times* sneered that Republicans had fallen so low they "actually procure a 'woman' for aid," and the *New Haven Register* scoffed, "Nothing popularizes any cause as a petticoat."[54] There was no denying, however, that Dickinson made an impact. Moreover, her inclusion by Republicans might have indicated a further movement toward abolitionism: Dickinson was devout in the cause and associated with William Lloyd Garrison.[55]

When the election results finally came in, Buckingham remained victorious, but with a margin of just 2,634 votes.[56] It was an outcome that might have been easily reversed had Republicans slackened their efforts for even a moment. Democratic opposition had been fierce. The *Courant* exulted in the result, declaring, "One of the most hotly contested political campaigns ever witnessed in Connecticut has just closed in a magnificent triumph for the Union. . . . Domestic treason has received a withering rebuke"; and "The whole nation will exult over the verdict pronounced in this State, yesterday." Under the headline "Victory! Victory!" the *Hartford Evening Press* wrote, "It was a voice for war. Let there be no mistake about it. Connecticut, small but compact and invincible puts her foot indignantly on every proposal of dishonorable peace. The South will well understand it."[57]

Democrats understood it, too, at least insofar as concluding that the election had been rigged. They charged that only Republican soldiers were given furloughs to go home and vote, and that vast amounts of money had poured into the state at the direction of the Lincoln administration. The *Times* made such charges clear in several articles: "The Democracy of Connecticut gallantly contended on Monday against all the virulent Abolitionists, the haters of the Union," yet Republicans utilized "the whole power of the federal administration; with MONEY in unlimited quantities . . . with over 2,000 *selected* soldiers from the army sent home to vote. . . . A FREE AND FAIR EXPRESSION OF THE POPULAR WILL WOULD HAVE RESULTED IN A DEMOCRATIC AND CONSTITUTIONAL TRIUMPH. But foul corruption and vile oppression—proved, and not denied—have been sufficient to turn the scale against us. . . . The Administration interfered directly in this election."[58] The *Register* concurred: "It is very evident from the election returns that the Democrats have been cheated out of it. Buckingham's majority of less than 2,500 falls short of the number of furloughed soldiers sent home to vote for him."[59]

There may have been some truth in Democratic accusations. Painfully aware of the nation's misgivings concerning the war, Lincoln looked to Connecticut with trepidation, as he had in 1860. In February, he summoned Thurlow Weed, a New York political boss, to the White House, writing, "We are in a tight place. Money for legitimate purposes is needed immediately; but there is no appropriation from which it can be lawfully taken. I didn't know how to raise it, and so I sent for you."[60] Only days later, Connecticut's Gideon Welles, the Secretary of the Navy, wrote in his diary that Weed was in town: "He has been sent for, but my informant knows not for what purposes of government. It is, I learn, to consult in regard to a scheme of Seward to influence the New Hampshire and Connecticut elections."[61] Although Weed's role is not proof of corruption in the election, anything was possible in a political contest fraught with such potentially dire consequences had Republicans lost.

The 1863 election was the Democrats' last real bid for state power. The military successes of 1863 blunted Copperhead strength, and for the 1864 gubernatorial election Democrats chose what they hoped was a more palatable, pro-war candidate, Origen S. Seymour of Litchfield. The strategy had little effect. Not only did O. S. Seymour lose by 5,658 votes, but Democrats also lost the New Haven city elections for the first time in eight years and, more significantly, William H. Eaton of Hartford, an outspoken Copperhead, lost his House seat in the Assembly.[62] The results represented a solid victory for Republicans, and they claimed it as such. "Throw high the cap of liberty! Connecticut has spoken in thunder tones to the nation and the world," announced the *Courant*. "Copperheadism in Connecticut has received its death wound." The South will hear us, insisted the paper: "Realizing the hopelessness of wearying the North into desistance, they will see before them the alternative of speedy submission or annihilation." The *Hartford Evening Press* announced that the Democrats were "finally nailed up and sent home in a box. . . . Union triumphant—no compromise with treason."[63]

Republicans lost little time in relaying the results to Washington. Governor Buckingham wrote President Lincoln immediately: "I beg leave to assure you that the election in this state yesterday may be regarded as a new pledge of the people to sustain your Administration in efforts to preserve national integrity." Buckingham continued, connecting the importance of Connecticut's political success to other Republican victories. "In the opinion of many our election in 1860 was the pivot on which events turned which led to the election of your Excellency to the Presidency and now if it shall lead to like results none will feel worse than the copperhead sympathisers [*sic*] with traitors in Conn[ecticut] and none rejoice more or give you a more cordial support than our loyal & patriotic citizens who have rolled up such a majority in favor of overwhelming the armies of the rebellion."[64]

Democrats blamed the losses on furloughed Republican soldiers, Republican treachery, and Democrats who stayed home from the polls. It was this last group that appeared most troubling. "It seems there are some voters who did not know the day on which it [the election] was to be held," lamented the *Hartford Times*. "Why should they slumber now, when the death knell of the Republic is uninterruptedly ringing, it is surprising to us. But they have slumbered this spring. Thousands who do not approve of this war, have not voted." The paper accepted that "the Abolitionists have swept the board by a majority," but reasoned that "the people looked upon an active canvass this Spring as useless, reserving their strength for the Presidential contest. In that struggle the great question of the preservation of the UNION will be directly presented, and then the people will rouse and act."[65]

That Democrats had lost their bid for control of the state did not mean that their movement failed to have influence. Discontent still ran high, evidenced by opposition to the draft. Indeed, when Governor Buckingham first implemented conscription he feared a riot similar to what had happened in New York, and subsequently announced it only after having secretly issued guns to loyal citizens in areas where the draft was to take place.[66] Even after it was instituted, Democrats managed to interfere with its effectiveness. Out of some 1,303 men drafted in Connecticut in 1863, 913 were exempted through medical certificates. The most notorious of the exempting doctors was a Democratic surgeon from Litch-field named Josiah G. Beckwith, who excused men for everything from "heart disease," "weak and feeble constitution," "general weakness," and "great nervous-ness" to "enlarged and diseased scrotum, of *long standing.*"[67]

As the war dragged on, Connecticut, like much of the North, seemed ex-hausted. By the summer of 1864, the bloodletting of the Wilderness and Cold Harbor Campaigns had shocked the nation and it seemed that Union forces sim-ply could not capture Atlanta. As fall approached and General Sherman finally took that city, along with Union success in the Shenandoah Valley, the northern malaise lifted in time for the November presidential election. The *Hartford Cou-rant* effectively captured the mood: "The political horizon has changed remark-ably. During the month of August despondency hung like a pall over the country." "To-day all is changed," continued the paper. "The current of dissatisfaction, and clamor, and gloom, whose treacherous waters were hurrying the nation toward the vortex of destruction, is arrested."[68]

Nonetheless, Democrats continued their attempt to carry the state. They fo-cused on the war's duration, promising that reelecting Lincoln would guarantee many more years of bloodshed and that the South could never be subjugated. The *Hartford Times* asked readers, "How many more years of war are we to have? How many more drafts? How many more thousands of millions spent? How long are our institutions to be crushed by military rule? How long is labor to be drained by the exhaustion of men and means?" The *New Haven Register* complained of taxation on everything: "And all this must be kept up, and be continued, and no one knows how long, to gratify the whim of a smutty joker [Lincoln]."[69]

Try as they might, Democrats were unable to match the intensity they had generated in the spring of 1863 when attempting to unseat Buckingham. This time there was no detailed letter campaign from soldiers and, overall, less heat in party papers, though in the final weeks of the campaign Democrats did or-ganize some three hundred meetings. The two leading Democratic papers tried to put the issue plainly. The *Hartford Times* ran the headline "A Republic or a Monarchy."[70] The *New Haven Register* announced:

The argument is closed—the case is made up, and tomorrow the jury will render its verdict,—a verdict upon which rests the fate of the country. Should it pronounce in favor of the election of General McClellan, we shall speedily have restored the Union, with peace reigning throughout our now distracted land; and we can then apply our energies to the work of restoring the happi-ness and prosperity which prevailed before the fell spirit of sectional fanaticism became a power in the land. Should it pronounce for Lincoln,—it will be an endorsement of the usurpations, corruption and outrages of which the Administration has been guilty—a declaration in favor of uncompromising war for Abolition—for unrelenting conscription and ruinous debt and taxation to carry out the policy of Garrison, Greeley, and Co. Was there ever a more momentous issue committed to the judgment of any people?[71]

Nationally, Abraham Lincoln won a resounding victory in the election. His popular vote exceeded McClellan's by almost half a million, and the electoral vote, 212 to 21, was devastating. The *Hartford Evening Press* derisively commented, "What was that man's name? McClellum, McPendlum, Micklelan, McClinelton—seems as if there was some such man, doing something or other the other day."[72] But the barb was not warranted by Connecticut's election returns. Out of almost 90,000 votes cast, Lincoln won by a mere 2,405 votes—a victory almost certainly secured by the fact that the General Assembly had passed an amendment to the state constitution authorizing soldiers to vote in the field.[73] Remarkably, the margin of the vote was actually smaller than in Governor Buckingham's victory in 1863, revealing that the Democratic movement may have been less outwardly explosive in 1864, but no less serious. What had been true at the war's outset and throughout the conflict remained true at the end of 1864: Connecticut was closely divided.

Certainly, more work needs to be undertaken to understand the full scope of the formidable Copperhead movement in Connecticut. It was no peripheral issue. Democratic resistance to Republican control was serious as early as 1860, when Governor William Buckingham narrowly defeated Thomas Seymour, and in doing so secured the state's support for Abraham Lincoln and the war that quickly followed his election. Democratic resistance exploded with remarkable speed once Fort Sumter was fired on, and increased following the Union failure at Bull Run. Neighbor faced off against neighbor in towns and cities throughout the state. Only a gubernatorial proclamation and swift action by the authorities stemmed the tide of violence and blunted Copperhead agitation in the form of peace flags and rallies. Yet the tide of Democratic animosity shifted just as abruptly and seriously with the announcement of the Emancipation Proclamation. Copperheads now saw what they believed was an open declaration for a war fought to promote abolition. The ensuing Connecticut gubernatorial election in 1863 was an all-out political offensive that witnessed an unprecedented effort to influence the electorate through the writings of soldiers, and an equally unprecedented outpouring of political feeling from those men on the front. Although

Republicans eked out a victory, Democratic opposition continued to hamper war efforts, such as the draft, and posed another astonishingly close contest in 1864, with President Lincoln barely taking the state.

The Democratic peace movement in Connecticut was no fringe action perpetrated by a small group and exaggerated by Republican fears. Rather, it was a tangible, sustained threat that hampered the Union war effort by politicizing every aspect of the conflict. Yet the occurrences in Connecticut do not reveal any sort of grand state or nationally orchestrated party plot. The peace movement was the natural political outflow of a two-party system that for decades had pitted citizen against citizen and state party organ against state party organ. The dissent that exploded in Connecticut was as much a grassroots movement as it was any directive by party leaders. That both parties attempted to exaggerate the actions and rhetoric of its foe was, again, a normal part of the party process. The fact that it was done amid the greatest conflict the nation had ever faced made it that much more harrowing and ripe for charges of conspiracy and collusion. That it negatively affected the Republican war effort cannot be denied.

One of the equally compelling issues is whether the Democratic peace movement can properly be called a "conspiracy," and thereby dismissed by historians as failed nationalism in a time of emergency. If one concludes that dissent in wartime is never appropriate, then Democrats were indeed guilty. If, however, dissent, even amid war, is a time-honored American tradition, then it is difficult to argue that the peace movement, at least as it existed in Connecticut, was some sort of conspiratorial-minded plot to overthrow the government.

"All Manner of Schemes and Rascalities"

The Politics of Promotion in the Union Army

Timothy J. Orr

In 1864, Orderly Sergeant George E. Andrews of the 12th Maine demanded a promotion to second lieutenant. Since 1861, Andrews had served as his company's senior noncommissioned officer, and he had been present with his regiment in its daring attack at Port Hudson, Louisiana. Sergeant Andrews probably would have received his overdue advancement that year, except that politics interfered. While in camp, the regimental field officers canvassed the regiment to determine which captains, lieutenants, or sergeants were entitled to promotion based on merit and seniority. However, when the 12th Maine's Democratic commander, Colonel William K. Kimball, forwarded a list of aspirants to the state capital in Augusta, he left off the names of any Republicans. Furious at being passed over on account of his politics, Sergeant Andrews fumed, "Col Bill Kimball is what I call a *Damd Copperhead* and . . . that is the reason that Capt Winder and others in Co D cant get a chance for promotion." At first, Andrews hoped that Maine's newly elected governor, Republican Samuel Cony, might refuse to send commissions to Democratic applicants. Unfortunately, as Andrews discovered, Cony—who had been a compromise candidate and until recently a Democrat—approved all of Kimball's recommendations without question. Writing to a family member, Andrews expressed hope that he could receive a furlough, return home, and confront the governor directly. Andrew vowed, "I shall go to Augusta to se[e] the Govenor and so will Some others go there to[o] and let him know what is the matter and if *he continues* to Commission every one that Col Kimball and Gen Lepley and Luit Col Ashley recomend I shall think that he is a Coperhead with them because he is not Obliged to Commission Every Drunken Democrat that is in the Regt." Furious at what he considered political discrimination, Andrews closed his letter, "I am so mad that I can't think of any thing to wright So Good Night."[1]

In the larger framework of the Civil War, Sergeant Andrews's quest for promotion was minor, but it represented a consistent and dangerous trend within the Union Army. Frantic arguments at the state level increasingly determined the course of promotions, affecting the quality and administration of the army. Scholars have not appreciated how northern state politics unavoidably intersected with Union military life. Throughout the war, northern partisanship affected the promotion of officers, hindering chances for the Union Army to operate as a full-fledged meritocracy. Although political spoils were hardly unknown to the U.S. Army, for forty years leading up to the war America's peacetime force attempted to adhere to a system of merit, whereby superiors made their appointments based on applicants' length of service, seniority, and accomplishments.[2] But the onset of the Civil War stifled this system of assessment. Because the Union Army chose to fill its ranks with "U.S. Volunteers"—state-organized troops transferred into federal service—little could be done to silence the reverberations of local and state party politics within the ranks of the Union's junior and senior officer corps. Essentially, state politics channeled partisanship into an institution that strived to be apolitical, and even the test of battle often failed to overrule the influence of political animosities in determining the advancement of military leaders.

Throughout the war, Republicans and Democrats formed themselves into civilian and military committees—or they organized themselves into secret political enclaves within the army—to advance party stalwarts, regardless of whether those men displayed capable military leadership. For four years, the administration of the Union Army became one great political squabble. The Confederate Army, by contrast, while not devoid of politics, operated under a system whereby the central government, not the states, approved commissions. The South also lacked a two-party system, further limiting institutionalized quibbling over promotions. In essence, the North suffered from debilitating political weaknesses within its officer corps, limitations that made it difficult for the Union's wartime army to filter its talent.

This essay challenges the reigning theory that the North's two-party system operated primarily to the Union's benefit. Since 1958, historians have been enamored with the notion that a two-party system offered the Union a "decisive advantage" over the Confederacy. That year, during a conference at Gettysburg College, David Potter tentatively suggested that the Confederacy's failure to establish a prominent opposition party may have stifled political initiative in the South. A few years later, Potter clarified his thesis in his now famous essay "Jefferson Davis and the Political Factors of Confederate Defeat," suggesting that the Union's political system, with alternative political leadership, may have been the key to military victory. Years later, Eric McKitrick and Joel Silbey separately sustained Potter's theory by examining party politics in the North. Both confirmed that a two-party system—a "give-and-take" dialogue between rival factions—assisted the Union war effort because the Democratic Party's "loyal opposition"—or "respectable minority," to use Silbey's words—emerged to subdue harsh measures enacted by paranoid Republican administrators. Recently, Potter's thesis received added support, albeit with modification, from Adam I. P. Smith's *No Party Now*, which advanced the claim that "antiparty discourse was critical to the process" of connecting the ruling party to the formation of American nationhood. Unlike McKitrick and Silbey, Smith found few constructive elements in the Democratic Party's conduct during the war, but nevertheless supported the belief that partisanship laid the foundation for the development of advantageous middle-ground politics, so embodied by the creation of the Union Party and the "fluidity . . . of antiparty patriotism."[3]

The records of the adjutant generals' offices of the various northern states do not sustain this theory. A simple reading of the state commission files paints a picture of a Union Army mired by political conflict, adhering to rigid customs of partisan patronage. As Mark Neely has argued in *The Union Divided*, the North's two-party system compelled rival groups to engage in fierce confrontations that nearly unraveled national affairs. In describing the operations of New York City's Custom House, Neely noted how easily anonymous workers and placemen could "resist the idealism of the party's leaders" and fight for patronage when leaders encouraged them to put aside partisanship for the good of the country. Not unlike customhouse workers, applicants for officers' commissions in the Union Army defied selfless antiparty sentiment for the sake of personal aggrandizement. Party discipline inflamed the ranks of the Union Army, and this irritation provided no great advantage. Due to the North's blending of promotions with patronage, though, some Union units struggled from an overdose of state politics.[4] The Union's senior officer corps—its generals—likewise suffered from political intrigue, but as will be revealed here, perhaps the more debilitating problem came from its junior officer corps. Political corruption in the Union Army, while often studied as a "top-down" process, perhaps came equally, if not more forcefully, from the "bottom up."[5]

When the Civil War began, Abraham Lincoln and Secretary of War Simon Cameron called up seventy-five thousand militiamen to serve for three months. Unprepared to field a large army, the War Department assigned quotas to the states, instructing each one to provide a specific number of regiments. Cameron held the governors responsible for selecting which militia regiments served. This early policy—wrought in a time of crisis and limited by the vague language of Article 1, Section 8, of the U.S. Constitution and the Federal Militia Acts of 1792 and 1795—left state militia laws to govern the organization and disciplining of the militia.[6] The federalized militia units followed a perplexing kaleidoscope of ideas about promotion. Each adhered to a set of bylaws, and although they often disagreed on method, these bylaws mandated the popular election of officers. Naturally, local politics influenced the appointment of officers in these units, leading Republicans to fear that too many Democrats, some of whom were critical of the war, would acquire positions of rank in the federalized militia.[7]

The president's call of May 3, 1861, asking for a new levy of forty-two thousand soldiers, represented a departure from the traditional policy of letting soldiers' elections determine promotions in the militia. Instead of relying on enlisted men to choose their officers, Lincoln and Cameron devised a system whereby state governors appointed them. To circumvent the state militia laws, the May 3 call expanded the army with U.S. Volunteers, the newly organized regiments sworn into federal service directly. By having appointed officers—instead of elected ones—the War Department hoped that the volunteer regiments would conform to a higher code of discipline than the seventy-five thousand militia then arrayed around Washington.

Although he had insisted on the May 3 call, Secretary Cameron believed he had no time to spare to inspect and appoint these new officer candidates. Thus, on May 4, 1861, he issued General Order Number 15, delegating the appointing power to the state executives. The primary goal of General Order Number 15 was to spell out the organizational plan for each new regiment of U.S. Volunteers. However, a pivotal sentence came in the fourth paragraph: "The commissioned officers of the company will be appointed by the Governor of the State furnishing it, and . . . [t]he field officers of the Regiment will [also] be appointed by the Governor of the State which furnishes the regiment."[8] Thus the U.S. Volunteers became an unusual administrative hybrid. Similar to the U.S. regular units, they fielded appointed officers whose qualifications were supposed to be based on merit, but like the militia, the state government directed their administration.

Cameron's order granted the Union's twenty-three loyal governors a wide berth when making their appointments. In effect, their pens alone had the power to approve or disapprove the leadership of the Union Army's junior officer corps. Moreover, each governor, to some degree, realized that General Order Number 15 offered incredible opportunity to reconfigure the boundaries of state political power. In peacetime, military service invariably translated into votes. Once the war was won, an infusion of veterans as candidates could conceivably reshape state politics. As the situation stood, the general order appeared to favor the Republicans because, out of twenty-three northern governors, all but six were affiliated with the party of Lincoln.[9]

Cameron's instructions to the governors suggested that the nation should put aside partisan differences for the benefit of the army, but the governors and their staffs did not always heed this injunction.[10] Within weeks governors began answering myriad patronage requests, appointing officers based solely on partisan allegiance.[11] This adherence to patronage over merit was hardly surprising. Young Republicans earned commissions largely because party heads spoke on their behalf. For instance, James Smith, a private in the 10th New York Zouaves, earned a lieutenancy because he had once been a member of the Central Republican Club of New York City and had been a campaign singer for Lincoln during the election of 1860. However suited—or unsuited—for military office, unblemished characters like Smith emerged as ideal choices, since, for the past seven years, Republicans had only heard—indeed, had only explicated—terrible propaganda about their opponents. If, as Republicans often argued, the Democrats won elections only through deceit and ballot stuffing, how could they be trusted to command men in battle? Thus governors generally approved men who exhibited honesty and faithfulness in civil life, but whose military qualifications were yet unproven.[12]

Tens of thousands of officers begged for their positions. It is impossible to comprehend the sheer amount of paperwork that engulfed the state offices during the Civil War. Hundreds of angry or forceful letters came across their desks daily. For instance, in 1861 alone, the state of New York organized 104 infantry regiments and eleven cavalry and mounted rifle regiments. To supply these units with their initial installment of officers, Governor Edwin D. Morgan commissioned more than 4,300 applicants. Of course, those commissions did not keep those regiments functional. Each week, officers resigned their commissions, fell ill during the campaign, deserted their units, or died in battle.[13] Brigadier General James Cooper, the commandant of all Maryland volunteers, expressed frustration even after he filled vacancies in only two regiments. Venting to Governor Augustus Bradford, Cooper wrote, "I was in hopes that the trouble and confusion produced by cliques would have terminated with the 3rd Regt. But I find both your Excellency and myself are to be annoyed by aspirants and disappointed applicants . . . in reference to the 3rd Infantry."[14]

The northern governors did not face their burdens alone. Each state executive possessed an appointed military staff of nine to twelve individuals to supplement his duties as "commander in chief."[15] Most important were the adjutants general,

The Power to Appoint. State governors alone held the power to commission junior officers in the Union Army. This image depicts the military staff of Pennsylvania's Governor Andrew Curtin (*seated, center*). Curtin's adjutant general, Andrew L. Russell (*seated, right*), was responsible for handling all the governor's commissions' files. (William H. Egle, *Life and Times of Andrew Gregg Curtin*)

who operated as the chiefs of staff.[16] They handled administrative paperwork, regulated other military departments attached to the governor's office, and analyzed military appointments made by the governor.[17] The pressing demands of the office required the adjutants general to become organization-driven fiends and effective judges of character.[18] Theoretically, the adjutants general imposed a sense of quality control in the appointment of army officers, but Democrats complained that Republicans used their offices to flood the volunteer forces with unqualified placemen. In August 1861, the *Boston Herald*, a Democratic newspaper, ran an article under the banner, "ABOLITIONISM AT THE STATE HOUSE." The editor complained that "no man, however well qualified can obtain favor from Governor Andrew or the military dandies about him, providing he is a Democrat." Naturally, such accusations—whether true or not—angered Republicans, who wanted to believe they had selflessly set aside their partisan animosities. In this case, the Republican *Boston Evening Journal* called the *Herald's* claims "utterly groundless." The editor argued, "From the best information we can obtain, it appears to us that political considerations have no weight whatever with the commander-in-chief [meaning Governor John Andrew]; that we think an examination of the real facts in the case will show that a desire to secure the utmost efficiency to the service has induced the Governor to make a majority of his appointments from the ranks of those who have always been his political opponents." To prove his point, the editor of the *Evening Journal* counted the colonels of the first fourteen infantry regiments from Massachusetts and asserted that only five of them were Republicans.[19]

Politicians and newspaper editors preferred to acknowledge selfless adherence to antiparty-ism, but they did not practice what they preached. Republicans rejected officer appointments based on partisanship, and the Democrats did the same when the roles reversed. New York City, with its unusual Democratic majority, spent much of the war castigating the Republican bastion at the state capital. In April 1861, Governor Morgan formed a "State Military Board" to assist his overworked staff. Democrats in New York City complained that "the object [of Morgan's Albany Board] . . . is understood . . . to provide their friends and favorites with colonelcies and majorities."[20]

Fearing that they would be deprived of commissions, some clever Democrats in Gotham appealed to the War Department in an effort to overrule Morgan. One savvy congressman, Daniel Sickles, went directly to Washington to request authority to recruit an entire brigade for federal service. On May 16, 1861, Lincoln granted Sickles's request, but when Governor Morgan learned of this, he complained that Lincoln's intervention violated General Order Number 15. Believing the law to be on his side, Morgan appointed officers to the five regiments assigned to Sickles's brigade, hoping that, by filling them with Republicans, he could oust Sickles from his command. Sickles appointed his own officers, each with commissions signed by Simon Cameron. Only Lincoln's intervention on behalf of Sickles ended this standoff.[21] The *New York Herald*, a pro-Sickles paper, exclaimed, "The snub that President Lincoln has given the Military Board . . . it is hoped will teach the members of this Albany humbug not to stand in the way of the movements of the people to maintain the government and the integrity of the Union."[22]

Democrats could also remove unwanted Republican officers through U.S. Army Examination Boards. After the fiasco at Bull Run, the War Department and Congress jointly created "boards of examiners." In reply to the panicked public outcry for better leadership, the War Department drafted two sets of General Orders, Numbers 47 and 49, authorizing, first, the "general in chief," and then later any commanding general of an army or independent garrison, to appoint boards of examiners to consist of three to five officers "whose duty it shall be to examine the capacity, qualifications, propriety of conduct, and efficiency of any commissioned officer of volunteers." As General Order Number 47 described, those "officers found to be incompetent will be rejected, and the vacancies thus occasioned will be filled by the appointment of such persons as may have passed examination before the board."[23]

Ideally, the boards were supposed to weed out ineffective officers, but instead the Union Army's senior leadership turned them into ad-hoc tribunals that removed officers allied with the Republican Party. Upon assuming command as general in chief in November 1861, Major General George B. McClellan put the provisions of General Orders 47 and 49 into effect.[24] One Republican officer fumed when his Democratic brigade commander began disqualifying his friends. "An officer," he wrote, "has no earthly hope, if summoned before the board, of passing simply that it is expressly understood that he is sent there to be broken if he does not resign."[25]

Fearing the army's examination boards would nullify the appointing powers of the governors, some states established their own boards to counteract them. Maryland's state board tried to stem a tide of removals from the 2nd Maryland after Major General Ambrose Burnside, a Democrat, purged eight from its ranks, including its colonel, all of whom belonged to Maryland's Union Party, the state's version of the Republicans. A faction of New York–born officers within the regiment—all of them Democrats—headed by Lieutenant Colonel Jacob Eugene Duryeé, convinced Burnside to initiate the anti–Union Party cleansing.[26] Burnside's examination board asked questions based on trifling military minutiae, so the Marylanders claimed, dismissing each officer who faced it. None from the Democratic faction ever faced examination. For the Union Party Marylanders in the 2nd Regiment, it appeared that the Democratic New York cabal meant to take over. Lieutenant Charles Bowen implored Governor Augustus Bradford, "Sir, if we had a Marylander for our commander we would be treated as soldiers and gentlemen. . . . All I want is justice and I hope the day is not far distant."[27]

Piqued by Bowen's lengthy account detailing the misdeeds of the Democrats, Governor Bradford initiated a state board to eliminate Duryeé's faction. It summoned one Democrat, Surgeon Edward Moroney, to stand examination—"without one moments time for preparation," Moroney later complained—and issued him a series of difficult questions that resulted in his dismissal. Moroney protested, writing, "To be handled so roughly . . . , with no opportunity whatever for preparation, I feel to be unjust in the extreme, and seriously reflecting upon ones whole future professional life."[28] When Governor Bradford sent a replacement to fill the 2nd Maryland's now vacant colonelcy, Lieutenant Colonel Duryeé contacted Burnside to have an army examination board prepared for him when he arrived. Even before Bradford's new appointee, Colonel Thomas B. Allard, set foot in camp, Burnside summoned him before this board, where its members found him incompetent to lead.[29]

Justified or not, Republicans considered themselves at the mercy of vindictive Democrats who dominated the senior officer corps. Governors appointed every officer from second lieutenant to colonel, but brigadier generals and major generals received their commissions from President Lincoln himself. President Lincoln did his best to keep the generalships free from unsightly mudslinging. Famously, he chastised one of the few Republican generals, Carl Schurz, who had blamed Lincoln for "plac[ing] the Army, now a great power in this Republic, into the hands of its' enemys," meaning the Democrats. Lincoln countered by arguing that few Republicans had professional military training. The president wrote, "It was mere nonsense to suppose a minority could put down a majority in rebellion. . . . It so happened that very few of our friends had a military education or were of the profession of arms. It would have been a question whether the war should be conducted on military knowledge, or on political affinity, only that our own friends (I think Mr. Schurz included) seemed to think that such a question was inadmissable. Accordingly I have scarcely appointed a democrat to a command, who was not urged by many republicans and opposed by none."[30]

Although Lincoln appointed men of suspect qualifications to the rank of general, he tried to respect military education and experience. This put the Republicans at a disadvantage. Most regular officers, particularly those educated at West Point, belonged to the Democratic Party. Formed in 1854, the Republican Party was too new to field a large number of professionals in the senior officer corps. Once at the front, the Republican Party's junior officer corps—the lieutenants, captains, majors, lieutenant colonels, and colonels—found itself at the mercy of hypercritical Democratic superiors. Also, by happenstance, certain army corps, which received regiments randomly, were filled with Democratic generals who intimidated Republican subordinates. One of the worst conglomerations of Democratic generals formed in the 2nd Corps under the command of Major General Winfield S. Hancock. In February 1864, a new regiment, the 183rd Pennsylvania, popularly known as the 4th Union League, joined this corps at its winter encampment at Brandy Station, Virginia. The Union League Club of Philadelphia, a forthright Republican organization, had recruited this regiment, recommending officer candidates to the governor. According to the officers of the 4th Union League, Democrats on the 2nd Corps staff resolved to mistreat the regiment upon its arrival. One officer from the 4th Union League complained that this overbearing attitude stemmed from "a report which preceded our advent in the Army, that we were a 'political organization,' 'of no account soldiers' and many other equally ridiculous sayings." Several of the Union League officers complained that the 2nd Corps staff officers were "faithless, hypocritical, canting, and selfish, it is difficult to conceive of a set of men combining characteristics more repulsive with an unscrupulousness so reckless: This essential element in their character probably never had a more forcible illustration than in their conduct toward our much abused Regiment. We have an evidence of this in the offensive and greedy recklessness which they seized upon every opportunity to annoy, embarrass, and misrepresent us." The Democratic officers attached to the corps staff denied these allegations, saying simply that the officers of the 4th Union League contrived excuses to cover up their incompetence.[31]

After the 2nd Corps staff officers accused the 4th Union League of cowardice at the Battles of the Wilderness and Spotsylvania Court House and threatened to confiscate the regimental colors, all the regimental field and staff officers resigned. They hoped for a vote of confidence from the club, but the Union League members banished them from further membership.[32] Stung by this bad publicity, the Union League Club attempted to find replacement officers. They offered the colonelcy to a U.S. Regular, but he refused it. Governor Andrew Curtin, a Republican, expressed disappointment that the Union League Club had refused to support the officers it had initially appointed. He wanted them to stand up to the Regulars and Democrats in the 2nd Corps. He chided them, "[I] Do not & [I] will not appoint officers of the regular service (and) when volunteer officers can be found acceptable & qualified." Ultimately, Curtin recommended a Republican officer from another regiment to stand in as the 4th Union League's colonel, and the Union League assented to his decision.[33]

When Democratic generals ruffled the feathers of Republican leaders, they took their case to the public media with varying levels of success. In 1862, the Republican press corps initiated a bold campaign to take down one of the most notorious Democratic cabals in the Army of the Potomac, the inner circle composed of the officers who led the brigades, divisions, and ran the staff of the 6th Corps. Republicans considered them a sly set of operatives, whose sole aim was to advance the ranks of young Democrats. Major General Joseph Hooker, a vindictive gossiper himself, once called them a cluster of "evil geniuses."[34]

The "evil geniuses" of this cabal earned disrepute as early as 1862, at a time before the "6th Corps" had even been officially recognized as a military force.

The 6th Corps Cabal. Although Republican politicians dominated northern state houses, Democrats tended to control the Union's senior officer corps. This image depicts the notorious Democratic enclave of the Army of the Potomac's 6th Corps led by Major General William B. Franklin (*seated, center*). Seated at the far right is Brigadier General John Newton, who involved himself in the controversial promotions of Gustavus Town and Adam King. (Library of Congress)

In January, Republicans assailed the reputation of a Delaware officer named Adam E. King, a young politician recently associated with the "Bayard Democrats." Dr. Arthur Harper Grimshaw, the postmaster of Wilmington, who moonlighted as editor for the *Delaware Inquirer*, took notice when King, then a private, received a commission as second lieutenant in the 31st New York. Displeased, Grimshaw sent a letter to King's brigade commander, Brigadier General John Newton, a member of the cabal. Grimshaw's discourteous letter censured Newton for promoting a traitor to lieutenant. Grimshaw declared, "This man [Adam King], participated in a Rebel meeting at Dover, on June 27th[.] I think, . . . he acted as no Loyal citizen should act. He cheered for Jeff. Davis after the battle of Bull's Run and is as much a secessionist as one dare be in Delaware." Grimshaw accused Newton of deliberately attempting to fill the Union Army with secessionists. Grimshaw continued, "I beg for your own sake that you will let me know about him and also deny the allegation that you are responsible for his appointment. A man who acted as this King has done is not to be trusted."[35]

On Lieutenant King's behalf, General Newton denied the charges of treason. He argued that Grimshaw had confused peace activism with sedition, thus censuring King for being a Democrat. To Grimshaw, Newton wrote, "I have an intimate persuasion that those of the opposition party in Delaware, who are not traitors in intention, could be converted into staunch defenders of our flag, in the field of battle, by a few words of friendly reason and argument." To Newton, Grimshaw's ill-considered letter seemed guided by blind faith in party politics, not by authentic alarm. The general scolded, "I cannot close without commenting on the extraordinary course you have thought proper to pursue in regard to Mr. King, and likewise to myself, in inviting an ex-parte and public prosecution of the case, in the columns of a party press. . . . You have chosen to appeal to popular passion, and the chances of a 'hue and cry' against Mr. King as the means, instead of a cool and impartial inquiry into the merits of the case, to expel him from the service and disgrace him irreparably."[36]

In receiving Newton's reply and his denial of the charges against him, Grimshaw got what he wanted, supposed "evidence" of a vast conspiracy to appoint traitors to the junior officer corps. Grimshaw sent another letter to Newton, in which he explained the details of King's treason, meaning his presence at the Dover meeting where he apparently dubbed Lincoln's administration a "military despotism."[37] Of course, Grimshaw could not get King's commission rescinded unless he appealed to the governor of New York. Thus he circulated dozens of anti-King broadsides, sending one to Albany. In large letters, the broadside read, "TRAITOR IN THE CAMP: The Case of Adam E. King." Grimshaw charged that King, then a lieutenant in the 31st New York, "is not a proper man to hold any position of trust or confidence under the United States Government."[38] An attached article from the *Inquirer* read, "Why such men should be appointed to places of responsibility and trust in a government which they have done everything they knew how to demoralize and destroy, I cannot imagine. When such appointments are made there must be 'something rotten in Denmark.' General Newton, of Fort Delaware, is the military God-Father of these traitors. Such acts sicken a Union Man."[39]

Grimshaw's accusations caught the attention of Adjutant General Thomas Hillhouse, who sent a letter to Colonel Calvin Pratt, King's regimental commander. Pratt, a Democrat, interviewed King and the generals belonging to the 6th Corps cabal.[40] King denied the charges of secessionism, and in turn blamed

Firestorm of Controversy. This image depicts Adam Eckfeldt King, a Delaware
Democrat who acquired a lieutenancy in the 31st New York Infantry. When Delaware Republicans learned of his promotion, they unleashed a vicious mudslinging
campaign to convince New York's Republican governor to rescind his commission. King weathered the disagreement, ending the war as brevet brigadier
general. (Library of Congress)

his accuser of "political hostility, intensified by personal hatred." In their letters
to Hillhouse, Colonel Pratt and Lieutenant Colonel William H. Browne insisted
on King's loyalty. The kingpin of the 6th Corps cabal, Major General William B.
Franklin, added, "The story which he [King] tells as to Dr. Grimshaw's enmity is
doubtless correct. I understand that political feuds are more bitter at present in
Delaware than in any other state."[41]

In King's case, the 6th Corps cabal protected a faithful officer from public
slander, but it often participated in malicious crusades of its own. In July 1862,
the 6th Corps officers tried to appoint a Democratic officer to command the 95th

Pennsylvania. On June 27, 1862, a vacancy opened in that regiment's colonelcy when its popular commanding officer, Colonel John M. Gosline, fell mortally wounded at Gaines's Mill, Virginia. With undisputed gallantry, Lieutenant Colonel Gustavus W. Town took command of the regiment on the field of battle and led it through the remainder of the Peninsula Campaign. In July, Town applied for the colonelcy of the 95th, but the 6th Corps cabal wanted its associate, Second Lieutenant John Baillie McIntosh, an Irish cavalry officer, to assume the position instead.

General Franklin sent a note to Governor Curtin, asking him to deny Town's application on account of his age (he was twenty-three), stating that "Col. Town is entirely too young and inexperienced to take care of the regiment under the difficult circumstances that now surround us." Franklin recommended McIntosh as Gosline's replacement.[42] Town's brigade commander, General Newton, also wrote a letter condemning the lieutenant colonel for his supposed youth and inexperience. Newton wrote that "Lieut. Col. Town is not in my opinion, of sufficient force, experience, or age" to be a leader.[43] Even the commander of the Army of the Potomac, Major General George B. McClellan, offered a damning assessment of Town's leadership. Having read Franklin's and Newton's letters, McClellan added, "I most cordially concur with the above & would regard it as my gift to the 95th to have McIntosh made its colonel."[44]

To Lieutenant Colonel Town and his men, the Democratic generals' wishes seemed unreasonable and tainted with favoritism. McIntosh was a second lieutenant, five grades below that of a colonel; he was a cavalryman, not an infantryman; and he had never served with the 95th Pennsylvania, not in battle, nor in camp. By contrast, Town had been with the regiment since the beginning of the war; he had led it gallantly at Gaines's Mill; and he held the rank of lieutenant colonel, the rank immediately below the vacant colonelcy. To the soldiers of the 95th, no other option seemed more logical than to elevate Town. When Town learned of the scheme to supplant him, he wrote to Adjutant General Andrew L. Russell to air his grievances: "I do not know that any one is attempting to undermine me, but it has every appearance of such. . . . My officers report to me that one of our Generals desiring to obtain a commission for a friend of his,—and knowing of the vacancy in the head of my Regiment, has requested Gov. Curtin to commission said friend colonel of this Regiment."[45]

Fighting to win the contested colonelcy, Town questioned the wisdom of appointing a cavalry lieutenant to command an infantry regiment. He concluded that "the dissatisfaction produced [by that move] would tend to much disorganize

Battle for Colonelcy. This image depicts Colonel Gustavus Washington Town, colonel of the 95th Pennsylvania Infantry. Town, a Republican, fought hard to receive
his rank. When Democratic generals blocked his bid for colonelcy, they caused an
uproar inside the Harrisburg State House and in his hometown of Philadelphia.
After weeks of intrigue, Town eventually secured a promotion. He led his regiment until his death at the Battle of Salem Heights in May 1863. (USAMHI-CWP
Collection, Record Group 98)

what has been considered one of the finest and best disciplined Regiments from
Penna., or in the service."[46] Town's fellow officers seemed to agree. On July 18, all
twenty-two captains, lieutenants, and surgeons in the 95th Pennsylvania held an
informal election, choosing Town as their new colonel. They sent their petition
to Governor Curtin, arguing that "well did he [Town] acquit himself, proving

that he possessed all the qualities of a true soldier. Devoted to his profession, at all times cool and self possessed, prompt and vigorous in all his movements, we regard him as the natural and fitting successor of that noble soldier the late Colonel John M. Gosline."[47] Even more surprising, forty-two officers from the three New York regiments in Newton's brigade signed a similar petition approving the decision made by the 95th Pennsylvania's officers.[48]

Of Town's friends, those who contacted well-known Republican officials counted most. For instance, Private Abel Thomas wrote to Pennsylvania's State Treasurer, demanding he take an interest in the appointment of officers to the 95th Pennsylvania. Thomas complained, "I have . . . learned that efforts are being made by certain politicians to set at naught the choice of the Regiment and put in an 'outsider' as Colonel. *I* am not a politician, and can only express my hope that you will use your influence with our worthy Governor to confirm the election of the Regt. Surely it is both wise and just to encourage regular promotions in the Army of the Republic, especially when approved by our brave soldiers."[49] Likewise, Private Thomas Noble wrote to a Republican state senator, arguing similarly:

I suppose you will be surprised at receiving a communication from me, but knowing that you feel an interest in the welfare of our Regiment, I will inform you of an imposition which rumor says is about to be penetrated upon our worthy and efficient Lieut. Colonel. . . . [Lieutenant Colonel Town] conducted the Regiment with bravery and skill through the numerous engagements which followed on Gaines' Hill, which has endeared him to the hearts of every officer and soldier in his command and it is the wish and expectation of them all that he will receive the reward justly due him, viz. a commission as colonel of the Regiment. Rumor says however that a certain Major General supposed to be Franklin is using his influence with Gov. Curtin to obtain the appointment of a favorite of his a 2nd Lieut. in the 5th Regular Cavalry who received his appointment to the position he now holds from civil life about one year ago and he has no more claim to the position of colonel of our Regiment than I have. All our officers say that they will not recognize him and should he receive the appointment it will cause a total disorganization of the Regiment, and knowing your influence with Gov. Curtin and at the request of many of your friends in that Regiment I have written this communication, hoping that you will give it your earliest attention.[50]

Republican State Representative Joseph Moore Jr. added to Governor Curtin's mailbag, writing, "I have heard from a number of my friends in the 95 Regt. that it is your intention to appoint a Lieut. of the 5th Regular Cavalry Col. of that (95) Regt., against the unanimous wish of the whole Regt. to have the gallant Lieut. Col. Town of the Regt. receive, as he ought, the command. I know you will not do such an act of injustice."[51]

Before Curtin could even fashion a response to these concerned citizens, Philadelphia's leading Republican newspaper censured him for his apparent decision to appoint McIntosh instead of Town. The *Philadelphia Inquirer* wrote, "The appointment of any other person to the command of the regiment would be greatly detrimental to its interests."[52] Lieutenant McIntosh happened to be in Philadelphia on the day the *Inquirer's* article appeared in print. After reading it that morning, he penned a brief letter to Governor Curtin withdrawing his name from consideration.[53] With no one contesting him, Town received the colonelcy and held it until his death at the Battle of Salem Church on May 3, 1863.

As the 95th Pennsylvania incident demonstrated, public opinion and judgments issued by Union high command influenced officer appointments, but the final decision always rested with the governors. In 1862, when Democrats in New Hampshire unleashed a wave of criticism against the Republican administration, Governor Nathaniel S. Berry dealt out retribution by refusing to appoint Democrat Thomas Whipple to colonelcy of the newly raised 12th New Hampshire. As the regimental historian recalled, "To withhold his commission was not only a great wrong to Col. Whipple and the men who had unanimously elected him, but an act of bad faith on the part of the chief executive himself."[54] Berry endured weeks of heckling and name-calling, but he refused to budge. As one soldier remembered, "Petitions and remonstrances, by tens and scores, . . . were sent in and piled upon the Executive table, all asking that Col. Whipple be commissioned colonel of the regiment or remonstrating against the Governor's refusal so to do. The large number of these papers, still to be seen filed away in the Adjutant General's office, are mute but convincing witnesses of the great pressure brought to bear upon Gov. Berry to move him from his negative position, and get him to comply with the popular demand." Berry never backed down, and the 12th New Hampshire went to war commanded by Colonel Joseph Potter.[55]

Aspirants watched the gubernatorial elections carefully. A change in the administration could determine which officers received promotions. In November 1862, the gubernatorial elections of New York and New Jersey went to the Democratic Party. Democratic soldiers who served in regiments from those states viewed the regime change as a godsend, and when they begged for commissions, they complained that bad policies of the preceding Republican administrations had unjustly held their rightful promotions in abeyance. For instance, several sergeants and corporals from the 176th New York grumbled that in 1862, Governor Morgan had selected a political hack, Mark Hoyt, and a band of contemptible cronies to command their regiment. According to the Democrats, Hoyt's placeholders had perpetrated "all manner of schemes and rascalities" to keep them from advancing in rank. To Governor Horatio Seymour, the soldiers wrote, "Cheating lying and swindling characterized them at home, and *drunkenness* and *incompetency* in the Field."[56] When it became known that the two new Democratic governors, Horatio Seymour and Joel Parker, made it policy to answer patronage requests, Democrats from Republican-governed states appealed to them. In 1864, eight Pennsylvanians requested a military chaplaincy—which was also an officer's rank—for a friend by writing to Seymour. They explained, "Had we a Democratic Executive in this once proud Commonwealth, your friendly office would not be invoked." These Pennsylvania Democrats continued, "You are the Governour of New York, a Democratic Governour. You have the appointment of Chaplains of Regiments. . . . [A]llow us to ask you, if you can spare such a place to our oppressed friend Miller, to give him one of these Chaplaincies. . . . The appointment will reflect no discredit on yourself, or the appointing power. We are slow to make this application as you are the Governour of another state,—but we come to you as Democrats, who can not find the help needed in our own."[57]

Republicans viewed the two Democratic victories as a threat to the Union Army. Although it had been their own policy to reward friends with commissions, when the Democrats did it, it seemed reprehensible to them. The Republicans considered it treason to offer military positions to individuals who criticized the war, and they considered it foolish when Seymour and Parker replaced the military staffs at Albany and Trenton. Seymour's adjutant general, John T. Sprague, for instance, handled his position competently, but Republicans considered him an unwise replacement for Thomas Hillhouse. When New Yorkers voted out Seymour in November 1864, replacing him with Republican Reuben Fenton, Republican Party leaders felt as if they had thrown off the yoke of tyranny. Only days after Fenton and his new adjutant general took office, Henry Liebenau Sr. wrote a letter demanding his son's overdue promotion to colonel. Liebenau, it seemed, had mistaken Adjutant Sprague's prickly demeanor as evidence of a conspiracy to ruin the state's military leadership. He wrote, "It was one of the tricks of the previous ("Copperhead") administration to dishearten patriotic citizens . . . by appointing and commissioning men who had not the slightest claim for positions—outsiders who had nothing to do with the organizing or getting up of the commands. . . . If [these] appointments or promotions therefore are approved of, the 'Copperhead' tricks of Seymour and Co. will be consummated."[58]

Both political parties believed that corruption, nepotism, and favoritism ran rampant, but were these merely paranoid fears? In some cases, the answer was yes. Some adjutants general, in fact, avoided corruption by adhering to a system of seniority. They dated all commissions, allowing them to establish a "pecking order" among the captains and lieutenants in the different regiments. Additionally, they graded sergeants and corporals to determine which noncommissioned officers were entitled to rise to second lieutenant. Later in the war, some adjutants general established a policy not to transfer men to fill vacancies in other units, thus avoiding the possibility of accusations of impropriety.

But fervent partisanship ruined this system of seniority, often elevating certain applicants ahead of more worthy candidates, meaning those entitled to their positions by duration of service or date of promotion. Field officers could easily outflank this policy. When recommending new candidates for second lieutenancies, field officers sent names of sergeants only from their own political party. A Republican sergeant who had been passed over for promotion several times by his Democratic colonel griped, "There is an old and true saying that 'Kissing goes by favours.' So it is in this regiment. There is too much partiality shown by some of the officers in this command."[59]

The question of seniority also fell apart when the governors and adjutants general tried to take talent and courage into account when making their decisions. One case in point involved two quarreling officers from the 83rd Pennsylvania, Major William Lamont and Captain Orpheus Woodward. In the summer of 1863, both men applied to fill the vacant colonelcy of their regiment. According to the right of seniority, Lamont should have assumed that position; however, Woodward stood out as the more capable candidate since he had led the regiment in more battles. Lamont had been absent from his regiment for several months, since he had been appointed to a divisional staff by friendly Democratic generals. Woodward, meanwhile, had capably led the 83rd Pennsylvania at the Battle of Gettysburg, and thus the line officers considered him the rightful commander. In late July, Major Lamont nominated himself to the colonelcy. In response, the other officers of the regiment sent Governor Curtin a letter demanding that he ignore Lamont's right of seniority and appoint Woodward. Curtin agreed with the officers' assessment—to him, Woodward was the superior leader—but the governor had to consider political factors. Six generals or brigade commanders, all of them Democrats, endorsed Lamont.[60] With a gubernatorial election in the offing, Curtin worried that by violating the generals' wishes he might lose the support of War Democrats in Erie County. Shrewdly, Curtin deferred his decision until after the election, at which time he advanced Woodward to colonel.[61]

Sadly, even obvious merit could take a backseat if partisan politics interfered. This happened in the 90th Pennsylvania, where an unfortunate first lieutenant found himself thwarted by rivals at every turn. First Lieutenant George W. Watson had mustered in as first lieutenant of Company H in 1861, and after the death of his captain at Second Bull Run, he found himself in command. By the summer of 1862, Watson emerged as the senior lieutenant in his regiment, and under the guidelines of promotion etiquette, he expected to receive the captaincy of Company H. Recognizing Watson's talent, bravery, and his right of seniority, Governor Curtin forwarded a captain's commission to him, but strangely, it never reached his encampment. A month after the Battle of Fredericksburg, Colonel Peter Lyle recommended fourteen officers for advancement, all of them Democrats. In this way, Watson—a Republican—discovered that another lieutenant, one who had been absent from the regiment for several months and who had participated in just one battle, was to take the command of his company.[62]

Watson might have buried his resentment had it not been for the intervention of Major Alfred J. Sellers, one of the regiment's few Republican officers. Sellers had been wounded at Fredericksburg and had returned to Philadelphia to recuperate. While he was absent, Colonel Lyle saw fit to recommend the fourteen officers for promotion. As Sellers explained to Governor Curtin, "You are no doubt aware that it is customary for the Field Officers of a Regiment to consult and canvass the merit and qualifications of those entitled to promotion, as vacancies have occurred from time to time. . . . At last, I have the misfortune to be absent from my command, then, apparently, *then*, the *opportunity* is embraced to make promotions." Sellers pointed out the injustice of promoting another officer over Lieutenant Watson. Sellers explained, "To be candid it looks as though merit is superseded by *other influences*." Stating it more plainly, he wrote, "Lieut. Geo W. Watson . . . has ably replied to the many constant expressions of opposition to the administration there by rendering himself *no doubt unpopular with his superiors*. Perhaps you can imagine his position."[63]

Governor Curtin made inquiries to Colonel Lyle, asking him if Watson had been unjustly ignored in his list of officers' candidates. Within days, Curtin received a caustic rebuke from twelve of the fourteen recently promoted Democratic officers, including Captain William Davis, the new commander of Company H. The officers chided, "Politics have never been broached in the regiment, and further . . . Colonel Peter Lyle is not acquainted with the political feelings of more than a few of us; and that but four of us, of the fourteen promotions, have ever, in any manner, been connected with the Democratic party."[64]

Curtin contacted Major Sellers, who discounted the officers' statement as hogwash; they had all lied about their political affiliations. Sellers contended, "I *have never* introduced politics in any of *my* communications, while on the contrary, the officers of the Regt. *have* introduced it, and therein they claim that 10 Republicans out of the 14 in the promotions, while it can be shown on oath that it is just the *reverse*." Convinced of Sellers's correctness, Curtin sent another captain's commission to Watson, commanding Colonel Lyle to honor it. The commission arrived sometime in late April 1863, and when Watson went to Lyle's tent to receive it, the colonel told him that he "had not the commission in his possession." Letters from Adjutant General Russell and Major Sellers had informed Watson otherwise, and it was then that the unfortunate lieutenant realized that Lyle had destroyed the commission. Before Watson left the tent, Colonel Lyle warned him not to complain anymore, as the question of promotions was "a matter between the Governor of Penna. and myself."[65]

Over the winter of 1863–64, Curtin sent yet another commission, and this time he instructed Watson to bring charges against Colonel Lyle if he refused to hand it over. Watson did as the governor suggested, but unfortunately, another campaign intervened. Just days before Watson planned to initiate a court martial against Lyle, the Army of the Potomac crossed the Rapidan River, commencing the bloody Overland Campaign. On May 5, 1864, the first day of fighting, Lieutenant Watson received a gunshot wound to the right thigh and fell into Confederate hands. Watson's sad experience—by no means a rarity among the files of the adjutants general—suggests that partisanship offered an unfortunate hindrance to military meritocracy. In many ways, this example is emblematic of the North's larger problem: that it suffered from an overabundance of politics. Political rivalries, perhaps functional in traditional settings, became malignant ulcers that produced turmoil and disagreement. Politics infected the Union Army with unhealthy competition, despoiling an arena where valor and courage were supposed to remain supreme.[66]

How did Union affairs match the situation in Confederate Army? It is important to note that the system of officer promotions operated differently in the southern armies. Unlike their Union counterparts, Confederate officers from second lieutenant to colonel received their commissions from the central government. Majors, lieutenant colonels, and colonels received formal confirmations from the Confederate Senate, but usually that governmental body followed the recommendations of its soldiers, meaning elections held in camp. Confederate generals, meanwhile, received their commissions from the president. Most surprising, in the Confederacy, the state governors had no appointing powers. Compared to their northern counterparts, southern governors had precious little state-level military power.[67] Certainly elections in the field riddled Confederate promotions with intrigue; however, because the Confederacy had no gubernatorial appointing powers and no two-party system, fewer accusations of impropriety emerged. With no rival party and no corrupt administration to blame, how could the Confederate army rival the political paranoia of the Union?[68]

Still, Confederate policy possessed certain disadvantages. While the popular election of officers inhibited rancorous infestations of partisanship, it eroded military discipline. Confederate soldiers, it appears, possessed a lower tolerance for abusive commanders. If an officer appeared too strict or too overbearing, the enlisted men convinced themselves of the right to remove him from camp. For instance, the Texas Brigade infamously humiliated each field officer appointed and confirmed by Davis and the Confederate Congress over the will of their popular elections. They even drove out one unfortunate contender by beating his horse with switches. In the spring of 1862, a private from the 5th Texas remarked that the enlisted men "fired colonels, lieutenant colonels, and majors faster than Mr. Davis could send them out." Recently, the historian Charles Brooks suggested that the Confederate volunteer's "rights of selection and election were an essential part of the tradition of citizen soldiering," a custom that "strengthened rather than weakened" the Confederate Army. It might be a pointless exercise to guess which system of promotion—by elections or by appointments—produced better officers, but the side effects of the Confederate scheme suggested that rebel commanders traded political infighting for disciplinary troubles. The Confederate system sustained merit over partisanship, but it may have lowered the de facto authority of the junior officer corps. Thus, for all the petty politics that saturated the Union Army, blue-clad officers could scarcely have imagined, or wanted, an army in which the enlisted men could remove an officer at the will of mob law.[69]

Despite the discipline problems irritated by the Confederacy's system of promotion, it was the Union Army that may have suffered more for want of proper leadership. Indeed, the Union fielded many cunning and fearless commanders during the war, but the North's pool of military talent was diluted by a system that allowed for a profusion of political hacks to wear officer's insignia. The adjutants general records prove that partisan conflict was a mainstay in the North's system of promotion; in essence, partisanship even caused applicants to receive their commissions. Thus in a way, the Union Army's bureaucracy functioned because of its squabbling. Although this patronage system may have played a role in the day-to-day operations of military administration—and it may also have elevated a few qualified men to command—partisanship and gubernatorial appointments in the North undoubtedly channeled more inexpert leaders into the Union Army than the centralized, single-party system in the South channeled into the Confederate Army. Far from becoming institutions where politics were fluid, the Union armies emerged as organizations where rigid partisanship became entrenched. The Union's policy of filling officers' positions with gubernatorial appointments made patronage a pivotal force in army life. As Union soldiers recognized, "all manner of schemes and rascalities" directed promotions inside the army of the republic.

"For My Part I Dont Care Who Is Elected President"

The Union Army and the Elections of 1864

Jonathan W. White

If there is any fixed star in our historiographical constellation, it is that the vast majority of Union soldiers had become "Lincoln men"—if not antislavery Republicans—by November 1864. The evidence seems simple and incontrovertible. Seventy-eight percent of the votes cast by soldiers in the field were for Abraham Lincoln and Andrew Johnson. Scholars see this statistic as clear evidence that the soldiers had joined the Republican cause by the end of the war. James M. McPherson, for example, has used the results of the soldier vote to suggest wide scale acceptance of the Republican policy of emancipation: "When Lincoln ran for reelection on a platform pledging a constitutional amendment to abolish slavery, he received almost 80 percent of the soldier vote—a pretty fair indication of army sentiment on slavery by that time." McPherson's student Jennifer L. Weber takes the argument a step further, claiming to trace "the politicization of Union soldiers . . . into lifelong Republicans," although she offers no evidence from the postwar period to substantiate her claim.[1] The arguments of McPherson, Weber, and others imply a linear evolution in the thinking of Union soldiers: they had represented numerous political positions when they enlisted in 1861 and 1862 but by 1864 had adopted Republican war aims as their own.

The story, however, is much more complex. Many soldiers opted not to vote in the presidential election, choosing instead to exercise their franchise by not supporting either candidate. Others reluctantly stumbled down the path of voting for Lincoln. Still others voted Republican only because they could not bring themselves to vote for the Democratic ticket, not because they actually supported the incumbent. And some Democratic soldiers were too intimidated by their Republican comrades to toe their party line. In short, while the army vote of November 1864 was cast overwhelmingly for Lincoln, it does not necessarily indicate that the soldiers had converted to the Republican Party or that they had become lifelong Republicans.

Soldiers casting ballots in the field was one of the defining events of the Civil War. Indeed, as the presidential election of 1864 was approaching, the eyes of all northern politicians turned toward the armies of the Union. Over the previous few years, nineteen northern states had passed legislation permitting volunteers from their states to vote in the field, and many politicians believed that the soldiers' votes would determine whether Abraham Lincoln would be reelected in November 1864. Never before had absentee voting existed on such a large scale in the United States, but with such a large portion of the electorate serving in the army, many politicians thought it necessary to extend the ballot to them.[2] Consequently, the votes of the soldiers became central to winning the election.

At their national convention in the late summer of 1864, Democrats chose General George B. McClellan as their presidential candidate for several strategic reasons. First, McClellan had been a popular officer in the Army of the Potomac during the first half of the war. Moderate Democrats hoped that a nominee with a strong war record like McClellan's would offset the Peace plank in their platform (which declared the war a "failure") and the selection of Peace Democrat George H. Pendleton for vice president. Despite their general aversion to the war, Democrats sought to make their candidates appear supportive of both the war effort and the troops by "getting up a 'war' record for Pendleton for the army," as well as "good McClellan military documents."[3]

The second reason Democrats chose McClellan was that their party had generally opposed allowing soldiers to vote in the field.[4] Some Democrats feared that their position on the soldier suffrage issue would alienate Democratic soldiers and that the army would only vote for the party that had supported their right to vote. In choosing McClellan, northern Democrats found a presidential candidate who had been loved by soldiers from both parties, and they hoped that this affection would be enough to win some of their votes on Election Day.[5]

Union soldiers watched intently as both parties jockeyed for their votes, but by 1864 many soldiers had grown weary of their political leaders. Many soldiers expressed disillusionment with the candidates and with politics in general in the weeks leading up to the election—particularly before the fall of Atlanta. Many doubted whether they would bother to vote at all. "I hardly think that Abraham Lincoln will be reelected the people are rather getting down on him," wrote one Vermont soldier. "For my part I dont care who is elected President if this war can be settled soon as possible but I dont see possible chances of settling under Lincoln's administration." An Illinois soldier, who could not vote because his state did not enfranchise soldiers, wrote his mother on Election Day, "I would not vote for McClellan for I think him a traitor and I'll be dambed if I would vote for Lincoln."[6]

These sentiments seem to have been expressed most often by Democratic soldiers who supported the Republican ticket during the war, many of whom moved slowly to the conclusion that they had to vote for Lincoln. "If I vote at all I shall vote most of the Republican ticket," wrote one soldier to his Democratic family on November 8, 1864. It is significant that even by Election Day he had not decided whether or how he would vote. A surgeon from Pennsylvania informed his mother that "politics are commencing to run quite high, but as for myself, not proposing to vote, I interest myself very little. Moreover, I really don't know whom I would vote for." Other Union soldiers were so discouraged that they were "ready to *vote* for *any* man that will put an end (or try to) to this awful butchery." In August this soldier cared for neither McClellan nor Lincoln, and did "not know who I shall vote for & I do not care whether I vote at all." By November he had changed his mind, however, and settled on President Lincoln as the best man to end the war. Similarly, a New York artillerist wrote his wife on September 29, 1864, from Atlanta, "You wanted to no who I was going to vote for. Most any body! I can't vote for old Abe. Tho, I think he will be elected. I can't go Maclelland, no way. The platform is made of copper, and I am no copperhead. So, I wont vote at all." In Atlanta this soldier observed that many southern women supported McClellan for president, "and for that verry reason I think the army should go for old Abe." So he decided to vote for Lincoln. "I can't support any copperhead candidate. I can't fite for the Union and vote against it. A house divided against it self can not stand. I go for the Union strart through. This is no time for party spirit to show it self. I am a Democrat, but I say hoora for old Abe and down with cesion." This soldier concluded that "the quickest way to end the rebellion is to elect Abe."[7]

This soldier touched on a sentiment that got to the motivation of many soldiers on Election Day. They voted for the candidate they believed would end the war quickly and honorably. "The Soldiers are all tierd of this war," wrote Michigan soldier Mack Ewing to his wife, Nan, in September 1864. "They are all (or the majority of them) are hurrahing for McLellon. they think if he is president that the war will stop." For himself, Ewing had "not made up my mind yet who to hurrah for. but I bet I am for the man that makes peace the Soonest." Surprisingly, he was even willing to support Peace Democrats like Clement Vallandigham of Ohio if they could make "an honorable peace" that would last. Thus, "if McLellon can compromise on honorable terms and make a lasting peace I say hurrah for McLelond for with old Abe there is compromise only to free the nigers and Nan I tell you that a niger is honestly looked on with more honor and esteemed higher and treated better by our rooling authorities than the Union Soldiers are."

Mack Ewing was upset that "this war has become a niger war instead of a union war," but as long as it was a war for emancipation, he concluded, "lett the niger help fight for his freedom and Shear the hard Ships of the Army." Ewing was willing to help free the slaves but he would not consent to be considered their inferior. And when peace came, he wanted to "lett the niger go to gina."[8]

One would not suspect that this soldier was an antebellum Republican, nor that he voted for Lincoln just two months after writing this letter, but he was and he did. Upon receiving this letter, his wife responded that she did not want him "to turn butter nut." He replied that he "almost begin to think that I cood not be a Republican any longer but I have made up my mind that Old Abe is the man for president any how." McClellan was losing support among the soldiers because of the Democratic platform, he said, and has "lost thousands of friends [in the army] which old Abe will find." He now declared himself "tru blue" and "for old Abe."[9]

Mack Ewing's sentiments do not match the standard narrative of the soldiers who voted for Lincoln. He had been a Republican prior to the war and had a Republican wife at home, yet two months before the election he was ready to support even the notorious Copperhead Clement Vallandigham. It took a stinging rebuke from his wife to convince him to vote for Lincoln. Usually historians have seen the opposite effect—that soldiers in the field reminded their friends and relatives at home to vote "loyally."[10] But communication about politics and loyalty was a two-way street. More important, the soldiers' political sentiments did not always follow a linear progression. They wavered and ebbed. Their feelings about the war improved in times of success and dipped when things were going badly.[11] And some, like Mack Ewing, had a loving spouse at home to help guide them back into the Republican fold.

Like many soldiers who voted for Lincoln, most soldiers who supported McClellan did so because they believed he would bring a speedy and honorable conclusion to the war. If McClellan was elected, one Massachusetts soldier told his wife, "I think the war will be over putey quick but if . . . Old Abe gets elected the war will last 4 [more] years."[12] A New York soldier believed "Gen McClellan will end it sooner and without embittering the two parties so much that they could never live happily together again." Similarly, a Pennsylvania soldier told his cousin that the general "is the only one that can settle the war. I hope you will not forget to put in a vote for little Mc and the union."[13]

Most soldiers who voted for McClellan saw themselves as Unionists, but they rejected the abolitionism of the Republican Party. One Wisconsin soldier, who knew he was voting against his father, brothers, and a majority of the army, voted for McClellan because he believed Mac was "best fitted to bring about an honorable Peace, and the Union as it was before the war."[14] Soldiers like this one wanted the Union restored with slavery intact. One of their main concerns was the economic consequences of emancipation. "If the negroes are freed what are we to do with them," wrote one Brooklyn soldier to his sister. "They will be the means of throwing the whites out of employment." Democratic soldiers' views of race permeated their criticism of their political opponents. Indeed, Democratic soldiers frequently conflated their hatred for Republicans with their disdain for African Americans. One Pennsylvania cavalryman expressed his opposition to emancipation by criticizing those "Dam Degreaded Wreches" up North who called McClellan "a trator to his Country. . . . You can tell all them Dam Sap headed nigrow Hug[g]ers up thear that i am a full Blooded McClelon man And Sow is Every good union soldier that Belongs to the Armey of the Potomac that is fighting for His Distracted Country."[15]

In like manner, not all soldiers who voted for Lincoln supported emancipation. We have already seen Mack Ewing's tepid support for emancipation. Other Lincoln voters felt the same. "I'm no abolitionist and if I had a vote and McClellan stood on a good old democratic platform I would vote for him, but as things are at present, if I had that vote it should be cast for Lincoln," wrote one Pennsylvanian stationed near Petersburg. "McClellan, standing alone or in connection with any good man, would gain the day, but as he stands in connection with the *traitor* Pendleton he must fail." Another Pennsylvanian who considered himself a "full Bloom" Republican admitted that "there are some things I do not like about Lincoln, one of them is why he does not exchange all the White Prisoners and let the Colored ones go if the south will not exchange them. I do not believe in having White Soldiers suffer to save a few Negroes."[16] Similarly, a Minnesota artillerist declared himself for Lincoln but against emancipation: "And whether slavery be right or wrong I dont believe in carrying on a bloody war for years for the sole object of Abolishing slavery . . . whenever [the South] can be made or Per[s]uaded to lay down their Arms & Return to their Allegiance the war should end but not before."[17] Following the election one soldier, who appears to have supported Lincoln, cursed abolitionists like Wendell Phillips for wanting "to make a nigger better than a white man."[18]

Many soldiers saw themselves as choosing between the lesser of two evils. After mailing home his ballot for Lincoln, one New York soldier remarked that he had no respect for either presidential candidate. Old Abe needed "a new set of brains" while McClellan had too many private interests to be trusted. The only reason he voted for Lincoln was because the war had to be fought and won, and he believed Lincoln would do that. Charles Francis Adams received a telling letter from his son who was serving in the 5th Massachusetts Cavalry: "Soldiers don't vote for individuals; they don't vote for the war; they have but one desire and that is to vote against those who delay the progress of the war at home; they want to vote down the copperheads." According to Adams Jr., soldiers decided how to vote based not on what they were *for*, but what they were *against*. "Look at the soldiers vote and that will show you what we think of your peace men," one Maine soldier told his wife, again implying that many voted against rather than for something. After commenting that he disliked both gubernatorial candidates in New York, but that he disliked the Republican "still more," Marsena Rudolph Patrick, the provost marshal general of the Army of the Potomac, commented, "It is a choice of evils—I vote for McClellan because I cannot vote for Lincoln."[19] Similarly, a War Democrat from New York decided to split his ticket, which was a rare occurrence in nineteenth-century elections. He feared the Peace Democrats, especially those who tried to portray themselves as supportive of the war. "I voted the Republican State ticket and if Gen McClellan had not been on the other should have voted for Lincoln as the less of *two evils*."[20]

The thought of a Peace Democrat on the ticket was more than most soldiers could bear. "The peace plank in the [Democratic] platform renders it untenable," observed one Republican soldier. "Army officers heretofore strong for McClellan say they cannot vote for an 'immediate cessation of hostilities.'" Similarly, a Rhode Island soldier noted in September that "six months ago a grait many of the soldiers would have voted for [McClellan] but he wont get as many now old abe is the man to finish this thing up." A New Yorker who had voted for the general noted that "McClellan would have got A greate many more votes in the army if he had not been in with pendleton[.] the soldiers dont like pendleton." A soldier in the Regular Army summed up what must have been the sentiments of many Democratic soldiers in a letter to his sweetheart: "You think perhaps I am a McClellan man yes I would rather fo[l]low him than any man on earth for I know him to pos[s]ess the true principle of the Soldier and a man, but I could not vote for him it is the wrong party that comes in to power with him if he is elected."[21]

A small number of soldiers were willing to overlook the peace plank in the platform if the Democratic Party would offer relief for some of the suffering and inconveniences they faced on the front. These soldiers were weary of the war and the Lincoln administration's handling of it. "I wish the Chicago convention or some other would have the effect of reducing the prices of Sutler's goods," wrote one New York soldier. He also remarked that his pay was seven months late and that a "new administration might do better by us." Another soldier noted that the troops "do not like [Lincoln] at all. He gives us very little to eat three hard tack and a pint of Coffee for breakfast, Three Hard Tack and a piece of Salt Horse for dinner, Hard tack and Coffee for supper. It is very hard for any kind of men to live on that." Others believed that McClellan would not provide "shoddy" equipment for the soldiers. Astute Republicans feared the effects of these issues on the army vote. The soldiers "are much dissatisfied because they have received no pay, they fear that they will not be paid at the end of their term of service as it seems has been the case with several regiments of that class," wrote one worried Republican to an Illinois congressman. "Unless something is done soon to counteract this evil, I fear that our candidate for President will lose many votes."[22] A wounded cavalryman at a hospital in Philadelphia similarly warned Pennsylvania's Republican governor that if the soldiers were not allowed to go home to vote (rather than vote at the hospital), many would refuse to vote at all and "some of the less intelligent even threaten to 'change their colors.'"[23]

At an even deeper level, many Democratic soldiers complained that Republicans at home did not understand what they were calling for when they urged the Lincoln administration forward until a peace was won. "'A vigorous prosecution of the war' sounds well to talk, it reads well in newspapers, and makes a good platform for political campaigns. But my God! do people know what it means? I do. It means every week or two to take out a few thousand men and butt them against the mud walls that surround Richmond, then march back to camp with from five to fifteen hundred [fewer] men than we went out with! . . . I am not in favor of withdrawing our armies and giving up everything, but think every honorable means that can be used to put an end to the war should be, and soon, too."[24]

Because of the suffering they had endured, Democratic soldiers and conservative supporters of Lincoln resented those at home who denounced anti-abolition soldiers as disloyal. A Kentucky soldier told his sister in August 1864, "All men opposed to Father Abraham's way of doing buisiness are not in favor of Jeff Davis' way—nor Vallandigham's. And all men that dislike the *service*, are not *cowards*, no, not even all that get out by dishonorable trickery." In July this soldier had said he would not vote for Lincoln "or anybody else" without having a change of mind. By October he appeared to come out in favor of Lincoln, but he still would not allow his sister to call McClellan a traitor. "Loyal men are in favor of McClellan and Slavery—who are willing to prove their loyalty by facing the enemy upon the Battle field." It was a truer loyalty to enlist in the cause of the Union and oppose emancipation than to stay at home campaigning for Lincoln and abolition, he cautioned. "So I will request you not to make any more charges like those contained in your last to the Genl. of 'Ignorance, Treason, & Cowardice.'"[25]

Most Democrats in the army probably opposed both the peace men of their party and the abolitionists of the other. An Indiana Democrat said he could indorse neither Vallandigham nor Lincoln: "I am a Douglas Democrat," he wrote in mid-1864 (three years after Douglas's death), "& will never vote for the mongrel, kinky headed abolitionists. I detest them." Another Democratic soldier, who believed party politics had a corrosive effect on the war effort, wrote, "I think the Peace Democracy are a despicable set, equally as bad as the worst abolitionist."[26]

Because so many soldiers expressed feelings of disdain toward politics and the presidential election, or uncertainty over whom to trust and vote for, the question of voter turnout must be examined.[27] Most scholars of Civil War politics and the Union military have taken this point for granted and merely assumed that the voter turnout in the Union Army mirrored the high voter turnout exhibited in the election as a whole. If the soldiers did not go to the polls in large numbers, however, then perhaps current understandings of soldier motivation and political affiliation need adjustment.

The sample of regiments in table 1 represents all the military units for which both election returns and complete morning reports for Election Day could be located. The sample reveals an estimated voter turnout of about 78 percent among the troops. This level of voter participation was typical for mid-nineteenth-century elections, but it is nevertheless telling that more than 20 percent of the soldiers eligible to vote chose not to do so. After all, voters at home might have to travel some distance to cast their ballots, but voters in the field had only to walk down their company street.[28] When the voter turnout from this sample is factored into the percentage of votes cast for President Lincoln, somewhere between 50 and 60 percent of the eligible soldier voters voted for Lincoln.

Tables 2 and 3 compare the results of several state and congressional elections with the votes of those states in the presidential election. These state and congressional elections were held in the weeks just before the presidential election. As can be seen, there were drastic increases in the voter turnout among the soldiers in the November presidential election, when compared with the September and October elections (with the exception of the Republican soldier vote in Maryland, which was an election in which voters had two days to cast their ballots). On average, the civilian vote of both parties increased by less than 9 percent from the state to the presidential election, whereas the Republican army vote increased almost 40 percent, and the Democratic army vote increased by nearly 100 percent. Table 4 reveals that soldiers who voted for president and Congress on the same day also showed a marked increase in turnout when voting for president (meaning that they "scratched" the names of congressional candidates from

Table 1. Estimated voter turnout in a sample of Union regiments

Total votes cast for Lincoln in sample	Total votes cast for McClellan in sample	Total votes in sample	Total present Nov. 8	Estimated eligible voters (80.8%)	Estimated voter turnout	Percentage of eligible soldiers who voted for Lincoln	Percentage of eligible soldiers who voted for McClellan
6,510	2,629	9,139	14,372	11,613	78.7%	56.1%	22.6%

Note: Table 1 contains statistics for all the regiments for which I could determine the total votes cast as well as the total number of men present on Election Day. The regiments included in this sample are the 16th Maine Volunteers; the 9th, 11th, and 12th New Hampshire Volunteers; the 57th, 69th, 84th, 88th, 91st, 97th, 99th, 100th, 107th, 110th, 116th, 118th, 140th, 150th, 190th, 203rd, 208th, 209th, and 211th Pennsylvania Volunteers; and the 6th, 11th, 17th, 20th, 23rd, 30th, 32nd, 37th, 42nd, and 43rd Wisconsin Volunteers.

I estimated the percentage that were eligible voters using statistics from Benjamin A. Gould, *Investigations in the Military and Anthropological Statistics of American Soldiers* (New York: Hurd and Houghton, 1869), 87. In a sample of soldiers from the army, Gould estimates that in July 1864 there were 116,440 men in the army between the ages of sixteen and nineteen; 80,590 who were twenty years old; and 681,970 who were twenty-one or older. In order to determine how many were voting age on Election Day in 1864 (roughly seventeen weeks after the sample), I took the total number of twenty-year-olds (80,590) and multiplied it by 0.35 (to account for the time between the sample and the election), and added that number (28,207) to the total of men who were already twenty-one (681,970), giving me an estimated 710,177 men who were of voting age in November 1864. I divided that number by the total men present in Gould's sample (879,000) to estimate that 80.8 percent of the men were eligible voters.

This sample likely overestimates the voter turnout in the Union Army. Six of the regiments in the sample produced a voter turnout of more than 100 percent. I have found evidence of numerous minors and other unqualified soldiers who voted.

Sources for Tables 1–4 include *Annual Report of the Adjutant General of the State of Michigan, for the Year 1864* (Lansing: John A. Kerr, 1865), 911–46; *Annual Report of the Secretary of State to the Governor of the State of Ohio, for the Year 1864* (Columbus: Richard Nevins, 1865), 19–46; *Maine Legislative Manual, 1865* (Augusta: Stevens and Sayward, 1865), 153–86; *Message of the Governor of Wisconsin, Together with the Annual Reports, of the Officers of the State, for the Year, A.D. 1865* (Madison: William J. Park, 1866), 164–69; Michael J. Dubin, *United States Congressional Elections, 1788–1997: The Official Results of the Elections of the 1st through 105th Congresses* (Jefferson, NC: McFarland, 1998); U.S. War Department, *The War of the Rebellion: A Compilation of the Official Records of the Union and Confederate Armies* (Washington, DC: Government Printing Office, 1880–1901), ser. 1, vol. 42, pt. 3; pp. 560–78; RG-19, Records of the Department of Military and Veterans Affairs (Morning Reports), PHMC; RG 94, Records of the Adjutant General's Office. Entry 115 (Book Records of Volunteer Union Organizations, Morning Reports), National Archives and Records Administration, Washington, DC; *Tribune Almanac and Political Register for 1865* (New York: Tribune Association, 1865), 46–67; William Blair Lord and Henry M. Parkhurst, eds., *The Debates of the Constitutional Convention of the State of Maryland*, 3 vols. (Annapolis: Richard P. Bayly, 1864), 3:1925–26.

Table 2. Comparison of soldiers' votes in the presidential and other 1864 elections (with percentage of increase in parentheses)

	Rep. home	Rep. army	Rep. total	Dem. home	Dem. army	Dem. total
Ohio election for secretary of state						
Oct. 1864	204,459	32,751	237,210	177,840	4,599	182,439
Nov. 1864 pres. election	224,008 (9.6)	41,646 (27.2)	265,654 (12.0)	195,811 (10.1)	9,788 (112.8)	205,599 (12.7)
Ohio congressional elections						
Oct. 1864	210,708	28,878	239,586	171,855	6,981	178,836
Nov. 1864 pres. election	224,008 (6.3)	41,646 (44.2)	265,654 (10.9)	195,811 (13.9)	9,788 (40.2)	205,599 (15.0)
Pennsylvania congressional elections						
Oct. 1864	247,423	17,888	265,311	244,919	5,232	250,151
Nov. 1864 pres. election	269,679 (9.0)	26,712 (49.3)	296,391 (11.7)	263,967 (7.8)	12,349 (136.0)	276,316 (10.5)
Maine gubernatorial elections						
Sept. 1864	62,529	3,054	65,583	46,287	116	46,403
Nov. 1864 pres. election	63,631 (1.8)	4,174 (36.7)	67,805 (3.4)	46,250 (−0.1)	828 (613.8)	47,078 (1.5)

(*continued*)

Table 2. *(continued)*

	Rep. home	Rep. army	Rep. total	Dem. home	Dem. army	Dem. total
Maine congressional elections						
Sept. 1864	62,212	3,099	65,311	46,417	72	46,489
Nov. 1864 pres. election	63,631 (2.3)	4,174 (34.7)	67,805 (3.8)	46,250 (−0.4)	828 (1050.0)	47,078 (1.3)
Maryland constitutional referendum (two days of voting in October)						
Oct. 1864	27,541	2,633	30,174	29,536	263	29,799
Nov. 1864 pres. election	37,353 (35.6)	2,800 (6.3)	40,153 (33.1)	32,418 (9.8)	321 (22.1)	32,739 (9.9)
Total of all state elections in this sample compared to the presidential election						
State & cong.	814,872	88,303	903,175	716,854	17,263	734,117
Sum of votes in pres. election from previous six examples	882,310 (8.3)	121,152 (37.2)	1,003,462 (11.1)	780,507 (8.9)	33,902 (96.4)	814,409 (10.9)

Note: After several years of searching, I have been unable to find official election returns from the 1864 congressional elections in Pennsylvania. The *Tribune Almanac and Political Register for 1865* lists the soldier vote as 7,635 Republicans and 2,500 Democrats, but it does not include every congressional district. Benton's *Voting in the Field* puts the number at 17,888 Republicans and 12,656 Democrats. While the *Tribune Almanac* is generally the most reliable source for election statistics in the nineteenth century, in this instance I believe it underestimates the actual vote. The other election returns in this table are taken from official reports published by each respective state.

Table 3. Maine regiments in the elections of 1864

Regiment	Gub. election, Sept. 1864		Pres. election, Nov. 1864	
	Republican	Democrat	Lincoln	McClellan
1st Infantry, Veterans	—	—	155	39
8th Infantry	133	3	179	15
9th Infantry	173	1	293	47
12th Infantry	122	6	108	26
13th Infantry	85	5	190	20
14th Infantry	26	0	44	13
15th Infantry	40	4	130	53
16th Infantry	114	1	152	61
17th Infantry	200	2	201	47
19th Infantry	107	0	129	31
20th Infantry	139	2	138	13
29th Infantry	138	3	175	40
30th Infantry	156	7	184	26
31st Infantry	56	6	108	20
32nd Infantry	54	0	68	31
1st Battery	—	—	32	31
2nd Battery	21	0	90	14
3rd Battery	73	4	77	5
4th Battery	46	11	59	34
5th Battery	33	0	36	8
6th Battery	59	0	58	3
7th Battery	60	0	78	90
1st Cavalry	243	7	289	46
2nd Cavalry	277	2	273	1
Detach at Cavalry Depot	54	8	59	8
1st Cavalry at Hospital	65	2	65	2
1st Heavy Artillery	132	5	149	23
2nd Battalion of Heavy Artillery	57	0	71	0
Base Hospital	36	3	44	0
Sickles Hospital	13	1	19	3
Camp Distribution	37	2	106	25
Campbell Hospital	14	1	24	5
Detach at New Orleans	51	1	52	1
2nd and 5th Corps Hosp.	73	3	78	3
Maine Agency in DC	64	5	93	7
Lincoln Hospital	11	0	35	9
City Point Hospital	29	6	33	7
Camp Stoneman	13	2	—	—
Ft. Washington	50	13	—	—
Soldiers at Annapolis	—	—	32	2
Co. A, Coast Guard	—	—	47	17
Detach at Pt. Lookout	—	—	21	2
Total	3,054	116	4,174	828

Note: The purpose of this table is to show that, for the most part, the same soldiers were given the opportunity to vote in both the state and national elections. The increased voter turnout, therefore, cannot be explained by an increased opportunity of soldiers to vote in November.

Table 4. Comparison of soldiers' votes in congressional elections held on the same day as the presidential election (with percentage of increase in parentheses)

	Rep. home	Rep. army	Rep. total	Dem. home	Dem. army	Dem. total
Iowa congressional election						
Cong. election	72,263	16,410	88,673	47,883	1,463	49,346
Pres. election	71,765 (−0.7)	17,310 (5.5)	89,075 (0.5)	47,675 (−0.4)	1,921 (31.3)	49,596 (0.5)
Wisconsin congressional election						
Cong. election	57,492	9,125	66,617	55,941	1,709	57,650
Pres. election	68,216 (18.7)	11,372 (24.6)	79,588 (19.5)	62,590 (11.9)	2,428 (42.1)	65,018 (12.8)

their tickets). Several explanations may help reveal why so few soldiers voted the Democratic ticket in the elections of 1864, and why so many Democratic soldiers who were willing to vote in the presidential election were unwilling to vote for state and congressional candidates.

First, as we have already seen, many soldiers expressed disillusionment about politics and apathy about the candidates. Some general officers noticed these sentiments among the enlisted men. "I note all you say of politics, but in the army we take but little interest except earnestly to wish the election was over," wrote General George Gordon Meade to his wife. "Until it is, nothing else will be thought of and no proper thought given to the war." Election commissioners canvassing the troops also got the impression that politics was not important to many of the boys in blue. One election commissioner was perceived as "rather disgusted with the result of his mission" because "very few of the soldiers had qualified themselves to vote and altogether appeared quite indifferent. He seemed to think the soldiers' vote would be very insignificant." Pennsylvania Commissioner David McKelvy recorded a similar observation in the journal he kept while canvassing the troops. The officers he met "were perfectly indifferent as to the election, and it was with some difficulty that they were urged in opening the polls yesterday and with more difficulty that they were to-day urged into the task of finishing out the forms. . . . They considered it just so much work put on them for nothing." After the state election in October, McKelvy determined that "getting the vote was a thankless job," and he did not wish to serve again as an election commissioner for the presidential election.[29]

These sentiments were present in the writings of enlisted men. Many soldiers wished the election were over for the sake of the war effort, while others paid no attention to it whatsoever. One invalid in a Philadelphia hospital believed that the rebellion was crumbling very fast but that "the rebels will striek and hang" on until the election was over. In line with this man's views, some soldiers lamented that politicians in Washington seemed to be more concerned with electioneering than with filling the ranks and winning the war. Other enlisted men simply revealed apathy about politics. A Democrat from New York remarked that "politics don't trouble us much," while another told his father that soldiers "have little opportunity of studying politics, and also have so much else to think of as to have little inclination for it."[30] Though many political issues were considerably relevant to the soldiers in the field, soldiers were often too busy to think about the issues, or simply did not have the information on hand with which to take educated positions. As if to underscore the lack of interest of some soldiers, one

Pennsylvania cavalryman recorded in his diary on Election Day, "Laying in camp today[;] nothing of importance."[31]

A second explanation for the increased turnout among the troops in November may be that the voters at home were more tied to particular party platforms than were the soldiers in the field. Perhaps the troops were more concerned with electing a commander in chief that would lead them to victory than they were with the two parties' positions on most of the political issues of the day. Electing the right commander in chief was the most important choice they would have to make—and for most soldiers, this was the only one worth voting for. Despite General McClellan's letter of acceptance in which he pledged to prosecute the war until victory was won, many soldiers had reason to believe that if McClellan was elected all their efforts in the field would come to naught. This belief was enough to convince more Republican soldiers to vote in November than in October, to get some Democrats to vote for Abraham Lincoln, and to keep other Democrats from voting at all. It also helps explain why so few Democratic soldiers voted in the state and congressional elections. A large number of Democratic soldiers, by 1864, had come to doubt their party's loyalty and Unionism. They could not bring themselves to vote for Democratic congressmen and state leaders. But many could still vote for McClellan because they believed he would fight to restore "the Union as it was." As one soldier explained, "I don't suppose for a moment that *any soldier* would go home and vote a *Copperhead ticket*, and on the other hand I wouldn't vote a *republican* ticket just merely because it *was* republican but I should most assuredly vote for the Union, and those that would maintain it, let the *principle* appear under any name whatsoever."[32]

Scholars who have used the soldier vote to support various conclusions about the army have almost invariably ignored the soldiers' votes in the non-presidential elections of 1864. By 1864, it seems that Republicans had maintained the support of their partisan friends in blue (the Republican Party did win a large majority of the soldier vote in September and October, too), whereas Democratic soldiers had lost confidence in both parties altogether. One New York soldier who cast his ballot for McClellan came to the sad conclusion that both parties were "equally corrupt, and equally far from my views in their extreme doctrines."[33] This soldier, like many of his comrades, believed he had to choose between the lesser of two evils. Some Democratic soldiers turned to Lincoln to finish out the war; some, like this one, voted for their party's candidate; and some opted to abstain from the franchise.

A third explanation for the low Democratic turnout among the troops—in both the state and the presidential elections—is voter intimidation.[34] Many

Democrats—both at home and in the field—complained that it was difficult to vote the Democratic ticket in the field. One soldier complained that his regiment received only Republican newspapers and that "some other regiments had no opportunity to vote any but the Republican ticket."[35] Indeed, some Democratic soldiers were court-martialed for distributing Democratic newspapers and pamphlets in camp.[36] A New York soldier groused that "such mean, contemptible favoritism or partisanship" was "shown for Lincoln, by many officers in the army, representatives of the Sanitary and Christian Commissions, etc." that "hundreds of soldiers have been literally proscribed from voting for McClellan by their officers, and they have been obliged to get McClellan ballots from other sources." On at least a few occasions Democratic politicians and electioneers were threatened and driven from military camps. Ohio Congressman Samuel S. Cox complained that "the camps [were] closed to us" and "the Barracks [were] used to keep us out & Republicans in." "The soldiers were hungry for our tickets," he exclaimed, "& the cry was for more, when the officers ordered us out! This in Columbus—a *free* state! Do you wonder how I am beaten. We left tickets there, when ordered out, but they were at once destroyed."[37]

Partisan soldiers took pride in this sort of behavior. One soldier wrote to his aunt that "I am going to do all I can for Abe." He described two Democrats who came into his camp "peddling McClellan tickets" but explained that they probably would not be back. "We all took tickets and when they had given the boys all [of the] tickets they were talking to us telling us what a good man McClellan is. We let them talk as long as we could stand it and then we burnt the tickets and told them iff they did not get out of ther[e] in less than 5 minutes we would ride them out on a rail."[38]

Some Democratic soldiers claimed to be discriminated against because of their political convictions. Democrats in Philadelphia learned from their election commissioners "that Democrats were threatened to be sent to the front if they voted." Testimony from soldiers corroborates this account. One soldier noted that his regiment was canvassed "to see how many would vote for Lincoln if they got a chance to go home."[39] An Ohio soldier believed "the majority of the Regt. will go for McClelland if they have a fair vote."[40] But many, of course, doubted there would be fairness.

Some of the harshest and most partisan restrictions on voting were in Unionist Tennessee. There, military governor and Republican vice presidential candidate Andrew Johnson required a test oath of voters that essentially branded all opposition to his Republican ticket as disloyal. After swearing to support and defend the Constitution and to oppose the Confederacy, a voter had to swear that "I will heartily aid and assist the loyal people in whatever measures may be adopted for the attainment of these ends." Striking directly at the heart of the Democratic platform, the oath taker further had to state "that *I will cordially oppose all armistices or negotiations for peace* with rebels in arms" (emphasis added) until the U.S. government had reestablished its authority throughout the land. An oath like this—which was a requirement to vote in Tennessee—incontrovertibly branded any Democratic opposition to the Lincoln administration as treason.[41] It also made it impossible for Democratic soldiers stationed in Tennessee to vote their party's ticket. This politicized oath was a tangible and logical outcome of the Republican rhetoric of loyalty that had taken hold in the North during the war. Opponents of the president—even Union soldiers—could lose their political rights because political opposition was treason.

In some cases Democrats faced court-martial, lack of promotion, or dismissal from the army for being a Democrat, or for writing allegedly treasonable letters home to Democratic newspapers.[42] McClellan and some of his supporters in the army believed they and their correspondence was being surveilled by Secretary of War Edwin M. Stanton and his Republican subordinates in the War Department.[43] Soldiers who attended a McClellan meeting near West Point were "confined in the guard house on their return, & as a punishment for holding the opinions of white men are now digging a drain for the Supt's water closet." Soldiers who attended Lincoln meetings, however, received no such punishment.[44] Evidence suggests that there was a great amount of pressure, and even coercion, for soldiers to toe the Republican party line. One Democratic artillerist worried that "a *poor cuss* like me might get shot" for his political opinions, and he felt he had to "keep silent" during the election. Indeed, testimony from several regiments reveals that Democratic soldiers were often too afraid to vote. A Massachusetts Democrat noted that his unit went for Lincoln "but a great many of the McClellan men did not vote. They are of the weak kneed kind."[45]

It took some mettle to be a Democrat in the army in 1864. One Democrat soldier recalled in later years that many soldiers "believed McClellan to be the man for the place and voted for him. Lincoln, however, was elected and his history shows was for the best of our country. Yet we always admired General George B. McClellan. This was our first vote and the proudest of our life. It took some nerve at that time to be a Democrat."[46] That many soldiers, like this one, realized later in life that Lincoln was the best man for the job does not necessarily mean that most of the soldiers felt so confidently in 1864. Over time, the martyred president assumed a status of national deity. At the time of the election, however, the consensus was not as certain. Many Americans who never would have voted for

Lincoln in 1860 or 1864 came to appreciate his greatness in the years after the war. "After all, I would not vote for him at the election," wrote one Democratic soldier in April 1865, "but I am glad that he was re-elected and am more glad to think he lived to know Richmond had been taken. He visited the Rebel City and sat on old Jeff's chair. Just as he was about to close the war, he has been cut down by the hand of a villain—a traitor who cried out after the fatal shot was fired that the South was revenged."[47] This soldier opposed Lincoln politically during the war and voted against him in 1864, but in the wake of his assassination felt empathy and a profound respect for the martyred president, feelings he had never held for Lincoln while alive.

If veterans did vote overwhelmingly Republican after the war, then their postwar party allegiance may have been based on postwar issues and not on a conversion to the war aims of the Republican Party in 1864. Party identification for many soldiers was still grounded more in the social and cultural variables of antebellum civilian life than in a changing of ideology during military experience.

The low turnout for McClellan among the troops and the even lower turnout in the earlier state and congressional elections suggests that Democratic soldiers lacked faith in the Democratic Party and its platform in 1864. While many soldiers loved George McClellan as a general, they frequently commented on their dislike of "the company he kept." Many soldiers just could not support McClellan's running mate, George H. Pendleton, who was among the numerous northern politicians who had branded the war a failure. It is likely that many Democratic soldiers consciously abstained from voting, rather than endorse a platform that denounced their efforts on the battlefield. In doing so they renounced both the "peace" platform of the Democrats and the "abolitionist" platform of the Republicans. At least one soldier wished he could vote for McClellan for president and Andrew Johnson, Lincoln's running mate, the War Democrat from Tennessee, for vice president.[48]

A final explanation for the low Democratic vote is that many Democrats may have left the army by November 1864. Many soldiers resigned or opted not to reenlist after the Emancipation Proclamation was issued.[49] Others deserted.[50] At least one soldier publicly—and quite foolishly—threatened to desert and flee to Canada, the West Indies, or the South, if Lincoln was reelected.[51] Shortly before the presidential election, McClellan noted that he had received "many letters from privates & *ex*-soldiers—*all* right."[52] His emphasis on "*ex*" soldiers suggests that many of his supporters had left the service by November 1864. Accordingly, more scholarly attention also ought to be paid to desertions, resignations, and reenlistments in the Union armies. If the army lost many Democratic soldiers after their three-year terms of enlistment were up, it would make the case even less tenable that the bulk of Democrats in the service had switched to the Republican Party during the Civil War.

The broader context surrounding the army vote during the presidential election of 1864 was more complex than how it is typically portrayed by scholars of the Civil War. To be sure, many soldiers were ardent and enthusiastic supporters of President Lincoln and emancipation, including some who had opposed Lincoln in 1860 and raged against abolitionism in the early years of the war. Nevertheless, scholars who see a steadily building wave of support for emancipation that eventually turned the soldiers into "lifelong Republicans" oversimplify the story. Soldier support for Lincoln and his policies rose and fell as the prospects for victory rose and fell. But even after the fall of Atlanta and Mobile in September 1864, many Democrats still could not bring themselves to vote for him.

New Perspectives in Civil War Ethnic History and Their Implications for Twenty-First-Century Scholarship

Christian B. Keller

Ever since the publication of Ella Lonn's landmark studies of northern and southern ethnic soldiers, *Foreigners in the Confederacy* (1940) and *Foreigners in the Union Army and Navy* (1950), Civil War scholars have increasingly acknowledged the significance of ethnicity in the creation, course, and resolution of America's greatest conflict. Over the last seventy years, ethnicity as an interpretive lens for analysis has steadily emerged, taking its place alongside race, class, and gender as a means by which we may more fully understand the complexities and nuances of the war. Indeed, considering some recent historiographical trends, ethnicity is becoming increasingly important to comprehending the realities and debunking the myths of 1861–65, especially in the North.[1]

Like its more popular interpretive siblings, however, ethnicity suffers from a few persistent problems. First, primary sources dealing with ethnic soldiers and civilians are scarce and not as readily obtainable as those written by Anglo-Americans. Scholars focusing on the African American or female experience in the war have run into the same issue. The Germans, Irish, Scandinavians, and other immigrant groups were minorities in the 1860s, albeit powerful and numerous, in a United States dominated by Anglo-Americans. Minority groups historically leave fewer historical records than do dominant core cultures, regardless of the host nation, and thus more easily fade into the woodwork when prominent historians, pushed by deadlines and publishers, write their landmark works. The language barrier—for example, understanding newspaper editorials written in old German script—can exacerbate this tendency. Such has been the case with ethnics in the Civil War.[2]

In the last thirty years, a growing number of scholars not as instantly recognizable have ushered forth much new and exciting scholarship on especially the Irish and the Germans. But again the reader in search of knowledge about ethnicity in the Civil War will encounter challenges. Like so many studies on race, class, or gender, much of this work is sequestered in professional journals or fragmentary monographs of particular geographic areas, regiments, or officers, or, alternatively, is just plain erroneous, founded on a truncated source base limited by the constraints of time, accessibility, or even preconceived notions. Not until the last ten years have we begun to witness a flowering of well-researched works of truly comprehensive scope. Walter Kamphoefner's and Wolfgang Helbich's *Germans in the Civil War: The Letters They Wrote Home* (2006), Susannah Ural's *The Harp and the Eagle: Irish-American Volunteers and the Union Army, 1861–1865* (2006), and Ural's *Civil War Citizens: Race, Ethnicity, and Identity in America's Bloodiest Conflict* (2010) are good examples. Previous attempts to provide overarching conclusions about ethnic Americans (or even one ethnic group) in the war—including Lonn's two important but flawed works—have been at best incomplete and at worst historically inaccurate.[3]

The second major challenge confronting scholars examining ethnicity in the Civil War regards argumentative significance. Why does the ethnic background of soldiers or civilians really matter in the greater course of the conflict? How does knowing about ethnic identity, for instance, create greater insights into the meaning of the war, how it was fought, and its outcome? These questions continually beg answering, or at least should be addressed, by anyone working on ethnic Americans in the war. The same questions can be asked of historians using race, class, or gender interpretations. Fundamentally, they challenge the scholar to justify why their research and writing deserves publication and why others should read their work. A lot of books and articles published since 1940 probably would fail this significance test, not just in the subfield of Civil War ethnic history, but also in the overall genre of Civil War historiography. So much has already been written on some subjects, like Abraham Lincoln or Gettysburg or the role of slavery in the coming of the war, that entire libraries could be filled with the volumes concerning just those topics. Considering this reality, did ethnic Americans really make that much of a difference and is it worth writing about them?[4]

That depends on whether one is studying primarily the Union or the Confederacy. For those seeking a greater comprehension of the social and military history of the North, the Germans, Irish, and other immigrants mattered a great deal. Very recent historiography, despite the aforementioned obstacles, has moved us toward a much deeper understanding of northern ethnicity, and simultaneously makes us aware of the enduring legacy of ethnic issues during wartime. The significance of analyzing the Union's foreign-born citizens thus extends well beyond the walls of academe and the bookshelves of amateur historians. It strikes at the very essence of American war-making and American society during times of national crisis.[5]

Recent Historiography: Where We Are Now

Three primary thrusts of inquiry characterize the most significant trends in the best research on northern Civil War ethnicity in recent years: the military effectiveness question, the allegiance question, and the assimilation question. All three of these analytical paths also lead to greater, even more substantive queries about the roles of minority citizens during wartime, their treatment by the majority population, and the future of American society in general. Because the vast majority of works have dealt with the two dominant ethnic groups, the Irish and the Germans, we will focus on them while acknowledging the existence of French, English, Polish, Swedish, Danish, Norwegian, Hungarian, Italian, Hispanic, and Chinese immigrants in the loyal states. Although comparatively small in numbers in 1860, these groups deserve much more scholarly attention than they have received heretofore.[6]

The Military Effectiveness Question

Susannah Ural, Lawrence Kohl, Paul Jones, and Frank Boyle, among others, have led the investigative charge into northern Irish military prowess. They have concluded that Irish American soldiers, especially in the East, were generally very good fighters. On the Peninsula, at Antietam, Fredericksburg, Gettysburg, and even in the 1864 Overland Campaign, the Irish Brigade and the few unconsolidated Irish units in the Army of the Potomac fought with bravery and an almost reckless abandon that earned them the stereotype that sticks yet today: the "fighting Irish." The casualty rates among the regiments attest to the valor of the soldiers: at Antietam, the Irish brigade lost over half its number attacking the Sunken Road, and a short three months later lost most of the rest in the gallant but futile charge at Fredericksburg's Marye's Heights. Private William McCarter of the 116th Pennsylvania, a regiment that had joined the brigade before Fredericksburg in order to bolster its depleted ranks, recalled that "it was simply madness to advance as far as we did and an utter impossibility to go further. . . . We lost nearly all of our officers. . . . In this assault, lasting probably not over 20 minutes . . . our division lost in killed and wounded over 2,000 men." The Irish brigade itself lost over half its remaining numbers, over 600 men, "mowed down like grass before the scythe of the reaper," another soldier lamented. That the brigade survived in name to help repel Longstreet's 2 July 1863 thrust toward the southern end of Cemetery Ridge at Gettysburg was due both to its bloody reputation in the army and Irish American politics—the Union high command could not "consolidate" such a storied organization. On 3 July, the 69th Pennsylvania Infantry, an Irish American unit in the famous Philadelphia Brigade, proved instrumental in repulsing the Confederate breakthrough at the copse of trees at the end of Pickett's Charge. Contemporary authors agree that on numerous other fields, Hibernian soldiers in blue, both in the Army of the Potomac and in the western Federal armies, in ethnically Irish units or not, overall served gallantly and earned the respect of their comrades and the northern public alike.[7]

Such was not the case with northern German American soldiers, who, like their Irish counterparts, believed they were excellent fighters, but received scant official or public approbation. The reasons behind this were varied, and unlike the Irish-born troops, who enjoyed a generally good fighting reputation in both the eastern and western theaters, the Germans found their military record was judged differently in the East than in the West. Chauncey Herbert Cooke served in the nonethnic 25th Wisconsin in the siege of Vicksburg and flatly exclaimed to his brother, "I have learned that the Dutch boys make the bravest soldiers. They don't do any bragging and they are ready for service no matter how dangerous." But as James Pula, Walter Kamphoefner, Wolfgang Helbich, Martin Oefele, Stephen Engle, and others have shown, perceptions of German American military contributions to northern victory were focused, again, on units in the Army of the Potomac, specifically the Eleventh Corps. Federal authorities and northern citizens alike closely examined the deeds of this organization, and its predecessor, Ludwig Blenker's "German Division," and found the Teutonic soldiers wanting in discipline, bravery, and leadership. Their military effectiveness was therefore seriously questioned as this, the largest concentration of German-born soldiery in the war, doggedly served from the 1862 Valley Campaign, to Second Manassas, Chancellorsville, and Gettysburg. Only after the Eleventh Corps boarded trains in August 1863 and transferred west to relieve the siege of Chattanooga did the aspersions begin to taper off. The disastrous Battle of Chancellorsville earlier in May, in which the outnumbered and poorly deployed corps was flanked and routed by Stonewall Jackson's Confederate divisions, created a veritable resurge in anti-German nativism among many Anglo-Americans in and out of the army. One Second Corps soldier, far from the scene of the Eleventh Corps struggle in that battle, put it thus: "This time I will not blame the generals. It was the men who bolted and run [and] 'disgracefully' is no word for it. It was Howard's Corps of _____ Dutchmen to whom [the defeat] is owed." The sting of such xenophobic censure receded only as the German regiments of the East joined those in the Armies of the Tennessee and Cumberland, and, in the afterglow of western Federal victories in late 1863 and 1864, left the public spotlight. The frustration, indignation, and feelings of betrayal that German American soldiers felt, regardless of whether they had fought at Chancellorsville, lingered for decades.[8]

A second area of inquiry regarding ethnic soldiers' effectiveness on the battlefield is the "raw numbers" argument. In 1869, War Department statistician B. A. Gould painstakingly compiled regimental returns and records and arrived at a total of 200,000 German-born and 160,000 Irish-born federal soldiers. These numbers amounted to 18 percent of all Union soldiers. Scholars in the first half of the twentieth century, some of them influenced by filiopietistic sentiments, tried to inflate these numbers. Ella Lonn accepted them with only minor tweaking, as did William Burton in the 1980s. Since then, more systematic research in original regimental records, and thoughtful considerations about what exactly constituted an "ethnic" Civil War soldier, have allowed us to revise Gould's tabulations. Susannah Ural argues that he was too optimistic, rounding down his numbers to 140,000 Irish American troops. Walter Kamphoefner, Wolfgang Helbich, and I contend that the German estimate may have been too low, especially when one considers that the majority—about 75 percent—of German-born soldiers served in predominantly Anglo-American regiments (often clustered together in ethnic companies). A related and highly intriguing question currently under debate regards whether we should include second-generation ethnic troops as ethnically German or Irish. These men were raised in ethnic households, speaking the German or possibly the Gaelic language from birth at home and among ethnic friends and neighbors, and clung to ethnic folkways despite greater immersion in the Anglo-American host society than their parents experienced. Regardless if these individuals served in all-German or -Irish regiments, they were still ethnic Americans, and, if nineteenth-century reproduction rates are to be believed, it is likely they outnumbered their parents. Even if a majority of them failed to serve in the war—a dubious assertion at best—it is still fair to claim at least some of them in the overall count of ethnic Union soldiers. With these considerations in mind, a conservative estimate therefore would place around 28 percent of all Federals under arms as German, Irish, or of another immigrant group. That is a significant number, and if true, raises questions about the importance of immigrant soldiers for the northern war effort. During the war, Confederate propagandists constantly expounded on the "damn Dutch mercenaries" or "brutish Irish" that composed, to them, the bulk of the enemy's armies. One rebel remembered that many who wore the blue "were only foreign hirelings, and were here to kill us merely for the greenbacks and gold they received." Perhaps such state-ments were not all hyperbole. Further, if one considers the criticality of African American troops to the Union war machine in the last two years of the war—and much has been said in scholarly circles about the 12 percent of Federals who were black—a reassessment, at the very least, may be in order regarding the added combat power created by ethnic American soldiers.[9]

The Allegiance Question

In the 1970s and early 1980s, scholars working on the immigrant experience dur-ing the Civil War era tended to focus on the political loyalties of the Germans, Irish, and Scandinavians before the war began, creating the "ethnocultural the-sis" that tried to explain ethnic voting behavior in the elections of 1856 and 1860. Michael Holt, Paul Kleppner, Bruce Levine, and Kathleen Conzen wrote some of the most influential and authoritative works on this topic, essentially agreeing that the more conservative religious denominations, such as the Irish Catho-lics and German Lutherans, voted mainly Democratic, whereas the more "re-formed" churches, such as the Scots-Irish Presbyterians and German Reformed, frequently supported the Republicans. In the last two decades, the ethnocultural thesis has been tested repeatedly in local and regional studies and found to be too generalized and in need of reform itself. Further, historians have switched their emphasis from political voting behavior prior to the war to examining political allegiance during the war itself. Kevin Kenny, David Gleeson, Kerby Miller, and Susannah Ural have led the way in their studies of the Irish, and Joerg Nagler, Martin Oefele, Stephen Engle, and I have broken scholarly ground on the Ger-mans. Research in original Irish and German American newspapers and per-sonal soldiers' and civilians' letters has convinced all these authors that most of the North's foreign-born citizens possessed a sort of "dual loyalty" during the conflict that obviously varied depending on the individual and the locality, but which included allegiance both to their ethnic group and to the Union. In this way, northern ethnics demonstrated complex loyalties during the war—loyalties that shifted depending on economic, political, and military events. An Irish American newspaper in Boston, *The Pilot*, claimed in 1861 that "the Celts might be hyphenated Americans in name, [but] were one one-hundred percent Amer-icans in deed." By mid-1863, however, that same paper was spouting repeated anti-American and pro-Irish editorials that complained of northern indifference to Irish American battlefield sacrifice and political anxiety. The idea that people during the Civil War changed or altered their loyalties or had numerous allegiances that sometimes conflicted with one another (e.g., state v. nation) is nothing new. Historians studying the border states and the Upper South in particular have more than clarified this phenomenon, and many of those concentrating on class or gender issues have arrived at the same conclusion. Not until recently have we applied this rubric to the North's immigrant population.[10]

For the Irish, as Ural explains, support for the Federal war effort had from the beginning been paired with an undying loyalty to the old home across the sea. Not just the Fenians—professed Irish revolutionaries who immigrated to the United States and swore to return home someday—but most Irish Catholics perceived fighting for the Union as a blow against England. They knew the South and the Confederacy stood for privilege, aristocracy, and a stratified class structure reminiscent of that which prevailed in British-controlled Ireland. Defeating the South therefore equated with helping the Irish cause, however indirectly. For the Fenians, many of whom actually served in the army, the Union offered military experience that could literally be transported back across the Atlantic and used to liberate Ireland. But when the northern cause appeared to morph from its original intent of preserving the old Union to one that espoused liberating slaves and enlarging the power of the federal government, drafting those who wished to stay at home while exempting the rich who could pay their way out, and wantonly killing large numbers of Irish soldiers in the process (as at Fredericksburg), the loyalties of the northern Irish began to change. By the spring of 1863, Irish American support for the Lincoln administration had severely waned; many Irishmen now questioned their identity as Americans in a country that had seemingly betrayed the values that had attracted them in the first place. One soldier summed up the new mood prevalent among his countrymen: "All is dark, and lonesome, and sorrow hangs as a shroud over us all." For many Hibernian immigrants, loyalties to one another and even to Ireland itself now outweighed a wavering loyalty to the North. As Iver Bernstein has noted, it was that weakening loyalty that helped ignite sparks that created the New York City draft riots of July 1863. In 1864, the northern Irish, especially in the big cities, voted overwhelmingly against the Republicans, and recruits for the Irish Brigade and other ethnic units all but dried up.[11]

German American loyalties, like those of the Irish, were also not monolithic. Lesley Kawaguchi and Stan Nadel have explained that Civil War–era German immigrants in Philadelphia and New York City possessed "crosscutting" allegiances that bound them concurrently to their state of origin in Europe, their neighborhoods, and their clubs. In 1861, loyalty to the Union emerged almost instantaneously with the firing on the flag at Fort Sumter, thereby adding another layer to most German-born citizens' already complex allegiance systems. Democratic and Republican Germans alike rallied to the colors and enlisted in ethnic and nonethnic regiments, and, until the obloquy following Chancellorsville, allowed loyalty to the Union cause to supersede most other allegiances. Indeed, as Kamphoefner and Helbich and Joseph Reinhart have shown in their edited collections of original German letters, for the first half of the war most northern German soldiers and civilians fervently supported the Federal cause. Sergeant Albert Krause of the 116th New York was typical when he wrote his family in 1862, "I am off to the fire filled with courage and enthusiasm. The United States have taken me in, I have earned a living here, and why shouldn't I defend them, since they are in danger, with my flesh and blood?" Yet even before the fateful spring of 1863, which changed the outlook of all of German America, Teutonic immigrants in the North began to detect the discordant but eerily familiar strains of nativism in some Anglo-American newspapers and in the official actions of certain native-born generals and government officials. Stephen Engle avers that Franz Sigel, the darling of German Americans everywhere, was an "iconic" symbol for his fellow countrymen, and when he resigned his generalship in early 1862 under the auspices of official anti-German prejudice, this created an uproar in German communities across the loyal states. Unfavorable reports in Anglo-American papers of Ludwig Blenker's German Division looting and despoiling the Shenandoah Valley in the spring of 1862 likewise raised concerns among many German leaders that the nativism of the 1850s had started to return.[12]

Their fears were confirmed in the anti-German vituperations that issued from both the Anglo-American press and the Army of the Potomac in the wake of Chancellorsville. A 5 May 1863 *New York Times* editorial characterized much of the reportage regarding the highly German Eleventh Corps: "Threats, entreaties and orders of commanders were of no avail. Thousands of these cowards threw down their guns and soon streamed down the road toward headquarters. General Howard . . . could not stem the tide of the retreating and cowardly poltroons." The correspondent for *New York Herald*, located nowhere near the point of attack on the Eleventh Corps, claimed "that the men, I am told, fled like so many sheep before a pack of wolves." Countless other, more local northern papers took the lead of the New York City press and unilaterally condemned the corps and its ethnic element for weeks, few editors able—or willing—to consult German-language and even some English-language accounts that spoke of German regiments standing and fighting to the last. German American newspapers and letters from the field were filled with such evidence, however, prompting many Teutonic immigrants to question why the greater northern population tacitly accepted such one-sided (and often erroneous) conclusions. Private Ernst Damkoehler of the 26th Wisconsin, a regiment that suffered a casualty rate of more 40 percent at Chancellorsville, bitterly complained, "The number of dead and wounded are sure evidence how the Regiment stood up," and Alexander Schimmelfennig, a brigadier in Carl Schurz's division, wrote an official report for his superior in which he stated that the "officers and men of this brigade of your division, filled with indignation, come to me, with [English] newspapers in their hands, and ask if such be the rewards they may expect for the sufferings they have endured and the bravery they have displayed."[13]

After Chancellorsville, the Germans of the North, like the Irish, turned inward as they attempted first to explain the resurgence of nativism to themselves and then unified—as best they could—in indignant defiance of Anglo-American verbal attacks. As they did so, the loyalties that had once been so unswervingly behind the northern cause began to dissipate and were frequently replaced by basic mercenary attitudes (i.e., being a soldier simply for the pay) or, more ominously for the Union, pan–German Americanism. Unquestionably, most German-born soldiers remained loyal to the flag and fought until their enlistment terms expired, but both they and their loved ones at home increasingly viewed themselves as Germans first and Americans second, and their actions and words proved it. One soldier, when asked by his brother if he would re-up in 1864, replied, "I did not forget about what was done to us last spring after the battle of Chancellorsville and will not forget it in the future. I shant re-enlist." Interestingly, as Engle and others have argued, many previous competing loyalties within the German neighborhoods, such as allegiances to the old German states of origin, likewise began to wane as a feeling of American "Deutchtum" waxed.[14]

The Assimilation Question

The loyalty question in recent historiography on northern ethnics has spawned much debate on what the Civil War meant for immigrants' identities in their adopted homeland. Were they more "American" after the conflict? Or did the war retard the assimilation process because of what they experienced in it? These are weighty questions, not only because of what we can learn about the importance of the Civil War in the demographic and cultural growth of the nation, but also because they offer further discussion on the significance of war in acculturating foreign-born citizens in democratic republics, and the role—or plight—of ethnic minorities in wartime.

There are two schools of thought on the assimilation question. The older and long-accepted analyses of Ella Lonn, John Higham, and William Burton, which appeared before the 1990s, essentially agreed that the war fully acculturated both the Irish and German immigrants who fought in it as well as the greater ethnic home front. Burton's title, *Melting Pot Soldiers: The Union's Ethnic Regiments*, pretty well sums up his opinion on the subject. The problem with his argument, as well as with Higham's, is that they relied strongly on Ella Lonn's findings, and Lonn, for all the credit she deserves for pioneering the subfield of ethnicity in the Civil War, relied too much on English-language sources, a few select newspapers (albeit some in foreign languages), and postwar memoirs that glossed over the nativism and difficulties of the war years and focused on glorifying the martial deeds of ethnic soldiers. Many of her sources, although written by actual participants, were tainted by filiopietism and an ethnic chauvinism that characterized much that was written by immigrant Americans in the decades after the war. Lonn also subscribed to a few too many stereotypes, such as the myth of the "drunken Irishman," without providing enough concrete evidence. In fairness to Lonn, many of the private letter and newspaper collections that have assisted modern researchers were not available to her, and she obviously could not check the veracity of every source she consulted. But her conclusions on the assimilation of the foreign-born have so influenced later scholars, and even basic conventional wisdom about the Civil War and immigration, that the "melting pot" school still has supporters today, such as Dean Mahin and Donald Allendorf.[15]

It is easy and pleasant to claim that the war acculturated the North's ethnic citizens: the United States is a nation based on immigration and, in the end, the Civil War–era Irish and Germans did assimilate into the greater American culture. However, scholarship in the last ten years, utilizing primarily foreign-language and -archived materials but also some previously unknown English-language sources, has strongly challenged the old assumption. Susannah Ural, Joseph Reinhart, David Gleeson, Stephen Engle, Walter Kamphoefner, Wolfgang Helbich, and I stand united in believing the historical record points decidedly in an antiassimilationist direction. The wartime letters, editorials, articles, and memoirs written by ethnic soldiers and newspaper editors, as well as those they wrote after 1865, provide the evidence. The war did not stop immigrant acculturation in the North, but did retard it, and nativism was primarily responsible for that. The situation of Captain Thomas Fitzgibbon of the 14th Michigan, for instance, is duplicated repeatedly in both Irish and German records. Fitzgibbon begged to be transferred to an ethnically Irish regiment in January 1862, protesting that his fellow officers "are partially American and bigotedly Protestant. In almighty God's name, if you can possibly do it," he wrote to his new prospective commander, "get us transferred to you, where we can be with and amongst our own people."

Both during and after the conflict, Irish and Germans, struggling to reconcile their blood sacrifice with Anglo-American wartime prejudice, created their own interpretations of their participation that at once glorified—and overemphasized—their ethnic identities and celebrated their deeds as new Americans. The bigotry of the war years could not easily be forgotten by the foreign-born, and therefore the process of becoming more American and less ethnic would occur in a way that was slower, more comfortable and self-adulating. German and Irish "contributions" to American society, both during the war and later, were touted as special gifts that only the immigrants could provide their new country, and the young United States was portrayed as badly in need of them. Ironically, ethnic leaders maintained in the postwar decades that Irish and Germans who retained their ethnic traits as long as possible would actually benefit their adopted homeland more than those who quickly absorbed American ways and blanched their ethnicity. One Dr. Welsch, frequent contributor to the *Deutsch-Amerikanische Monatshefte*, a literary, cultural, and historical journal for German Americans, boldly exclaimed in 1867, "The German immigration does not force the natives to Germanize . . . but it also rejects the demand to Americanize, because it possesses too much pride in its own worth, too much independent strength and too much confidence in its future" than to "make other concessions to cocky nativism." This "culturally pluralistic" view of the Civil War era and ethnic assimilation was first hinted at by Kathleen Conzen in the 1970s and 1980s, but since 2000 recent historiography has confirmed the correctness of her ideas. The melting pot thesis is, however, melting away only grudgingly, and future scholars will likely have to stoke the fires of research even further to see if it can stand the heat of the revisionists.[16]

The Future of Ethnic Civil War History

The study of ethnicity in history is becoming ever more popular, and nowhere is this more evident than in the subfield of Civil War scholarship. The growing number of authors choosing to evaluate ethnicity at least partially in their research is a testament to its historical significance. The bottom line, clear to all who have a good contextual understanding of the mid-nineteenth-century United States, is that ethnic background mattered a great deal to the majority of the northern population. The rise and enduring power of the nativist movement, embodied politically by the Know-Nothing Party in the mid-1850s, clearly indicates that many Anglo-Americans cared about ethnicity. Obviously, Irish and German immigrants also cared—or, as much modern scholarship has shown, were forced to care about it. These facts alone make studying ethnicity in the Civil War era a worthy pursuit for future scholars. What is left to extract, however, from the increasingly well-mined archival mountains?[17]

The recent historiographic themes, identified earlier, are a good place to begin answering that question. Ethnic fighting prowess, loyalty, and assimilation during the war all offer further avenues of historical research that may still enlighten us a great deal about Irish and German participation in the Civil War era, and, more significantly, help us better understand the war in the context of the robust diversity it encompassed. If we poke and prod a little deeper, we may also glean some insights into the nature of democratic polities at war, and specifically the role of minorities during wartime. The German American reaction to the Battle of Chancellorsville offers an admirable case study to address these issues.

Ethnic Battlefield Performance: Context Is King

Captain James W. Vanderhoef of the German 45th New York thought his regiment and his corps had fought as well as possible at Chancellorsville on 2 May 1863. In a letter to his sister fifteen days after the battle, he defended the military performance of his ethnic command: "But for what the papers say we the 11th Corps do not care a snuff. We strove to do our duty as good soldiers and have lost meny [*sic*] a good and brave comrade. And those who brand their name and memory as cowards had better lay aside the pen and take rifle to help swell the strength of the Eleventh Corps that they can better stand the shock of Forty Thousand the next time (but of course they can't see it)." Private Adolph Bregler of the 27th Pennsylvania, another ethnically German regiment farther from the point of the initial Confederate attack, wrote that "our division did not have enough time to correctly deploy before the running rebels hurled themselves at us, but we held firm as long as we could, and pushed them back hard several times." Sergeant Otto Heusinger of the 41st New York, whose regiment was almost immediately overrun by Stonewall Jackson's charging rebels, made no apologies in his 1869 reminiscences, frankly admitting that "a panicked fear overcame us, how crazily we plunged away, the rest of the division running with us." Each of these soldiers, survivors of Chancellorsville, frankly admitted what they perceived had happened in the part of the battle they participated in. They were echoed by dozens of other German American veterans who attempted to describe, as best they could, the shock and horror of an overwhelming flank attack. Few tried to embellish their reports, especially those written directly after the campaign closed, and all believed they had fought as best as could be expected considering the circumstances. Their perceptions were backed up by some Anglo-American letters, often written by native-born soldiers serving in the Eleventh Corps itself, which lend credence to German claims of adequate military performance on that bloody spring day. William Wheeler, serving in one of the corps' batteries, wrote his mother on 14 May that it was "absurd" that the Germans "would not fight. . . . Any corps so scattered, and strung along an extended line, could not have failed to be overwhelmed by a force brought so suddenly against it. . . . I know that the regiments by our Battery, viz., McLean's Brigade, fought as well as men can fight, and only fell back when further fighting was madness."[18]

Most Anglo-Americans, however, in and out of the army, roundly accused the Germans of the Eleventh Corps of cowardice and dishonorable conduct. The initial reports printed in the leading New York City newspapers were copied over and over again, embellished, and spread throughout the Union, where average northerners read about the "flying Dutchmen" and found both a scapegoat for yet another failed federal campaign and vindication for previously held stereotypes and prejudices. The Philadelphia *Public Ledger* declared that the "losses sustained by this corps, either in killed or captured, could not have been great—they ran too fast for that." Another paper labeled the Germans' performance "unaccountable and inexcusable," adding that "somebody is to blame for this disgraceful affair," and then immediately exonerated both Army Commander Joseph Hooker and Eleventh Corps Commander Oliver Howard. In the Army of the Potomac itself, the loudest condemnations came from soldiers located far from the Eleventh Corps on the evening of 2 May—men who had never served with the Germans and who could not have known of the three successive stands conducted by elements of the corps. These stands, each lasting approximately twenty minutes, were critical in holding up Stonewall Jackson's onslaught as darkness fell over the battlefield and Confederate chances for crippling the Union Army slipped away. Charles Parker, serving on the staff of a colonel in the First Corps, wrote on 15 May that "we found out that the 11th Corps, composed of *Dutchmen*, the Blenkerites . . . had stampeded shamefully [and] broke and run, the contemptible cowardly vagabonds who had more done for them and made more of by the government and the people at large than any other portion of the Army." Parker's comments are representative, and even mild, compared to other non-German accounts. James T. Miller of the 111th Pennsylvania professed that the Federals would have won if the Eleventh Corps had only stood and fought: "We think very little of the dutch sons of bitches that used to brag they 'fight mit Sigel' and I don't know but they might have fought well with [Sigel] but they did not fight worth shit under Howard." Daniel O. Macomber in the blue-blooded 1st Massachusetts went a step further, claiming that his officers apprehended fleeing German American soldiers "and made them fall into our Regt and every one of them happened to get shot." Reports of Anglo-American officers shooting at fleeing refugees from the Eleventh Corps appear in several letters and postwar accounts, making Macomber's ominous statement contextually viable.[19]

As Third Division Commander Carl Schurz wrote to Joseph Hooker after the battle, "The spirit of this Corps is broken . . . too much humiliation destroys the morale of men."[20] Schurz, Schimmelfennig, and nearly all the officers and men of the Eleventh Corps, German-born or not, believed they fought as well as possible at Chancellorsville. Yet nearly all Anglo-Americans in other corps of the Army of the Potomac and at home vigorously refuted that notion, influenced by rumor, poor geographic location, specious initial newspaper reports, or outright prejudice. Clearly this is a case of irreconcilable differences, and the historical record is, with only a few exceptions, starkly divided along German- and Anglo-American lines. Where does the truth lie? For future scholars interested in ethnicity in the Civil War, the implications are clear: to fully evaluate the foreign-born on the battlefield, whether in the eastern or western theaters, early or late in the war, both ethnic and nonethnic sources must be consulted, and the geographic location of the writer matters. A decent reading knowledge of a foreign language, at the least, will be required to consult German, Swedish, French or other non-English letters, diaries, and newspapers. Simply checking secondary sources that have translated such original documents is not enough. The date of those sources matters as well: those written quickly after the military event in question are likely more accurate portrayals of what actually happened. Additionally, Civil War soldiers of all types read newspapers, and most of the time had reasonable access to them. It would not take long for their thoughts of the last battle to be tainted by what they read. Thus, when examining Anglo-American soldiers' commentaries on ethnics, historians should be aware of when the commentary was made and the likelihood of influence from newspapers. Ethnic soldiers themselves often turned to their newspapers for information on battles they had participated in, and in the cases of Chancellorsville and Gettysburg, often read hyperbolic editorials about their contributions to victory or exculpating apologies for weaker performances. Sometimes they wrote letters to these same papers, which eagerly sought direct word from the field to promote sales. Letters written long after the smoke cleared away, especially those published in ethnic newspapers, should therefore be read cautiously. Finally, nineteenth-century America was a bigoted, prejudice-ridden land by twenty-first-century standards. It is simple to ridicule Anglo-Americans for their lampooning of the Germans or the Irish, but the modern historian should be wary of judging too quickly sources as nativistic or bigoted (although many were). Terminology such as "damn Dutch" or "paddy" may not have been necessarily flung as an epithet but rather as a descriptor of foreign-born soldiers. As in most historical research, understanding the context of such verbiage—who said it, where they were, when, and under what conditions—is key.

Ethnic Wartime Loyalty and the Salience of Nativism

The Highland, Illinois, *Highland Bote*, a German-language newspaper with considerable influence in the Midwest, wrote following the battle that the "bigots, witch-burners, temperance men, and Know-Nothings that hate the German population from the bottom of their soul now have their much wished-for opportunity to attack the 'cowardly Dutchmen.'" The Pittsburgh *Freiheitsfreund* argued that the "nativist Halleck" and other anti-German leaders in the Lincoln administration had forced former Eleventh Corps Commander Franz Sigel to resign, an event that then caused the disaster at Chancellorsville, which "the nativist perfidy of the correspondent of the New York Times" had brewed into an anti-German firestorm. Yearnings for Sigel combined with stalwart defenses of the German regiments' battle performance in the German-language press in May and June 1863. The fault for the debacle was unilaterally thrown on the Anglo-American leaders of the Eleventh Corps: "For the idiocy of the commanding generals the poor Corps must now take the fall. Hooker and especially General Howard are to blame. . . . [These] generals are not worth a shot of gunpowder—and yet they would have been worth that," hissed the *Pittsburger Demokrat*. The *Highland Bote* arrived at the same conclusion a week later, and its editor further urged Germans to "watch out." German speakers needed to look after one another in the wake of Chancellorsville: "The Know-Nothings and Temperance men left us alone for a while because they needed us Germans for voting and fighting. Now the humbug is back again. . . . It is high time the local German element unifies a little. Otherwise we will be spied upon, criticized, and labeled 'traitors' right and left." Throughout all these editorials, a theme of indignant resignation arose that urged German readers to think carefully about where their loyalties truly lay: with fellow German immigrants and the troops now so bitterly maligned by Anglo-Americans, or with the North and the Union cause in general. It was possible to walk a middle path, and few German American leaders advocated withdrawing support from Lincoln's war effort, but the aftershocks of Chancellorsville forced many German speakers to gravitate closer to one another and question their commitment to the federal cause.[21]

Loyalty in wartime is not easy for the historian to quantify or track. It is by its very nature a highly personal and subjective notion, influenced by a potentially limitless number of variables that can change on a moment's notice. What a soldier feels toward his country, fellow soldiers, his leaders, or his ethnic group is not a static emotion; as John Keegan, Paul Fussell, Reid Mitchell, and James McPherson have shown, it is likely to change over time. Such was the case with most German American soldiers and civilians. With the exception of a few radical Republican Germans in Missouri and other locations and isolated enclaves on the Great Plains, the great majority of German-born Americans seriously examined their allegiances after Chancellorsville and decided that the time for petty squabbling among themselves had passed. Now was the time to unify against the nativist threat and protect their own. Loyalties to one another, caused by what Stephen Engle calls a "heightened consciousness" of their ethnic identity, equaled or superseded loyalties to the Union cause. Democratic and Republican Germans would still be suspicious of one another, Catholics and Protestants preferred not to rub shoulders together, but in the end the overarching specter of a resurgent American nativism forged bonds of mutual understanding and cooperation that lasted throughout the rest of the Civil War and well into the postwar period. The Frémont political movement grew largely in response to western German American frustrations with a Lincoln administration that increasingly ignored ethnic concerns, including nativism. German-speaking soldiers huddled together in ethnic companies to avoid unnecessary interaction with Americans, and the ethnically German regiments, reduced in numbers, with recruits all but dried up and struggling to avoid amalgamation, vigorously defended their ethnic integrity as far as possible—even to the point of dispensing reverse prejudice to nonethnics drafted into them. The student of ethnicity in the nineteenth-century United States should therefore be aware of the powerful influence nativism had in directing ethnic behavior during the war, both politically and culturally. Ethnic allegiances did not emerge and change in an ethnic vacuum. Loyalties often shifted, before, during, and after the war, based on ethnic Americans' perception of the nativist threat they faced locally and nationally. Much more research needs to be completed on this topic to make any absolute conclusions, but it appears ethnic loyalty—especially for the Germans but also for the Irish—was primarily reactive in nature. Future scholars may confirm this trend for Scandinavian or other smaller northern ethnicities, and in so doing should bring us closer to the historical truth of the matter.[22]

Postwar Assimilation: Who Speaks for Whom?

For Civil War historians, the term "unity" usually conjures up discussions of whether the Union or Confederacy fought the war with the support of the majority of its population. An analysis of unity can be easily extended into the postwar period, also, as many fine studies of Reconstruction remind us. But what about ethnic unity in the postwar era? How did the experiences of the Civil War affect ethnic Americans after it was over? In response to the reality that the nativism unleashed by the Civil War would not easily fade away, German Americans in the postwar decades reacted by celebrating their German-ness wherever possible. Americanization would occur on immigrants' terms and in their own good time. German political and literary leaders exhorted their followers to recognize that "the blood of our heroes has dearly bought for us this country as a homeland. We are not foreigners in America, in that we are fully equal with the natives. . . . Our nature, our individuality and customs have the same entitlement as all the others." Friedrich Lexow, one of the strongest advocates of a culturally pluralistic vision for his countrymen after the war, wrote in the *Deutsch-Amerikanische Monatshefte* in 1866 that "Germans who Americanized too quickly are not among the best citizens of the republic." Hold on to your unique ethnic traits and mores, he implored his readers in article after article; only then can you truly be a good American citizen. "Behind us lies a time we do not fondly remember," he said. "The German word was not cherished and cultivated, the banner of German custom not held high in victory. Far too many immigrants [plunged] into that which [they] understood as Americanism," but "this time of humiliation has been overcome. A better recognition of what lies ahead for us in America is now leading the way, and what was once the rule has become the shameful exception." One year earlier, the popular Forty-Eighter Friedrich Kapp echoed the same message when he told the attendees at the Ninth German Saengerfest in New York City that "the times are happily over when the German hurls from himself as quickly as possible his entire history and education so that he may fast become a practical American. The Knownothing movement has had the positive effect of negating the idea that there is no higher plane of existence than to sink to being the disciples of Americanism." He concluded, "Let us work towards the good and betterment of the Unites States in correspondence to the spirit of our past and character."[23]

Examining how the Civil War affected immigrant assimilation is a new arena of research for Civil War and ethnic scholars. Only a few souls have ventured into this area, and thus much room for further research remains, especially for the North's smaller ethnic groups, but also for the Irish and the Germans. Systematic, methodical research in surviving veterans' records would probably bear much fruit, as would a comprehensive review of all the regimental books of the major ethnic regiments located in the National Archives and in some of the state historical societies (to trace ethnic dilution or discrimination against nonethnics). Besides this quantifiable information, more research of postwar ethnic American newspapers would assist immensely in determining public attitudes toward Americanization. But here the future scholar will likely encounter a familiar methodological question that all who have studied ethnic political and social behavior have wrestled with: do ethnic leaders, such as newspaper editors, truly speak for their constituency or readership? Most German American scholars have long argued that they do in nearly all circumstances, but others disagree, and there is merit to such protests.[24] For the Irish, who spoke and wrote almost entirely in English, leaders would have been aware that their comments could be read not only by their own people but also by Anglo-Americans. How much did this affect their statements? For the Germans, secure in knowing that a small minority of non-Germans could understand their language, it is likely that leaders spoke their minds more freely, but this cannot be conclusively proven. For ethnic leaders of any ilk, what they said in front of or for the benefit of one group might not be the same message delivered to another. This truism should put the future researcher on alert to evaluate the context of public statements carefully. Additionally, like all Americans in the nineteenth century, ethnics were strongly influenced by local economic, political, and social conditions that may have set the stage for overt but temporary antiassimilative feelings and actions. How long did these persist, and can they be correlated with other locales? Only by tracing recurrent themes and ideas over time and space will we be able to concretely and fully make the case that the Civil War reinforced ethnic identity among the North's immigrant populations more than it weakened it. We have a strong start in that direction, and much good work has been done, but much more research remains to be completed to fully debunk the melting pot thesis.

As the twenty-first century slides into its second decade, the greatest lesson, perhaps, that we can draw from the ethnic experience in the Civil War concerns the long-term effects of estranging a minority group during wartime. For both Irish and German Americans, the nativism of the war years was not easily forgotten and contributed mightily to their culturally pluralistic assimilation process in the postwar decades. Being more German or more Irish was viewed in most ethnic circles as a good thing, and it took fifty years for another cataclysmic war—World War I—to break the ethnic strength of German American communities. It is arguable that Irish ethnic consciousness was never seriously damaged and still lingers proudly today. Naturally, strong German and Irish immigration in the 1880s and 1890s contributed to both groups' endurance, replenishing ethnic communities with new immigrants as old ones died or their sons and daughters chose more assimilative paths. That said, most recent scholars researching the Germans in the Civil War era now agree that the conflict retarded the acculturation of that ethnic group by strengthening its ethnic consciousness. For the Irish the verdict is less clear but still points in a similar direction. Regardless of one's opinion about whether ethnic groups should assimilate quickly in modern American society, it appears we may be witnessing a similar process among some Americans of Middle Eastern ethnicity as the United States enters the second decade of its global War on Terror.

The younger, resource-rich, and geographically protected United States of the late nineteenth century could afford cultural pluralism, and indeed may have benefited from it by the very nature of the country's growth patterns. It is debatable if the United States of the early twenty-first century can follow suit, but as a nation founded on immigration—and mindful of the lessons of the past—perhaps we will all rise to the challenge.

The Black Flag and Confederate Soldiers

Total War from the Bottom Up?

Michael J. Bennett

The Civil War possesses the odd reputation of being the last gentlemen's war and the first modern war. It is known as a war of restraint and a war of violence. Historians argue back and forth whether the war was total, limited, hard, soft, destructive, or rosewater. This discussion arises in part from a scholarly frustration that seeks to understand how soldiers showed great compassion on one hand and brutality on the other. The historians of this issue have typically limited their analysis of total war to acts against civilians mandated from the policy makers on down. Yet during the conflict soldiers often waged total war. It was not waged consistently. Its nature changed from regiment to regiment and from army to army. It occurred throughout the war, North and South, East and West, and by men of all rank and standing. Between 1861 and 1865, Confederate soldiers waged total war against Yankee soldiers. Yet soldiers did not use the term "total war." They referred to total war by a number of names: "black flag," "no quarter," and "take no prisoners." The acts of this war were called "atrocities." Southern nurse Kate Cumming, after watching a wounded Confederate officer return to his sick bed after shooting a Union prisoner of war dead outside her hospital, wrote in her diary that she wished that she could say it was only the Yankees who committed such acts. The sad truth for Cumming was that the South was just as guilty as the North in authoring what she called the war's "dark pages."[1]

To examine the morality of American atrocities during the Civil War is not, as is often done in military history, a quasi-historical trial of guilt and innocence. Instead, it might be more useful to understand the interplay of values and events that occur during war. Atrocities, as idealistic onlookers might hope, did not appear and then disappear without warning or reason. On both sides, men greatly feared that the war would coarsen them. They feared that the grinding nastiness of the war would turn their darker impulses loose. In short, they worried that the war would turn them into bad men who did bad things. They were right to be scared. The exposure to hardship and violence as well as the freedom to act provided by war threatened their prewar selves. This fear coupled, with the high expectations of family and friends, were heavy burdens.

An examination of atrocities is even more relevant given the current revisions to the numbers of Civil War dead. The study of atrocities can confirm, revise, or reject the war's "killed, wounded, or captured" figures. Of those 600,000 or so Union soldiers killed in action, how many were momentary prisoners? Of those 400,000 or who later died of wounds from battle how many were wounded after the fighting ceased? What explains the 200,000 or so Union soldiers the Surgeon General and the Adjutant General's records concluded died from murder, accidents, or suicides? Were there autopsies done? If yes, how many were there and what were the results?[2]

The treatment of the killed, wounded, and captured touches on the broader argument as to whether the Civil War was a total war. Notable Civil War historians such as James McPherson and Edward Hagerman, influenced by the parallels of destruction between the Civil War and World War II, have read the concept backward into the war. In reaching his conclusion, McPherson focuses on the involvement of the civilians, the huge loss of life, the material devastation, and the radical social changes to validate the Civil War as a total war. For Mark Neely, the issue is more complex and rests on processes rather than outcomes.[3]

Civil War soldiers would side with Neely. In the mid-nineteenth century, the phrase "total war" was not used. Civil War soldiers and civilian leaders called a war where there was limited or no differentiation between combatants and civilians an "un-Christian war" or "black flag war." Like McPherson, Civil War soldiers did consider the encroachment of war on ordinary civilians and property as characteristics of a total war. Unlike McPherson, Civil War soldiers considered the mistreatment of combatants, living and dead, as evidence of a total war. It was a fluid process marked by internalized prewar restraints that ebbed and flowed between civilization and barbarism.

The official policy of the Union and Confederate governments was to respect the surrenders of enemy soldiers. Each side promised to give to the other adequate medical care and a decent burial. Unofficial policies proved more elusive. Despite these ambiguities, soldiers on both sides showed restraint in dealing with prisoners of war. In some instances, they were capable of acts of mercy. Neither government offered incentives for soldiers to take prisoners, however, and punishments for the mistreatment of prisoners were rare.[4]

Instead, a number of unofficial restraints protected prisoners on the battlefield. These restraints, as Mark Neely has recently demonstrated in *The Civil War and the Limits of Destruction*, included army discipline, societal mores against murder, and commonality of race. Neely, however, fails to assess those core American values that did the most to keep a lid on mindless violence: Christian, republican, and rural values. Specifically, antebellum Americans firmly believed that religion made good soldiers. In fact, Christianity had been a long-standing supporter of soldier restraint. The Peace and Truce of God was a movement of the Catholic Church that applied spiritual sanctions in order to limit the violence of war since the Middle Ages. The Peace of God was a proclamation issued by local clergy that granted immunity from violence to noncombatants who could not defend themselves. Civil War soldiers acknowledged the continuing influence of this heritage. In their letters and journals, soldiers claimed to be bound by Christian values to extend mercy to defenseless women, children, and disarmed soldiers.[5]

The Peace of God movement had grown amid a European society that was paradoxically becoming both more religious and more militaristic. Added to this dynamic was a peasant class that lived exposed on their farms. As a result, death was a regular event on a farm and therefore taken seriously. Most soldiers, North and South, lived on farms before the war. They were familiar with the killing of animals. Rules existed on farms during slaughtering time that farmers were expected to follow. Participants and onlookers were expected to treat the animals with respect. Taunting or the torturing of the animals was forbidden. Farmers were expected to use the swiftest means possible to slaughter the animal with the least amount of suffering. Those persons that violated these old rites suffered severe reprimands and elicited the worried whispers of family and friends.[6]

These restraints ultimately created a prewar disposition in Americans not to kill. Part of the training for Civil War armies sought to obviate the moral dilemma by permitting killing under certain circumstances. These "permissions to kill," as Drew Gilpin Faust notes in her book *The Republic of Suffering*, included military necessity and just war theory.[7] These permissions were balanced with informal rules adopted to protect soldiers in similar defenseless situations. Soldiers on both sides adopted an informal "live and let live" policy on prisoners and off-duty soldiers as a form of life insurance when they themselves were off-duty. The killings of soldiers who were sleeping, eating, or relieving themselves were serious violations of this "unwritten code of honor."[8]

Joseph Glatthaar in *General Lee's Army* argues that the value system of Confederate soldiers flowed from the bottom up. Southern culture featured an especially violent streak that reared its head from time to time. Even in Lee's army, there were a number of "bad characters." Lee himself witnessed numerous "depredations" during the Seven Days' Battles.[9]

Southern prewar culture freed men to pursue every individual impulse. Open displays of anger and quick resorts to violence were common. In a war, these traits proved valuable in the short run. They made southerners ferocious fighters. Over the long run, they made for poorly disciplined soldiers. On the battlefield, for every courageous individual act of bravery that furthered the cause an equally self-serving act injured the Confederate effort. Southern soldiers did what they wanted, when they wanted to do it. If they wanted something, they took it from foe or friend. If they did not like an order, they ignored it. If they won a battle, they walked home. It was no wonder that Southerners were so effective at guerilla warfare. Its part-time, unrestrained, acquisitive nature was tailor-made for the southern spirit.[10]

The fuel for bad acts lay dormant in a preexisting hatred for northerners. Southern political leaders had demonized northerners as greedy, demonic abolitionists. This hatred had been stoked by Jefferson Davis to unify southerners in February 1861. As Union armies moved south in July, it was heated by Confederate propaganda that characterized invading northerners as ruthless barbarians. This campaign proved so effective that civilians and slaves were initially terrified of Yankee troops. Often they would look for horns under their caps. Before the First Battle of Bull Run, P. G. T. Beauregard warned his troops that the Yankees would wage an "uncivilized war" against women and children.[11]

The letters and journals of Confederate soldiers exhibited this hatred. Rebs called northerners "Hessians," "vandals," "Dutch," "thieves," "robbers," "hirelings," and "wretches." "Mother," wrote Harry Lewis of the 16th Mississippi, "I am getting to hate the Yankees in earnest." One soldier called them the "lowest and most contemptible race upon the face of the earth." Another called Yankees "vile and inhuman wretches." A Georgia soldier wrote to his wife that she was to "teach my children to hate them with that bitter hatred that will never permit them to meet under any circumstances without seeking to destroy each other." "I desire above all things on earth," wrote one Alabama rebel "to drive a Bayonet to the heart's Blood" of Yankee soldiers. Richard Watkins of the 3rd Virginia Cavalry wrote to his wife, "I am more willing to kill as many of them as God will permit me."[12]

One of the most dramatic exhibitions of this hatred took place after the Army of the Potomac's defeat at Fredericksburg. Nearly one thousand Union dead were sprawled out in the front of the stone wall on Marye's Heights. Lee granted Burnside's request for a truce on December 14 to tend to the wounded and to gather the dead. Members of the 48th Pennsylvania collected the bodies. As they arrived at the wall they were appalled: the Confederates had stripped and mutilated the bodies of the dead. Union soldiers worked angrily but silently. Unable to resist taunting, one Confederate officer yelled over, "You Yankees don't know how to hate—you don't hate us near as much as we hate you." Pointing at the desecrated bodies, the man continued, "Is that not very revolting to you? Don't you think it terrible?" The Pennsylvanians replied that only an uncivilized people would abuse the dead. "Indeed," the Confederate replied, "I could not be to any other save a Yankee."[13]

Black flag warfare also meshed with the southern spirit. Private James Painter of the 28th Virginia admitted to his brother that "when they Fight under a Black flag they don't take any prisoners; they kill every man they get a chance." The flag was supposed to be displayed before battle to let the other side know the rules. Southerners often waited until a successful attack to reveal it or did not display one at all. Sometimes it was a personal decision. Louisiana cavalryman Sergeant Edwin Fay wrote to his wife that "I don't intend ever to take any prisoners." One Texas soldier warned that if any Yankee ever crossed his path, "he need not petition for mercy. . . . If he does I'le give him lead."[14]

Throughout history, the use of the black flag in battle has been rare. Pirates used it when a captured crew had refused to surrender immediately. On Easter Sunday, 1525, six thousand peasants stormed the city of Weinsberg and killed the nobility there during the German Peasants' War (Deutscher Bauernkrieg). Northerners expected that a southern rebellion would be fought under the black flag.[15] South Carolina initially adopted the black flag as its official policy. Only after Robert E. Lee pressured the state did it retract its decision to hoist the black flag.[16]

Political support in Richmond for a black flag policy varied. Two factions within the Confederate Congress fought over the adoption of the approach. "Cats" or radicals supported adoption of the black flag; the "snakes" or conservatives did not. Within the many manifestations of Davis's cabinets there was never a consensus. Cats included Confederate Secretary of War James Seddon, Postmaster General John Reagan, and Josiah Gorgas, Confederate Ordnance Chief. However, according to John Jones, a clerk in the Confederate War Department, the government's actual approach to the war was that "no mercy can be shown the enemy."[17]

Southern newspapers openly urged the Confederacy to fight the war without restraints. The *Richmond Examiner* told its readers that northerners must be made to understand that "there is a God that punishes the wicked and the Southern army is His instrument." Editorials rang with admonitions to southerners to run the black flag and show no mercy to invading Yankees. *The Lynchburg Republican* believed that the motto of the Confederacy should be "the entire extermination of everyone who has set foot upon our sacred soil."[18]

Individual regiments made the decision to fight under the black flag. Soldiers elected their own officers and designed their own uniforms. It made sense then that soldiers chose the way they would fight the war. Support among the rank and file for the black flag proved mixed. Those soldiers that opposed the practice often feared they would be hanged if caught.[19] Those soldiers that supported the policy did so out of the belief that it might end the war sooner. Corporal John Power from the 1st Alabama wrote, "I sincerely believe that if the Black Flag is hoisted there would be peace in less than six mos."[20] Those in favor often defied orders. Before the Battle of Shiloh, Confederate officers rejected their soldiers' requests to fight without rules. When the officers refused, some men took a slightly less radical approach. They took off red pieces of clothing and hung them like flags. A red flag meant that the Confederates would fight to their deaths.[21]

Regiments from the Old Southwest were more inclined to adopt the black flag. Louisiana, Tennessee, Virginia, Georgia, Alabama, and Texas all contributed black flag regiments to the Confederate armies. Some of the more infamous were the 12th and 16th Tennessee Cavalry Battalions (also known as "Rucker's Legion"). Another was the 8th Texas Cavalry, better known as "Terry's Texas Rangers" and "Shannon's Scouts." They arrived in Richmond in September 1861, promising no quarter and carrying a black flag. A group of backwoods Alabamians carried a black flag and old mill saws to shear away the heads and limbs of Union troops.[22]

Louisiana produced at least three black flag regiments, two of which were composed of free blacks. Both of these were formed in New Orleans, where 45 percent of the citizens were free blacks. On March 1, 1861, more than a month before the firing on Fort Sumter, prominent free blacks of New Orleans met to discuss their course of action after secession. They decided that they should support the new Confederate government and volunteered for military service. Most were free men of mixed-race bloodlines whose families had been given their freedom by the federal government when New Orleans became an American possession in 1803. Governor Thomas D. Moore accepted the regiment as part of the Louisiana militia on May 2, 1861.[23]

The first, the "Black Flag Riflemen," volunteered to defend Louisiana. Qualifications for membership mandated that each recruit must agree to fight under the black flag and furnish his own uniform, rifle, and hunting knife. The other free black, black flag regiment was the "Native Guards." Also formed in March 1861, its 1,500 members carried a black flag that proclaimed, "We give and take no quarter."[24]

But in January 1862, uneasy Confederate authorities denied the Native Guards the opportunity to defend New Orleans. However, Louisiana's governor called the regiment back into service when Union warships began sailing up the Mississippi River in April 1862. Union soldiers contended they fought black Confederate soldiers at Baton Rouge. Union soldier Henry Howe of the 35th Massachusetts wrote home of two occasions where he encountered Confederate soldiers under the black flag fighting around Baton Rouge. There were also reports that at the Battle of Antietam, a black Louisiana regiment killed Union wounded as they lay suffering. Richard Yates, governor of Illinois, complained in a telegram to Lincoln that Confederates had armed southern blacks as soldiers.[25]

The most famous black flag regiment from Louisiana was "Wheat's Tigers." Also known as "Lions," "Grave-Diggers," and "Yankee-Slayers," the regiment was comprised of Irish "wharf-rats, cutthroats, and thieves" of New Orleans. Many claimed to join the war just to kill people. After the Battle of Williamsburg, a number of Confederate soldiers had gathered around a group of wounded Federals, one who had been shot thru the bowels and was begging to be put out of his misery. Several of Wheat's men had been passing by and stopped to see what was going on. One of them pushed his way to the front and approached the wounded Federal. One of Wheat's men said, "Put you out of your misery? Certainly sir." At which point he used the butt of his musket to smash in the Union soldier's skull. The executioner then looked around at the remaining wounded and said glibly, "Any other gentleman here'd like to be accommodated?"[26]

The first instance of black flag warfare occurred at Bull Run. The typical narrative of the battle showcases the bravery of the Confederates and in particular Stonewall Jackson. Missing from the narrative was how viciously southern soldiers fought. During the height of the battle, Union soldiers saw Confederate soldiers and cavalry stab the struggling wounded with bayonets. This was often done multiple times. Union soldiers called this infliction of pain on a wounded man "rewounding." Union soldiers who suffered non-mortal wounds had a higher probability of being killed by rewounding. At Bull Run, Confederates pinned men onto the ground and onto trees. Private Lewis Francis testified that Confederate soldiers stabbed him fourteen times, including once in the testicles. Private Joseph Sweigart testified that soldiers at Bull Run impaled wounded soldiers "against treas with their buynetts": "I have seen more than I ever expect to see and more than ever want to see again."[27]

"The Rebels Bayoneting Our Wounded on the Battlefield of Bull Run" (*Harper's Weekly*, August 17, 1861)

Henry Hill was a chaotic scene. Confederate soldiers executed those wounded not able to walk. Men begged for their lives to no avail. Some were killed using pistols. Others were speared to death. After one such lancing a Confederate soldier pulled out his bayonet and uttered, "There damn you, learn something." Appalled at these atrocities, a company of Fire Zouaves led three Confederate prisoners into a hollow and methodically shot them in the back of the head.[28]

Confederate medical staff committed some of the most vicious acts. Acting on orders from Brigadier General Pierre T. G. Beauregard, surgeons were barred from performing surgeries on the wounded.[29] Instead, he ordered that physicians' assistants amputate arms and legs. Dr. J. M. Homiston of the 14th New York testified before the Joint Committee on the Conduct of the War that these assistants "performed the operations in a most horrible manner, some of them absolutely frightful." Lewis Francis of the 14th New York reported that the amputation of his leg had been done so poorly that bone of his amputated leg continually ruptured through the sutures of his wound.

After the battle, Confederate soldiers mutilated the bodies. They decapitated the heads and threw them in pots to boil off the flesh. The most popular form of mutilation done to the living and the dead was a throat cut from ear to ear, called a "Confederate smile."[30] Confederates also cut off ears, tongues, and noses for trophies. Fingers were severed to remove rings. Private James Painter bragged in a letter to his brother that "[some of] us roasted the grease out of their heads." Some, including Painter, even pulled out teeth. Another soldier wrote to his sister that he wanted to pull the fingernails off of Yankee dead so that she could make a basket.[31] A worried U.S. Sanitary Commission reported that its agents had tried to investigate the treatment of Union troops but were barred for days from the battlefield.[32]

How can these accounts be folded into the current narrative of the war? The answer is that they cannot. The best way to reach an understanding of what really happened at Bull Run and the events that followed is to rethink what soldiers went through in combat. Watching GIs commit "un-American acts" against German soldiers in Italy during World War II pushed the combat artist George Biddle to seek a reassessment of the soldiers' combat ordeal. He wrote that it was unfair for civilians to think of soldiers as heroes or stars. Instead, he thought it more appropriate that soldiers be viewed as survivors of a great disaster like a mine collapse or a burning building. Only then could civilians truly understand the desperate circumstances and decisions under which soldiers fought.[33]

Generally, soldiers were expected to accept men trying to surrender as prisoners and show care for the wounded. This was easier said than done. Civil War battlefields were often places of detached consciousness. Assaults happened quickly and soldiers often had to make split decisions about who was still fighting, who had surrendered, and who was injured. Both sides acknowledged that in the "heat of battle" mistakes were made. The primary uncertainty surrounded the question of when should a soldier stop killing. As soldiers grew to understand, from a win–loss perspective, it did matter if they stopped too soon. History is littered with losers who thought the battle was over only to discover otherwise. Civil War armies were no exception and often resembled mobs at the end of a battle.

Oddly enough, trying to surrender may have been one of the most difficult transactions on a Civil War battlefield. Prospective prisoners had to decide whether they would survive the capture and the captivity. The uncertainty of surrender often frightened soldiers from surrendering, even when they found themselves in hopeless situations. Prospective captors had to decide whether to accept the surrender or slay the enemy. Often this was decided by captors balancing the risks posed by taking prisoners versus shooting the prisoners. Since the same armies tended to fight over and over, captors worried if they did not take prisoners this time what would happen if after the next battle they fell prey.[34]

Confederate soldiers tended to be sticklers for the formalities of surrender. In order for Union soldiers to surrender alive they had to drop their weapons, raise their arms, display a white flag, and ask for mercy. If a soldier failed one of these steps he might be killed. Stories of disarmed Yankees being gunned down grew so rampant that when Sir Arthur James Fremantle, a Royal Army officer traveling with the Confederate Army, met Jefferson Davis he asked him about it. "I have yet to hear of Confederate soldiers putting men to death," Davis weaved, "who have thrown down their arms and held up their hands."[35]

Succumbing to the heat of battle may explain some Confederate executions of Union wounded at Bull Run. The heat of battle referred to the most violent and intense stage of combat. Soldiers did not immediately emerge from the haze of battle. In that condition, they were in a berserk state. More animals than human soldiers, they tended to strike out at any perceived threat. Under this exception, soldiers were excused from any accidental killings they may have committed in the crazed aftermath of combat. Once an assault had been successfully completed and the passions had cooled, however, the rules changed. The killing of prisoners or wounded after the cooldown period was seen as closer to murder than an act of war. Acts that seemed to serve no military purpose drew suspicion.[36]

Separating heat-of-battle deaths from summary executions proved nearly impossible. Unless there were eyewitnesses, the sheer numbers of dead and wounded made criminal investigations unrealistic. However, the eyewitness accounts of Confederates shooting the lame wounded are compelling. In addition, Union soldiers' testimony and newspaper accounts of the prevalence of rewounding make it clear that rebel soldiers committed numerous atrocities at Bull Run.[37]

Confederates also learned a valuable lesson about atrocities: such acts were so abhorrent that most people refused to believe them. Union soldiers told newspapers, told Congress, and wrote home to their families about what had happened at Bull Run. Union surgeons who had examined the bodies testified before Congress about rewoundings and malicious amputations. These accounts were dismissed as propaganda by southerners and as fantasy by some northerners. To this day, historians such as James McPherson still dismiss the accounts of Confederate atrocities at Bull Run as mere talk. Union soldiers also learned a lesson after Bull Run: better to file the information in the back of their minds and put it to good use later.[38]

It was probably no coincidence that two proponents of black flag warfare held important commands at Bull Run, P. G. T. Beauregard and Stonewall Jackson. In particular, Jackson lobbied for the black flag three times during the war, May 1861, August 1862, and September 1862. "I have always thought that," Jackson wrote, "we ought to meet the Federal invaders on the outer verge of just right and defence, and raise at once the black flag." Jackson believed that a black flag war would be the most efficient way to fight. It would eliminate the messy collection of prisoners and the round up and treatment of the wounded. Each side's soldiers would know they would have to fight to the death or be killed.[39]

Jackson applied this approach during his famous 1862 Valley Campaign. At the battles of Front Royal and Winchester he refused to take prisoners. On May 23, 1862, his army slammed into elements of the 1st Maryland (Federal), 29th Pennsylvania, and 5th New York Calvary at Front Royal. As Jackson's soldiers surrounded the 1,100 men, they unfurled a black flag. They killed all those trying to surrender.[40]

The scene replayed itself in Winchester on May 25, 1862. As soldiers from the 2nd Massachusetts retreated through the streets of Winchester, soldiers threw hand grenades and shot weapons from windows. In the streets, Turner Ashby's 7th Virginia Cavalry routed and then shot the wounded. Later, in a sweep of the homes in Winchester, Confederates bayoneted injured Union soldiers in their beds with the order of "give no quarter to the damned Yankees."[41] After one hard fight during Jackson's 1862 Valley Campaign, a subordinate officer asked Jackson if they should spare at least brave Union soldiers. Jackson responded angrily, "Shoot them all; I don't want them to be brave."[42]

Jackson's men fought with a ferocity that became the stuff of legend. In fact, one of the lasting impressions of the war has been the unmatched courage and fearlessness of the Confederate soldier. It seems that Jackson's soldiers as well as other rebel soldiers had help in achieving this superior level of performance. Starting at Bull Run, Confederate soldiers used a mixture of whiskey, gunpowder, and opium to reach a frenzy before combat. Joseph Field wrote that the mixture made rebels "crazy" and they fought with "no thought of their lives." Among prisoners and the dead, Yankee soldiers found canteens filled with this concoction of whiskey, gunpowder, and opium. The whiskey and opium acted as initial euphorics and stimulated men to fight like "demons." These canteens were found at Bull Run, Fair Oaks, Seven Days, Milliken's Bend, and Atlanta.[43]

The use of stimulants to prod men to kill and be killed was not new. Their use explains the ferocity of southern soldiers and their high casualty rates. Fighting under the influence might also explain rewoundings, prisoner executions, and use of the black flag. Certainly, the use of "blue pills and black powder," as soldiers called the potion, also vividly illustrates the seriousness of the war's violence and the desperation of southerners. The fact that this phenomena has not been revealed until now reflects the grip the "Lost Cause" myth has on the war.

But Confederates were desperate, particularly after emancipation. In a letter to W. Parker Miles, a member of the Confederate Congress, Beauregard urged that it was "time to proclaim the black flag." "Let the execution begin," Beauregard wrote, "with the garrote." Private James Painter wrote to his brother that after the defeat at Antietam, rumors abounded that the black flag phase of the war was about to begin.

On December 24, 1862, Jefferson Davis issued as close to a black flag proclamation as the Confederacy ever did, General Order No. 111. Davis declared that any white officer captured in command of black troops were to be given no quarter. Black soldiers were not to be afforded prisoner-of-war status and could be re-enslaved or executed. In May 1863, the Confederate Congress passed a resolution that black soldiers and white officers could be executed as retaliation. Lincoln considered the policy an official embrace of no quarter, and in response he issued his "Eye for an Eye Proclamation" on July 30, 1863. He promised to execute a Confederate soldier for every Union soldier killed as lawful retaliation. Davis withdrew his order but he did not discipline commanders who employed it. When presented with allegations of misconduct, Davis either denied them or had his officers issue warnings, but little more.[44]

The problem of atrocities grew more complex as the war continued. Under current practices and customs, the lawful retaliation for an atrocity was one for one or "an eye for an eye." But each Confederate atrocity produced a ripple effect that generated multiple Union retaliations. These Union retaliations mushroomed into Confederate counter-retaliations that Union soldiers treated as additional atrocities demanding retaliation. Some soldiers committed atrocities based on acts that had occurred months before or based on episodes that they had only heard about. This created an unending circle of violence. George Burkhardt in *Confederate Wrath, Yankee Rage* concludes, "Confederates massacred white Union troops in the last two years of the war in every theater."[45]

This spiral of violence pushed Henry W. Halleck to ask Francis Lieber to draft a legal framework for war. On April 24, 1863, General Order No. 100 went into effect. Known also as "Lieber's Code," it set forth, in writing, the first recital of the laws of war in human history. The code prohibited fighting under the black flag and permitted that troops that flew the black flag could be put to death up to three days after capture. The code also banned pre-mortem rewounding, throat cutting, and any other act intended to cause "the infliction of suffering for the sake of suffering."[46]

Lieber's Code seemed to have little immediate impact. One of the most gruesome episodes of the war took place at the Battle of Chickamauga. Like Bull Run, the battle ended with panicked Union soldiers running for their lives. Braxton Bragg's men abused the wounded and captured after the battle. Bragg's chief of staff, Daniel G. Brent, blamed Bragg in his diary for the commission of atrocities. Brent wrote that Bragg's prebattle address told his men that they should fight to the death. This "squints at the black flag," Brent wrote. He was right. Confederate soldiers executed men trying to surrender. Some wounded men were buried alive. For six days, Confederate soldiers denied the wounded food, medical treatment, and shelter. By the sixth day, men succumbed to infected wounds and disease. One man lamented that "the rebels don't seem to care how many of us die."[47]

Many did not. A Texas officer, after examining the blackened and bloated Union corpses on the Chickamauga battlefield, wrote that "it actually done me good to see them laying dead." When Union troops regained the Chickamauga area they saw ghastly sights. Bragg's soldiers had mutilated the bodies of the dead. The heads of dead soldiers had been placed on poles and tree stumps. Mutilated bodies hung on trees, splayed open. Union soldiers were horrified and angered. They swore not to take another Confederate soldier alive.[48]

Chickamauga reinforced the notion that southerners hated Yankees and enjoyed seeing them dead. "I certainly love to live to kill the base usurping vandals," wrote Chris Kendrick to his father. Lieutenant Colonel Porter Alexander commented to a fellow officer that "I always feel like kicking their prisoners around. [I]t is my greatest comfort to know I have killed some of them with my own hands." Some Confederate soldiers even admitted that the sight of dead bodies brought them pleasure. Osmun Latrobe, an officer serving in Longstreet's corps, confided that seeing "severed limbs, decapitated bodies, and mutilated bodies" was "doing my soul good." Private James Painter bragged in a letter to his brother that he took delight in trampling on the dead bodies of Union troops at First Bull Run: "I could walk over them like they was brutes—smelled like brutes."[49]

The mutilation of bodies took the war to another unfamiliar level. Evangelical Christianity's emphasis on the resurrection made the human body sacred. From Bull Run to the end of the war, Confederate soldiers mutilated bodies. They did so for a number of reasons. First, they liked to take body parts as trophies and mementoes of combat.[50] Second, they sawed off bones to make pieces of jewelry. In fact, bone jewelry proved quite popular among soldiers. Union soldiers sometimes discovered these souvenirs in private homes as they moved deeper into the South. The taking of these items matters. They denote a brutal people or a people brutalized by war. Canteens and bullets were not enough. Only a skull or a bone ring could adequately memorialize the experience of the war.[51]

"Historic Examples of Southern Chivalry, Illustrated by Thomas Nast, Dedicated to Jeff Davis" (*Harper's Weekly*, February 3, 1863)

On a more profound level, the mutilation of the body signified disrespect. Bodily mutilations sought to negate the Christian rituals that gave death its power. Such acts were associated with savages. For southerners, the ritual of mutilation was not unfamiliar. Postmortem dissection was the fate of many of marginal people in prewar Southern society. It was designed to humiliate and desecrate the bodies of people deemed inferior. This included slaves, criminals, and white people who violated the Old South's honor code.[52]

Other factors play a role in understanding atrocities. Such acts tended to occur within small units. Moreover, small units that had survived the war with their core intact tended to be more likely to commit atrocities. Shared friendships often reinforced the impulse to avenge shared wrongs.

Physical environments that reduced large-scale battles to small unit actions also were conducive for atrocities. Four battles that represent this phenomenon took place at Seven Days, Stones River, Chickamauga, and the Wilderness. In all these engagements, the physical environment broke large unit fighting into uncoordinated, isolated assaults. To soldiers, these fights looked and felt like ambushes rather than coordinated battles. One soldier stated that at Chickamauga the battle was more like "guerrilla warfare on a vast scale." Instead of a unified effort, the fight was more like "one army was bushwhacking the other."[53]

The breakdown of big battles into small ones also occurred at the Wilderness. Hidden in burning underbrush, Lee's riflemen used the low ground cover to shoot Yankee wounded between the lines. Northern soldiers tried to rescue the wounded without a truce. Sharpshooters then began shooting would-be rescuers. Soon the bodies of the wounded and their rescuers were clumped between rifle pits. When Union soldiers managed to drag a wounded comrade back to the line without being hit, huge celebratory cries erupted from the northern lines. When launching attacks, rebel soldiers picked up Union wounded and used them as human shields during close-quarter fighting.[54]

The most dangerous of these small units was the Confederate cavalry. Under Joseph Wheeler, Wade Hampton, and S. W. Ferguson, the cavalry used size, speed, and ferocity to launch fatal attacks on foragers, teamsters, pickets, and sentries. Union soldiers that fell behind on a march often were found killed and mutilated. On April 23, 1864, at Nickajack Trace near Ringgold, Georgia, a detachment of Joseph Wheeler's cavalry overran the pickets of the 92nd Illinois (Mounted). Five men were killed after surrendering, and several wounded were cruelly butchered as they lay on the field. An investigation of the incident disclosed that several federals were shot for not running fast enough.

In September 1864, Brigadier General S. W. Ferguson of the 2nd Alabama Cavalry, after the fierce fighting in the Atlanta campaign, skirmished in Sherman's rear almost daily. In one such action, Ferguson captured ten of Sherman's men. Ferguson had served under Nathan Bedford Forrest and was present at Fort Pillow. He ordered all ten prisoners to be executed immediately by firing squad. Subordinate officers questioned the execution order and asked Ferguson to reconsider. When he refused, they threatened to resign. Members of the Provost Guard refused to participate in the firing squad. Captain Frank King labeled the shootings "cold-blooded and deliberate murder."[55]

Other Confederates who killed Union captives in Georgia were the 8th Texas and Joseph Wheeler's cavalry. One of Wheeler's men said that Wheeler "did not give them any quarter but shot them down as we overtook them." By the end of the March to the Sea, rebel troops captured and murdered at least 173 Union soldiers. This lack of "sival warfair," as one Ohio infantryman called it, did not end when Sherman left Georgia. Union soldiers were captured and mutilated near Robertsville, Columbia, and all along the march through South Carolina. At least fifty Union soldiers were captured, murdered, and mutilated. Robert

Wallace echoed the thoughts of many soldiers when he wrote, "It was no good time to be taken prisoner."[56]

Interference by Confederate partisans and guerillas often triggered atrocities. Guerillas would kill a Union soldier; Union soldiers would then retaliate against the first Confederate force they encountered. If this victimized force was a conventional unit, it would treat the retaliation as an atrocity and respond in kind. In areas where guerilla and regular soldiers both operated, like along the Mississippi River and the Shenandoah Valley, atrocities and reprisals lost any semblance of logic or restraint. Add to this Phil Sheridan's mission to eradicate the area's military usefulness in July 1864, and it's easy to see how some of the war's most unprincipled acts occurred.[57]

In the Shenandoah Valley, the retaliation for the execution of Union sentries, foragers, teamsters, and stragglers was the burning of civilian houses within five miles of the event. As counter-retaliations for these "burnings," Confederate soldiers and guerrillas executed Union prisoners. On August 19, Colonel John Singleton Mosby captured thirty members of the 5th Michigan Cavalry after a burning. The men tried to surrender but were shown no mercy. With screams of "no quarter," Mosby's men herded their captives into a ditch and shot them to death point-blank. Three men were shot in the face.[58] In retaliation, General George Custer seized seven of Mosby's men in Front Royal on September 22, 1864. General Lee then authorized Mosby to execute seven more of the 5th Michigan using a death lottery. Men pulled numbers out of a hat to see which seven of the remaining men would die. On November 6, Mosby decided three would be hanged and three would be shot in the back of the head at Rectorsville. A note pinned to one of those executed read simply, "Measure for Measure."[59]

One of the last brutal episodes, called the "Apple Jack Raid," occurred in December 1864. On December 7, 1864, Grant sent the Army of the Potomac's V Corps—twenty-five thousand soldiers—south of Petersburg to destroy the last rail connection, Weldon Railroad, between Richmond and Wilmington, North Carolina. The raid required that Union troops make a forty-mile trek in cold and icy weather. The discovery of an abundance of hard cider called "apple jack" made it a particularly sloppy march. Many men fell off the march and went to sleep it off.[60]

Many of them never woke up. Drunken, sleepy stragglers made prime targets for Wade Hampton's cavalry. Most of V Corps made it to the railroad by December 9. It spent the next two days tearing up seventeen miles of track. Amid another winter storm on December 11, the soldiers began the return trip to the Petersburg lines. It was then that they discovered what had happened to their stragglers. The march back was a horror show of naked, mutilated, and frozen bodies of the dead. One group of soldiers had been stripped naked, forced to kneel in the snow, and were shot execution-style in the back of the head. Corporal Smith McDonald of the 110th Pennsylvania found four of his friends with their throats cut. Other men had been clubbed to death. Some of the corpses had been hung up for display along the road. At Sussex Court House the nude bodies of half a dozen Union soldiers were found lying on the courthouse grounds, while another dead Federal had been discovered pinned to the ground by a stake driven through his mouth. The worst discovery was those soldiers who had their hearts cut out and their penises cut off. The penises had been stuffed in their mouths. Total casualties for the expedition numbered 200 infantry and 130 cavalry. Of this number, 225 Union men were listed as missing.[61]

Confederate accounts justified these actions as retaliation for Union thefts and rapes that occurred on the march in. The problem was that Union soldiers of the V Corps committed retaliations on the way out. As they had done in the Shenandoah Valley, Union soldiers burned the homes of civilians within five miles of the atrocities. "Coming back," wrote Captain Benjamin Oakes, "we made clean work of the buildings."[62] The proliferation of atrocities pushed Stanton to adopt a radical policy with regard to retaliations. Starting in 1864, Stanton ordered that all retaliations be executions sub rosa. Executions of Confederates as reprisals were carried out in secret in order to prevent retaliations to reprisals.[63]

Atrocities have not been a popular subject among Civil War scholars. One reason is they represent everything that the war was not supposed to be about: treachery, brutality, and killing without meaning.[64] Unlawful killings also made it more difficult to disguise the true nature of war. Through atrocities, the interior nature of war becomes visible. Atrocities cannot be dressed up in ideology, politics, or courage. The disintegration of soldiers' principles, restraint, and discipline was roughly revealed. In this respect, however, the study of atrocities provides another lens through which historians can view the "modernization" of war. Or, to paraphrase Mark Neely, the question of whether the Civil War was a total war can be examined on the ground level. How Confederates treated Yankee soldiers when they were not armed spoke volumes about where the war was in terms of its totality, violence, and the breakdown of the values its participants endured.

Liberia and the
U.S. Civil War

Karen Fisher Younger

H. W. Dennis, an African American emigrant in Liberia, wrote to an acquaintance in the United States on June 24, 1861, "I regret much to learn of the sad condition of things in your country. I should judge that by this time the conflict has commenseds and that there must be an awful state of things, and which I cannot contemplate without being exercised with feelings of deep and sad regret."[1] Burke's commiseration about the impact of the American Civil War on Liberia underscores a problem—and opportunity—in Civil War–era historiography. Surprisingly little attention has been given to how the American Civil War affected the lives of those in Liberia, a nation with unique ties to the United States. The American Colonization Society (ACS), founded in 1816, labored throughout the nineteenth century to relocate African Americans to Liberia, which the U.S. government had helped establish in 1822. By the beginning of the Civil War, black American emigrants and their descendants, known as Americo-Liberians, had asserted their authority over the African population and established their cultural, political, and economic domination in the land. The symbols of the republic—its flag, motto, and seal—as well as its government were modeled after those of the United States. Its leaders declared Liberia the "promised land" for African Americans. But the republic was far from paradise. Wars between natives and Americo-Liberians plagued the infant nation. Farmers could not produce enough food to meet demand. Wages remained low and the cost of living high. Disease and death haunted its residents. One female missionary characterized the country this way: "Things do not last long here."[2]

Considerable scholarly attention has been paid to the history of the ACS and Liberia, Lincoln and colonization, and the black response to colonization. A growing number of historians are reexamining the ACS and immigration to Liberia to give equal weight to both the American and African experience. We know now, for example, the important role emigrants, especially those from Virginia and North Carolina, played in making Liberia part of the greater Atlantic community. Claude Clegg's examination of North Carolina emigrants expertly demonstrates the value of exploring the colonization movement from the van-

tage point of two continents. Similarly, Richard Hall's *On Afric's Shore*, an examination of Maryland in Liberia, shows the tenacity and ingenuity that characterized early settlers. One of the few works to examine the role of women and
colonization, Marie Tyler-McGraw focuses on Virginia settlers and shows how
their presence shaped the Liberian historical narrative in a way similar to how
white Virginians contributed to the American narrative.[3]

We know that the majority of African Americans did not want to immigrate
to Liberia before, during, or after the war. But we also know that there was never
a unified opposition to emigration and that black American interest in emigration intensified in the 1850s and in the post-Reconstruction years. Most recently,
Kate Masur has explored the great debate among blacks in Washington DC over
colonization, and how, at least for a time, some leaders favored colonization.[4] We
know that public discourse on colonization contributed to a sense of black national
identity within the United States, and that emigrants carried a black construction
of racial identity to Africa. Richard Newman's *Transformation of American Abolitionism* portrays colonization as central to both northern black identity formation and the contribution black Americans made to reshaping antislavery reform.
Randall Miller's edited study of the Skipwith family letters from Liberia reveals the
Skipwiths' American perspective. Other scholars such as Gus Liebenow and Amos
Beyan have been quite critical of American settler attitudes that refused to extend
civil rights to the majority ethnic groups.[5] We know that in post-Reconstruction
America most prominent black leaders continued to oppose African migration,
but for many ordinary black Americans, Liberia became a symbol of new life.
Kenneth Barnes, in *Journey of Hope*, traces the hopes and disappointments of
Arkansas freedmen who emigrated in the 1880s and 1890s, and explores the role
of poor black farmers in the creation of a black nationalist identity in Liberia.[6]

We know that African colonization disrupted slavery whenever emancipation for the purpose of colonization took place.[7] The best example of this argument is Eric Burin's *Slavery and the Peculiar Solution*. After assessing all the ACS-
sponsored immigration to Liberia, Burin concludes that colonization tended to
undermine slavery. We also know that Lincoln's prolonged devotion to colonization cuts against his historical image as a pragmatic politician. Considerable
attention has been given to Abraham Lincoln's views on race and African American colonization. Scholarship has illuminated his long association with the idea
of colonization and shown that from the beginning of his presidency, Lincoln
considered ways of laying the groundwork for colonization. As president, Lincoln flirted with an array of wild colonization schemes to remote areas of Texas,
Florida, Haiti, Liberia, and Central America.[8]

Yet we do not know enough about the effect of the Civil War on Liberia and its American emigrants. Scholars have begun to show how the Civil War was far from merely a national story confined to the United States, but affected millions of people outside the country. An analysis of the connections and interactions between the two nations raises new questions for historians of the Civil War era. How, for instance, did Americo-Liberians, who in immigrating to Liberia had given up hope for black civil rights in the United States, react and respond to the events transpiring across the Atlantic when the tide of freedom swept their homeland? How did the tentacles of a national crisis reach across a vast ocean to touch those living in the struggling nation? An examination of the interface between Liberia and the United States will not only enhance our understanding of ocean-based connections, it will also deepen our understanding of the national debate over race and the place of African Americans in the United States in the Civil War years and beyond.

African Americans first landed on the West African coast in March 1820, the result of a joint effort of the ACS and the U.S. government.[9] In 1819, three years after the formation of the ACS, Congress approved a new slave trade law. The Slave Trade Act of 1819 sanctioned cruising along the African coast by the U.S. Navy and established a system of awarding prize money to naval personnel for the capture of slave ships. Most important, it authorized the president to arrange for the return of Africans rescued from U.S. vessels to Africa rather than state authorities. The act also provided for appointing an agent in Africa to facilitate the resettling of the Africans and a $100,000 appropriation. Practically, the act allowed President James Monroe to make the federal government a partner with the ACS and support its efforts to establish a settlement site for black Americans. Colonization supporters urged Monroe to interpret the act as granting authority to purchase territory and establish an African colony. Although Monroe was a strong advocate of colonization, his cabinet members, specifically John Quincy Adams, argued that colonization—to establish and possess colonies—was unconstitutional. The compromise was that the federal government would appoint an agent and send a warship with workmen and agricultural implements to the coast to establish an African agency, and the ACS would purchase the territory. The administration acted as though the expedition was a step toward suppression of the slave trade, but it also marked the beginning of the colonization effort. The United States chartered and paid for the first vessel sent to search for a settlement site. The first agents in the colony received salaries from the government. And in February 1820, the *Elizabeth*—carrying tools, supplies, and eighty-eight African Americans (thirty-three men masquerading as hired laborers, and their wives and children)—left for the shores of West Africa under the protection of the U.S. sloop of war *Cyane*.[10]

For the next twenty-five years, Liberia remained a colony of the ACS, presided over by an appointed white agent and assisted by an elected council of settlers. The early years were treacherous for new emigrants; nearly a quarter of them died within the first year of settlement. Faced with a malaria-infested environment, surrounded by external threats from the indigenous population, unfamiliar with the soil and without the proper agricultural tools, and often without adequate food and clean water, emigrants struggled to survive in their promised land. Nevertheless, yearly reinforcements brought new emigrants, and in time, the settlement expanded.[11] By the beginning of the Civil War, nearly thirteen thousand black American settlers had come to Liberia. Scattered settlements stretched along 250 miles of coastline. Compared to the millions of Africans who remained in the United States, the number of black American emigrants resettled in Liberia appears insignificant. Yet these few adventurous men and women who braved an ocean voyage and confronted the hardship of frontier life created something unique. They built—albeit at the expense of the indigenous population—the first black republic in Africa.

By the mid-1840s it had become clear to Americo-Liberians that a colony supported by the ACS, a private philanthropic society, had little legal and diplomatic standing. In 1847, the Americo-Liberians voted to separate from the ACS in favor of self-government; by this time, they had asserted their authority over the native African population and had established their cultural, political, and economic domination. The Liberian Constitutional Convention adopted a Declaration of Independence on July 16, 1847, and ten days later the convention adopted a new constitution modeled on that of the United States. It was ratified in September, and the first president of the Republic of Liberia, Joseph Jenkins Roberts, took office on January 3, 1848.

By the beginning of the Civil War, the Republic of Liberia was a lightning rod of controversy in America's black and white communities. To some, Liberia symbolized everything that was wrong with race relations in the United States. Many black Americans and white abolitionists believed Liberia was tangible proof that white Americans could not imagine a place for black Americans outside of slavery. Others—some black Americans and many more white Americans—viewed Liberia as a symbol of black ingenuity, a place where black people ruled themselves.[12] The controversial nature of the nation is illustrated by the refusal of the United States to recognize the republic until Abraham Lincoln, in December 1861, urged Congress to establish official relations with the republic, four-

teen years after it became an independent nation. Americo-Liberian Tobias M.
Oatland, a farmer living in Clay-Ashland, a town ten miles northeast and inland
of Monrovia, predicted the importance of Lincoln's election and a change in Liberia's status: "We are glad to hear out here of Mr. Lincoln's election, and hope he
will . . . place us on the same commercial footing with other nations."[13]

U.S. recognition is one of the most important outcomes achieved in relation
to Liberia during the Civil War, yet hardly any scholarly attention has been given
to the nation's delayed diplomatic recognition and the forces that prompted Lincoln's action. The consensus is that the Civil War removed the principal objec-
tors—southern Congressmen—who did not want a black envoy in Washington
DC. While this is partially true, the evidence suggests a more complicated story
line. Liberian independence presented an enormous conundrum for the United
States. Some Americans—especially African colonization supporters—believed
that the United States had a unique obligation to Liberia. After all, the ACS, with
the help of the federal government, had sent thousands of persons out from the
United States. For colonizationists, Liberia symbolized the great Christian work
of civilizing and Christianizing Africa even as it uplifted black Americans. Nevertheless, the U.S. government's relationship with Liberia had been ambiguous
during the nineteenth century. Despite official assistance, the U.S. government
refused to recognize Liberia as an American colony and remained aloof when
the British government ignored Liberian land claims.

The real problem for the U.S. government was that recognition exposed the
country's hypocrisy to its citizens as well as the world. The very existence of an
independent Liberia revealed the U.S. government's doomed attempt to pacify
both North and South and the slave owner and antislavery proponent in order to
preserve peace and the Union. Liberia had a population as large as California and
a coastline extending the distance from Boston to Charleston. It was developing
agriculture, manufacturing, and trade. It had a militia, a school, and an eccle-
siastical system. Americo-Liberians had written a constitution, implemented a
republican government, elected officials, and had articulate spokesmen like Alexander Crummell and Edward Blyden. Moreover, England, France, and Prussia
recognized Liberia. Regardless of whether the U.S. government acknowledged
the new nation, it was there for the entire world to see. Day after day and year
after year, the people of Liberia exposed the fallacy that blacks were incapable of
caring for themselves and were unfit for voting, work, or government. Liberian
independence implied a censure on the doctrine of black inferiority, and the idea
that dependency on whites was the true and natural condition of black men and
women. New Jersey Senator Jacob Miller, in a speech before the Senate in March

1853, pinpointed the problem that recognition posed: "I have heard it suggested as an objection to the recognition by this Government of the independence of Liberia, that it would reflect upon the legal institutions of domestic slavery . . . that we cannot admit the capability of the African race for self-government, and at the same time justify ourselves before the world in holding a portion of that race in bondage."[14] African Americans also identified slavery as the root problem: "The presence of a black minister at Washington would be more pregnant with mischief to our peculiar institutions than the whole emigrated population of Liberia could be, scattered over this nations in the capacity of free negroes." Slavery, argued this anonymous writer, "will prove an effectual barrier to any full recognition of the independence of Liberia, or of St. Domingo."[15]

Many of the calls for recognition presented to the House and Senate asking Congress to recognize the independence of Liberia in the 1850s came from colonization-supporting state legislatures, colonization societies, and citizens who supported African colonization. By far the most petitions came from the Ohio legislature, a strong advocate of colonization in the 1850s. In February 1850 Henry Clay, a longtime colonization supporter, presented several petitions from citizens of that state. Greene County and Cedarville, Ohio, places with strong colonization sentiment, sent petitions in 1850 and 1853. In the years that followed, calls for recognition came from states with vocal contingencies of colonization supporters, including New York, Pennsylvania, and Massachusetts. All of these were referred to the Committee on Foreign Relations. Complicating matters, James Mason, an author of the Fugitive Slave Law of 1850, defender of slave traders' rights, and later a Confederate minister to England, was the Foreign Relations Committee's chair from 1851 to 1861. Mason was unlikely to encourage action on a petition to recognize a country settled by former slaves. Despite continued pleas from states and individuals, no action was taken until Lincoln's call for recognition in 1861.[16]

Correspondence between ACS agents and Liberian officials show that the ACS desperately wanted the United States to acknowledge Liberian independence as much as, if not more than, Liberians did. Letter after letter from William McClain, the corresponding secretary of the ACS in the 1850s, updates Liberian officials on Congress's deliberations or lack of action on the part of Liberia. Explanations to Liberian officials for the failure of the United States to officially acknowledge Liberia almost unanimously blame the heated political atmosphere of the 1850s. Early in 1852, ACS leaders believed recognition was eminent. Daniel Webster, a longtime colonization supporter, had been appointed secretary of state by Millard Fillmore, also a colonization supporter. At a dinner hosted by the New York businessman Anson Phelps, Webster was asked to give his views on Liberia. The *New York Express* and *Boston Courier* reported that Webster remarked, "Liberia has certainly given proof of the power of self-government . . . and I do not see why we should not recognize them as a government, as we recognize countries possessing a people inferior in intelligence." Word spread quickly among ACS leaders, and not long after, they communicated the good news to Liberian officials. "I think I hazard nothing in expressing to you my earnest conviction that the time is drawing near when I shall have the pleasure of informing you that our Government has recognized the Independence of yours!" wrote McClain to President Joseph J. Roberts.[17] But Liberians took a more cautious approach to such news. "I confess," wrote Roberts, "having been so often disappointed in my hopes in regard to this matter—I have now but little expectation of seeing our wishes, in this respect, realized."[18] Roberts had good reason to doubt McClain's judgment. Just a year later McClain wrote to Roberts, "I am sorry that I am not able to speak something encouraging touching the acknowledgment of the Independence of Liberia by our Government. I fear the present administration is more indisposed to do it than any of the preceding ones have been."[19] Referring to the Pierce administration, ACS officials and the Liberian government would not seriously entertain hope of recognition again until Lincoln's election, despite continued petitioning.

Lincoln's December 1861 State of the Union message calling for extending diplomatic recognition of Liberia and Haiti, is best understood in the context of war, emancipation, and the border states. Certainly Lincoln viewed recognition as a way to improve prospects for black immigration to Liberia or Haiti. Besides calling for extending recognition, he also urged Congress to provide funds for the colonization of slaves freed under the First Confiscation Act as well as slaves that the border states might decide to free.[20] On February 4, 1862, Charles Sumner, Massachusetts senator and chairman of the Senate Committee on Foreign Relations, introduced bill S.184, "authorizing the President to appoint Diplomatic Representatives to the Republics of Haiti and Liberia respectively."[21]

Debate over the bill took place in the context of the disintegration of slavery in parts of the South occupied by the Union Army, thousands of "contrabands" within Union lines, and the emancipation of Washington DC slaves. Lincoln's call for recognition, originally intended to encourage colonization and black emigration, received almost universal rejection as a bill from Democrats and representatives from the border states—states that had strongly supported colonization before the war. Moderate and Radical Republicans overlooked their differences on the propriety of colonization and universally supported the bill, arguing it was long overdue and a simple act of justice to recognize the countries that all the other major nations had already acknowledged. Democrats and Lincoln opponents reduced the bill to a referendum on racial equality. They mocked, scoffed at, and ridiculed the people of Liberia and Haiti in an attempt to excite racial fears and turn voters against the administration. Southern Unionist John Crittendon argued the bill was part of the larger plan of Radical Republicans to abolish slavery and introduce racial equality. "It comes in connection with a series of measures obviously designed for the abolition of slavery," asserted Crittendon, "and as intended to introduce at once the idea of negro equality by establishing diplomatic equality with the negroes of Liberia and Hayti."[22] Charles Biddle, of Pennsylvania, best summarized the Democratic position: "I object to the establishment, at this time, of diplomatic relations with Hayti and Liberia, because it will be taken, and by those who at this time are its prime movers, it is intended, as an acknowledgment of the equality of the races."[23] This sentiment was expressed in harsher terms in some instances. "But unless gentlemen here propose equality, unless they intend abolition entire, there is nothing logical in their pressing this bill," argued Samuel Cox of Ohio. "How fine it will look, after emancipating the slaves in this District, to welcome here at the White House an African, full-blooded, dressed in court style, with wig and sword and tights and shoe-buckles and ribbons and spangles and many other adornments which African vanity will suggest."[24]

The political debate over recognition featuring harsh racial discourse was a portent of the fall midterm elections, where rising sensational racial fears yielded great electoral dividends for the Democrats. It was also a harbinger of things to come, as it highlighted the central problem that neither the Civil War nor Reconstruction solved. Although the war freed slaves and Reconstruction gave black Americans a claim to citizenship and black American men the right to vote, neither provided the moral energy required for rooting equal rights in American society. It would take another revolution, led principally by black American clergy during the civil rights movement, to change public policy.

Americo-Liberians hoped recognition would achieve two objectives. The first was increased emigration from the United States. The majority of Americo-Liberians remained committed to Liberia even after the tide of freedom swept the United States during the Civil War and, in fact, believed—or at least hoped—black Americans would come to Liberia en masse. The one thing that Liberia needed throughout the nineteenth century was workers. Early in 1862, the nation's congress commissioned two of its most towering figures to recruit black Americans to immigrate, whose ideas about Africa and its relationship to black Americans shaped debate for much of the nineteenth century: Alexander Crummell, a freeborn New Yorker and Episcopal minister who immigrated to Liberia in 1853; and Edward Blyden, who was born on the island of St. Thomas, went to the United States for theological training, and, when denied admission, immigrated to Liberia in 1851. Both men were deeply committed to the idea that black Americans should return to Africa and wrote extensively and convincingly on the topic. Throughout summer 1862, the men traveled through the major cities of the North, presenting the advantages of emigrating at well-attended meetings of black Americans. Yet their tour through the northern states resulted in no surge in emigration. Americo-Liberians expressed dismay throughout the war that black Americans, especially newly freed slaves, appeared uninterested in emigrating. "It is especially surprising to me to perceive that no applications are made for emigrating to this Country," wrote C. L. Randamie in January 1862. "The north will necessarily be flooded with the fugitives from the south, & though they may not wish to leave America just now I am almost confident that they can not stay there, & will be obliged sooner or later to leave."[25]

Americo-Liberians had always retained a keen interest in and exhibited an impressive political awareness of the United States, which they viewed as the "mother country." U.S. newspapers and letters from family and friends sent aboard steamers helped keep settlers well-informed. The *Liberian Herald*, Liberia's official newspaper, filled its pages with news concerning the United States. When war broke out in the United States, Americo-Liberians expressed a deep empathy for America. Citizens were "much grieved," voiced "deep and sad regret," reported being "down in spirit because of the dreadful state of things in the U.S," and were "ever anxious to learn the state of affairs" in America.[26] William C. Burke, an African American emigrant in Liberia, wrote to an acquaintance in the United States after hearing news of war, "This must be the severest affliction that have visited the people of the United States and must be a sorce of great inconvenience and suffering and although we are separated from the seane by the Atlantic yet we feel sadly the effects of it in this country."[27]

Letters from government officials as well as citizens indicate that Americo-Liberians viewed the Civil War from its inception as a referendum on slavery. At a time when Abraham Lincoln, and most Union troops and white northerners, would have said the war was about restoring the Union, emigrant H. W. Dennis, writing in June 1861, believed it was being fought for the destruction of slavery and the liberation of the slaves: "I trust that the great Governor of the universe will so order things as that American Slavery may be speedily and totally abolished and that peace and prosperity be restored to your great and glorious country."[28] Others saw the war as part of a providential plan to end slavery. "Humanity sickens at the sight of so much blood," declared Dr. J. S. Smith, "but it is clear that the hand of Providence is in it and that it will rebound to his glory and to the advancement of his kingdom on earth."[29] At the war's end, H. M. Davis, who called the conflict "the greatest contest the world has ever seen . . . in favor of Liberty and Justice," believed the outcome the result of "the visible manifestation of [God's] guiding hand, and sustaining power."[30] J. H. Deputie was willing to endure the hardships that the U.S. war inflicted on Liberia in order that the "Right triumphant." He wrote, "Though without a dollar in the world, with no prospects, and sick. I must be content with my life. . . . The war is a just war—which will eventuate in the good of my race, and I am willing to bear my share of the inconveniences."[31]

America-Liberians also hoped U.S. recognition would achieve improved trade with the United States and stimulate capital investment. Indeed, some America-Liberians prospered from the war. As Martha Ricks observed, "Liberia has and is still feeling the effects of your war, and it has caused her to arise up to help herself, and to call for wheels, cards, and looms. . . . Coffee is being raised in large quantities. They are enlarging their sugar plantations every year."[32] Coffee and sugarcane cultivation grew dramatically during and after the Civil War. Liberia's sugar production had intimate ties with the United States. Serious sugar production began there in the 1850s; during the Civil War, Liberian planters saw a greater opportunity to sell their sugar in the United States, as the American sugar trade was disrupted and sugarcane farms were destroyed. So great was interest in sugar production among America-Liberians during the Civil War years that the *Liberia Herald* labeled it a "mania for sugar estates."[33] In 1862, William Spencer Anderson, an emigrant from Wilmington, Delaware, in the 1850s stated, "During this year there has been shipped to the United States about fifty thousand pounds."[34] The mania for sugar created a rapid rise in the price of land in the 1860s. For example, the price of land on the St. Paul River increased about 300 percent between 1859 and 1864. Yet the rapid increase in production and trade of sugar in the 1860s ended in the 1870s. The reordering of the U.S. industry by 1880 proved to be a disaster for Liberian farmers, who were unable to complete with the much larger and better-financed U.S. sugar producers.

While sugarcane farmers were setting up mills and sugarhouses, an even larger number of America-Liberians manifested an interest in coffee cultivation. Liberian interest in growing coffee is almost entirely the result of the Quaker Edward S. Morris, a Philadelphia businessman and officer of the Pennsylvania Colonization Society. In 1863, he visited Liberia, bringing samples of machines he had designed for cleaning and hulling coffee. He delivered addresses in Monrovia and again upriver in Clay-Ashland on February 15, 1863. Liberian coffee gained rapid acceptance in the world market, in large part because of Morris's promotional campaign, and cultivation thrived throughout the 1870s. In September 1863, Reverend William C. Burke, of Clay-Ashland and a former slave of Robert E. Lee, remarked, "The planting of coffee is now receiving attention from every farmer in Liberia. I regret, and it seems to be the regret of almost every farmer, that they did not attend to planting coffee many years ago."[35] During the Civil War years, the price of coffee increased for the first time in a number of decades: a pound of coffee sold for forty-two cents by the end of the war, having risen from fourteen cents in 1861.[36] In the 1870s, coffee cultivation continued to thrive. Yet by the close of the nineteenth century coffee, like sugar, had fallen into decline because of international competition and chronic labor shortages.

At war's end, Liberia's President Warner expressed his optimism in his annual message to Congress: "Liberia is yet to be the asylum for the oppressed American negro."[37] And he had reason to hope. In the fall of 1866, just months after the end of the war, nearly one thousand black Americans applied to immigrate to Liberia under the auspices of the ACS. Applications remained high through the end of the 1860s; however, by the end of the Civil War, the ACS had essentially ceased operations. Revenues had sharply declined during the Civil War, state auxiliaries no longer existed, and the society's leaders had grown old and died. So, while momentum to emigrate was growing among mostly poor black southerners, the ACS didn't have the funds to transport them.

Black Americans expressed a variety of motives for wanting to leave the United States. Some expressed frustration with the lack of opportunities, the prejudice, and the persecution. In April 1868, A. E. Wilhelm, Willis Fort, and William Rhoades explained that the "K.K.K. are going on outrageous and every body wants to leave the country."[38] Others wanted to reunite with family members who had already emigrated. Still others articulated more altruistic motives, such as the desire to convert Africans to Christianity, help build a black nation free of white prejudice, or return to what they believed to be their home. Edward Hill, a former slave from North Carolina, called Africa "my home" and hoped to "to reach that land before I do die."[39] The pressure from whites and blacks to remain in the United States, however, was fierce. Southern whites desperately wanted to secure freedmen as laborers. Many black leaders also tried to stop emigrant parties from forming. By April 1868, Charles Snyder of Halifax, North Carolina, had gathered a group of three hundred potential emigrants but reported that the "leading colored men of the republican party" were going throughout the country "trying to brake down the party from going to Liberia."[40]

The desire to emigrate was so intense among some black Americans in the years immediately following the war that they turned to the U.S. government for help. Thousands of potential emigrants from Mississippi, North Carolina, South Carolina, Georgia, and Alabama sent petitions to Congress. A group from Alabama sent three different petitions to Congress, which went unread. They concluded that Thaddeus Stevens and Charles Sumner were "pretended friend[s]."[41] In the end, Congress did nothing with the petitions.

Even when emigrants were able to secure passage through the ACS, logistical difficulties discouraged groups. Almost without exception, emigrants planned to leave the United States as groups of friends and family. If a family member became too sick to travel, the entire company would often wait to leave. Communication problems (such as confusion over the day of departure, which often changed with little notice), difficulties transporting groups and their belongs from scattered rural locations, and debt all hampered emigration. Edward Hill decided against leaving because he was unable to repay his debts. He fell $75 in debt after the war and wrote that he "did not see no way to pay it and I do not want to leave a bad name behind me."[42]

Black interest in emigration in the nineteenth century fluctuated but never disappeared, as measured by the number of letters of interest to the ACS. Correspondence is especially frequent in the years 1867–68 and again in the 1880s. Yet the post–Civil War mass exodus of black Americans to Liberia and the political and economic support that Americo-Liberians had hoped for—and needed—never materialized. When slavery existed in the United States, the United States refused to recognize Liberia as a sovereign state because of the political complications that would follow. After slavery was finally abolished and Liberia was recognized, the United States failed to produce what the country needed most: settlers. Not only did black Americans "not seem so willing to migrate there," as Abraham Lincoln noted, but it was clear the U.S. government would not finance a mass exodus of its most prized source of low-wage labor, or provide to Liberia the economic support it desperately needed. More than this, for most Americans the abolition of slavery in the United States shattered the republic's justification for existence, thereby sealing the fate of the nation. Throughout the nineteenth century, the United States ignored Liberia as it struggled to carve out a "promised land" while warding off the encroachment of European colonizationists. Tragically, Liberia would remain plagued by political and economic turmoil late into the late twentieth century.

"No Regular Marriage"

African American Veterans and Marriage Practices after Emancipation

Andrew L. Slap

C hauncey Taylor offered to resign as chaplain of the 3rd United States Colored Heavy Artillery Regiment in November 1865. After describing to General Lorenzo Thomas his personal reasons for wanting to resign, Taylor wrote that "my services as chaplain of this regiment may be spared without material determent to the religious and moral interests of the men." He explained that each of the other two African American regiments stationed at Fort Pickering in Memphis "has its chaplain on the ground and we all use the same house of worship in common, so that none of the men will be without the opportunity of religious services every Sabbath." The somewhat self-serving letter of resignation stands in marked contrast to the chaplain's correspondence with Thomas four months earlier. At that time Taylor reported that during his year of service—which included a month's leave—he had "married 300 of the men of his regiment and their wives." Taylor considered the prospects of most couples good because "many of them lived together as husband and wife before the war." Most of the soldiers in the regiment were former slaves, so while they had formed families before the war they had been unable to marry legally. Maybe Taylor thought that enough soldiers in the regiment were now legally and happily married. Taylor's letter suggests, however, that the regiment might still require a chaplain, for he warned that the government needed a new law "to provide for divorce in cases of adultery by one of the parties." He explained that "he had a great many such cases brought before him" and did not "know what to do with them." With his resignation accepted, Taylor returned to his home in Iowa and no longer had to contemplate the seeming contradictions and complexities of African American marriages during the Civil War era.[1]

Scholars, though, have spent generations trying to understand how emancipation affected African American marriage practices. In 1965 Daniel Patrick Moynihan argued that centuries of slavery had disorganized African American families and directly caused many of their contemporary problems. John W. Blassingame and Herbert Gutman were among the many historians who challenged Moynihan's thesis. Blassingame examined the slave family in his 1972 *Slave Community: Planation Life in the Antebellum South*. He concluded, "Although it was weak, although it was frequently broken, the slave family provided an important buffer, a refuge from the rigors of slavery. . . . The family was, in short, an important survival mechanism." Gutman directly contested Moynihan's findings in his 1976 *Black Family in Slavery and Freedom*. He estimated the number of slave couples that legalized their marriages after the Civil War by comparing the number of ex-slave marriages registered in Virginia and North Carolina to the number of adult slaves in the 1860 census. He concluded that "blacks in diverse social settings . . . placed a high value on legal marriage, at least as high as their urban and rural white neighbors." In addition, he asserted that "the choices so many made immediately upon their emancipation and before they had substantive rights in the law did not result from new ideas learned in freedom."[2]

It is understandable that historians in the late twentieth century would want to see African Americans as empowered actors, but it seems odd not to think that generations of slavery followed by sudden emancipation would have major effects on the construction and understanding of African American families. Nevertheless, for the next couple of decades major works on Reconstruction and nineteenth-century African American history relied on Gutman's findings, with the likes of Leon Litwack, Eric Foner, and Peter Bardaglio directly citing his work to demonstrate the enthusiasm recently freed slaves had for legalizing their marriages. Bardaglio, for instance, contends that "African American couples rushed to legalize their marriage bonds. Most African Americans viewed the ability to solemnize their customary ties as a badge of freedom, a powerful symbol of their newfound status as citizens." Litwack describes how "mass wedding ceremonies involving as many as seventy couples at a time became a common sight in the postwar South."[3]

Historians started using new sources like pension records in the 1990s to re-examine African American marriage during the Civil War era. While adding some nuance, though, many have come to the same conclusions as earlier historians. For example, Keith Wilson contends that during the war the "enthusiasm to legitimize marriage by documenting it continued, with increased fervor, in the army." Elizabeth Regosin argues that after the war, "although some resisted and resented the government interference in their familial relationships that legalization represented, most freedmen and freedwomen embraced it and the protection it afforded their families." In 2010, Tera Hunter discussed her project on nineteenth-century African American marriage on National Public Radio. While acknowledging some resistance, she repeatedly insisted that "most African Americans did want to embrace the idea of formalization and legalization of their marriages." On March 3, 2012 Henry Louis Gates Jr. asked his Harvard colleague Annette Gordon-Reed about African American marriage right after the Civil War on his PBS show *Finding Your Roots*. Gordon-Reed explained that "enslaved people wanted to be able to form families and so this was a way of affirming their humanity and affirming their right to one another." When Gates inquired whether there was a rush for freedpeople to become legally married, Reed stated, "Oh, there was a rush. . . . This is something that was one of the things that they looked forward to so they were going to take advantage of it as quickly as possible." Thus the idea that most African Americans quickly adopted legalized marriages after the Civil War continues to be a widely held interpretation.[4]

An increasing number of historians since the mid-1990s, however, have questioned the traditional interpretations of slave family composition and how many freedpeople legalized their slave marriages after the Civil War. An important finding has been that there was not a monolithic African American attitude toward or practice of marriage during the Civil War era. Brenda E. Stevenson was in the vanguard of post-Gutman revisionism with her 1996 *Life in Black and White: Family and Community in the Slave South*. She was one of the first people to stress the diversity of slave family patterns, emphasizing the extent and importance of households headed by single women—what she treated as "matrifocal" families. Noralee Frankel thoughtfully proposes that "the attitudes of freedpeople toward marriage were more complex than historians have suggested," and offers a well-argued reappraisal in her study of black women and families in Civil War–era Mississippi. She contends that "historians have exaggerated the number of slave couples who remarried each other after the Civil War." While finding that "evidence from the pension records suggests that they were comfortable with their community sanctioned slave marriages," she thinks that "on the whole, freedpeople favored legalization." According to Frankel, younger African Americans creating new relationships in the aftermath of the war were even more likely to embrace legal marriages. She asserts that "the decisions of young freedpeople to wed under legal auspices after the war showed how quickly they adjusted to the concept of formalized wedlock." This is an important generation distinction, suggesting that after emancipation most new marriages were formal and legal.[5]

Anthony Kaye likewise finds a more nuanced evolution of post-emancipation relationships in Natchez, Mississippi. He contends that "many couples who had lived together in good standing during slavery days saw no reason to pronounce themselves husband and wife in law after emancipation." And it was not just relationships formed in slavery, for "romantic unions persisted in some variety through the 1870s. More than a few men and women who got together in those years preferred taking up or living together to marriage." Ultimately, though, Kaye thinks that "legal marriage, buttressed by the pillars of church and state, held considerable sway with freedmen and -women," and that "freedpeople's reservations about legal marriage had nothing to do with any hankering for slave marriage. Couples did not deem themselves married solely on employers' and neighbors' say-so." It is important to note here, as Kaye does, that the term slave marriage did not refer only to negative aspects of African American marriage under slavery, such as the power of the owner. Slave marriage also encompassed aspects of informal marriage that some may have found positive, such as the importance of community approval and the ability of spouses to quit a marriage without getting a divorce.[6]

Some historians have even more provocatively asserted that many African Americans continued practicing non-legalized marriage for decades after emancipation. Laura Edwards, for instance, contends that "many refused to marry legally" and that "the pension records of black Civil War veterans indicate that poor African Americans in North Carolina lived with these same marital precepts well into the twentieth century." Nancy Bercaw likewise finds in the Mississippi Delta that "while many men and women formalized their relationships by marrying during and after the war, almost as many built on slave traditions of household, emphasizing a wide range of relationships." Donald Shaffer dedicates most of his chapter on black veterans' families to challenging directly Gutman's thesis. Shaffer asserts that "slave marriage customs survived for many decades after the Civil War. Although informal marriage had been the only option during slavery, former slaves voluntarily continued the practice in the postwar period."[7]

None of the historians challenging the dominance of legalized marriage questions the importance of family or committed relationships among African Americans in the years after the Civil War. For example, Laura Edwards states that for freedpeople "marriage was no joke." Knowledge of the flexible attitudes toward marriage, however, changes our understanding of African American life in the second half of the nineteenth century. Brenda Stevenson, for instance, finds that during slavery "a woman's role as the head of a matrifocal family mandated that she make some of her family's most vital decisions." Nancy Bercaw and Donald Shaffer both agree that the persistence of informal marriages, which continued slave-era approaches to relationships, "provides evidence of the limits of male power in the postwar black family." The continued practice of traditional intimate relationships like sweethearting and informal marriage can also help us understand things like the transition from slavery to freedom, and the contours of African American communities after the Civil War. The analysis of African American marriages around Memphis during the Civil War era in this essay continues the efforts of the post-Gutman revisionists to explore the many types of intimate relations African Americans created during both slavery and the age of emancipation.[8]

Ann Horn's experience illustrates the wide range of relationships African Americans participated in throughout the Civil War era. When Horn filed for a widow's pension in 1897, she probably did not expect to have to wait seven years for it to be approved. The special examiner investigating the case caused some of the difficulties, such as not accepting certain evidence and requiring Horn to prove negatives. Eventually, the assistant secretary of the pension office intervened and found that "the action of rejection was erroneous and is hereby reversed." While such a reprimand was unusual, the complicated nature of Horn's case—and relationships—was common.[9]

Born a slave in the 1830s outside of Nashville, Horn lived there until her owner, Banks Burrow, died when she was about fifteen years old. Napoleon Burrow, who seems to have inherited Horn, then took her to Arkansas. In the next three years she was sold five times before ending up with Joseph Clark. According to her, "I had not been long on the Clark place before Madison Brown, who also belonged to Mr. Clark, asked him for me as his wife, and he gave his consent and so we went together and lived together till Madison went off to the Yankees. We had no ceremony of any kind." The Civil War changed things. A couple of Horn's friends testified that "they were married in slave time and after Madison Brown enlisted in the army of the U.S. were married again by order of the military commander at Vicksburg." Life did not turn out happily ever after for the new legally married couple, for in 1877 Madison Brown froze to death in a Mississippi jail. Still, so far this case fits the standard Gutman interpretation.[10]

It became more complicated because Horn was applying for a pension for herself based on the service of her second husband, Manuel Horn. Born a slave in Tennessee in the mid-1820s, Horn somehow ended up in Holly Springs, Mississippi, by 1855. Like Ann Horn, he was married as a slave, but his wife died just as the Civil War ended. Horn moved fifty miles to Memphis, where he enlisted in the 3rd United States Colored Heavy Artillery Regiment at the end of March 1865 and started a relationship with a woman named Bettie. The exact nature of the relationship between Horn and Bettie became one of the central issues of Ann Horn's pension application. She testified that Manuel Horn had told her that "while a soldier in Memphis he had a 'woman' named Bettie just for a sweetheart, but that she was dead." She acknowledged that the sweethearts had lived together, but she did not know for how long.[11]

The use of the term "sweetheart" is significant for a couple of reasons. First, it connoted a relationship or household structure that was common during slavery, but historians disagree over how prevalent it was after emancipation. Anthony Kaye argues that "antebellum intimate relations at the boundaries of commitment—sweethearting and marriage—changed most radically after emancipation. Freedpeople ceased to associate sweethearting with the first stirrings of youthful desire and instead attached its clandestine quality to infidelity. An unfaithful man was often said to have a wife and a 'sweetheart.'" Nancy Bercaw, though, finds that "not limiting 'family' and 'household' to formal marriage vows, African Americans recognized the validity of at least three household structures connecting men and women—'taking up,' 'sweethearting,' and marriage. Each involved sharing a house, work, skills, and in most cases, love." The second reason for the significance of the term "sweetheart," and a major reason it is difficult for historians to determine how prevalent the relationship was after emancipation, was that Ann Horn had a clear interest in having her husband's earlier relationship not classified as a marriage. If the woman Bettie was married to Manuel Horn while he was a soldier and there was not an official divorce, then she, and not Ann Horn, would have claim on the pension.[12]

Manuel's former comrades disagreed about the nature of his relationship with Bettie. One thought that they had been married, or at least appeared so. He testified that "all I know of his wife is that while in the army a woman frequently came to the camp to see him and we took her to be his wife." The veteran explained that "after muster out he worked in the cotton sheds and we were frequently thrown together. He was living then in an alley behind Union and Monroe [in Memphis] with the same woman and she passed for his wife." Another comrade, however, recounted that Horn "said he had lived with a woman not his wife." Ann Horn and the two veterans did agree that she and Manuel Horn were married. She swore, "I was fully and lawfully married to Manuel Horn." Interestingly, one of the former comrades did not mention whether Ann and Manuel Horn's marriage was legal, but stressed that "they lived together and were recognized as husband and wife by each other and by the community in which they lived." While relying on community to sanction a marriage was a tradition from slavery, it is unclear from the deposition the definition or composition of the community this veteran was referring to in 1897.[13]

The community was a little better defined in the case of Phillip and Josephine Bellfield. A private in Company E of the 63rd United States Colored Troops, Phillip Bellfield probably spent most of his time stationed in Natchez, Mississippi, and he and Josephine Bellfield were still residing Mississippi in the late 1880s. Morgan Black and Clem Willis had lived on "adjoining places" to Phillip Bellfield since 1845 and testified on behalf of his widow in 1891. The neighbors stated that "in 1880 Philip married the claimant. The fact is that he was not legally married to the claimant, but simply married her as was formerly prevalent among slaves—he took her to his home and gave notice to all his friends & acquaintances that she was his wife. Everybody, black and white, who knew them, regarded them as man and wife." The neighbors stressed what constituted marriage in their community, insisting that "there can be [no] doubt of this fact that the claimant was his wife—socially and morally—if not legally." Thus fifteen years after emancipation at least some African Americans still followed the practice of marriages sanctioned by community but not law.[14]

Many of these same phrases and situations from the Horns' case appear in Millie Davis's 1906 pension application, which reveal that both her and her former husband had been in either unlegalized marriages or sweetheart relationships after the Civil War. Millie Davis was born a slave in Arkansas during the late 1840s. She explained that two years after the Civil War, "for about one year, (no More), I lived as man and wife with Henry Hackett, although no regular marriage ceremony was performed in our case." She added, perhaps to make it seem more acceptable, that "this prior marriage was such a one as was commonly entered into by colored people during the period immediately after the close of the Civil War." Millie later described how Henry visited the plantation she lived on and "asked my ma for me and my ma made supper for us and we went to living together." Though at least a couple of years after emancipation, it is clear that Millie and Henry Davis were still following many of the practices of a slave marriage, with the major difference being that the mother—not the owner—gave permission.[15]

The marriage even ended in the manner of a slave marriage, showing how many different aspects of traditional marriage customs survived after emancipation. During slavery African Americans created the term "quitting" for nonlegal but community-recognized divorce, though it was often permissible for a spouse to quit a marriage without the other's approval. Millie Davis stated, "I left him at the end of about one year, in 1868 or thereabouts, and never lived with him after that, because he misused me, and was not a good man." This is similar to how and why Rebecca Saulsbury ended her first marriage, to George Jackson. She was about eighteen years old at the end of the Civil War when "a colored preacher" married her and George Jackson on the Avery Plantation in Iberville, Louisiana. "I lived with George Jackson seven or eight years and had five children by him," recounted Rebecca Saulsbury in 1898. "We parted because he treated me bad and was a man who ran about after other women. We did not have a license to marry and we did not get any divorce. He went off up the river after we quit and I don't know whether he is alive or dead." The ability to quit a non-legalized marriage would have been a major source of empowerment for women in the mid-nineteenth century, particularly those who found themselves in abusive relationships. At this time, divorces were still rare and courts often favored husbands in marital disputes. The decision in an 1868 domestic assault and battery case in North Carolina demonstrates the judicial attitudes that helped make getting a divorce so difficult. The judge found for the husband because he did not wish to "inflict upon society the greater evil of raising the curtain upon domestic privacy, to punish the lesser evil of trifling violence." There were thus some tangible advantages for African American women to maintain traditional, nonlegal relationships after emancipation. Millie Davis's brother stressed that "she was never formally married to him." While there was no formal wedding ceremony and the marriage was never legal, Millie Davis insisted, "I considered Hackett my husband, and he was too, when I lived with him and my ma made supper for us. He was my husband till I left him. No, I never had a divorce from him. We never knew of such a thing in them days."[16]

Reverend Anthony Isbell married Millie and Owen Davis on October 24, 1875, in Memphis. Millie Davis made clear that "I got a marriage certificate when I was married to Davis. Had none when I got married to Hackett. They did not have them then." Of course, legalized marriages were available in the late 1860s, but Millie Davis may have known that a previous legal marriage, particularly without an official divorce, could jeopardize her chances of getting a pension as Davis's widow. Millie Davis and her rural Arkansas, African American community, though, may not have known of legal marriages for African Americans in the immediate aftermath of the Civil War. The same cannot be said for Owen Davis. Though born a slave in rural Missouri during the mid-1840s, he was living in Memphis by at least 1862 and soon joined the 3rd United States Colored Heavy Artillery Regiment. During Owen Davis's time with the regiment the chaplain had married three hundred soldiers in the regiment, including some of the soldiers in Davis's company, indicating that he would have known many comrades who were formally and legally married during the Civil War. Even with the knowledge and opportunity to legally marry, though, Owen Davis did not choose that option in his relationship with a woman named Eliza that started in the late 1860s. It is interesting to note that both Owen Davis and Manuel Horn started these relationships in a major city and not the countryside. Donald Shaffer has contended that "informal marriage appears to have survived most strongly among poor and rural African Americans," which appears to make sense but is not true in these instances. This may be another case where we need to investigate more deeply the migration and interaction between rural and urban areas in the nineteenth century.[17]

One of Owen Davis's sisters testified in July 1907 that "I am positive he never had a wife and never lived with any woman before he married Millie Rawlings." The pension examiner was probably a bit surprised a few days later when one of Owen's brothers contradicted his sister's statement. "I am sure he was never married before he married Millie Rawlings," explained the brother. "I recollect he lived for a while with a woman called Lizzie but I understood they were not married. I think it was two or three years after the close of the war that they began living together. I can't say just how long they lived together. They had one child called George Davis. He died after Owen and Lizzie separated. I don't know what became of that woman. Her name was Eliza not Lizzie." Upon questioning, the brother responded both, "Yes, I am sure they lived in a house together as man and wife," and "Yes sir, I am quite sure they were not married." The pension examiner quickly returned to the sister, who said, "Well, I knew about it but I did not think that woman 'counted in this matter.' I thought you was just inquiring about Owen Davis's wife or wives. I am sure he was not married to Eliza. He just run in and out like sweethearts they lived together awhile, then apart awhile, then together again and so on and off for two or three years." Without hearing from Owen Davis or Eliza, it is difficult to determine the exact nature of their relationship, whether it was sweethearts, an informal marriage, or something else. The nature of the relationship was important, however, since if Owen Davis and Eliza were married then she, and not Millie Davis, might be entitled to the widow's pension. Millie Davis's relationship with her in-laws, and their desire to help or hurt her chances of getting the pension, could have affected their testimony and accounted for their different recollections of the relationship between Owen Davis and Eliza. Using legalistic and Victorian standards, the pension examiner concluded, "In the absence of a record of their marriage I am led to believe that they lived in adultery, just as stated by the witnesses." Of course, despite their differences neither witness stated that Davis or Eliza lived in adultery. The white pension examiner was imposing his definitions of relationships and marriage, which were different from those of the African Americans in this case.[18]

Different attitudes toward marriage, however, also existed among African Americans. Black churches became the most important institution in African American society in the decades after emancipation. For a variety of reasons, black churches became the most powerful advocate for African American couples to adopt formal and legalized marriages. More than just enforcing their view of moral behavior, many black churches and clergy saw legalized marriage as a defense against both white stereotypes of African American sexual promiscuity and white harassment of black women. Black churches commonly withheld membership from couples living together in an unlegalized marriage, and one freedwoman recounted that after two years of living together "we got married by license, because the church we joined required everyone to be married by license."[19]

The struggle within African American communities over legalized marriage lasted decades after emancipation, as seen in the case of Elizabeth and Henry Vass. Elizabeth Vass was born in King George County, Virginia, around 1848 and lived there until her early twenties, when in 1870 she moved sixty miles north to Washington, DC. That was the same year she met Henry Vass, ten years her senior and a veteran of the 2nd United States Colored Calvary. Though the couple did not marry until July 3, 1890, she told a pension examiner that "about eight yrs prior to my ceremonial marriage to the soldier I began to cohabit and live with him as his wife. For something more than two years prior thereto I began keeping house for him—he owned a little home and was a single man. I did not live there all the time but went back and forward. It was when I first went there to keep house for him that we began to have carnal knowledge of one another. That intimacy continued . . . until I moved to his house about eight years prior to my marriage to him."[20]

Elizabeth and Henry Vass had a couple of children and lived together for almost a decade without a seeming need to legalize their relationship, for according to her, "there was no discussion of the question of marriage between us until just prior to the time we were married by the Rev. W. J. Howard." Before the wedding Elizabeth Vass used her maiden name, Conway, and recounted, "I was not introduced by the soldier to his friends and acquaintances as Mrs. Vass until after my marriage July 3, 1890. I was at times called Elizabeth Vass or Mrs. Vass by some who knew I was living with him in the capacity of wife." Eventually though, she said, "I had got tired of living with him in the capacity of a wife without being married to him." There may have been many reasons Elizabeth Vass wanted to get legally married, but her testimony in the pension application suggests that the primary motivation was to avoid being ostracized by her church. She explained that "some four or five years prior to our marriage I had been 'turned out' of the church for living with him without being married to him. I wanted to rejoin the church and could not do so until I was lawfully married to him."[21]

The couples discussed above each had a sweetheart relationship or unlegalized marriage after the Civil War, when African Americans could formally and legally marry. While we are still not sure how common this was overall, these do not appear to be isolated instances. Elizabeth Regosin and Donald Shafer, for example, have found cases as late as the 1880s, suggesting that at least in some places these practices lasted for decades. In her study of Mississippi, Noralee Frankel finds that "after the Civil War, African American and white southerners used the term took-up (the expression originally used to describe slave marriages) to refer to any nonmarital relationship," and that these constitute approximately 16 percent of the intimate relations referred to in the pension files. She quotes a Freedmen's Bureau agent reporting that "I find the rites of matrimony among them seldom solemnize[d] or legalized, but when they choose, they call themselves married and live together until they take a notion to separate."[22]

The language historians use to describe African Americans who did not adopt formal and legal marriage practices after the Civil War era is interesting—and possibly revealing. There are phrases like "freedpeople contested the state's narrow definition of marriage"; they "resisted and resented the government interference in their familial relations"; "many reportedly ignored both legal procedures and moral norms"; "many refused to marry"; "others came to it slowly, if at all, clinging to older ways." How should we interpret words like contested, resisted, ignored, refused, and clinging? These all seem to imply the existence of a dominant Victorian, middle-class paradigm of marriage that these African Americans consciously rejected—or a dominant historiographic paradigm that dictates that behavior contrary to social norms is resistance to those norms. The emphasis on formal and legalized marriages for African Americans after the Civil War marginalizes the experiences and importance of freedpeople who continued such relationships as sweethearting and informal marriage. The language and tone of the depositions discussed here, though, does not suggest either conscious rejection or marginalization—and recall that these were taken in the 1890s and early 1900s. As the brother of one of the widows explained, they "lived as was customary during those days among the colored people in the South."[23]

In the last two decades, historians have increasingly found that legal marriage was not universal, as either a practice or an ideal. As Shafer points out, there has been little work done on the nature of common law marriage practices in the United States. Brenda Stevenson explains that in the antebellum South, "poverty, legally sanctioned instability, and growing white hostility meant that free men and women who were black continuously had to rely on alternative familial and marital styles." In a larger sense, Stevenson contends that living in a race-based slave society, "blacks and whites in the old South rarely understood the contours of the other's life—even the significance of some of the most profoundly important aspects of one's existence eluded the comprehension of the other." It would seem to make sense that many freedpeople would continue the types of intimate relationships that had developed over the preceding centuries, and that this appeared alien to whites or northern blacks. For these freedpeople, this behavior was probably not a form of resistance, but rather just living in the reality they knew and experienced.[24]

Recognizing the continued existence of sweethearting, informal marriage, and other types of intimate relationship among freedpeople has profound consequences. First, it de-marginalizes the experiences of many freedpeople, making it easier to understand their lives from their own perspectives. Many of the African Americans continuing to practice traditional antebellum relationships after emancipation seem to have left fewer records than did members of the African American middle class, press, politicians, or clergy. It is difficult enough to give voice to the voiceless without also marginalizing their perspectives and histories, thus limiting our ability to understand the wider African American experience.

Taking into account a broader African American experience during the Civil War can affect the meaning of the conflict itself. For the past generation, historians like Eric Foner and James McPherson, often synthesizing the work of earlier generations, have argued that the Civil War was a transformative event that created a modern state and society in the United States, an interpretation that has been the reigning paradigm for decades. The continuation of long-standing African American marriage practices for decades after emancipation would suggest that maybe the Civil War did not constitute as sharp a break with the past as historians have thought. Even more far-reaching, much of the paradigm of the Civil War as a central point in the modernization of the United States rests on viewing the South and slavery as antimodern.

As Frank Towers has recently argued, it may be time to reevaluate the South, slavery, and even the definition of modernity. More than a decade of social history, according to Towers, has been "discrediting modernization's premise of the United States as an exceptional liberal–capitalist society resisted by a distinctly anti-modern South," and perhaps the most significant work situates slavery "as a constituent element of modernization rather than a lagging sector." He contends that "this reorientation of slavery's place in U.S. history works with a more open-ended definition of modernity that decenters Western Europe as its exemplar and recognizes that the broad pattern of change summed by the term modernization took multiple forms."[25]

Ironically, the Victorian middle-class definitions of marriage that historians have privileged as modern now look rather antiquated in Western society. For possibly the first time in U.S. history, in 2005 a majority of women were unmarried and married couples became a minority of all American households. These changes in marriage rates at the beginning of the twenty-first century do not indicate that people are increasingly living alone, for according to the Census Bureau, in 2010 the sharp decline in marriage has been accompanied by a rapid increase in the number of cohabiting couples. Maybe many of the freedpeople were more "modern" than the rest of nineteenth-century American society. Such an interpretation would fit with the work of cultural scholars like Paul Gilroy, who argues that slavery was at the heart of modernity, and that the hybrid, transnational black Atlantic culture that emerged was at the cutting edge of this modernity. Without trying to fit African American relationships in the age of emancipation into preconceived and arbitrary concepts of modernity, we are better able to understand the African American experience during the Civil War era—and understanding the broader African American experience can reshape our perspectives about the nature and meaning of the Civil War.[26]

"She Is a Member of the 23rd"

Lucy Nichols and the Community of the Civil War Regiment

Barbara A. Gannon

Amid the Spanish American War in 1898, the *Salem* (Indiana) *Democrat* reported on a reunion of a Civil War regiment—the Twenty-Third Indiana Volunteer Infantry. The newspaper did not use this gathering to remind their readers of how these men's heroism might inspire contemporary U.S. soldiers, as some might have thought. Nor did the reporter promote sectional reunion by neglecting the role of race and slavery in the causes and consequences of the Civil War, as some scholars might have expected. Instead, the article included a lengthy description of a former slave, "Aunt Lucy Nichols, an aged colored lady, who is known and loved by every member of the regiment." She "attached herself to [this unit] at Bolivar, Tenn., in 1862." Nichols served as a nurse in the regimental hospital and returned to New Albany, Indiana, with the Twenty-Third after the war ended. While this essay focuses on her wartime service, her obituary in the *New York Times* emphasized the government's recognition of her status. She was "pensioned by the Government for her service in the civil war as a nurse." The *Salem Democrat* explains both her status at the reunion and her government pension. She "attracted more attention . . . than any other one member of the regiment—for virtually, she is a member of the 23rd," a surprising characterization for an African American woman. A close examination of Lucy Nichols's life and that of her comrades reveals that "actually" is a better word than "virtually."[1]

Most students of the Civil War would reject the notion that Lucy Nichols was a member of the regiment, since gender and race mattered in these organizations. Lucy could not have belonged because she was a woman, and only men were accepted in Civil War units. Even if she disguised herself as a man, as some women did, the Twenty-Third was a white regiment and did not enroll African Americans. Moreover, membership in the regiment was clearly defined as the men who appeared on the muster roll—those legally enlisted in its ranks—and

Lucy had not officially enrolled in the regiment. Finally, the regiment's temporal boundaries were its wartime existence; it was born on the day it recruited its first member, and it died when it mustered out of service and its soldiers went home. Even if she was a member of the Twenty-Third in wartime, she could not be considered a member thirty-three years after the war ended. Much of the focus of this essay might have been on how Lucy's membership in this regiment transcended race and gender roles; instead, it will explain what her membership says about the regiment—the Civil War's primary military organization.[2]

The community of the regiment, as understood by its members, was not always the same as the official military organization defined by the army. Instead, membership in a regiment had more to do with the shared suffering of men and, in this case, a woman, than with the official muster roll. Moreover, it was not so much the "red badge of courage"—battlefield wounds—that created this fellowship; instead, it was suffering that occurred between battles by soldiers who were on the march, exposed to the elements, and subject to diseases that were endemic to Civil War regiments. In a unit that lost twice as many men to disease as combat, it is not surprising that Lucy Nichols's service as a nurse in the regimental hospital explains her status in the Twenty-Third Indiana. After the war, the survivors of this regiment, including men whom Lucy had treated in the hospital, fought to obtain a pension for her service, rejecting the government's official definition of membership in the regiment. While the struggle for Lucy's pension demonstrates her status in the regiment, it also explains the regiment's enduring nature. By the Twenty-Third's 1898 reunion, she and her comrades had suffered for decades in peacetime from the wartime diseases—one of the lesser-known legacies of the Civil War. Because she both alleviated and shared these men's suffering, it would have been difficult to imagine that Lucy would have been considered anything but a member of the community of the regiment. While this study represents the story of one woman and one regiment, it suggests new ways to examine these organizations. If an African American woman was considered a member of an all-white, all-male unit, we may need a more expansive definition of the community of the Civil War regiment.

The communal nature of a Civil War regiment makes more sense if you understand that Civil War regiments were recruited in local communities. According to its regimental history, "The 23rd Regiment [was] raised in the southern part of the State of Indiana, . . . its entire enlistment having come from the border counties of Floyd, Clark, Harrison and Crawford, with the exception of a large portion of one company and a few members of the other companies who came from Washington County, and a score or more loyal Kentuckians." In the twentieth century, the U.S. Army turned away from this practice, partially because of the disproportionate impact of heavy casualties incurred by locally recruited units on American communities. While this was one disadvantage of the practice, localized recruiting also had advantages. Civilians readily enlisted in volunteer regiments because the community expected them to do so. Moreover, long after recruits' initial enthusiasm waned in the face of war's harsh reality, soldiers continued to fight because they feared the judgment of their neighbors and the stigma of cowardice. The membership of an African American woman from Tennessee in a regiment composed of white men from small towns in southern Indiana can be explained only by a more expansive definition of the community of the Civil War regiment.[3]

To understand why Lucy Nichols belonged to the Twenty-Third, you must understand the nature of the Civil War regiment—both the official regiment constructed by the Federal Army, and the reality of the regiment shaped by the experience of the Civil War. While states recruited volunteer regiments, they did so according to army regulations. This guidance, provided by the national government, varied based on the unit's purpose. While the government organized cavalry and artillery regiments differently, most Civil War soldiers served in infantry regiments comprising one thousand soldiers—ten combat-oriented companies of one hundred men. Despite the army's notion of what constituted an ideal regiment, few Civil War regiments met this standard. Instead, they usually enrolled closer to three hundred or four hundred soldiers. The official regiment did not last long in the reality of Civil War campaigning, as soldiers were lost to illness, wounds, desertion, and death.[4]

The Twenty-Third Indiana was no different from most Civil War regiments; it was considered a "regiment" with far less than the full complement of one thousand soldiers. Officially, it mustered in July 1861 and was accepted for federal service at full strength as a three-year regiment. At the end of three years of hard campaigning, the regiment had fewer than 500 men; only 280 veterans reenlisted and served until the end of the war. Official records document some of these losses. The Twenty-Third suffered four officers and sixty-eight enlisted men killed in action or died of wounds, and two officers and 143 enlisted men died of disease. If the regiment started with one thousand men, and by 1864 it had five hundred men, at least three hundred men were not accounted for in this calculation. The regimental historian, its former adjutant, discussed these missing soldiers and argued that uncounted in the official record were "the great numbers that were necessarily discharged from service on account of disease contracted and wounds received." Even this broader definition ignores another type of casualty, soldiers who were sickened but stayed in the ranks. Men like Granville Holtsclaw suffered from a painful bladder disease and left the regiment only when his enlistment ended. His disease was not documented until he filed for a pension decades after the regiment mustered out. The diseases that affected men like Holtsclaw explain why the Twenty-Third in 1865 was not the same regiment that left Indiana, convinced that the war would end quickly after a few short and relatively bloodless battles. The regiment in 1861 had no place for an African American nurse. In contrast, the community of the regiment in 1865, ravaged by four long years of campaigning, embraced Lucy Nichols and accepted her into its fellowship.[5]

Who was Lucy Nichols, and how did she end up joining an all-white, all-male regiment? Like most African American men and women accompanying the Union Army, she was a former slave. We know more about her than did many of her compatriots because her owners died and, like any other piece of property, others inherited her. An inventory of property documented Lucy's birth on April 10, 1838, in Halifax, North Carolina. Later she and her owners, a husband and a wife, moved to Tennessee, where the couple died. Because her new owner, the couple's daughter, was a minor, Lucy lived with her owner's guardian in Mississippi. In 1848, litigation prompted a judge to order Lucy, known as "said property," turned over to the minor; once again Lucy moved, this time back to Tennessee. Lucy was ten years old, and it is likely she never saw her family again. Slavery may have destroyed her first family, but in Tennessee she tried to recreate another, though slavery limited her ability to do so. She had a husband, but slaves were not legally married. She also had a child, whose fate was out of her hands. In 1860 another legal action involving heirs threatened her family. Fortunately, she and her child stayed together. This reminder of her family's vulnerability may explain why, in the summer of 1862, she escaped with her husband and baby and joined the Twenty-Third Indiana at Bolivar, Tennessee. She may have been hesitant about fleeing; Lincoln had not even announced the preliminary Emancipation Proclamation, so at that point the war was for Union, slavery and all. But she may have been willing to take this risk. Lucy understood that her family had no legal protection; her owner could die and "said property" would be scattered among heirs. Sadly, this desperate measure failed; her husband and baby both died during her service with the Twenty-Third Indiana.[6]

Before these twin tragedies, Lucy Nichols found her place in the Twenty-Third as a nurse in the regimental hospital. Because the ideal Civil War regiment that mustered in at the beginning of the war had been designed for combat, it did not have enough personnel to provide important support functions such as cooking, cleaning, and building fortifications. Since white soldiers were trained for combat duties, and likely unwilling to perform these other functions, Civil War regiments hired formerly enslaved African Americans to provide these services. Unlike Lucy, these men and women were considered employees and never became part of the regiment. Lucy was different because she worked in the hospital as a nurse, as opposed to a laundress or cook, and because she was not actually an employee. She had no official status in the hospital because she could not—female nurses were not officially allowed in frontline regiments. Magnus Brucker, the surgeon who hired her, left no explanation for why, in the face of this prohibition, he employed her as a nurse. It is only a matter of conjecture, but he likely required more staff; officially, a regimental hospital staff consisted of a surgeon, an assistant surgeon, and a hospital steward. But a surgeon needed more than two men to assist him as he dealt with battlefield casualties and the day-to-day medical needs of a Civil War regiment. Because she had no official status, Lucy never received any money for her service during the war, and in its aftermath she struggled to obtain a nurse's pension.[7]

Her postwar efforts to receive recompense for her wartime service documented Lucy Nichols's role in the community of the regiment. Despite her unofficial status, the men of the Twenty-Third supported her efforts to obtain a pension. Benjamin Welker testified to her service: "I was sick in the regimental hospital and claimant waited on, gave me medicine, and took care of me in every way." He also observed her "waiting on and caring for the sick and wounded soldiers." An assistant surgeon, who served for less than a year in the hospital, agreed: "She was a good and faithful nurse rendering great aid and comfort to the sick." John S. McPheeters, who replaced Brucker when he was promoted to brigade surgeon, also testified to her service. By the time he joined the regiment in 1863, she had been a nurse for at least eight months. When he arrived, "She was waiting on the sick in the hospital and I got the impression she was regularly employed by the surgeon." When McPheeters became surgeon, he must have realized that Lucy had no official status, particularly when he was not required to pay her any salary. The coming and goings of Brucker and McPheeters suggest one reason the regiment accepted Lucy: she was one of the few permanent fixtures in this important institution. Because she played such a central role in caring for the sick and injured, over such a long period, she was considered part of the community of the regiment, even though she never formally enlisted in this unit.[8]

Enlisted or not, Lucy Nichols provided an important service to the Twenty-Third Indiana; like most Civil War regiments, it had its sick and its wounded.

Magnus Brucker described the regiment's first significant engagement—the Battle of Shiloh—to his wife: "You will have heard about the bloody battle, details you can best find out from the newspapers. My regiment lost 8 men and 42 injured, my hospital was three times surrounded by the enemy on Monday." The regimental historian explained that the "loss of the 23rd [at Shiloh] was not extremely heavy"; however, this experience might have prompted Brucker to reassess his medical staff and, later that year, hire Lucy. Since Shiloh was the regiment's first battle and certainly not its last, Lucy would have her chance at caring for the wounded. In fact, the regiment's greatest battles occurred during the Vicksburg Campaign, when Lucy served as a regimental nurse. In May 1863 the Twenty-Third fought at Port Gibson, and Brucker described the battle: it "lasted the whole day on the first of May, it was a terrible . . . my regiment had 4 dead, and 23 injured, a few of those will still die." He had not yet seen the regiment's worst day; at Raymond on the road to Vicksburg, 127 officers and men were killed, wounded, or missing. Lucy's nursing would have been critical to the survival of wounded soldiers that terrible day.[9]

Despite its participation in these battles, the Twenty-Third was not considered one of the hardest-fighting regiments of the war. Given the nature of the regiments' official organization, it was designed for battle; the fact that regiments were assessed based on their performance in combat is not surprising. While there is no official rating for Civil War regiments, William Fox's study *Regimental Losses in the Civil War* set the standard for identifying hard-fighting regiments, and the standard was difficult to meet. To be considered a hard-fighting regiment, Fox declared, a unit must have "lost over 130 in killed and died of wounds during the war, together with a few whose losses were somewhat smaller, but whose percentage of killed entitles them to a place in the list" of hard-fighting units. Because most Civil War regiments did not meet this requirement, Fox recognized that "large casualty lists are not necessarily indicative of the fighting qualities of a regiment; that on many occasions, regiments have rendered valuable service and achieved a brilliant success with but slight loss." Since, in the long run, more soldiers died of disease than wounds, combat may be only one way to assess the sacrifices of Civil War regiments. This was certainly true in a regiment like the Twenty-Third, which lost twice as many to disease as it did in battle.[10]

While the ideal regiment was organized for and judged by its combat performance, in reality, combat represented a series of short segments in the life of most Civil War regiments, including the Twenty-Third Indiana. This regiment served long and hard in the western theater of operations; it was recruited in the summer of 1861 and it mustered out in summer of 1865. Ultimately, the regiment campaigned for more than 1,400 days. Outside of long sieges at Vicksburg and Atlanta, the experience of battle represented about 1 percent, or 14 days, of the regiment's service; sieges, 123 days, not even 10 percent. Not surprisingly, members of the Twenty-Third evaluated their regiment based on the harsh campaigning that occurred between battles—the 1,000 days of marching, through long summers and harsh winters.[11]

More than remembering a fighting regiment, soldiers and veterans of the Twenty-Third Indiana remember their unit as a marching regiment. The notion that marching is as important as fighting is evident in the regimental history, which places as much emphasis on the regiment marches as it does on their battles. In fact, the regimental historian argues that marching may be the Twenty-Third's most distinguishing characteristic: "Was [there] any regiment whose campaign was more extensive or covered so vast a territory as that of the 23rd? When it is considered that in leaving its rendezvous at New Albany Indiana, for the field, it marched *west* and during the succeeding four years accomplished a complete circle of fully 3,000 miles, returning home from the *east*, and at no time retracing its steps except in detours from its great circular journey." The regimental historian begins the narrative of a marching regiment with its first short march. Though it was only eight miles, he explains, it "was an extremely severe one" because the men carried "heavy knapsack and personal belongings that the raw recruit was want to equip himself—though he learned better later." As time passed, the raw recruit became hardened. By November 1861, the historian explained, the Twenty-Third "marched consecutively forty-one hours without even time to cook a meal." By spring 1862, the regimental historian argued, it was marching as much as fighting that hardened this unit's raw recruits. Describing the regiment before its first battle at Shiloh, Tennessee, he explained that though the "23rd had not been engaged in the heated contest of any great battles," it was a veteran regiment because "it had a severe campaign experience in the way of arduous marches and a number of skirmishes." He defined the regiment based first on marching and second on its skirmishes—minor, short-lived engagements with the enemy. If marching, not fighting, defines the regiment, someone like Lucy Nichols, who marched all the way from Bolivar, Tennessee, through the heart of the Confederacy, and back to Indiana, could be considered a member.[12]

While the regimental historian looked back on the Civil War from a distance, letters from the men of the Twenty-Third Indiana during the war confirmed that the dominant factors in their life related to the periods between battles, particularly their life on the march. Lucy Nichols left no letters; she was illiterate during the war and illiterate thirty years later when she applied for a pension. However, two men who served by her side wrote letters: the doctor who hired her, Magnus Brucker, and his successor, Dr. John S. McPheeters. In March 1862, Brucker opened his letter to his wife with news of the march: "Dear wife, after a 3 day march, 25 miles every day . . ." Civil War letters often open with a commentary on the soldier's most recent march. Similarly, in March 1864, his colleague Dr. McPheeters began his letter home in this way: "My dear wife, we arrived in camp from our long march." In the same letter, McPheeters explains why marching may have been more important than fighting in this regiment: "We marched nearly two hundred miles into the heart of the confederacy without a regular battle." If a unit marched that far and did not fight a single major engagement, it is not surprising that its members defined their service and their sacrifice based on marching and not fighting. Finally, the article in the *Salem Democrat* identified the Twenty-Third as a marching regiment when explaining Lucy's status: "For three years she accompanied the gallant old regiment in all of its weary marches. She was present at every siege and battle in which the regiment was engaged." The weary marches of this long-serving regiment created a regimental community that included Lucy, even if she was not officially enrolled in the regiment.[13]

When these men marched, they also were exposed to the elements; they trudged over thousands of miles through four long winters. While letters sent home seemed less willing to burden the home front with the suffering endured on the march, the regiment's history and postwar pension records describe the harsh conditions these men experienced as they marched through the heart of the Confederacy. The regimental historian begins in the regiment's first winter in 1861: "The troops were compelled to ford numerous streams, often more than waist-deep, and wagons and artillery were buried in the mud and swamped in the streams, to the extent that compelled the infantry at all times to furnish assistance in order that the wagon trains might be moved at all. . . . The entire distance going and returning was scarcely 150 miles, yet it required the greatest of effort, constant labor and much suffering to complete the journey in twelve days." Early in 1862, the weather worsened, "snow fell to the depth of six inches, freezing at night and thawing in the daytime." Lack of proper equipment exacerbated this suffering. "The regiment was absolutely without blankets or other protection than ordinary clothing." It was no better in the winter of 1863; according to the regiment's historian, the weather "was extremely severe, because of the extraordinary cold and heavy snows followed by thaws that made the roads impassable." The evidence of soldiers' pension claims supports the regimental history. A veteran of the Twenty-Third described the harsh conditions that led to his postwar illness. In "February 1862 [the regiment] marched through snow, ice, and mud" and "had to wade through icy streams several times, and at night [slept] at night in wet clothing, with no shelter. Snow and rain falling, we had to spend the night as best we could, not even having an ax to cut fuel for fires. We spent a miserable night, from the effects of which I contracted a severe cold."[14]

A marching regiment may not have experienced as many injuries from battle, but it certainly suffered due to the diseases endemic in Civil War regiments that strained the limited resources of a regimental hospital. We know something about the typical workload in the Twenty-Third's hospital because Dr. McPheeters's letters include an account of the number of men in the hospital and how this related to the health of the regiment. In September 1863 he wrote his wife that "the health [of our regiment] seems to be getting better, at least we have not so many sick now, there are only four in the hospital now and none of them are very sick." Later, in December 1863, he described the health of the regiment as "pretty good . . . we have six [patients] in the hospital." Since regimental hospitals usually had room for eight patients, resources must have been inadequate when the regiment was not in good health. Despite McPheeters's favorable report, he describes two of his six patients as "not out of danger, yet," suggesting that the regiment could be in relatively good shape while some of its members were gravely ill. Based on McPheeters's statements, both made when the regiment was in relatively good health, we can assume that the hospital may sometimes have had more patients than it could reasonably handle, placing quite a burden on Lucy Nichols and her colleagues.[15]

While the letters of the regimental surgeons, McPheeters and Brucker, survived to document life in the regimental hospital, neither man provided a full accounting of this organization because neither man stayed with this regiment as long as Lucy Nichols did. None of the official staff stayed for long: surgeons and assistant surgeons resigned or were promoted, and enlisted men assigned to the hospital on temporary duty came and went. Ironically, it was because she had not officially joined the regiment that she stayed at the hospital. Since she had not been assigned, she could not be reassigned. Given her longevity and the endemic nature of disease in a Civil War regiment, Lucy may have cared for almost every man in her regiment at one point or another. Lorenzo Emory, who supported Lucy's pension application, described his own service in the hospital; he served as an orderly for eight months. Emory explained that after he left, Lucy "still remained a nurse in the hospital until said regiment was mustered out." It was Lucy, more than anyone else, who stayed in the hospital, across a continent, with

Sherman to the sea, and beyond. Lucy was a permanent fixture in the regimental hospital through more than one thousand days of its service.[16]

Lucy Nichols's place in the regiment relied on understanding that not all members of the regiment were equal; the way the unit measured a person's service favored Lucy. Longevity mattered in the Twenty-Third Indiana; distinctions were made based on when you enlisted and how long you stayed. The evidence of this inequality is found in the muster roll the regiment published after it mustered out, a document that reflected the community of the regiment's understanding of the relative merit of its members, and not the army's categorization of enlisted personnel. The army had one rank for men who were neither noncommissioned nor commissioned officers; they were privates. In contrast, the postwar regimental muster had another designation: recruit. The postwar roll divided enlisted soldiers into two broad categories: those who joined the regiment in 1861 were privates; in contrast, men who came to the regiment after its first term expired were listed as recruits. In addition, the roster carefully noted whether a private reenlisted and was a "veteran," as opposed to someone who left after his first term. Moreover, if a soldier was drafted or served as a substitute, this point was also noted in the margins. The muster role for Company A listed Christ Holschward as a private and a veteran; he enlisted July 1861 and mustered out July 1865. Joseph Heirizman enlisted at the same time as Holschward, and he was also considered a private, but not a veteran. He mustered out after three years and did not reenlist. Finally, William C. Aspy was drafted in October 1864 and designated as a recruit. Since he served until the regiment mustered out in July 1865, he was not an inexperienced soldier—in modern terms, a recruit—when the war ended. Based on these distinctions, Lucy was a veteran; she enlisted in the regiment during its first term and stayed with it for another term. As a woman, she was subject to neither the draft nor service as a substitute. She could not have been accused of enlisting for a bounty or any other financial motive; the men probably knew she received no compensation for her service. If a substitute who came to the unit in the last year of the war was included on this roster, Lucy, a veteran volunteer, must have been considered a member of the regiment.[17]

Ironically, Lucy Nichols's status as a veteran was confirmed by the time she spent away from the hospital. She accompanied members of the Twenty-Third Indiana home on furlough in 1864, a privilege given only to veterans who reenlisted for the last year of the war. The regimental history notes this important milestone: "In the latter part of March [1864] the regiment left Vicksburg on the regulation 30-day furlough and returned in a body . . . to New Albany . . . and the members dispersed to various homes for a much needed rest." When members of the Twenty-Third needed evidence to prove her service, they often used this furlough to bolster their case. John Sandlewick cited both her service and her break in service when he supported her pension claim: "Dr. Brucker employed her to attend to the sick and wounded, she made a useful and industrious nurse. The regiment was furloughed after the surrender of Vicksburg, and came home, and they told me that [Lucy] came home with them and went back when they went back." Sandlewick suggest that her time on furlough, as much as her work in the hospital, demonstrated that she deserved a pension. Lorenzo Emory drew the same connection when he provided evidence of Lucy's service. She "came with them to New Albany on a veteran furlough and went back with the regiment. She was a good nurse and was with the regiment at Atlanta and Vicksburg." Emory goes one step further than Sandlewick and describes her participation in the furlough before he discusses her service in some of the regiment's hard-fought campaigns.[18]

While furloughs were an intermission, mustering out—when their regiment and its soldiers were discharged from the service—represented the war's final act. Though Lucy Nichols did not enlist, she and other members of the Twenty-Third claimed that she mustered out with the regiment in Indianapolis. Going home with the regiment on furlough and coming back to the front lines may have been unusual, but someone who had not enlisted in the regiment might have made the trip. In contrast, being "mustered out" was a specific term that referred to the government's need to discharge soldiers and complete other important administrative tasks, such as calculating a veteran's final pay. Despite the fact that Lucy did not enlist and did not need a discharge, members of the regiment insisted that she mustered out with the regiment. John McPheeters, among others, mentioned this final process when he supported Lucy's pension. Lucy, he claims, "was with the regiment as a nurse till we were mustered out in 1865." Lorenzo Emory explained that after the furlough, and after the regiment's extended campaigning in the South, Lucy arrived in "Indianapolis, Ind. where she was relieved when we were mustered out." Lucy uses the exact same language in her deposition—"we were mustered out"—to describe the end of her Civil War service. Lucy's participation in the final muster of the regiment cements the notion that the regiment in 1865 was not what the army said it was by 1861; instead, it was a community whose members created its boundaries.[19]

After the Twenty-Third Indiana, the volunteer infantry regiment organized by the state of Indiana, mustered out, the community of the regiment did not. While the bonds of friendship and the memory of their shared service explained some of this longevity, their suffering in the postwar era explains the survival of the regiment decades after the war ended. Members of the regiment who had reported for sick call to the Twenty-Third Indiana's regimental hospital continued to suffer because of their wartime service. Of course, these veterans were not alone; all Union soldiers suffered. One indicator of their postwar misery was the pensions the government gave to veterans for their service. No one should be surprised that, according to a report on pensions submitted to Congress, the greatest number of pensions—117,947—had been awarded for gunshots or shell shots. The number of pensions given to soldiers in the next largest pension category, those made chronically ill by the war, may be more remarkable. The government awarded 55,125 pensions for one of the greatest killers of veterans, chronic diarrhea, and 40,790 pensions were awarded for rheumatism. The battered survivors of the regiment, including Lucy, qualified for these benefits.[20]

The government did not give her this pension without a fight. Only a concerted effort by the community of the regiment allowed her to receive these payments. It was not that there were no benefits for women who had served; after 1892, nurses received pensions from the government. Lucy Nichols seemed a natural candidate because of her long service in a frontline regiment. Ironically, her service in a combat unit hurt her application. Women were not supposed to be in regimental hospitals. This explains why she did not have an official status in the regiment: there were no positions for a female nurse in the formal bureaucratic entity of an infantry regiment. Only nurses with an official status in the army, those who served further from combat, received pensions.[21]

The men and the woman of the Twenty-Third Infantry did not let this bureaucracy stop them. Members of the regiment swore affidavits testifying to her service. They were able to do so because, to give credit where credit is due, the government did not immediately reject her claim. As part of the government's review, the Pension Bureau appointed a special examiner to adjudicate her case. He gathered a number of affidavits from members of the Twenty-Third, including Dr. McPheeters, Lorenzo Emory, and John Sandlewick; earlier discussions of Lucy Nichols's wartime service used these depositions to describe her wartime activities. Ultimately, the special examiner decided that she deserved this pension. The pension examiner agreed that Lucy "has no documentary evidence of her employment by anyone having authority of the War Department"; however, "her claim is one of merit and should be allowed." He was overruled by his superiors, and she did not receive her pension. The men and woman of the Twenty-Third refused to accept this limited definition of Civil War service and turned to

Congress for a solution. More than fifty members of the Twenty-Third Indiana, one of whom could only sign his name with an *X*, petitioned Congress, and a special bill passed granting Lucy a twelve-dollar-a-month pension.[22]

While this pension could be understood as a token of their gratitude for her wartime service, or as an act of charity for an elderly woman, a close examination of Lucy Nichols's pension records and that of her comrades demonstrate that they all suffered from the same type of chronic illnesses—a lasting legacy of their wartime service. In addition to experiencing the same debilitating conditions, members of the Twenty-Third needed one another to testify to the severity of their condition and its connection to their wartime service. The battered survivors of the Twenty-Third relied on the community of the regiment to support their efforts to receive much-needed pensions.

Lucy Nichols's files and that of the men in her regiment support the Pension Bureau's report to Congress; chronic diarrhea was the most common ailment. According to her physician's affidavit, Lucy suffered from "Chronic Diarrhea, Chronic Bronchitis, and rheumatism, among other ailments." While Lucy, like most veterans, reported more than one ailment, she and her comrades seem best able to prove the debilitating nature of diarrhea. Her doctor relied on this condition to verify that she was unable to work, a critical factor in receiving a pension: "She has periodical attacks of trouble with her bowels, and those attacks are very debilitating, during which she is confined to her bed and is not able to work at all." Lucy Nichols was not alone. An examination of the pension records of the men who supported Lucy's pension fight revealed that diarrhea seemed to be a common problem. Lorenzo Emory, who testified to Lucy's service as nurse, received a pension for this illness. A friend describes the debilitating effect of this disease on Emory: "I have known him to have a spell of diarrhea so that he is confined to the house and at these times have frequently visited him. This has been his condition ever since his discharge and at times it has been worse than at others." Alexander Banks, who also supported Lucy's application, "live[d] on bread toasted and mashed potatoes because of this condition." Benjamin B. John may have backed Lucy's petition because he spent time in the regimental hospital with chronic diarrhea. A witness testified to the effect of this illness during the war: "He came home on furlough about the poorest living human that I ever saw suffering with chronic diarrhea from which he has been a continual sufferer ever since his discharge from the Army." Decatur S. Jocelyn suffered from chronic diarrhea, though his doctors did not agree on how often it occurred. One doctor claimed it was once a month, another once a week. After examining the pension files, it is evident that chronic diarrhea may have been the number-one reason the government awarded pensions, since it was easy to prove. Diarrhea affected the rectum in a very visible way. John's physician detailed the effect of this disease: his "rectum is inflamed, sensitive and bleeding; inflammation will not admit use of instrument." Recruits who mustered into the Twenty-Third in 1861 might have been less enthusiastic if they knew that the price they would pay for their service included a decades-long struggle to control their bowels.[23]

The importance of the community of the Twenty-Third may be illustrated by the challenges faced by a veteran who had moved away from Indiana. Charles Kepley served in the Twenty-Third, but at some point he moved to Chicago, far from other members of his regiment. Like many of his comrades, Kepley suffered from chronic diarrhea and rheumatism. In addition, he had two hernias— one from his Civil War service, and another from a workplace accident. Unlike most pensioners with chronic diarrhea, he had difficulty proving it. One set of doctors confirmed the diagnosis; another set decided it was cured. Similarly, some physicians found his hernias; others did not. All doctors agreed that he was "feeble, anemic, and emaciated," suggesting that he had some serious illness. Because of this confusion, the government stopped his pension, and he had to fight to get it back. A careful reading of this file demonstrates the obstacles confronting pensioners who did not have the support of their regiment when confronting the pension bureaucracy.[24]

Remaining a member of the community mattered, because a successful pension application usually included some reference to the applicant's wartime service, so veterans relied on the testimony of other members of their regiment for this evidence. This was particularly true when the disability's connection to wartime service was difficult to prove. Granville Holtsclaw needed support when he applied for a pension based on severe bladder and kidney problems. He relied on his comrade Beal Spurrier to support his claim. Spurrier remembered an incident on picket duty near Vicksburg. Holtsclaw "retired a short distance to urinate. He noticed that Holtsclaw while urinating "groaned and ground his teeth and seemed to suffer great pain." Later, Spurrier noticed that Holtsclaw's "urine . . . was quite bloody, [and] seemed at least half blood and was scant in quantity." When John Knowland claimed he "contracted blindness in both eyes while on Sherman's march to the sea," he agreed that the connection to his wartime service might be tenuous. He could not "assign any particular cause, only the hardships of said march." To support his claim, he called on witnesses from his regiment to demonstrate that this disability occurred during his service. In response, one veteran remembered that Knowland "sometimes had to be led as he complained that he could not see how to travel on account of his bad eyes." More specifi-

Lucy Nichols (*center*) at a reunion of her regiment, circa 1890s. (Courtesy of the
New Albany–Floyd County Public Library)

cally, Dr. John McPheeters stated authoritatively that Knowland "was afflicted by
blindness in the service" and that he "contracted [this disease] while in the line
of duty . . . with the regiment on 'Sherman's March to the Sea.'" A pension examiner wrote "good" on McPheeters's affidavit. The community of the regiment
remained intact, if for no other reason than to support its members' efforts to
receive pensions for service-related illnesses decades after the war ended.[25]

Perhaps the most tangible way a regiment defined itself in the postwar world
was at reunions, like the one described by the *Salem Democrat*. Perhaps the reporter described Lucy Nichols as "virtually" a member of the regiment because
he could not challenge the notion that the regiment was anything but a military organization that excluded an African American woman. Despite his re-
luctance, the members of the Twenty-Third left their own record of a reunion
that proved her membership in this organization. The pension examiner who
supported Lucy's claim cited this evidence as proof that she deserved a pension:

"As evidence of the esteem in which she is held by the regiment for her attention and professional proficiency in nursing the sick and wounded the regiment at a recent reunion they had themselves photographed with claimant the central figure in the group." In this picture, in the center of the regiment, surrounded by the men of the Twenty-Third was the woman of the Twenty-Third. Confident of her place in the community of her regiment, she stands at the end of long journey that began as a slave, passed around by the guardians of white children, and ended when she marched all the way home to New Albany, Indiana. While she died at the beginning of the twentieth century, the memory of Lucy and her regiment live on in the twenty-first. The Carnegie Center for Art and History in her hometown hosts a permanent exhibit honoring Lucy Nichols's life and legacy. A regiment can live forever, if only in the hearts of its community.[26]

Afterword:
On Mark Neely

An Appreciation

Harold Holzer

When I first encountered Mark Neely some thirty-three years ago, he was half-submerged in a snowdrift.

Along with the late architectural photographer Joseph Farber, I had arrived in what was then his base, Fort Wayne, Indiana, the previous night in the teeth of a raging winter storm, on the last flight in before the airport shut down. The next morning, we somehow commandeered a taxi from our motel to the Lincoln National Life Foundation to keep our appointment with its director. Our prearranged plan was to research and photograph the institution's Lincoln sculptures. But we found the sidewalks unplowed, the doors locked.

Cell phones had yet to be invented—it was 1978—but somehow our driver found a nearby phone booth, from which I called the missing director at home. "You're actually here?" Mark Neely asked, clearly astounded. "Well, my street has not been cleared yet. Can you pick me up on the corner?"

Off we drove again, to the intersection nearest his address. After five minutes, out of a large, undisturbed field of white, emerged a tall, blade-thin figure wearing earmuffs, a long scarf, a dark-gray overcoat now dappled with white snow, and knee-high rubber boots. Within minutes he had agreeably cleared a path toward the museum doors and opened its treasures to us. No one else ventured inside that day.

I do not recall how long this diversion took, but I do know that Mark has never kept me waiting since. Over three decades marked by repeat visits to Fort Wayne, frequent collaborations, long phone conversations, research trips throughout the country, and public events in Gettysburg, Washington, North Carolina, Virginia, New York, New England, and countless other venues, in fair and foul weather alike, he was never, ever late. Mark Neely is the most reliable man I've ever known. He does not commit to do everything. But if and when he does, he arrives on time and performs at full throttle. And as I have said many times over the years, when he is at his best, which is often, no one is better. He is a consummate professional.

When Mark Neely arrived at the foundation in the mid-1970s to become its director, he brought those already-high standards to a major collection still arranged around the principles of a mid-sized house museum. Mark plunged himself into bringing coherence to the displays and scholarly insight to the newsletter, meanwhile extending a welcome mat to fellow historians. He was the third director to bear the title of "Doctor," but the first to have earned the PhD in postgraduate studies (his predecessors held, respectively, a divinity degree and an honorary one).

Mark never drove this disparity home, but I knew it meant something to the scholars who quickly benefited from the rigor he brought to the archives and the publications. I suspect it meant something to Mark as well—until, that is, in an incident I only heard about second-hand, he was awoken from a deep sleep one night at one of the motels he frequented on his Lincoln's Birthday lecture tours. "Dr. Neely, come quickly," came the voice on the other end of the phone. "A guest is sick and this is an emergency." Thereafter he instructed his assistant to register him as *Mr.* Mark Neely.

Those lecture tours were never the favorite part of the job for Mark—difficult as it is to believe that one would not want to leave a warm house and comfortable office in the middle of February to tool around the Midwest by car. Even so, Mark performed at peak energy, even if inclement crowds limited attendance to a handful.

I cannot recall with precision how we arrived at the idea of collaborating on a book about Lincoln iconography. I know we had communicated often during the early 1980s on the subject of Lincoln print portraits. He was invariably encouraging about the early articles I contributed to magazines and journals—though if pressed, he allowed himself to offer a useful critique as well.

These were the days before scans and PDFs. I was forever borrowing foundation photographs (at bargain prices, thanks to Mark) to use as illustrations for these articles. I think that eventually I mentioned I might like to do a book. The only known "competition" was an outdated, overpriced catalogue raisonné of which, inexplicably, only the second volume had ever been published. Mark, who had already authored *The Abraham Lincoln Encyclopedia* (still, along with *The Collected Works of Lincoln*, the most used and weather-beaten book in my library), said he would be interested in doing so, too. I had a choice: head off on my own with Mark merely as a resource for photoreproductions and advice, or suggest joining forces. I made the right decision.

Iconography was still a virgin field, and almost anything we contributed would have been an improvement over the handful of existing titles on the subject. We began with a goal of making a start—but in the back of our heads was the idea of doing something not only fresh but, hopefully, definitive. Mark initially brought two great assets to the project: a huge collection (from which we could publish without fees), and a word processor (the first between us) together with an assistant to do the final typing. Above all, he also brought infectious enthusiasm, sophisticated ideas, sharp insights, breathtaking knowledge of the sources, a great eye for pictures, and an authoritative and delightfully original way of expressing himself in writing.

Best of all, we quickly discovered that we shared a passion for research and an inexhaustible ability to go at it, frequently side by side at the Library of Congress or some other repository, for hours on end with few breaks in between. (Those who know Mark, even if they do not know me, will understand that like most people, I do require more food and at more frequent intervals than he does.) We quickly and wisely brought the historian Gabor Boritt into our triumvirate, and together enjoyed hours of travel in pursuit of the best examples of Lincoln engravings and lithographs, and the most useful data to document their use and detail their impact. Some wag dubbed us the "Nairobi Trio" (a dated reference, perhaps, but familiar to anyone who remembers the comedian Ernie Kovacs and his simian jazz band from early television). Because I got top billing on our first book, someone else nicknamed us "Harold, 'et,' and 'al.,'" which of course Mark found amusing and unthreatening.

Astonishingly, thinking back on it, the three of us seldom worked in the same room at the same time, whether in the library or at the typewriter. Relying on marathon phone calls, frequent debate, one ten-hour rewrite session at a motel in Gettysburg, and mutual editing distributed by mail, we produced what I think was a groundbreaking book that not only still holds up but, just as we hoped, has inspired new respect for visual sources and renewed interest in the field of Civil War–era iconography. We squabbled from time to time, as expected, but I can honestly say I have never had so much fun at any other time of my professional life. The day we opened an accompanying exhibition of original Lincoln prints at Gettysburg College we managed—thanks mostly to the pictures, not us—to bring the subject to life as seldom before: long-stored prints back on the walls where they had inspired the awe and reverence of religious icons during the Lincoln era. We had written about their impact. Now we, and the exhibition's visitors, really saw it for the first time ourselves.

Happily, the trio went on from *The Lincoln Image* (1984) to collaborate on *Changing the Lincoln Museum* (1985), long articles for the *Winterthur Portfolio* and the *American Art Journal*, and then another book, *The Confederate Image*

(1987), accompanied by another challenging print exhibition (it opened in a heat wave and power failure, which we feared would curl the paper). Boritt was the first to leave the team. Mark and I went on to coauthor *The Lincoln Family Album* (1990), *Mine Eyes Have Seen the Glory: The Civil War in Art* (1993), and *The Union Image* (2000). Some are actually still in print, and others have emerged from the backlists to become collectors' items on eBay. If you live long enough . . .

When I was asked by New York Governor Mario M. Cuomo to choose the best Lincoln scholars in the country to assemble a volume of Lincoln's writings on freedom and opportunity, I naturally enough turned to Mark for the chapter covering the signal years 1862–63. He developed theories about Lincoln's view of the Constitution and presidential power that have characterized his work, too. And Cuomo, a pretty fair writer himself, made certain we all got together twice, in New York City and Albany, to discuss the historical problem among ourselves, and with the public. The resulting book, *Lincoln on Democracy*, has appeared in English, Polish, Hebrew, Japanese, and even Indonesian.

I remain extremely proud of the work we did together. It was an enormous pleasure to research and write with so gifted and passionate a historian, and to share lecture stages at venues from the Metropolitan Museum of Art (my own longtime base) to rather more unexpected places, including the medical school at Richmond; the Jimmy Carter Presidential Library in Atlanta; a Southern-style barbecue in Dallas, North Carolina; and a Civil War group in Bromley. England, not to mention Lincoln Groups and Civil War Round Tables in New York, Washington, Chicago, Milwaukee, and Providence.

For me, though never averse to public speaking, the best of times were the research trips, in perennial search for what we called the "pistolette fumiere"— the holy grail of a single smoking gun discovery. These were the trips on which we battled restrictive house rules (infuriatingly, only five prints a day, apiece, at the Library of Congress), confronted occasionally indifferent librarians ("You want me to call up *what*?"), and then admired our own defiance over a glass of wine at day's end. Long ago, Mark suggested we keep a diary of these often frustrating trips and write an exposé on hostile curators and institutions that inhibit, rather than encourage, scholarship. Ultimately we decided that it should be our *final* project, published only when we were ready to hang up our spikes and never enter a research institution again. Fortunately, we are not ready yet.

A few years ago, to my delight, a university press approached me with the idea of bringing out an updated, corrected edition of *The Lincoln Family Album*, a volume issued initially by a major New York publisher, but marred by poor reproductions (bad news in a book about pictures). I knew that the family album project had always been dear to Mark's heart. It had been inspired by, and filled with, photographs from the long-unknown collection Mary Lincoln and her descendants had amassed from the 1850s until well into the twentieth century. Mark had purchased the originals for the museum in Fort Wayne years earlier, and its acquisition was perhaps the biggest of his curatorial career. Even so, I cautiously approached my old friend and colleague, who by this time had collected a couple of generations of students, a Pulitzer Prize for *The Fate of Liberty*, and a reputation for going at his projects quietly, and alone.

With a bit of gentle prodding, Mark agreed to coauthor a new introduction and go back to the original to weed out problems, and even to add a few illustrations we omitted from the commercial edition for lack of space. A good ten years had passed since we had last worked together, but we went at it as if we had merely poured tea, left the table to answer the front door, and returned a few minutes later to add milk and sugar. The beverage, not to torture the metaphor, was still hot. As always, we wrote individually (still essential since he now lived in Pennsylvania and I remained in New York), then compared and edited each other's texts, melded them together, and found a common voice that merged our distinctive styles into a voice that sounded a bit like each, but without revealing the secret of who composed what. (Note to prospective coauthors: we've always kept to ourselves the details of who held responsibility for which chapter. It works.)

It was like old times, only now via e-mail (it is extraordinary, maybe a tad depressing, to contemplate the technological innovations that have come—and in some cases, gone—since we first began working together). Here again were the vigorous discussions, the moments when we savored each other's latest research discovery or turn of phrase (it is good to know we have remained a mutual admiration society), the satisfaction in new themes robustly explored. Such experience never gets old, even when their authors do.

This ends—for now, I can always hope—my account of working with this amazing fellow. I have purposely ended with a phrase bracketed by an em dash as a bit of a private joke: Mark never liked em dashes, and loved to call me on my overuse of them. Sorry, Mark—one more for the road. I hope we have more opportunities in our dotage. As we used to write when we reached an impasse in our manuscripts and elected to skip to something else and resume the challenge later, "TK." Until then, I'm comforted to know from my new relationships with some of your students and disciples that you have made an equally strong impact on their lives, too, and now I cherish the activities I conduct with them. You have molded a class of historians devoted to your exacting standards and manifest professionalism. Like you, as the dazzling contributions to this book reflect, they are highly original and write beautifully. And as I have discovered, not surprisingly, they are always on time.

In one of the countless influential articles he has contributed over the years to the leading scholarly journals in the field, Mark E. Neely Jr. once revisited J. G. Randall's famous question, "Has the Lincoln Theme Been Exhausted?" He then laid out the challenges and opportunities for the new generation of scholars. It was more than a vague rallying cry to rescue the field for the future. Here, he declared, were precise subjects that needed study, revision, reinterpretation, and professional attention. That was more than three decades ago, and reflecting on the literature published since, it is simply staggering to note how many of Mark Neely's suggestions have in fact inspired important scholarship and publications.

Not surprisingly, many of the topics have been explored by Mark himself. And yet one remains convinced that the best is yet to come.

Notes

Introduction: New Answers for Old Questions
about the Civil War–Era North
Andrew L. Slap and *Michael Thomas Smith*

1. Eric Foner, *Reconstruction: American's Unfinished Revolution, 1863–1877* (New York: Harper & Row, 1988), xxiv, xxvii; James M. McPherson, *Battle Cry of Freedom: The Civil War Era* (New York: Oxford University Press, 1988), vii–viii.

2. Foner, *Reconstruction*, 23; McPherson, *Battle Cry of Freedom*, viii.

3. Avery O. Craven and James G. Randall were among the most prominent advocates of the "blundering generation" thesis (the phrase comes from the title of an article by Randall). See Thomas J. Pressley, *Americans Interpret Their Civil War* (New York: Free Press, 1962), 289–328; Arthur M. Schlesinger Jr., "The Causes of the Civil War: A Note on Historical Sentimentalism" *Partisan Review* (October 1949), 969–981; Allan Nevins, *The War for the Union*, 4 vols. (New York: Charles Scribner's Sons, 1959–71), 4:394–95. Michael F. Holt has advanced a neo–blundering generation interpretation with some of his work, most particularly *The Fate of Their Country: Politicians, Slavery Extension, and the Coming of the Civil War* (New York: Hill and Wang, 2004).

4. Melinda Lawson, *Patriot Fires: Forging a New American Nationalism in the Civil War North* (Lawrence: University Press of Kansas, 2002), 3, 181. For an excellent overview of some of this scholarship see Eric Foner, "Slavery, the Civil War, and Reconstruction," in Foner (ed.), *The New American History*, revised and expanded edition (Philadelphia: Temple University Press, 1997), 85–103.

5. James McPherson, *For Cause and Comrades: Why Men Fought in the Civil War* (New York: Oxford University Press, 1997), 120, 124; Chandra Manning, *What This Cruel War Was Over: Soldiers, Slavery, and the Civil War* (New York: Vintage, 2007), 219–21.

6. David W. Blight, *Race and Reunion: The Civil War in American Memory* (Cambridge: Harvard University Press, 2001), 2.

7. Heather Cox Richardson, *The Greatest Nation on Earth: Republican Economic Policies during the Civil War* (Cambridge: Harvard University Press, 1997), 1, 5.

8. Michael Vorenberg, *Final Freedom: The Civil War, the Abolition of Slavery, and the Thirteenth Amendment* (New York: Cambridge University Press, 2001), 6.

9. David W. Blight, *American Oracle: The Civil War in the Civil Rights Era* (Cambridge: Harvard University Press, 2011); David Goldfield, *America Aflame: How the Civil War*

Created a Nation (New York: Bloomsbury Press, 2011), 1; Adam Goodheart, *1861: The Civil War Awakening* (New York: Random House, 2011), 19.

10. Edward L. Ayers, *In the Presence of Mine Enemies: The Civil War in the Heart of America, 1859–1863* (New York: Norton, 2003), xx; Edward L. Ayers, "Worrying about the Civil War," in Ayers, *What Caused the Civil War? Reflections on the South and Southern History* (New York: Norton, 2006), 128–30.

11. Gary W. Gallagher, *The Confederate War: How Popular Will, Nationalism, and Military Strategy Could Not Stave Off Defeat* (Cambridge: Harvard University Press, 1999); Gallagher, *The Union War* (Cambridge: Harvard University Press, 2011), 153, 80–81.

12. Eric Foner, "Why the North Fought the Civil War," *New York Times Book Review*, May 1, 2011; Frank Towers, "Partisans, New History, and Modernization: The Historiography of the Civil War's Causes, 1861–2011," *Journal of the Civil War Era* 1, no. 2 (2011): 248, 238, 256.

13. "I wish the administration all success in its almost impossible task of governing this Distracted & anarchical People." William T. Sherman to John Sherman, April 8, 1861, in Brooks D. Simpson and Jean V. Berlin (eds.), *Sherman's Civil War: Selected Correspondence of William T. Sherman, 1860–1865* (Chapel Hill: University of North Carolina Press, 1999), 67.

"A Press That Speaks Its Opinions Frankly and Openly and Fearlessly": The Contentious Relationship between the Democratic Press and the Party in the Antebellum North
Matthew Isham

I would like to thank Dan Crofts, Andy Slap, and Michael Smith for providing helpful and constructive feedback on a previous draft of this essay. I also would like to thank Michael Green, who offered an incisive critique and numerous helpful suggestions for reframing and revising this piece. Any remaining shortcomings in the essay are, of course, attributable to me alone.

1. *Cleveland Plain Dealer*, 18 August 1851.

2. Mark Wahlgren Summers, *The Press Gang: Newspapers and Politics, 1865–1878* (Chapel Hill: University of North Carolina Press, 1994), 52; Thomas C. Leonard, *The Power of the Press: The Birth of American Political Reporting* (New York: Oxford University Press, 1986), 92. On the history of the American press, see Frank Luther Mott, *American Journalism: A History of Newspapers in the United States through 250 Years, 1690 to 1940* (New York: Macmillan, 1941); Leonard, *News for All: America's Coming of Age with the Press* (New York: Oxford University Press, 1995); Michael Schudson, *The Good Citizen: A History of American Civic Life* (New York: Free Press, 1998); David Paul Nord, *Communities of Journalism: A History of American Newspapers and Their Readers* (Urbana: University of Illinois Press, 2001); Kevin G. Barnhurst and John Nerone, *The Form of the News: A History* (New York: Guilford Press, 2001); and Jeffrey Pasley, *"The Tyranny of Printers": Newspaper Politics in the Early American Republic* (Charlottesville: University Press of Virginia, 2001).

3. Yonatan Eyal, *Young America and the Transformation of the Democratic Party, 1828–1861* (New York: Cambridge University Press, 2007). Eyal suggested that Young America, a somewhat militant, nationalist movement, created a more dynamic Democratic Party, one that fought for expansion, promoted internal improvements, and embraced the development of a powerful market system built on free trade.

4. This territory included present-day California, Nevada, Utah, Arizona, and New Mexico, as well as parts of Colorado and Wyoming.

5. Jonathan H. Earle, *Jacksonian Antislavery and the Politics of Free Soil, 1824–1854* (Chapel Hill: University of North Carolina Press, 2004), 5–15, 36, 60, 136–41. Arthur Schlesinger Jr. and Sean Wilentz both located the genesis of Democratic radicalism in the urban workingmen's movements in the North in the 1820s and 1830s. In contrast, Earle located such radicalism in the countryside. See Schlesinger Jr., *The Age of Jackson* (New York: Little, Brown, 1945); and Wilentz, *The Rise of American Democracy: From Jefferson to Lincoln* (New York: Norton, 2005).

6. Richard John has provided an excellent history of the Postal Service's subsidization of newspaper expansion in *Spreading the News: The American Postal System from Franklin to Morse* (Cambridge: Harvard University Press, 1995). In 1832 newspapers accounted for 95 percent of the weight of all postal freights but only 15 percent of postal revenues. See *Spreading the News*, 38.

7. *Maine Washingtonian Journal and Temperance Herald*, 9 November 1842. The Washingtonian society initially promoted temperance through moral suasion and voluntary abstinence. The *Journal* and other such papers in the state eventually mobilized reformers into a powerful political organization that elected temperance crusader Neal Dow mayor of Portland, Maine, in 1851.

8. Glenn Altschuler and Stuart Blumin, *Rude Republic: Americans and Their Politics in the Nineteenth Century* (Princeton: Princeton University Press, 2000), 108.

9. James W. Carey, *Communication as Culture: Essays on Media and Society* (Boston: Unwin Hyman, 1988), 20. On the communal nature of newspaper reading, see Leonard, *News for All*, 12–21, 43–50.

10. Jean Harvey Baker, *Affairs of Party: The Political Culture of Northern Democrats in the Mid-Nineteenth Century* (Ithaca: Cornell University Press, 1983), 145.

11. Wilentz, *Rise of American Democracy*, 440. On Whig principles and their economic program, see Daniel Walker Howe, *The Political Culture of the American Whigs* (Chicago: University of Chicago Press, 1979); and *What Hath God Wrought: The Transformation of America, 1815–1848* (New York: Oxford University Press, 2007). Democratic opposition to internal improvement schemes intensified after the Panic of 1837, a severe credit contraction that nearly bankrupted several northern states that had overextended their treasuries in constructing elaborate and often-unproductive improvement systems.

12. "The Governor's Message," 19 May 1847, 27th Legislature, *Acts and Resolves Passed by the Legislature of the State of Maine*, Raymond H. Fogler Library, University of Maine.

13. Democrats shepherded the charter bill through the legislature, whose bipartisan support allowed it to pass with an astounding 104–10 vote. The only opposition came from radical Democrats centered in the state's mid-coast region, far removed from the location of the proposed railroad. See Phineas Barnes to John Neal, 8 February 1845, Atlantic &

St. Lawrence Railroad Company Records, George J. Mitchell Department of Special Collections and Archives, Bowdoin College Library. The Canadian portion of the railroad was chartered separately in Canada as the St. Lawrence and Atlantic Railroad.

14. Three bills entitled Portland to extend $1.5 million in credit to the railroad in the form of interest-bearing city scrip or notes. The bills were passed in two-year intervals from 1848 to 1852. See *Charter and By-Laws of the Atlantic and St. Lawrence Railroad Co.* (Portland: Bearce, Starbird, Rich and Co., 1855).

15. *Belfast Republican Journal*, 11 October 1850. Daniel Walker Howe noted that Democratic rhetoric condemning state involvement in speculative ventures resonated with journeymen and other small producers who opposed "government favoritism toward a national bank or other mixed corporations," which they often equated with monopolies. See *What Hath God Wrought*, 544.

16. See Reuel Williams, John D. Long, and John Otis (Directors of Kennebec and Portland Railroad) to the President and Directors of the Atlantic and St. Lawrence Railroad, 30 March 1847, 5 April 1847, 3 May 1847, and 28 April 1848. For the Atlantic and St. Lawrence Railroad's reply, see Directors of the Atlantic and St. Lawrence Railroad to the Directors of the Kennebec and Portland Railroad, 24 April 1847 and 16 March 1848. All in Atlantic & St. Lawrence Railroad Company Records, George J. Mitchell Department of Special Collections and Archives, Bowdoin College Library. See also John A. Poor, *Memoir of Honorable Reuel Williams: Prepared for the Maine Historical Society* (Cambridge, MA: H. O. Houghton and Co., 1864), 47. Williams was a Whig legislator who came out of political retirement in 1848 in an unsuccessful bid to break the Atlantic and St. Lawrence's railroad monopoly and charter competitor rail lines.

17. In this case, the Charles River Bridge Corporation had obtained an exclusive charter in 1785 to maintain a toll bridge over the Charles River, connecting the cities of Charlestown and Boston, Massachusetts. However, after fifty years of operation, that bridge could no longer accommodate the foot traffic of these burgeoning cities, and the state licensed the Warren Bridge, a free structure, to serve the two communities. The Charles River Bridge Corporation had sued on the grounds that the state violated its charter and unlawfully appropriated its property (the tolls paid by its customers) when it chartered a competing corporation.

18. First quotation from *Portland Eastern Argus*, 27 February 1845. Second quotation from *Bangor Whig and Courier*, 5 March 1845.

19. The road's officers made no secret of their pretensions. Portland's entrepreneurs initially faced competition from counterparts in Boston, who also sought to forge a rail connection between their city and Montreal. John Neal, one of the founders of the Atlantic and St. Lawrence, wrote of the necessity "to drive Boston out of the business and secure [a] monopoly" of the traffic between Montreal and New England. See John Neal to J. P. Cutler, F. G. Butler, et al. (Farmington, Maine), 9 March 1845. Atlantic & St. Lawrence Railroad Company Records, George J. Mitchell Department of Special Collections and Archives, Bowdoin College. See also Poor, *Memoir of Honorable Reuel Williams*, 47.

20. Poor, *Memoir of Honorable Reuel Williams*, 45. Poor's brother, Henry Varnum Poor, made a successful career of collecting and providing statistics and insurance for railroads. He later founded the Standard and Poor's corporation.

21. See *Portland Eastern Argus*, 19 September 1845.

22. *Portland Eastern Argus*, 8 January 1849. The quotation comes from a letter to the *Argus* by "Justice." The writer argued that "while capitalists of our State and city stood aloof" when stock was first issued for the railroad, "the mechanics, farmers, and working men subscribed freely for the stock" and gave the project its start. In a cruel irony, rents and real estate valuations had increased dramatically after the railroad's groundbreaking in 1846, before the road itself brought increased business or higher wages to the city. Thus, while small investors now struggled to meet their assessments, the city's wealthy speculators and property lords grew fat off advancing real estate values.

23. On Holden's promotion of the auction, see *Portland Eastern Argus*, 5 May 1849. Auctioned shares were sold at rates of seventy-one to seventy-six cents on the dollar (*Portland Eastern Argus*, 13 March 1849). Holden attempted to balance his support for the divestment of small stockholders by supporting passage of a bill to increase the value of property exempted from seizure for debt. See *Portland Eastern Argus*, 23 April and 21 August 1849.

24. On Croswell's early life, see Richard H. Manning, "Herald of the Albany Regency: Edwin Croswell and the *Albany Argus*, 1823–1854," PhD diss., Miami University, 1983. On Croswell's encouragement of railroad building in New York, see *Albany Argus*, 3 July and 11 July 1845.

25. Quotations from *Albany Argus*, 13 September and 11 July 1845.

26. Radical Democrats had passed laws that prohibited railroad corporations from accruing debt greater than their subscribed capital. For Croswell's criticism of these laws, see *Albany Argus*, 2 August 1845.

27. *Albany Argus*, 22 April 1846. Even as late as 1850, when the political influence of the *Argus* had begun to decline, it still claimed nearly sixteen thousand subscribers, while the *Atlas* logged a mere seven thousand. See Joseph C. G. Kennedy, *Catalogue of the Newspapers and Periodicals Published in the United States . . . Compiled from the Census of 1850* (New York: J. Livingston, 1852), 26.

28. Until the adoption of a new constitution in 1846 (which took effect in 1847), state cabinet officers (secretary of state, attorney general, treasurer, comptroller, state engineer) were not elected at large, but elected through joint ballot of the legislature, giving the majority party in the state house tremendous power to install loyal members in those positions.

29. The Anti-Rent crisis of 1845–60 only exacerbated the internecine conflict between the Democratic factions and further obscured party principles. During the crisis between twenty-five thousand and sixty thousand tenant farmers in eleven counties resisted the collection of rents in arrears and refused to abide by the feudalistic terms by which they tenanted land on enormous, privately held Hudson River manors. The Regency, beholden to the political support of the manor lords, eschewed radial egalitarianism and resorted to the state militia to suppress Anti-Rent agitation. Sensing opportunity, commercially oriented Hunkers and Whigs scrambled after the support of disgruntled tenant farmers, portraying themselves as agrarian populists. Charles McCurdy has written the best, most comprehensive account of the Anti-Rent crisis. See *The Anti-Rent Era in New York Law and Politics, 1839–1865* (Chapel Hill: University of North Carolina Press, 2001).

30. For an account of the violence at New Scotland, see *Albany Argus*, 8 April and 11 April 1846. Hunkers held forty-eight of the seventy seats. Several men were indicted for their roles in orchestrating the violence. John Van Buren only narrowly escaped indictment, which required the unanimous vote of the seventeen-member grand jury. A majority favored including him in the indictment. See Manning, "Herald of the Albany Regency," 286.

31. *Rochester Republican*, 24 August 1847. See also *Rome Sentinel*, 9 July and 23 July 1847. Ironically, Barnburners had sponsored the articles in the 1846 state constitution that made Flagg's post and other cabinet positions elective by the people at large. The 1847 state canvass thus gave Hunkers their first opportunity to remove Flagg from power through the nomination process.

32. See Eric Foner's excellent explication of the sources of the Proviso in "The Wilmot Proviso Revisited," *Journal of American History* 56, no. 2 (1969): 262–79. Despite its name, the famed Proviso largely had been authored by the Barnburner Congressman Preston King of New York and radical Democrats Jacob Brinkerhoff of Ohio and Hannibal Hamlin of Maine. Angered by the extreme pro-slavery positions of some southern politicians, like John C. Calhoun, who argued that war with Mexico was necessary to promote the expansion of slavery, these radical Democrats offered the Proviso as a means by which northern Democrats could loyally support the war without seeming to acquiesce to the demands of the pro-slavery South.

33. Samuel Young (ed.), *Herkimer Convention. The Voice of New York* (Albany: Albany Atlas, 1847), 5. The epithet doughface connoted a northern man with supposedly southern principles. It was a starkly gendered term, suggesting that doughfaces were not strong, independent men, but mere tools, who were easily cowed and manipulated by stronger personalities. Leonard Richards offered perhaps the most convincing etymology of the term, suggesting that it derived from a children's game in which they would apply dough to their faces to make grotesque masks with which to shock and frighten one another. Richards, *The Slave Power: The Free North and Southern Domination, 1780–1860* (Baton Rouge: Louisiana State University Press, 2000), 85–86. On the breakup of the Syracuse convention and the birth of Free Soil, see Schlesinger, *Age of Jackson*, 460–461. Sean Wilentz echoed Schlesinger's moralistic account in *Rise of American Democracy*, 609.

34. It was not merely Flagg's failure at nomination that weakened the Barnburners. The Syracuse convention also installed a new state central committee with a Hunker majority, giving that faction effective control over future party conventions. See Walter L. Ferree, "The New York Democracy: Division and Reunion, 1847–1852," PhD diss. University of Pennsylvania, 1953, 60–83. On the Herkimer resolutions, see *Herkimer Convention*, 8. Joseph Rayback described the Free Soil Party as the first American political party founded on a sincere humanitarian impulse. Rayback, *Free Soil: The Election of 1848* (Lexington: University Press of Kentucky, 1970), 230, 249. Frederick Blue, on the other hand, has described Free Soilers as a mix of opportunistic young politicians and those on the outs seeking a new, expedient path to office. See Blue, *The Free Soilers: Third Party Politics, 1848–54* (Urbana: University of Illinois Press, 1973). Joel Silbey recently has argued that the Free Soil revolution exerted little impact on the party system, as the "dominant players" on the political scene in 1848 remained the traditional parties. See Silbey, *Party over*

Section: The Rough and Ready Presidential Election of 1848 (Lawrence: University Press of Kansas, 2009), 153.

35. Unable to rely on unpredictable patronage to keep their journals afloat, partisan editors like Holden secured valuable funding and labor through a succession of business partners.

36. *Portland Eastern Argus*, 14 and 17 May 1850.

37. *Cleveland Plain Dealer*, 25 January 1847.

38. *Cleveland Plain Dealer*, 10 February and 3 March 1846.

39. *Cleveland Plain Dealer*, 4 January 1848. Johnson was a crony of Polk's and had represented Tennessee for fourteen years in Congress. The *Times* had published a single special issue that it mailed to its subscribers and all known Democrats in Cleveland and its surrounding communities, and the paper subsequently used that circulation figure to claim a greater customer base than the *Plain Dealer*. See *Cleveland Plain Dealer*, 2 October 1847.

40. *Cleveland Plain Dealer*, 4 January 1848. This was not the first time Gray had failed to win the Post Office's coveted advertising contract. When he had failed in a similar bid in 1846, he condemned the institution's method of dispensing patronage as thoroughly corrupt. See *Cleveland Plain Dealer*, 22 September 1846.

41. For the growth of Gray's printing business, see *Cleveland Plain Dealer*, 17 July 1851. Gray's postmaster position appears in *Spear, Dennison and Co.'s Cleveland City Directory for 1856* (Cleveland: Spear, Dennison and Co., 1856), 48; and William H. Boyd, *Cleveland City Directory* (New York: Boyd Directory Publisher, 1857), 86.

42. *Cleveland Plain Dealer*, 21 January 1848. Anticipating the topic of his meeting with Postmaster General Johnson the previous December, Gray had intimated that the ends of the Wilmot Proviso could be achieved by other means. See *Cleveland Plain Dealer*, 24 December 1847.

43. *Cleveland Plain Dealer*, 6 June 1848. Gray obliquely suggested that existing Mexican law, which prohibited slavery and still prevailed in the territories, ensured the territories' continued freedom. That this law would appear to obstruct popular sovereignty itself did not appear to trouble the editor.

44. *Cleveland Plain Dealer*, 24 May 1848.

45. See *Portland Eastern Argus*, 13 February 1847; and *Hallowell Free Soil Republican*, 21 September 1848. The *Free Soil Republican* had been a Liberty Party organ, called the *Liberty Standard*, until reluctantly joining the Free Soil Party after its Buffalo convention in August 1848.

46. Croswell had launched an independent newspaper in New York City and had begun to entrust the *Argus*'s operations increasingly to his assistant as he labored to make his new paper a success. He had effectively ceased his regular involvement with the *Argus* long before he agreed to step down as its editor. See Manning, "Herald of the Albany Regency," 297–311. For examples of the periodic but unsuccessful attempts at reuniting the Democratic Party, see *Rochester Republican*, 18 January 1848 and 29 November 1849; and *Rome Sentinel*, 12 September 1849.

47. *Portland Eastern Argus*, 22 March 1849.

48. *Cleveland Plain Dealer*, 30 August 1847.

49. *Cleveland Plain Dealer*, 18 August 1851.

Abraham Lincoln, Manhood, and Nineteenth-Century
American Political Culture
Michael Thomas Smith

1. Gail Bederman proposes that the Victorian ideal of manliness as self-restraint gave way by the end of the nineteenth century to a more aggressive, primal conception of masculinity in *Manliness and Civilization: A Cultural History of Gender and Race in the United States, 1880–1917* (Chicago: University of Chicago Press, 1995), 18–19. Amy S. Greenberg suggested that the seemingly incompatible visions of restrained and aggressive manhood "competed for men's allegiances" throughout the mid-nineteenth century in *Manifest Manhood and the Antebellum American Empire* (Cambridge: Cambridge University Press, 2005), 10. Lorien Foote emphasizes the contested nature of American manhood in the Civil War era and the ambiguities that make it difficult to entirely separate the different variations in practice, or to determine which was dominant at any given time, in *The Gentlemen and the Roughs: Violence, Honor, and Manhood in the Union Army* (New York: New York University Press, 2010), 178–79.

2. (Washington) *National Intelligencer*, July 27, 1861; *Cleveland Plain Dealer*, July 12, 1864; (New York) *Old Guard* (February 1863), 32.

3. G. T. Allen to Lyman Trumbull, December 14, 1864, Lyman Trumbull Papers, Library of Congress; Francis B. Carpenter, *Six Months at the White House with Abraham Lincoln* (New York: Hurd and Houghton, 1866), 68–69.

4. *Cleveland Plain Dealer*, April 18, 1864; Michael F. Holt, *The Rise and Fall of the American Whig Party: Jacksonian Politics and the Onset of the Civil War* (New York: Oxford University Press, 1999), 728, 732; David Herbert Donald, *Lincoln* (New York: Touchstone, 1995), 281.

5. Lydia Maria Child to John Greenleaf Whittier, September 22, 1861, Lydia Maria Child Papers (microfiche edition); Fessenden quoted in Doris Kearns Goodwin, *Team of Rivals: The Political Genius of Abraham Lincoln* (New York: Simon and Schuster, 2005), 487; Howard K. Beale (ed.), *The Diary of Edward Bates, 1859–1866* (Washington: Government Printing Office, 1933), 269; Donald, *Lincoln*, 399–406.

6. (Boston) *Commonwealth*, February 20, 1863; (Boston) *Liberator*, November 13, 1863; *Cleveland Plain Dealer*, March 15, 1864; (New York) *Old Guard* (July 1864), 158; Gideon Welles, *Lincoln and Seward* (New York: Sheldon and Company, 1874), 8, 7.

7. (New York) *Round Table*, May 7, 1864; Benjamin Sherwood to Benjamin S. Hedrick, March 29, 1864, Benjamin Sherwood Hedrick Papers, Perkins Library, Duke University; (Boston) *Commonwealth*, October 8, 1864; Michael Thomas Smith, "The Meanest Man in Lincoln's Cabinet: A Reappraisal of Montgomery Blair," *Maryland Historical Magazine* 95 (Summer 2000): 191–206.

8. Douglass quoted in William Lee Miller, *Lincoln's Virtues: An Ethical Biography* (New York: Vintage, 2002), 415; *Cleveland Plain Dealer*, August 21, 1863; Ulysses S. Grant, *Personal Memoirs of U.S. Grant* (1885; reprint, New York: Modern Library, 1999), 608–9.

9. *Pittsburgh Post*, May 30, 1862; Daniel S. Dickinson to Henry W. Rogers, July 31, 1864, in John R. Dickinson (ed.), *Speeches, Correspondence, Etc., of the Late Daniel S. Dickinson of New York*, 2 vols. (New York: G. P. Putnam and Son, 1867), 2:651.

10. Tyler Dennett (ed.), *Lincoln and the Civil War in the Diaries and Letters of John Hay* (1939; reprint, Cambridge, MA: Da Capo, 1988), 29.

11. Salmon P. Chase to William Sprague, November 26, 1863, Salmon P. Chase Papers, Library of Congress; Donald, *Lincoln*, 264, 483.

12. Michael Burlingame, *Abraham Lincoln: A Life*, 2 vols. (Baltimore: Johns Hopkins University Press, 2008), 2:632–33, 690; Andrew Rolle, *John Charles Frémont: Character as Destiny* (Norman: University of Oklahoma Press, 1991), 233.

13. (Boston) *Commonwealth*, February 20, 1863; Benjamin F. Butler to Sarah Hildreth Butler, September 9, 1862, in Jesse Ames Marshall (ed.), *Private and Official Correspondence of Gen. Benjamin F. Butler during the Period of the Civil War*, 5 vols. (Norwood, MA: Plimpton Press, 1917), 2:629; Boutwell quoted in Adam Gurowski, *Diary*, 3 vols. (1866; reprint, New York: Burt Franklin, 1968), 3:154, 86–87; Donald, *Lincoln*, 478. See also Michael Thomas Smith, "The Beast Unleashed: Benjamin F. Butler and Conceptions of Masculinity in the Civil War North," *New England Quarterly* 79 (June 2006): 248–76.

14. (Boston) *Commonwealth*, December 20, 1862; Casper Butz quoted in *Albany Argus*, April 4, 1864; *New York Evening Express*, June 9, 1864; *Brooklyn Eagle*, June 6, October 31, 1864.

15. Donald, *Lincoln*, 427; *Chicago Times*, February 25, 1864; *Chicago Times* quoted in *Albany Argus*, August 16, 1864.

16. Donald, *Lincoln*, 244–245; Kenneth J. Winkle, "Abraham Lincoln: Self-Made Man," *Journal of the Abraham Lincoln Association* 21 (Summer 2000): 1–16; Grace Bedell to Abraham Lincoln, October 15, 1860, Abraham Lincoln Papers, Library of Congress.

17. William Dean Howells, *Life of Abraham Lincoln* (1860; reprint, Bloomington: Indiana University Press, 1960), 21, 35, 40.

18. The offending letters were probably written or cowritten by Mary Todd. Burlingame, *Abraham Lincoln: A Life*, 1:190–94.

19. *Pottsville Miners' Journal*, July 13, 1861; Burlingame, *Abraham Lincoln: A Life*, 2:257; Diary of Joseph T. Mills, August 19, 1864, in Roy P. Basler (ed.), *Collected Works of Abraham Lincoln*, 8 vols. and supplements (New Brunswick: Rutgers University Press, 1953–55), 7:507; Stevens quoted in *Brooklyn Eagle*, December 31, 1864.

20. Donald, *Lincoln*, 575.

21. *Atlantic Monthly*, July 1862, 47–48; *Albany Evening Journal*, June 27, 1862; Lydia Maria Child to Charles Sumner, July 31, 1864, Child Papers; (New York) *Round Table*, June 11, 1864.

22. (Boston) *Commonwealth*, December 11, 1863; *Boston Advertiser*, January 30, 1864; Sylvanus Cobb to Abraham Lincoln, December 27, 1862, Lincoln Papers.

23. Dennett, *Lincoln and the Civil War in the Diaries and Letters of John Hay*, 91, 76; *London Review* quoted in William C. Harris, *Lincoln's Last Months* (Cambridge: Harvard University Press, 2004), 241.

Damnable Treason or Party Organs? Democratic Secret Societies in Pennsylvania
Robert M. Sandow

1. Richard Hofstadter, "The Paranoid Style in American Politics," *Harper's Magazine* (November 1964), 77–86.

2. Jennifer L. Weber, *Copperheads: The Rise and Fall of Lincoln's Opponents in the North* (New York: Oxford University Press, 2006). Weber summarizes her thesis—that dissent was a central issue and that "Copperhead" opposition materially undermined the war effort—in her introduction, pp. 1–2.

3. Ibid., 195, 165.

4. The thesis that two-party rivalry was an advantage to the Union can be traced to seminal work by David M. Potter, "Jefferson Davis and the Political Factors in Confederate Defeat," in *Why the North Won the Civil War, ed.* David H. Donald (Baton Rouge: Louisiana State University Press, 1960), 91–112; and Eric McKitrick, "Party Politics and the Union and Confederate War Efforts," in *The American Party Systems: Stages of Political Development, ed.* William Nisbet Chambers and Walter Dean Burnham (New York: Oxford University Press, 1967), 117–51.

5. Mark E. Neely Jr., *The Union Divided: Party Conflict in the Civil War North* (Cambridge: Harvard University Press, 2002), 59.

6. Edward L. Pierce, *Memoir and Letters of Charles Sumner*, 4 vols. (Boston: Roberts Brothers, 1877–93), 4:114.

7. A number of studies grapple with categorization of Democrats. Jean Baker questioned the traditional division into war and peace factions, arguing that most supported war as necessary to restore the Union and few sought "peace at any price or recognition of Southern independence." Jean H. Baker, "A Loyal Opposition: Northern Democrats in the Thirty-Seventh Congress," *Civil War History* 25, no. 2 (1979): 143–44. See also Herbert H. Wubben, *Civil War Iowa and the Copperhead Movement* (Ames: Iowa State University Press, 1980), ix–xi; and Joanna D. Cowden's analytic overview "The Ideological Assault against Lincoln," in *"Heaven Will Frown on Such a Cause as This": Six Democrats Who Opposed Lincoln's War* (Lanham, MD: University Press of America, 2001), 1–23.

8. John A. Logan, *The Great Conspiracy: Its Origins and History* (New York: A. R. Hart, 1886), 562, 555, 560. Logan indulged in a half-page footnote about the Knights of the Golden Circle, whose purported aim was "to hamper, oppose, and prevent all things possible that were being done at any time for the Union Cause, and to encourage, forward, and help all things possible in behalf of the Rebel Cause." Relying on a controversial federal exposé of the organization, Logan repeated the fanciful estimate of half a million members. See pp. 499, 559.

9. John Russell Bartlett, *Dictionary of Americanisms: A Glossary of Words and Phrases Usually Regarded as Peculiar to the United States*, 4th ed. (Boston: Little, Brown, 1889), 145. Less partisan interpretations could be found as well.

10. The most penetrating and analytically useful historiographical essay on Copperhead studies, at least in the Midwest, is Robert H. Abzug, "The Copperheads: Historical Approaches to Civil War Dissent in the Midwest," *Indiana Magazine of History* 66, no. 1 (1970): 40–55.

11. James Ford Rhodes, *History of the Civil War, 1861–1865* (New York: Macmillan, 1917), 350–55. Rhodes had a fascinating perspective on the subject of Copperheads. In letters to fellow academics, he admitted that his own father was a Douglas Democrat and Ohio Copperhead. This partial sympathy helps explain why Rhodes seemed to play down the

real threat of dissenters. Joseph Borome, ed., "James Ford Rhodes and Historical Scholarship," *New England Quarterly* 21, no. 3 (1948): 379–83.

12. William A. Dunning, "Disloyalty in Two Wars," *American Historical Review* 24, no. 4 (1919): 628.

13. Abzug, "Copperheads," 42.

14. For a discussion of the impact of World War I on Civil War studies, consult Thomas J. Pressly, *Americans Interpret Their Civil War* (1954; reprint, New York: Collier Books, 1962), 291–93, 305–6.

15. Milton's book did not even contain any source citations. George Fort Milton, *Abraham Lincoln and the Fifth Column* (New York: Vanguard Press, 1942).

16. Roy P. Basler, ed., *The Collected Works of Abraham Lincoln*, 9 vols. (New Brunswick: Rutgers University Press, 1953–55), 6:266.

17. Wood Gray, *The Hidden Civil War: The Story of the Copperheads* (New York: Viking, 1942), 224. A useful discussion of the context of these works can be found in Frank L. Klement, "Copperheads in the Upper Midwest during the Civil War: Traitors, Politicians, or Dissenters?" in *Lincoln's Critics: The Copperheads of the North* (Shippensburg, PA: White Mane Books, 1999), 3–5. See also Abzug, "Copperheads," 48–50, for a more nuanced summation of Gray's work.

18. The quotation comes from Nevins's presidential address at the annual dinner of the American Historical Association. Allan Nevins, "Not Capulets, Not Montagus," *American Historical Review* 65, no. 2 (1960): 259.

19. Examples include Henry Clyde Hubbart, *The Older Middle West* (New York: Appleton-Century Co., 1936); Albert L. Kohlmeier, *The Old Northwest as the Keystone of the Arch of American Federal Union: A Study in Commerce and Politics* (Bloomington, IN: Principia Press, 1938); and Kenneth M. Stampp, *Indiana Politics during the Civil War* (Indianapolis: Indiana Historical Bureau, 1949).

20. Abzug, "Copperheads," 50–51.

21. Curry called for more quantitative analysis, further research into other regions of the Union, and more careful scrutiny of ideological diversity in the ranks of Copperheadism. Richard O. Curry, "The Union as It Was: A Critique of Recent Interpretations of the 'Copperheads,'" *Civil War History* 13, no. 1 (1967): 34–39.

22. Klement, *Lincoln's Critics*, 239–51.

23. Mark E. Neely Jr., *The Fate of Liberty: Abraham Lincoln and Civil Liberties* (New York: Oxford University Press, 1991), xii.

24. Joel H. Silbey, *A Respectable Minority: The Democratic Party in the Civil War Era, 1860–1868* (New York: Norton, 1977); Jean H. Baker, *Affairs of Party: Political Culture of Northern Democrats in the Mid-Nineteenth Century* (Ithaca: Cornell University Press, 1983).

25. Richard Orr Curry, *A House Divided: A Study of Statehood Politics and the Copperhead Movement in West Virginia* (Pittsburgh: University of Pittsburgh Press, 1964). Robert M. Sandow's *Deserter Country: Civil War Opposition in the Pennsylvania Appalachians* (New York: Fordham University Press, 2009) examines economic, political, and social factors for opposition rooted in an Appalachian context.

26. Weber, *Copperheads*, 6, 25–26. Weber acknowledged only "three major books" on the subject: Gray, *Hidden Civil War*; Milton, *Abraham Lincoln and the Fifth Column*; and Frank L. Klement, *The Copperheads in the Middle West* (Chicago: University of Chicago Press, 1960). For her brief summary of motivations, see pp. 17–23.

27. Ibid., 2, 25–26.

28. Baker, "Loyal Opposition," 140.

29. Francis Lieber, *No Party Now, but All for Our Country* (Philadelphia: Crissy & Markley, 1863), 11.

30. The case against Gainer P. Bloom, George Rousher, Benjamin Boyer, Henry Yoas, and Charles Keller, General Court Martial, Order. No. 184, Adjutant General's Office, War Department, Washington, 13 April 1865, National Archives Building (NAB), Washington, DC, Record Group (RG) 153, Records of the Office of Judge Advocate General (Army), 1792–1981, MM 1607, Court-Martial Case Files, 1809–1894.

31. Henry W. Bellows, *Unconditional Loyalty* (New York: Anson D. F. Randolph, 1863), 5.

32. Mark Neely described the appearance of the Union Leagues and their publication campaign as a "revolt against politics"—a reaction to the rise of partisanship in late 1862. He argued that they were not specifically campaign tactics because they were not conducted in key election years. Neely also suggested that "most Americans expected parties to cease operation if the country were invaded or faced a major rebellion," and that this was a legacy of the Founding Fathers. See Neely, *Union Divided*, 48, 8–9. Adam I. P. Smith's *No Party Now* stresses the novelty of this Republican endeavor. He tied together the origins of the Union Leagues, their equation of partisanship with treason, and their campaigns to "re-forge patriotism" around unquestioning support for the government—an "antiparty nationalism." See *No Party Now: Politics in the Civil War North* (New York: Oxford University Press, 2006), 68–79. For his discussion of the failure of Democratic "loyal opposition" rhetoric, see pp. 157–62.

33. A number of recent studies have highlighted the origins, development, and lasting significance of this new nationalism. See Melinda Lawson, *Patriot Fires: Forging a New American Nationalism in the Civil War North* (Lawrence: University Press of Kansas, 2002), 2–11, 66–68; Jorg Nagler, "Loyalty and Dissent: The Home Front in the American Civil War," in *On the Road to Total War: The American Civil War and the German Wars of Unification, 1861–1871*, ed. Stig Forster and Jorg Nagler (New York: Cambridge University Press, 1997), 335–38; Peter J. Parish, "Partisanship and the Construction of Nationalism," in *The North and the Nation in the Era of the Civil War*, ed. Susan Mary-Grant and Adam I. P. Smith (New York: Fordham University Press, 2003), 118–122; Robert H. Churchill, *To Shake Their Guns in the Tyrant's Face: Libertarian Political Violence and the Origins of the Militia Movement* (Ann Arbor: University of Michigan Press, 2009), 6–7, 108–11.

34. Weber drew parallels between the crises of September 11 and the Civil War in an author interview posted on the Oxford University Press website: "I was at the Clements Library at the University of Michigan when the planes hit. After that, there was almost a surreal quality to working on this book. I'd spend the day reading material from the early 1860s, and then I'd go home at night and hear about the exact same issues and concerns on the news." Weber emphasized that analogies to the war in Iraq were "super-

ficial." Some conservative blogs, however, described Bush administration opponents as "Neo-Copperheads." See http://blog.oup.com/2006/10/a_few_questions_5/. Weber also articulated this "modern" conception of nationalism in *Copperheads*, paraphrasing Carl von Clausewitz that "civilians must back the war, and they need to maintain the will—the morale—to continue it." See *Copperheads*, 11.

35. Churchill, *To Shake Their Guns in the Tyrant's Face*, 8–9.

36. Neely, *Union Divided*, 124.

37. Fredrickson argued that the reevaluation of "loyalty, patriotism, and nationality . . . led to a harvest of political thought which is among the most interesting intellectual products of the war." George M. Fredrickson, "The Doctrine of Loyalty," in *The Inner Civil War: Northern Intellectuals and the Crisis of Union* (New York: Harper & Row, 1965), 132.

38. Examples include Curry, "Congressional Democrats," 229; and G. R. Tredway, "Democratic Loyalty," in *Democratic Opposition to the Lincoln Administration in Indiana* (Indianapolis: Indiana Historical Bureau, 1973), 56–69.

39. As evidence of this view, Democrats in Congress did not block passage of military bills including conscription. Congressional Democrats could unite as an opposition and did so on bills that sanctioned emancipation, black troops, and infringements of civil liberties by the executive branch. As Jean Baker summarized, Democrats did vote for peace conventions and peace commissioners and spared no opportunity to vilify their political opponents. But "bills involving men, money, and materials gained an overwhelming (but not universal) Democratic support." Baker credited the Democratic example of "loyal opposition" as "the Northern Democrats' contribution to American political culture." By analyzing roll call votes from the 37th Congress, Leonard Curry and Jean Baker came to the same conclusion. Curry, "Congressional Democrats"; Baker, "Loyal Opposition," 143, 152.

40. "'Administration' vs. 'Government,'" *Clearfield Republican*, 11 September 1861.

41. Lawson, *Patriot Fires*, 5, 66–67.

42. Weber, *Copperheads*, 195, 165. Ella Lonn's classic study *Desertion during the Civil War* (Gloucester, MA: American Historical Society, 1928; reprint, with an introduction by William Blair, Lincoln: University of Nebraska Press, 1998) paraphrased these initial reports, giving the impression that they were truths. See pp. 205–6.

43. Richard I. Dodge to James B. Fry, Washington, DC, 1 November 1864, U.S. War Department, *The War of the Rebellion: A Compilation of the Official Records of the Union and Confederate Armies*, 127 vols., index, and atlas (Washington, DC: Government Printing Office), ser. 1, vol. 43, pt. 2: 525. Hereafter all references are abbreviated as *OR* with appropriate series and volume numbers.

44. Richard I. Dodge to James B. Fry, Washington, DC, 10 August 1864, *OR*, ser. 3, vol. 4: 607.

45. The author is extremely grateful to colleagues who shared their unpublished writings and research notes on the Fishing Creek Confederacy. Richard A. Sauers generously shared primary sources, offered his counsel, and provided the author with the manuscript for his forthcoming book "Murder, Mayhem, and Mystery: The True Story of the Fishing Creek Confederacy," coauthored with Peter Tomasak. Jonathan W. White likewise has given significant insight and source material along with an unpublished essay on the sub-

ject titled "Reconstructing the 'Confederacy': Memory and Community in the North's Civil War." For published work on Columbia County, consult William W. Hummel, "The Military Occupation of Columbia County: A Re-examination," *Pennsylvania Magazine of History and Biography* 80, no. 3 (1956): 320–38. Many primary sources on the event can be accessed in John G. Freeze, *History of Columbia County, Pennsylvania, from the Earliest Times* (Bloomsburg, PA: Elwell and Bittenbender, 1883).

46. For a more detailed assessment of the context of Clearfield dissent as well as a fuller narrative of the military expeditions and their results, consult Sandow, *Deserter Country*.

47. Much of this literature is found in essay form. Good examples include Joan E. Cashin, "Deserters, Civilians, and Draft Resistance in the North," in *The War Was You and Me: Civilians in the American Civil War*, ed. Joan E. Cashin (Princeton: Princeton University Press, 2002), 262–85; Kenneth H. Wheeler, "Local Autonomy and Civil War Draft Resistance: Holmes County, Ohio," *Civil War History* 45, no. 2 (1999): 147–59; Paul A. Cimbala, "Soldiering on the Home Front: The Veteran Reserve Corps and the Northern People," in *Union Soldiers and the Northern Home Front: Wartime Experiences, Postwar Adjustments*, ed. Paul A. Cimbala and Randall M. Miller (New York: Fordham University Press, 2002), 182–218.

48. For a more complete examination of these patterns in Clearfield, see Sandow, "Everyday Resistance in Pennsylvania's Deserter Country," in *Deserter Country*, 99–116.

49. The Democratic Club in question met in Stillwater, northern Columbia County. See "Resolutions," *Columbia Democrat*, 11 April 1863.

50. Kenneth Wheeler saw the same pattern in Ohio: "The Holmes County draft rebellion of 1863 . . . reflects an explicit ideology of localism that undergirded resistance to federal authority." "Local Autonomy and Civil War Draft Resistance," 195.

51. "Correspondence," *Columbia Democrat*, 20 August 1864. Editor Tate had the phrase typeset as "Abolition Slavery" in these two editorials from the summer of 1864. While I have interpreted them both as errors, he may well have meant to imply an enslavement to abolitionism.

52. "Peace Propositions," *Columbia Democrat*, 30 July 1864.

53. "Mutual protection society" was a contemporary term, and their existence has been noted variously across the North. Scholars that addressed them include Klement, *Copperheads in the Middle West*, 146–47, 161–63. G. R. Tredway offered an identical assessment to Klement about their origins and purpose in Indiana. See G. R. Tredway, *Democratic Opposition to the Lincoln Administration in Indiana* (Indianapolis: Indiana Historical Bureau, 1973), 113–19. Writing about Iowa, Hubert H. Wubben was more tentative, writing that "some secret organizations probably existed, but they, most likely, were entirely home grown" and located in the southern counties. His description credited them with more earnest talk than action. See *Civil War Iowa and the Copperhead Movement*, 120–23. For Pennsylvania, see Sandow, *Deserter Country*, 92–94.

54. For more details about the release incident, read Sandow, *Deserter Country*, 92–94. See also the court martial case against Bloom et al., NAB, Washington, DC, RG 153, MM 1607.

55. "The Maugh Chunk, PA, Rioters," *New York Times*, 5 February 1864.

56. Basler, *Collected Works of Abraham Lincoln*, 6:266.

57. "Let Us Organize," *Columbia Democrat*, 4 April 1863.

58. "The Columbia County Invasion," *Columbian and Democrat*, 4 February 1870.

59. Testimony of Peter Kase, 2 October 1864, NAB, Washington, DC, RG 393, Records of United States Army Continental Commands, 1817–1940, Entry 4663 Department of the Susquehanna, Office of the Judge Advocate, Letters and Reports Received, 1863–1865.

60. "The Monster Meeting," *Clearfield Republican*, 17 August 1864.

61. Summary report of Addison A. Hosmer, Bureau of Military Justice, to the War Department, 25 July 1865. The court martial case against Bloom et al., NAB, Washington, DC, RG 153, MM 1607.

62. Testimony of George Kerb, ibid. See also the court martial case against Patrick Curly, Samuel Lownsberry, and Jacob Wilhelm, NAB, Washington, DC, RG 153, OO 348.

63. "Is Justice Cheated? Or Is This Despotism?" *Clearfield Republican*, 29 March 1865.

64. For a fuller treatment of the Democratic Castle and subsequent military investigations and tribunals, consult Sandow, *Deserter Country*, 86–94.

65. "Meeting of the Democratic Standing Committee of Columbia County," *Columbia Democrat*, 13 June 1863.

66. "The Monster Meeting," *Clearfield Republican*, 17 August 1864.

67. For more on the investigations into Bigler and Wallace, see Sandow, *Deserter Country*, 90–91.

68. "The Monster Meeting," *Clearfield Republican*, 17 August 1864.

69. Scholars of Copperheadism have long been mindful of the importance of a radical memory of the Revolution. Opposition speeches are replete with the language of and historical references from that pivotal period. See Klement, *Copperheads in the Middle West*, 20–21. Churchill's more sustained work on this subject recounted its intellectual origins as well as its application and controversy through time. While his narrative sought to uncover the foundations of the modern militia movement, earlier chapters covered the early republic and Civil War eras. For the latter, Churchill focused most closely on contentious and problematic Indiana, where the government broke up a suspected secession plot in 1864. Churchill, *To Shake Their Guns in the Tyrant's Face*, 5–6, 28–31.

70. *Proceedings of the Nob Mountain Meeting, Held in Columbia County, PA, on the Last Three Days of August, 1865* (Philadelphia: McLaughlin Brothers, 1865), 121.

71. Gray, *Hidden Civil War*, 214. For more on Burr and the *Old Guard*, consult Frank L. Mott, *A History of American Magazines, 1850–1865*, 5 vols. (Cambridge: Harvard University Press, 1938), 2:544–46.

72. Churchill's study also examines how the libertarian memory of the Revolution was contested in earlier challenges to the government, notably Fries's Rebellion. For passages that relate directly to the Civil War, consult Churchill, *To Shake Their Guns in the Tyrant's Face*, 7, 107–11.

73. Neely, *Union Divided*, 59.

74. Robert H. Clark to Andrew Curtin, telegram, Bloomsburg, August 15, 1864, Military Dispatches, July 1–August 31, 1864, Record Group 19, Pennsylvania State Archives, Harrisburg.

75. "Loyal Leagues," *Pittston Gazette*, 16 July 1863.

76. Charles H. Stewart to Richard I. Dodge, 24 August 1864, Charles H. Stewart, Compiled Service Record, NAB, Washington, DC, RG 94, Records of the Adjutant General's Office.

77. For a brief summary of the failures of the expedition in Clearfield, see Sandow, *Deserter Country*, 135–38.

78. "Was Not the Sending of Soldiers to Clearfield a Fraud upon the Government?" *Clearfield Republican*, 8 February 1865.

79. In fact, it incriminated every free state except Massachusetts and Vermont. Joseph Holt to William H. Seward, 8 October 1864, *OR*, ser. 2, vol. 7: 930–53. For a lengthy discussion of the Holt report, consult Frank L. Klement, *Dark Lanterns: Secret Political Societies, Conspiracies, and Treason Trials in the Civil War* (Baton Rouge: Louisiana State University Press, 1984), 136–50. Klement also examines the Knights of the Golden Circle; see pp. 7–33. Once exposed, the KGC was reported to have undergone various rebirths into the Order of American Knights or the Order of the Sons of Liberty. There is no evidence of these organizations in Pennsylvania either.

80. "Keep It before the People," *Brookville Republican*, 10 June 1863.

81. Arnold Shankman, *The Pennsylvania Antiwar Movement, 1861–1865* (Rutherford: Fairleigh Dickinson University Press, 1980), 17, 19, 148.

82. James M. McPherson, *Battle Cry of Freedom: The Civil War Era* (New York: Oxford University Press, 1988), 599.

83. Nagler, "Loyalty and Dissent," 329.

Copperheads in Connecticut: A Peace Movement That Imperiled the Union
Matthew Warshauer

1. A. A. Pettingill to William A. Buckingham, August 24, 1861, RG 005, Governor William A. Buckingham, Connecticut State Library, Hartford.

2. Wood Gray, *The Hidden Civil War: The Story of the Copperheads* (New York: Viking Press, 1942); George Fort Milton, *Abraham Lincoln and the Fifth Column* (New York: Vanguard Press, 1942); Frank L. Klement, *The Copperheads in the Middle West* (Chicago: University of Chicago Press, 1960); Frank L. Klement, *The Limits of Dissent: Clement L. Vallandigham and the Civil War* (New York: Fordham University Press, 1998); Frank L. Klement and Steven K. Roqstad, *Lincoln's Critics: The Copperheads of the North* (Mechanicsburg, PA: White Mane Publishing, 1999).

3. Jennifer L. Weber, *Copperheads: The Rise and Fall of Lincoln's Opponents in the North* (New York: Oxford University Press, 2008).

4. Mark E. Neely Jr., *The Union Divided: Party Conflict in the Civil War North* (Cambridge: Harvard University Press, 2002); Adam I. P. Smith, *No Party Now: Politics in the Civil War North* (New York: Oxford University Press, 2006).

5. See William A. Croffut and John M. Morris, *The Military and Civil History of Connecticut during the War of 1861–1865* (New York: Ledyard Bill, 1869); Joanna D. Cowden, "The Politics of Dissent: Civil War Democrats in Connecticut," *New England Quarterly* 56, no. 4 (1983): 538–54; J. Robert Lane, *A Political History of Connecticut dur-*

ing the Civil War (Washington: Catholic University of America Press, 1941); John E. Tallmadge, "A Peace Movement in Civil War Connecticut," *New England Quarterly* 37, no. 3 (1964): 306–21.

6. See Jarvis M. Morse, *A Neglected Period of Connecticut's History, 1818–1850* (New Haven: Yale University Press, 1933); Michael F. Holt, *The Rise and Fall of the American Whig Party* (New York: Oxford University Press, 1999).

7. New Hampshire was the earliest election. *The Tribune Almanac and Political Register for 1862* (New York: Tribune Co., 1862), xxx. Rhode Island was close to Connecticut, holding its election on the first Wednesday in April. The next election did not occur until September.

8. J. Robert Lane discusses the extent to which other states and commercial interests in New York watched and, to some extent, interfered with Connecticut's election. See *Political History of Connecticut during the Civil War*, 109–10. The historian Albert E. Van Dusen concurred: "The spring election campaign attracted national attention since it was considered by seasoned political observers as a weather vane for the presidential race in the fall." *Connecticut* (New York: Random House, 1964), 222.

9. "Obituary: Ex-Gov. Thomas H. Seymour, of Connecticut," *New York Times*, September 4, 1868; Thomas H. Seymour, biographical information available on the website of the National Governors Association, http://www.nga.org/.

10. James A. Briggs to Abraham Lincoln, February 29, 1860, Abraham Lincoln Papers, American Memory, Library of Congress, http://memory.loc.gov/ammem/alhtml/malhome.html. Lincoln had initially traveled east to visit his son Robert, who was attending Phillips Academy in New Hampshire, and he decided to use the trip to introduce himself to voters in New York, the home of his chief rival for the Republican nomination, William H. Seward. Lincoln delivered his famous Cooper Union address and several speeches in New Hampshire before arriving in Hartford. See Gene Leach, "Glimpses of Lincoln's Brilliance," *Hog River Journal* 3, no. 4 (2005): 26–31; Lewis K. Parker, "Abraham Lincoln in Connecticut," *Connecticut Lawyer* 19, no. 6 (2009): 16–21; J. Doyle Dewitt, *Lincoln in Hartford* (Hartford: Civil War Centennial Commission, 1961).

11. "Abe Lincoln at the City Hall! Another Republican Rally! THE HALL CROWDED TO EXCESS! The Question of Slavery Philosophically Considered! THE DANGER OF INDIFFERENCE," *Hartford Daily Courant*, March 6, 1860; "Lincoln at Meriden; TREMENDOUS ENTHUSIASM 3000 IN THE TOWN HALL! Torchlight Procession! Extra Train from New Haven!" *Hartford Daily Courant*, March 9, 1860; "The Wide Awakes," *Hartford Daily Courant*, March 3, 1860; "The Wide Awakes," *Hartford Daily Courant*, March 20, 1860. For more on the Wide Awake movement, see Julius G. Rathbun, "'The Wide Awakes': The Great Political Organization of 1860," *Connecticut Quarterly* 1 (October 1895): 335; Jon Grinspan, "'Young Men for War': The Wide Awakes and Lincoln's 1860 Presidential Campaign," *Journal of American History* 96, no. 2 (2009): 357–78.

12. Abraham Lincoln to Lyman Trumbull, March 26, 1860, in Lincoln, *Collected Works*, ed. Roy P. Basler et al. (New Brunswick: Rutgers University Press, 1953–55). Lincoln's *Collected Works* are available at http://quod.lib.umich.edu/l/lincoln/.

13. James F. Babcock to Abraham Lincoln, April 8, 1860, in Lincoln, *Collected Works*. See also *The Connecticut Register: Being an Official State Calendar of Public Officers and*

Institution (Hartford: Brown and Parsons, 1859–66), 18. On charges of voter fraud, see Lane, *Political History of Connecticut during the Civil* War, 120–21.

14. John Niven, *Gideon Welles: Lincoln's Secretary of the Navy* (New York: Oxford University Press, 1973), 291.

15. William A. Buckingham, *Message of His Excellency William A. Buckingham, Governor of Connecticut, to the Legislature of the State, May Session, 1860* (New Haven: Carrington and Hotchkiss, 1860), 17–20.

16. *Hartford Times*, November 7, 1860.

17. "Editorial," *New Haven Register*, May 6, 1861; "News Item," *New Haven Register*, May 21, 1861.

18. "Negroes Contraband of War," *New Haven Register*, June 3, 1861; *New Haven Register*, June 7, 1861. See also "Editorial," *New Haven Register*, July 5, 1861, in which the *Register* charges that those pushing the war are "the most detestable traitors are those who hate the Union and have been working for its overthrow for the quarter of a century. . . . We have such traitors now in Connecticut, and throughout the Northern States. They have been long in league with the rabid Abolitionists Garrison and Wendell Phillips."

19. "News Items," *New Haven Register*, May 7, 1861; *Hartford Times*, June 3 and 6, 1861. See also Croffut and Morris, *Military and Civil History of Connecticut during the War of 1861–1865*, 103; Tallmadge, "Peace Movement in Civil War Connecticut."

20. Quoted in "Gov. Seymour's Peace Offering," *Hartford Weekly Times*, July 22, 1861.

21. "A Marked Warning," *Litchfield Enquirer*, June 27, 1861. I have been unable to determine the difference between a white peace flag and a secession flag. The Confederate "bars and stars" was not yet in use. A secession flag may have simply been a white flag or a South Carolina palmetto flag, both of which appeared in Connecticut.

22. Ibid. See also Cowden, "Politics of Dissent."

23. "Peace Movement in Bloomfield," *Hartford Weekly Times*, August 10, 1861.

24. Quoted in Croffut and Morris, *Military and Civil History of Connecticut during the War of 1861–1865*, 106.

25. A. A. Pettingill to William A. Buckingham, August 24, 1861.

26. Croffut and Morris, *Military and Civil History of Connecticut during the War of 1861–1865*, 100–110, provides an excellent account of the peace movement and the reactions to it. See also Tallmadge, "Peace Movement in Civil War Connecticut"; Cowden, "Politics of Dissent."

27. Quoted in Lane, *Political History of Connecticut during the Civil War*, 180.

28. George A. Oviate to William A. Buckingham, August 27, 1861, RG 005, Governor William A. Buckingham, Connecticut State Library, Hartford. Just prior to and at the outset of the war, a number of Connecticut arms companies continued to do a rather brisk business with the South. There is not enough space in this chapter to go into such details. For more on this, see Matthew Warshauer, *Connecticut in the American Civil War: Slavery, Sacrifice, and Survival* (Middletown: Wesleyan University Press, 2011).

29. "A Proclamation: By His Excellency the Governor," *Hartford Daily Courant*, September 2, 1861. Mark Neely notes that many Republicans advocated shutting down Democratic newspapers. See *Union Divided*, chap. 4.

30. On September 3, Carr wrote to Secretary of War Simon Cameron that he had stopped circulation of the *New York Daily News* in New Haven. On the eleventh, he reported that the order was being defied by "a noisy secessionist" named George A. Hubbard, who continued to sell the newspaper on trains of the Naugatuck Railroad. Carr requested approval to arrest Hubbard and did so on the twentieth. Hubbard's brother, however, had connections in the Republican Party, and Secretary of State Seward ordered his release. See Barruss M. Carnahan, *Act of Justice: Lincoln's Emancipation Proclamation and the Law of War* (Lexington: University Press of Kentucky, 2007), 57.

31. On August 29, Ellis B. Schnabel was arrested and charged with "making treasonable harangues at peace meetings . . . and with publicly denouncing the government." *The War of Rebellion: A Compilation of the Official Records of the Union and Confederate Armies*, 128 vols. (Washington, DC, 1880–1901), 2nd ser., 2:620.

32. Phineas T. Barnum to Abraham Lincoln, August 30, 1861, Abraham Lincoln Papers. Barnum also noted, "Those who one week ago were blatant secessionists are to day publicly announcing themselves as 'in for the country to the end of the war.' The '*strong arm*' has a mighty influence here."

33. "It Will Stand," *Hartford Daily Courant*, October 19, 1861; "Toucey and Seymour," *Hartford Daily Courant*, October 29, 1861; "CONNECTICUT DISGRACED," *Hartford Times*, October 16, 1861. The resolution allowed the portraits to be restored when the legislators were satisfied of Toucey and Seymour's loyalty to the Union. See Croffut and Morris, *Military and Civil History of Connecticut during the War of 1861–1865*, 136.

34. 1818 Constitution of the State of Connecticut, art. 3, sect. 5, http://www.sots.ct.gov/sots/cwp/view.asp?a=3188&q=392280. The 1864 amendment was passed in August, as Article 13 of the constitution; it applied solely to soldiers during the "present war." See also Josiah Henry Benton, *Voting in the Field: A Forgotten Chapter of the Civil War* (Boston, 1915), 175. The *Hartford Times* made a brief mention of the judges' decision in its January 1, 1863, edition.

35. Interestingly, Mark Neely notes that when a similar soldier letter and resolution campaign occurred in Illinois, Democratic newspapers did not respond: "The Democrats were left speechless by the soldiers' resolutions—another remarkable and unparalleled fact. Their newspapers mustered little response. The resolutions—threatening a coup d'état rather than warning against one—lay well outside the rules of the political game as usually played. They may have struck genuine fear in the hearts of Democrats. Whatever the case, the Democratic press regarded them as somehow unanswerable." *Union Divided*, 47. The situation in Connecticut did not play out in the same manner.

36. "An Appeal from the Republican State Central Committee," *Hartford Daily Courant*, February 12, 1863. See also Lane, *Political History of Connecticut during the Civil War*, 221–24.

37. "The Convention," *Hartford Times*, February 17, 1863. Eaton referred to Lincoln as an accidental president because he had been elected due to the Democratic Party split, and he had not won the majority of the popular vote.

38. "Democratic Caucus: The Administration Denounced: The Rebels not Denounced," *Hartford Daily Courant*, February 18, 1863.

39. "Copperhead Sentiments," *Hartford Daily Courant*, March 12, 1863.

40. "The Reaction," *Hartford Evening Press*, February 20, 1863; "What Do 'Peace Men' Want?" *Hartford Evening Press*, February 3, 1863. The *Courant* wrote, "We would like to inquire what plan of settlement the Peace party propose. Is the Confederate *usurpation* to be indulged in all its demands?" (January 23, 1863). In another article, the *Courant* insisted, "Peace propositions and compromises are a cheat and a snare, cunningly devised by men who have always opposed the Administration and given aid and comfort to the rebels." "An Appeal from the Republican State Central Committee," *Hartford Daily Courant*, February 12, 1863.

41. "The Soldiers and Their Feelings," *Hartford Times*, January 20, 1863; "What Some of the Soldiers Say," *Hartford Daily Courant*, February 9, 1863; "Letter from a Republican Soldier," *Hartford Times*, February 20, 1863.

42. There are too many articles to cite in a single note, though many are cited throughout this chapter, and a thorough search of the *Times* and *Courant* for the month of March will show the letters and resolutions. See also Laura Lawfer, "'Do Not Place Us between Two Fires': Connecticut Soldiers, Connecticut Newspapers, and the Gubernatorial Election of 1863," paper presented at the "Symposium on 19th Century Press, the Civil War, and Free Expression," at the University of Tennessee, Chattanooga, November 8–10, 2007. Ms. Lawfer was kind enough to share a copy of her paper.

43. "Echoes from the Army Address of the 20th Connecticut, Army of the Potomac," *Hartford Daily Courant*, March 2, 1863; "Soldier's Letters," *Hartford Daily Courant*, March 26, 1863.

44. "From the Soldiers," *Hartford Daily Courant*, March 4, 1863; "What the Soldiers Think of the Copperheads," *Hartford Daily Courant*, March 10, 1863; "An Appeal to the Men of Connecticut!" *Hartford Daily Courant*, March 14, 1863; "Soldier's Letters," *Hartford Daily Courant*, March 17, 1863.

45. "How Soldiers Feel," *Hartford Daily Courant*, March 18, 1863.

46. "A Voice from the Ninth Corps: Patriotic Appeal from Five Connecticut Regiments," *Hartford Daily Courant*, March 21, 1863. See also "The 19th Army Corps:—A Patriotic Appeal," *Hartford Daily Courant*, March 25, 1863.

47. "The Latest Dodge: Republican Misrepresentation of the Soldiers!" *Hartford Times*, March 12, 1863. "Hear the Soldiers: The Truth against Abolition Lies," *Hartford Times*, March 20, 1863. In response to the letter concerning the 22nd, Private William Pearson wrote, "The writer is very ignorant—not much acquainted with the minds of his fellow soldiers (in Co. B, especially,) or he is awfully addicted to saying and writing that which is not true." "Still Another Voice," *Hartford Daily Courant*, March 19, 1863. Another soldier insisted, "I wish to say that that article is an unmitigated falsehood, and that the writer has not the courage to make his name known. . . . If a vote was taken nearly every man would vote for Buck." See "Another Voice from the 22d:—The Outrageous Course of the *Hartford Times*," *Hartford Daily Courant*, March 19, 1863.

48. "A Statement from Major Glafke," *Hartford Daily Courant*, March 25, 1863; "The Times Rebuked," *Hartford Daily Courant*, March 23, 1863.

49. "What a Soldier Thinks of Seymour's Nomination," *Hartford Daily Courant*, February 27, 1863.

50. [Samuel Fiske], *Mr. Dunn Browne's Experiences in the Army* (Boston: Nichols and Noyes, 1866), 118–19.

51. Frederick A. Lucas, *Dear Mother from Your Dutiful Son: Civil War Letters, September 22, 1862 to August 18, 1865, Written by Frederick A. Lucas to His Mother*, ed. Ernest Barker (Goshen, CT: Purple Door Gallery, 2003), 70.

52. Benjamin Hirst, *The Boys from Rockville: Civil War Narratives of Sgt. Benjamin Hirst, Company D, 14th Connecticut Volunteers*, ed. Robert L. Bee (Knoxville: University of Tennessee Press, 1998), 94.

53. "The National Platform! Purposes of the War!" *Hartford Times*, April 4, 1863. See also "A Great Meeting: *Outpouring of the Democracy!* Immense Enthusiasm: 'Seymour and the Constitution,'" *Hartford Times*, March 20, 1863; *Hartford Times*, March 26, 1863.

54. *New Haven Register*, March 26, 1863.

55. J. Matthew Gallman, "An Inspiration to Work: Anna Elizabeth Dickinson, Public Orator," in *The War Was You and Me*, ed. Joan E. Cashin (Princeton: Princeton University Press, 2002), 159–82; J. Matthew Gallman, *America's Joan of Arc: The Life of Anna Elizabeth Dickinson* (New York: Oxford University Press, 2006); Lane, *Political History of Connecticut during the Civil War*, 232–33; Joseph Duffy, "Anna Elizabeth Dickinson and the Election of 1863," *Connecticut History* 25 (1984): 22–38; Joseph Duffy, "A Quaker Firebrand Swings An Election," *Hog River Journal* 2, no. 4 (2004): 18–23.

56. There is a minor discrepancy regarding the actual number of votes. I follow *The Connecticut Register*, which provides the following numbers: Buckingham: 41,031 votes; Seymour: 38,397 votes; total votes: 79,428; margin: 2,634.

57. "The Election," *Hartford Daily Courant*, April 7, 1863; "Well Done, Hartford!" *Hartford Daily Courant*, April 7, 1863; "Victory! Victory!" *Hartford Evening Press*, April 7, 1863.

58. "Unwelcome Truths," *Hartford Times*, April 8, 1863; "The 'Government' Outrage on the People of Connecticut," *Hartford Times*, April 10, 1863. See also "Connecticut Election: The Result," *Hartford Times*, April 7, 1863.

59. "Cheated out of It," *New Haven Register*, April 8, 1863. The *Register* had written earlier, "The Republicans, knowing well that the popular tide is against them, now depend upon money and a large influx of furloughed Republican soldiers to carry them through. The Democratic soldiers are to be kept on duty, and the Republicans, to a large extent, sent home to vote. All this won't save them. The people are moving." "Take Notice, Democrats," *New Haven Register*, March 24, 1863.

60. Abraham Lincoln to Thurlow Weed, February 19, 1863, in Lincoln, *Collected Works*, 6:112–13.

61. Quoted in Lincoln, *Collected Works*, 6:112–13n1. See also Stephen F. Knott, *Secret and Sanctioned: Covert Operations and the American Presidency* (New York: Oxford University Press, 1996), 147–48, 222. Lane, *Political History of Connecticut during the Civil War*, 237, discusses accusations that Mark Howard, a Republican Party insider, raised money for bribery. See also Joanna Dunlap Cowden, *"Heaven Will Frown on Such a Cause as This": Six Democrats Who Opposed Lincoln's War* (Lanham, MD: University Press of America, 2001), 48–49.

62. Thomas and Origen Seymour may have been cousins. Buckingham received 39,820 votes to Seymour's 34,162. See *The Connecticut Register*.

63. "The Result in Hartford! COPPERHEADISM ON ITS LAST LEGS! Wm. W. Eaton Defeated! A GLORIOUS DAY'S WORK!" *Hartford Daily Courant*, April 5, 1864; "BUCKINGHAM AND UNION," *Hartford Daily Courant*, April 5, 1864; "Victory Again," *Hartford Evening Press*, April 5 1864. See also "The Great Victory," *Hartford Evening Press*, April 5, 1864.

64. William A. Buckingham to Abraham Lincoln, April 5, 1864, Abraham Lincoln Papers.

65. "The State Election," *Hartford Times*, April 5, 1864.

66. John Niven, *Connecticut for the Union* (New Haven: Yale University Press, 1965), 88–90; Croffut and Morris, *Military and Civil History of Connecticut during the War of 1861–1865*, 459.

67. "List of Certified Cowards in Woodbury! As Per Surgeon's Certificates," Museum of Connecticut History, Hartford. This list provides medical exemptions by name and malady. At the height of the exemption controversy over the notorious Josiah Beckwith, the doctor sent a justification of his actions to the *Litchfield Enquirer*, arguing that "many absurd as well as unjust reports are in circulation in relation to the manner in which certificates of exemption were obtained in the Litchfield office." "A Card from Dr. Beckwith," *Litchfield Enquirer*, n.d. The Litchfield Historical Society also owns all of Dr. Beckwith's medical journals, which list the men he exempted and the reasons he gave for doing so. Josiah Gale Beckwith, Journals, Beckwith Family Papers (unprocessed collection), Helga J. Ingraham Memorial Library, Litchfield Historical Society, Litchfield, Connecticut. For more on draft evasion in Connecticut, see Croffut and Morris, *Military and Civil History of Connecticut during the War of 1861–1865*, 241–45; Lane, *Political History of Connecticut during the Civil War*, 206–8; Niven, *Connecticut for the Union*, 82–86.

68. "Brightening Prospects," *Hartford Daily Courant*, September 8, 1864.

69. "How Many More Years of War!" *Hartford Times*, October 20, 1864; "Lincoln vs. Sherman," *New Haven Register*, September 16, 1864.

70. "A Republic or a Monarchy," *Hartford Times*, November 7, 1864: "Elect GEORGE B. MCCLELLAN, and the days of Peace, tranquility, prosperity, and happiness will dawn their glorious light upon our country. The war will stop, the good old Union will be restored, and, God be praised, Liberty and the Constitution will be again triumphant and the most glorious jubilee that ever rejoiced the heart of man will burst forth upon this people, redeemed, disenthralled and standing up in all the splendid attributes of a Heaven-inspired manhood."

71. "Close up the Campaign of 1864," *New Haven Register*, November 7, 1864.

72. "Victory," *Hartford Evening Press*, November 9, 1864.

73. By 1864, nineteen states had passed legislation allowing soldiers to vote in the field. In New York and Connecticut, these votes provided the margin for Lincoln's victory. See James M. McPherson, *Battle Cry of Freedom: The Civil War Era* (New York: Oxford University Press, 1988), 804–5; 1818 Constitution of the State of Connecticut, art. 3, sect. 5. See also Benton, *Voting in the Field*, 175. Connecticut election results were 44,693 for Lincoln and 42,288 for McClellan. Connecticut Election Results, http://www.uselectionatlas.org/RESULTS/state.php?year=1864&off=0&elect=0&fips=9&f=0. William Frank Zornow noted

that of the votes for Lincoln, some 2,898 were cast by soldiers, thus assuring him victory. See *Lincoln and the Party Divided* (Norman: University of Oklahoma Press, 1954), 201. Weber also notes that "the soldier vote probably tipped the balance in New York and Connecticut to Lincoln's favor." *Copperheads*, 252.

"All Manner of Schemes and Rascalities": The Politics of Promotion in the Union Army
Timothy J. Orr

1. G. E. Andrews to Freeman Andrews, 24 March 1864, Civil War Miscellaneous Collection, U.S. Army Military History Institute, Carlisle, Pennsylvania (hereafter USAMHI); Henry Chase, *Representative Men of Maine* (Portland, ME: Lakeside Press, 1893), xlvii.

2. For a survey of politics in the antebellum army, see William B. Skelton, "Officers and Politicians: The Origins of Army Politics in the United States before the Civil War," in Peter Karsten, ed., *The Military in America: From the Colonial Era to the Present, New Revised Edition* (New York: Free Press, 1986), 112–30. Skelton argued that "military and political life interpenetrated at all levels," but the "regularization of the military administration after the War of 1812 somewhat restricted the scope of political patronage. . . . Seniority strictly governed regular promotions through the grade of colonel."

3. David M. Potter, "Jefferson Davis and the Political Factors in Confederate Defeat," in David Donald, ed., *Why the North Won the Civil War* (Baton Rouge: Louisiana State University Press, 1960), 111; Eric McKitrick, "Party Politics and the Union and Confederate War Efforts," in William Nisbet Chambers and Walter Dean Burnham, eds., *The American Party Systems: Stages of Political Development* (New York: Oxford University Press, 1967); Joel Silbey, *A Respectable Minority: The Democratic Party in the Civil War Era, 1860–1868* (New York: Norton, 1977); and Adam I. P. Smith, *No Party Now: Politics in the Civil War North* (New York: Oxford University Press, 2006), 7.

4. Mark E. Neely Jr., *The Union Divided: Party Conflict in the Civil War North* (Cambridge: Harvard University Press, 2002), 27.

5. For a survey of political maneuvering in the Union Army's senior officer corps, see Thomas Joseph Goss, *The War within the Union High Command: Politics and Generalship during the Civil War* (Lawrence: University Press of Kansas, 2003).

6. As they arrived at the seat of war, each militia regiment adhered to a different set of state-imposed guidelines. They showed up wearing different uniforms, wielding different weapons, fielding differently sized companies and battalions, and commanded by different numbers of corporals, sergeants, lieutenants, and majors. For instance, Ohio's militia law of 1857 defined a "company" as no less than twenty men, but no more than one hundred; New York's militia law, meanwhile, considered a company to be no less than thirty-two men but no more than fifty. Ohio's law prescribed three lieutenants per company; New York's law allowed only two. For the full descriptions of state antebellum militia statutes, see *Militia Law of Ohio, Being an Act to Organize and Discipline the Militia and Volunteer Militia, Passed March 28, 1857* (Columbus: Richard Nevins, State Printer, 1857), 1–48; *Militia Law of the State of New York, an Act Passed for the Enrollment of the Militia and*

the Organization of Uniform Corps, and the Discipline of the Military Forces of this State, Passed April 17, 1854 (Albany: Weed, Parsons & Company, Printers, 1854), 1–107.

7. While there were many differences among the antebellum state militia laws, one thing they all had in common was that the governors, even when operating as "commanders in chief" of the militia, had limited roles to play in the promotion of officers. Generally, state governors approved the election results in the militia regiments and no more. Each state militia law delineated the process of election, but they sometimes followed different methods. For instance, the laws in Maine, Massachusetts, New York, and Pennsylvania required enlisted men in each company to vote for their lieutenants and captains. These lieutenants and captains elected the majors, lieutenant colonels, and colonels of the regiments. In those states, elections stopped at colonel; the state legislatures chose the brigade and division commanders, except in New York, where the appointment of major generals of the state militia remained with the governor. Conversely, Ohio's antebellum militia law required all officers, from second lieutenant to major general, to stand for popular election. Neither did these militia laws remained fixed for lengthy periods of time. Pennsylvania, for instance, revised its militia law four times in the 1850s, the largest alteration coming on April 21, 1858. This revision expanded the statute to more than one hundred sections. On April 21, 1861, six days after Lincoln made his first call for troops, the Pennsylvania legislature amended its militia act yet again. *Militia Laws of the State of Maine, with Extracts from the United States and State Constitutions and the Laws of the United States in Relation Thereto* (Augusta: Fuller and Fuller, State Printers, 1856), 1–84; *Digest of the Militia Laws of Massachusetts, Extracts Relating to the Militia from the United States and State Constitutions and the Laws of the United States* (Boston: Dutton, Wentworth, State Printers, 1851), 1–121; Frederick C. Brightly, John Purdon, and George Coode, *A Digest of the Laws of Pennsylvania from the Year One Thousand Seven Hundred to The Tenth Day of July One Thousand Eight Hundred and Seventy-Two, Tenth Edition, Volume 2* (Philadelphia: Kay and Brother, 1873), 1038–65.

8. Thomas M. O'Brien and Oliver Diefendorf, *General Orders of the War Department Embracing the Years 1861, 1862, and 1863, Volume 1* (New York: Derby and Miller, 1864), 32–33. Under these orders, each infantry company would now consist of one captain, two lieutenants, five sergeants, eight corporals, two musicians, one wagoner, and between sixty-four and eighty-two privates apiece. Ten infantry companies, so organized and combined, constituted a regiment, which would, in turn, be led and administered by a staff of thirty-six commissioned officers and noncommissioned staff officers. Cavalry regiments followed the same model, but they fielded between seventy-nine and ninety-five aggregate per company, and they consisted of four to six squadrons apiece. (Two cavalry companies constituted a squadron.)

9. In 1861, Democrats had control of the executive offices in Kentucky, Delaware, Missouri, Oregon, and California. The American Party controlled one executive office, that of Maryland.

10. The potential for political mischief was great, but Cameron tried to make it clear that political favoritism in the Union Army would not be tolerated. He instructed the governors to choose their junior officers based on military merit, not partisan affiliation. On May 22, 1861, Cameron wrote to John Andrew of Massachusetts, instructing him to,

"1st. . . . commission no one of doubtful morals or patriotism and not of sound health. 2d. To appoint no one to a Lieutenancy (second or first) who has passed the age of 22 years or to a captaincy over 30 years, and appoint no field officers (Major, Lieutenant Colonel, Colonel) unless a graduate of the United States Military Academy or known to possess military knowledge and experience, who have not passed the respective ages of 35, 40, 45 years." See Simon Cameron to John Andrew, 22 May 1861, Adjutant General's Papers, Massachusetts State Archives, Boston (hereafter MSA).

11. For instance, G. G. Ferguson, a Pennsylvania clergyman, wrote Governor Andrew Curtin, "With your approval, I will stump the state if necessary to fill my regiment. I know of parts of Cos, squads of men in different sections, and these with proper influences can be brought into the service. . . . I might not say that we are nearly all Republicans and *Curtin men*." G. G. Ferguson to Andrew Curtin, 19 October 1861, Record Group Nineteen, Adjutant General's Papers, Pennsylvania State Archives, Harrisburg (hereafter PSA).

12. Clerk of the Courts Edward Skidmore wrote a glowing letter to Governor Edwin D. Morgan, endorsing James Smith's appointment. The rhetoric of his letter was typical of the hundreds of thousands of endorsements that flooded into the governors' offices during the opening months of the war. Skidmore enthused, "He [Smith] is an ambitious young man, and left his wife and family in this city in defense of his country. He is also a man of responsibility and good standing and deserves a higher place than a private. I trust that his merits as a soldier may entitle him to favor at your hands. Ex. Judge Culver, Hon. Benj. Wade and other prominent men of our state, I am informed, are personally acquainted with Mr. Smith, and traveled with him and Cooke's Glee Club during the last presidential canvas. At the request of the friends of Mr. Smith, I take the liberty of bringing him to your notice." Edward Skidmore to Edwin Morgan, 11 September 1861, Office of the Adjutant General's Correspondence, New York State Archives, Albany, New York (hereafter NYSA). Some ambitious applicants spoke for themselves, often proudly. For instance, Augustus B. Sage of New York City cajoled Governor Edwin D. Morgan, promising, "I respectfully apply for the position of second lieutenant in one of our state regiments, now at the seat of war. If appointed to the position, I will immediately donate to the state library a fine collection of coins, medals, &c." Impressed by Sage's willingness to sacrifice—in this case, to share his collection of medals and books—Morgan honored his request. In fact, the governor elevated him to captain. Augustus B. Sage, 11 September 1861, NYSA.

13. Container List, Record Group B0462, Adjutant General's Office, Correspondence and Petitions, 1821–1896, NYSA. Boxes 25–97 contain the Civil War–era correspondence. During the war, New York organized 194 infantry regiments, twenty-seven cavalry and mounted rifle regiments, sixteen heavy artillery regiments (each with fifteen companies and two additional majors), sixty light artillery batteries (each with five officers), and dozens of sundry independent organizations that required officers. Considering the fact that some companies fielded more than a dozen different officers during the war, the scope of administrative paperwork is nothing short of mind-blowing. Presently, the commissions' files kept at the New York State Archives consist of approximately seventy boxes of correspondence. Each box contains twenty-two to twenty-nine folders and each folder contains thirty to forty letters or groups of letters relating to commissioning.

14. James Cooper to Augustus Bradford, 19 April 1862, Adjutant Generals Papers, Maryland State Archives, Annapolis (hereafter MDSA).

15. Only Vermont deviated from the norm in that its legislature elected—its governor did not appoint—the state military staff.

16. In some states, such as Vermont, the adjutant generalship became a part-time clerkship, an unnecessary station that posed a minor drain on the state treasury (it paid a mere $75 per year). *H. Henry Baxter, Born January 18, 1818, Died February 17, 1884* (New York: Atlantic Public and Engraving, 1884), 16; Stephen C. Hutchins, *Civil List and Constitutional History of the Colony and State of New York* (Albany: Weed, Parsons, and Company, 1880), 153–54.

17. Some adjutants general owed their posts to political favoritism, but others owed their appointments to a blend of political and military experience, sparse though it was. New Hampshire's adjutant general, Natt Head, descended from an illustrious military family, served as a sheriff and as president of the New Hampshire State Agricultural Society, and had once held memberships in five antebellum militia units. As one biographer said, "Inheriting military taste and enthusiasm from three generations," it was no surprise to see him "following in the footsteps of distinguished and patriotic ancestors." Thomas Hillhouse, New York's first adjutant general of the war, had been a state senator and an anti-secession pamphleteer. A biographer said of him, "Much of his leisure was devoted to the study of military and political science." Hillhouse's replacement, John T. Sprague, who ascended to the position after a new administration took office in late 1862, had been a lieutenant in the Florida Wars. John Badger Clarke, *Sketches of Successful New Hampshire Men* (Manchester: J. B. Clarke, 1882), 223–28; *Prominent Families of New York* (New York: Nichol and Roy, 1897), 278; Hutchins, *Civil List and Constitutional History of the Colony and State of New York*, 153–54.

18. William Schouler, long heralded by self-serving Massachusetts eulogizers as the most effective adjutant general of the war, apparently possessed the ability to select good officers. As one admirer said of him, "He knew the stuff of which our regiments were made." *H. Henry Baxter*, 7; James Schouler, *Historical Briefs* (New York: Dodd, Mead, and Company, 1896), 263.

19. The editor of the *Evening Journal* argued that five other colonels harbored Democratic loyalties, three more aligned with the Bell–Everett ticket, and the remaining colonel had no discernible political loyalties whatsoever. See *Boston Evening Journal*, 22 August 1861. The *Evening Journal* quoted the *Herald*'s article. The fourteen regiments in question were the 1st, 2nd, 7th, 9th, 10th, 11th, 12th, 13th, 14th, 15th, 16th, 18th, 19th, and 20th Massachusetts Infantry.

20. *New York Times*, 9 May 1861.

21. A. Howard Meneely, *The War Department, 1861: A Study in Mobilization and Administration* (Cranbury, NJ: Scholar's Bookshelf, 2006), 160–61.

22. *New York Herald*, 20 May 1861. This did not end the disagreement between Sickles and Morgan. Under a provision granted him as commander in chief of state forces, Morgan refused to authorize the departure of Sickles's regiments unless the officers held official commissions signed at Albany. At this point, Sickles kept quiet, and throughout

June and July, he let Morgan appoint officers to the brigade, known as the "Excelsior Brigade"; but after the Battle of Bull Run, when Morgan authorized the brigade's departure to Washington, Sickles purged the officer corps of all persons loyal to Morgan. When the governor sent a package of commissions to the brigade's encampment, Sickles intercepted it and turned the official documents into "waste paper" for his orderlies. Governor Morgan pursued no further action. Already overburdened with paperwork, and with the Union Army reeling from its defeat at Bull Run, Morgan left the Excelsior Brigade alone, apparently unconcerned with who officered it. Thomas A. Smith to Edwin Morgan, 20 December 1861; J. L. Palmer to Nelson Taylor, 17 March 1862; Nelson Taylor to Thomas Hillhouse, 19 March 1862; William H. Tingley to Thomas Hillhouse, 23 March and 3 April 1862, NYSA; James Stevenson, *History of the Excelsior Brigade or Sickles' Brigade* (Patterson, NJ: Van Derhoven and Holmes, 1863), 5–7.

23. U.S. War Department, *The War of the Rebellion: A Compilation of the Official Records of the Union and Confederate Armies, Series 1, Volume 23* (Washington, DC: Government Printing Office, 1880–1901), 349, 380–83 (hereafter *OR*). The War Department issued GO 47 on July 25, 1861, and then on August 3, it issued GO 49, this just after Congress passed an act, "for the better organization of the military establishment," mandating a change in the way the army determined competency. This GO followed the directions of the Congressional Act.

24. Ostensibly, both Congress and the War Department wanted McClellan to appoint experienced U.S. Regulars to preside over these examination boards and keep them devoid of partisan sentiment. Also, according to the regulations set forth by Congress, each board could not consist of less than two officers of a higher rank than those summoned to examination. (Essentially, each board had to consist of at least two lieutenants.) Finally, these boards had to avoid conflicts of interest, as the orders described "that no officer shall be eligible to sit on such board or commission whose rank or promotion would in any way be affected by its proceedings." This meant an officer sitting on the board had to excuse himself in the event that the board examined a member of his own regiment.

25. Ariovistus Pardee Jr. to Father, 7 January 1863, Pardee-Robison Collection, USAMHI.

26. Described by one Marylander as "a Northern adventurer," Duryeé and his cabal, which included a number of other New York–born officers, promised to "oust every one of us [Marylanders] if possible"—so complained Lieutenant Charles Bowen of Company D. Charles Bowen to Augustus Bradford, 4 June and 23 July 1862, MDSA.

27. Ibid.

28. Edward Moroney to Augustus Bradford, 21 April 1862; Charles Bowen to Augustus Bradford, 4 June and 23 July 1862; Andrew B. Brunner to Augustus Bradford, 17 July 1862, MDSA.

29. Bowen to Bradford, 23 July 1862. Once again thwarted by the New Yorkers, Lieutenant Bowen believed, "the whole proceedings were gotten up expressly for Colonel Allard; such a thing was unprecedented in the Division; the like had never been done before." Bowen, however, had to endure the situation as it stood. Like it or not, Duryeé commanded the regiment.

30. Abraham Lincoln to Carl Schurz, 10 November 1862, in Roy P. Basler, ed., *The Collected Works of Abraham Lincoln, 1809–1865*, Volume 5 (New Brunswick: Rutgers University Press, 1953), 493–95.

31. George P. McLean et al., to Andrew Curtin, 25 June 1864, PSA.

32. These discouraged Republicans returned to Philadelphia to state their case before the members of the Union League, but then a sequence of letters written by prominent Democratic generals—including Seth Williams, George Gordon Meade, Winfield Scott Hancock, and Colonel Nelson Miles—laid the blame on the haughtiness of the 4th Union League's officers. When it came time to make a decision regarding the reputation of the resigned officers, the Union League Club members unexpectedly sided with the 2nd Corps staff. "Believing without question," their public minutes stated, "the statements of those officers contained in their letters, . . . the committee have reluctantly come to the conclusion, notwithstanding the testimonials, which induced the committee to approve your commissions in the regiment, that you have merited the reproach now of record at the hands of your superiors in command. . . . It is only necessary to add that the committee consider that its official relations with you to be properly terminated with this reply to your communication." Union League Club to George P. McLean et al., 22 November 1864, Union League Club Library, Philadelphia (hereafter ULCL).

33. George H. Crosman Jr. to George H. Crosman Sr., 30 May 1864; Andrew Curtin to Union League Club, 30 May 1864, ULCL.

34. *OR*, ser. 1, vol. 32: 467–69.

35. A. H. Grimshaw to John Newton, 29 January 1862, in "Traitor in the Camp," undated broadside, NYSA.

36. John Newton to A. H. Grimshaw, 7 February 1862, in "Traitor in the Camp," undated broadside, NYSA.

37. Grimshaw chided, "Resolution 1st repudiated the war in any case, and preferred a peaceable recognition of the Confederate States to the shedding of blood. For this Adam E. King voted. Because we have Adam E. King's *et id genus omne* we have *Rebellion*." A. H. Grimshaw to John Newton, 11 February 1862, in "Traitor in the Camp," undated broadside, NYSA.

38. A. H. Grimshaw public statement, 13 February 1862, in "Traitor in the Camp," undated broadside, NYSA.

39. *Delaware Inquirer*, 25 January 1862.

40. The 6th Corps did not come into official existence until May 18, 1862. The Adam E. King episode occurred during January and February 1862.

41. Adam E. King to William E. Browne, 13 February 1862; William E. Brown to Thomas Hillhouse, 13 February 1862; William B. Franklin to Thomas Hillhouse, 13 February 1862; O. F. Pratt to Thomas Hillhouse, 14 February 1862, NYSA.

42. William B. Franklin to Andrew Curtin, 16 July 1862, PSA.

43. John Newton to Andrew Curtin, 16 July 1862, PSA.

44. George McClellan to Andrew Curtin, 16 July 1862, PSA.

45. Gustavus Town to Andrew Russell, 14 July 1862, PSA.

46. Ibid.

47. Officers of the 95th Pennsylvania Infantry to Andrew Curtin, 18 July 1862, PSA. The officers included six captains, nine first lieutenants, five second lieutenants, one surgeon, and one assistant surgeon.

48. Officers of the 18th, 31st, and 32nd New York Infantries, n.d., PSA. Speaking of Colonel Town, the New York officers wrote, "We have been associated with him for eight months, have seen him in all the varying scenes of a soldier's life, and bear willing tribute to the commendable manner in which he conducted himself in all of them. We desire expressly to bear testimony to his management of the regiment. . . . Well did he perform that duty throughout the memorable week of trials which succeeded the above mentioned battle. At all times cool and self possessed, exhibiting sleepless vigilance and untiring activity, he proved himself to be a fitting leader and fully worthy of being the successor of the lamented Colonel John M. Gosline."

49. Abel Thomas to Henry Moore, 22 July 1862, PSA.

50. Thomas Noble to Jeremiah Nichols, 15 July 1862, PSA.

51. Joseph Moore Jr. to Andrew Curtin, 23 July 1862, PSA.

52. *Philadelphia Inquirer*, 25 July 1862.

53. John McIntosh to Andrew Curtin, 24 July 1862, PSA.

54. Asa W. Bartlett, *History of the Twelfth New Hampshire Volunteers in the War of the Rebellion* (Concord: Ira C. Evans, 1897), 8–9.

55. Ibid.

56. George C. Canek, William Coxson, William Wade, Thomas Byrd, and Charles Rogers to Horatio Seymour, 31 August 1863, NYSA.

57. Moses McClean, H. J. Stahle, J. C. Weed, D. Ziegler, G. Swope, J. A. Swope, E. B. Buehler, and W. A. Duncan to Horatio Seymour, 18 August 1864, NYSA.

58. Henry F. Liebenau Sr. to Reuben Fenton, 23 January 1865, NYSA.

59. This soldier was Sergeant Francis L. Morgan, and his commander was Colonel Andrew H. Tippen of the 68th Pennsylvania. William H. Morgan Jr. to Joseph Moore, 10 February 1863; Francis L. Morgan to William H. Morgan Jr., 29 January 1863; Andrew H. Tippen to Eli Slifer, 1 February 1863; Joseph Moore to Colonel Roberts, 6 February 1863, PSA.

60. The six Democratic officers were Brigadier General Alexander Webb, Major General George G. Meade, Brigadier General James Barnes, Colonel Jacob Sweitzer, Brigadier General Daniel Butterfield, and Major General Charles Griffin.

61. George E. Deutsch, "The Politics of Command in the 83rd Pennsylvania Volunteer Infantry and the Bizarre Case of Major William H. Lamont," *Gettysburg Magazine* 40 (January 2009): 111–22.

62. George Watson to Andrew Curtin, 20 February 1863, PSA.

63. Alfred Sellers to Andrew Curtin, 12 January and 3 February 1863, PSA.

64. William P. Davis et al., to Andrew Curtin, 19 March 1863, PSA.

65. Unhappily, in the spring of 1863, before Watson could remonstrate through official channels, the Army of the Potomac commenced three grueling campaigns: Chancellorsville, Gettysburg, and Mine Run. All the while, Watson found himself persecuted by Democratic officers who wanted to drive him out of the regiment. In December 1863, Watson lamented, "By my efforts in a just and legal manner to obtain my rights I have of-

fended some of the Officers in command over me in my Regt., who if they be foolish, or prejudiced, or dishonest, or have a spite, they have the opportunity of bearing hard on me, and I have most dangerous enemies to deal with." Alfred Sellers to Andrew Curtin, n.d.; George W. Watson to Andrew Curtin, 18 December 1863 and 9 February 1866, PSA.

66. George W. Watson to Andrew Curtin, 9 February 1866, PSA.

67. It should be noted that the Confederacy fielded three general forces: the Provisional Army of the Confederacy, the Army of the Confederacy, and the State Militias. The Provisional Army and the Army of the Confederacy performed the bulk of the combat action, with the War Department and Confederate Congress administrating regiments organized under their direction. Confederate governors wielded stricter control over the militia, or "Home Guard," as they were derisively known. Thus, when referring to the "Confederate Army," most scholars never mean to include the militia. The process of promotion in Confederate high command is explained more fully in John H. Eicher and David J. Eicher, *Civil War High Commands* (Stanford: Stanford University Press, 2001), 66–71.

68. This evidence might help explain a theory from the early twentieth century, that "states' rights" weakened the Confederacy. The lack of an appointing power might explain why certain Confederate governors—Joseph Brown and Zebulon Vance, especially—resisted the Confederacy's central government so viciously. See Frank L. Owsley, *States Rights in the Confederacy* (Chicago: University of Chicago Press, 1925).

69. Charles E. Brooks, "Popular Sovereignty in the Confederate Army: The Case of Colonel John Marshall and the Fourth Texas Infantry Regiment," in Aaron Sheehan-Dean, ed., *The View from the Ground: Experiences of Civil War Soldiers* (Lexington: University Press of Kentucky, 2007), 209, 216.

"For My Part I Dont Care Who Is Elected President": The Union Army and the Elections of 1864
Jonathan W. White

1. James M. McPherson, *For Cause and Comrades: Why Men Fought in the Civil War* (New York: Oxford University Press, 1997), 129; Jennifer L. Weber, *Copperheads: The Rise and Fall of Lincoln's Opponents in the North* (New York: Oxford University Press, 2006), 2. For other scholars who follow this general interpretive trend, see Chandra Manning, *What This Cruel War Was Over: Soldiers, Slavery, and the Civil War* (New York: Random House, 2007); and William C. Davis, *Lincoln's Men: How President Lincoln Became Father to an Army and a Nation* (New York: Free Press, 1999).

2. Josiah Benton, *Voting in the Field: A Forgotten Chapter of the Civil War* (Boston: Plimpton Press, 1915).

3. Geo. W. A. to Manton Marble, September 27, 1864, Manton Marble Papers, Manuscript Division, Library of Congress, Washington, DC (hereafter LC).

4. See, for example, Jonathan W. White, "Canvassing the Troops: The Federal Government and the Soldiers' Right to Vote," *Civil War History* 50 (September 2004): 290–316; White, "Citizens and Soldiers: Party Competition and the Debate in Pennsylvania over Permitting Soldiers to Vote, 1861–64," *American Nineteenth Century History* 5 (Summer 2004): 47–70.

5. Barlow to Marble, August 21, 1864, Marble Papers.

6. Napoleon Bonaparte Hudson to Nathaniel, August 28, 1864, Hudson Letters; and Frederic Henry Kellogg to Mother, November 8, 1864, Kellogg Letters, both in Civil War Miscellaneous Collection, U.S. Army Military History Institute, Carlisle, Pennsylvania (hereafter MHI).

7. Harvey Reid to Father, November 8, 1864, in Frank L. Byrne, ed., *Uncommon Soldiers: Harvey Reid and the 22nd Wisconsin March with Sherman* (Knoxville: University of Tennessee Press, 2001), 198; Daniel G. Brinton to Ma, September 12, 1864, Daniel G. Brinton Letters, Chester County Historical Society, West Chester, Pennsylvania; John F. L. Hartwell to Wife, August 14, 1864, in Ann Hartwell Britton and Thomas J. Reed, eds., *To My Beloved Wife and Boy at Home: The Letters and Diaries of Orderly Sergeant John F. L. Hartwell* (Madison: Fairleigh Dickinson University Press, 1997), 270, 308; Leaner E. Davis to Wife, September 29 and October 21, 1864, Davis Letters, Civil War Miscellaneous Collection, MHI.

8. Henry McKendree "Mack" Ewing to Nan Ewing, September 6, 1864, Archives of Michigan, Lansing (available through http://seekingmichigan.org/).

9. Mack to Nan, September 25, 1865, ibid.

10. There are many instances where soldiers sought to influence their friends and family at home. See, for example, Robert E. Bonner, *The Soldier's Pen: Firsthand Impressions of the Civil War* (New York: Hill and Wang, 2006), chap. 4, esp. p. 127.

11. On the rise and fall of morale in the armies at various points in the war, see McPherson, *For Cause and Comrades*, 155–62.

12. Samuel Brooks to Wife, November 4, 1864, Brooks Letters, Civil War Miscellaneous Collection, MHI. See also Carl Uterhard to Mother, September 5, 1864; Christopher Monn to Brother et al., December 9, 1863; Christian Bonsel to Parents et al., January 29, 1865; and G. W. Schwarting to Brother, August 15, 1864, all in Walter D. Kamphoefner and Wolfgang Helbich, eds., *Germans in the Civil War: The Letters They Wrote Home* (Chapel Hill: University of North Carolina Press, 2006), 172, 273, 330, 443; H. J. H. Thompson to wife, March 27 and November 27, 1864, quoted in John G. Barrett, *The Civil War in North Carolina* (Chapel Hill: University of North Carolina Press, 1963), 226.

13. John Berry to Samuel L. M. Barlow, September 3, 1864, Barlow Papers; Daniel Helker to George Miller, November 2, 1864, George Miller Collection, MHI. See also John Borry to Daniel Musser, September 12, 1864, Daniel Musser Papers (MG-95), Pennsylvania State Archives, Harrisburg (hereafter PHMC).

14. Martin G. Ellison to Parent and Sister, October 1, 1864, Martin G. Ellison Papers, Research Center, Wisconsin Veterans Museum, Madison. See also George F. Morse to Father, November 6, 1864, Morse Letters, Civil War Miscellaneous Collection, MHI; Charles A. Coward to Father, January 25, 1863, Coward Letters, Civil War Miscellaneous Collection, MHI; John Berry to Barlow, August 27, 1864, Barlow Papers.

15. John Morton to Mother, January 13, 1863, and August 31, 1864, Morton Letters; and Morris W. Chalmers to Sister, September 26 and October 27, 1864, Chalmers Letters, both in Civil War Miscellaneous Collection, MHI; Charles Henry Morgan to Susannah Miller, September 23, 1864, Chester County Historical Society, West Chester, Pennsylvania.

16. John S. McVey to Horace Subers, October 15, 1864, McVey Letters; and Thomas C. Bowman to Sister, October 20, 1864, Bowman Letters, both in Civil War Miscellaneous Collection, MHI.

17. Brigham Foster to Wife, November 9, 1864, Foster Letters, Civil War Miscellaneous Collection, MHI. This soldier also believed that the southern people would never be willing to end the war while Lincoln was president and his emancipation policy was the law of the land.

18. Jacob B. Dannaker to Mother, December 28, 1864, Dannaker Letters, Civil War Miscellaneous Collection, MHI.

19. Edward King Wightman to Brother, October 26, 1864, in Edward G. Longacre, ed., *From Antietam to Fort Fisher: The Civil War Letters of Edward King Wightman, 1862–1865* (Madison: Fairleigh Dickinson University Press, 1985), 212–13; Charles Francis Adams Jr. to Father, October 15, 1865, in Worthington Chauncey Ford, ed., *A Cycle of Adams Letters, 1861–1865*, 2 vols. (New York: Houghton Mifflin, 1920), 2:204; Charles H. Smith to Wife, October 20, 1864, Charles H. Smith Letters, Civil War Miscellaneous Collection, MHI; Patrick, diary entry for October 25, 1864, in David S. Sparks, ed., *Inside Lincoln's Army: The Diary of General Marsena Rudolph Patrick, Provost Marshal General, Army of the Potomac* (New York: Thomas Yoseloff, 1964), 433.

20. John Berry to Samuel L. M. Barlow, November 4, 1864, Barlow Papers. On the rarity of ticket splitting in the nineteenth century, see Richard Franklin Bensel, *The American Ballot Box in the Mid-nineteenth Century* (New York: Cambridge University Press, 2004), chap. 2.

21. Adam Badeau to Harry, September 4, 1864, Badeau Papers; John Preston Campbell to Sister, September 11, 1864, Campbell Letters; Edward Cotter to Parents, November 15, 1864, Cotter Letters; and Samuel J. Marks to Carrie, October 1, 1864, Marks Letters, all in Civil War Miscellaneous Collection, MHI.

22. Hermon Clarke to Father, September 11 and October 3, 1864, in Harry F. Jackson and Thomas F. O'Donnell, eds., *Back Home in Oneida: Hermon Clarke and His Letters* (Syracuse: Syracuse University Press, 1965), 161, 166; Morris W. Chalmers to Sister, October 27, 1864, Chalmers Letters; and George W. Lewis to Henry S. Jay, August 29 and September 3, 1864, Henry S. Jay Papers, both in Civil War Miscellaneous Collection, MHI; A. Beeler to Elihu Washburne, October 6, 1864, Elihu Washburne Papers, LC.

23. H. K. Smith to [Andrew G. Curtin], October 12, 1864, RG-19 (Records of the Department of the Military), Subgroup: Office of the Adjutant General, Series 19.29 (General Correspondence), PHMC.

24. Hermon Clarke to Father, November 13, 1864, in Jackson and O'Donnell, *Back Home in Oneida*, 176–77.

25. Robert Winn to Sister, July 16, August 1, October 19, 21, and 26, 1864, Winn–Cook Family Papers, Filson Historical Society, Louisville, Kentucky.

26. William Allen Clark to Parents, June 5, 1864, in Margaret Black Tatum, ed., "'Please Send Stamps': The Civil War Letters of William Allen Clark Part IV," *Indiana Magazine of History* 91 (December 1995): 420; Andrew Knox to Wife, February 22, 1863, Knox Letters, Civil War Miscellaneous Collection, MHI. See also George D. Williams to Henry S. Jay, March 24, June 20, and August 18, 1864, Henry S. Jay Papers, Civil War Miscellaneous Col-

lection, MHI. For an excellent analysis of the effects of party competition on the Union war effort, see Mark E. Neely Jr., *The Union Divided: Party Conflict in the Civil War North* (Cambridge: Harvard University Press, 2002).

27. On antiparty sentiment in the North during the Civil War, see Adam I. P. Smith, *No Party Now: Politics in the Civil War North* (New York: Oxford University Press, 2006).

28. Bensel, *American Ballot Box in the Mid-nineteenth Century*, 35–37, 139, 167, 206–7, 229.

29. George G. Meade to Wife, October 7, 1864, in George Gordon Meade, *The Life and Letters of George Gordon Meade*, 2 vols. (New York: Charles Scribner's Sons, 1913), 2:232–34; Margaret McKelvy Bird and Daniel W. Crofts, eds., "Soldier Voting in 1864: The David McKelvy Diary," *Pennsylvania Magazine of History and Biography* 115 (July 1991): 404, 410.

30. Meade to Wife, October 7, 1864, in Meade, *Life and Letters of George Gordon Meade*, 2:232; Hermon Clarke to Brother, October 9, 1864, in Jackson and O'Donnell, *Back Home in Oneida*, 169; Jesse Brown to Sister, October 23, 1864 (GLC3523.15.19), Gilder Lehrman Institute, New York (hereafter GL); Edwin Weller to Nett, October 15, 1864, in William Walton, ed., *A Civil War Courtship: The Letters of Edwin Weller from Antietam to Atlanta* (New York: Doubleday, 1980), 115–16; Harvey Reid to Pa, September 19, 1863, in Byrne, *Uncommon Soldiers*, 91.

31. G. D. McCormick to Margaret Williams, September 28, 1864, Evan Williams Civil War Letters, Historical Collections and Labor Archives, Paterno Library, Pennsylvania State University, University Park; Meade, *Life and Letters of George Gordon Meade*, 2:239; John W. Rowell, *Yankee Cavalrymen: Through the Civil War with the Ninth Pennsylvania Cavalry* (Knoxville: University of Tennessee Press, 1971), 196.

32. George W. Tillotson to Wife, November 21, 1863 (GLC4558.124), George W. Tillotson Papers, GL.

33. Allan Nevins, ed., *A Diary of Battle: The Personal Journals of Colonel Charles S. Wainwright* (New York: Harcourt, Brace & World, 1962), 473.

34. Jean H. Baker has also linked low voter turnout among the troops to voter intimidation: "Only 3,121 of approximately 15,000 Union soldiers [from Maryland] took advantage of this opportunity [to vote]," writes Jean H. Baker, "although certainly some soldiers received convenient furloughs and returned home to vote. The voting procedures in the field, which permitted officers to collect ballots, probably intimidated some Democrats from voting." *The Politics of Continuity: Maryland Political Parties from 1858 to 1870* (Baltimore: Johns Hopkins University Press, 1973), 131n59.

35. Hermon Clarke to Father, October 16 and 17, 1864, in Jackson and O'Donnell, *Back Home in Oneida*, 171, 173; Robert Emmet Doyle to Barlow, October 27, 1864, Barlow Papers; "From the Headquarters of the Army of the Potomac," September 22, 1864; Geo. W. A. to Mr. Croly, September 22 and 25, 1864; Horatio Seymour to August Belmont, September 26, 1864; Geo. W. A. to Marble, September 27 and October 2, 1864, all in Marble Papers; Wilhelm Mobus to Parents et al., November 4, 1864, in David L. Anderson, ed., "The Letters of 'Wilhelm Yank': Letters from a German Soldier in the Civil War," *Michigan Historical Review* 16 (Spring 1990): 81; Peter Curley to Andrew Curtin, October 11, 1864, Slifer-Dill Papers, Dickinson College, Carlisle, Pennsylvania.

36. See, for example, RG 153 (Records of the Judge Advocate General [Army]), Court-Martial File LL-1359, National Archives and Records Administration, Washington, DC (hereafter Court-Martial Case file).

37. George Breck to Ellen, October 23, 1864, in Blake McKelvey, ed., *Rochester in the Civil War* (Rochester, NY: Rochester Historical Society, 1944), 141; S. S. Cox to Marble, October 12, 1864, Marble Papers; Cox to Barlow, October 11, 1864, Barlow Papers.

38. James S. Graham to Aunt Ellen, November 7, 1864, in William H. Bartlett, ed., *Aunt and the Soldier Boys* (Santa Cruz, CA: privately printed, 1973), 152. Democrats could also be guilty of such behavior. See Fitz-John Porter to Barlow, June 3, 1863, Barlow Papers. Republican soldiers from New York also believed they would be defrauded of their votes by unscrupulous state agents in Baltimore and Washington. See William P. Forman to William H. Seward, October 28, 1864, William H. Seward Papers, LC; Jonathan W. White, "Canvassing the Troops: The Federal Government and the Soldiers' Right to Vote," *Civil War History* 50 (September 2004): 303–9.

39. William B. Reed to Barlow, October 18, 1864, Barlow Papers; Nelson G. Huson to George T. Huson, August 14, 1864, HM29119, Huntington Library, San Marino, California. This sort of electioneering had occurred in previous elections as well. See Jonathan W. White, "Citizens and Soldiers: Party Competition and the Debate in Pennsylvania over Permitting Soldiers to Vote, 1861–64," *American Nineteenth Century History* 5 (Summer 2004), 57.

40. Gideon R. Viars to Mary Viars, September 21, 1864, Viars Family Papers, Filson Historical Society; "Kentucky Unionist" to August Belmont, September 27, 1864, Marble Papers.

41. *The American Annual Cyclopaedia and Register of Important Events of the Year 1864*, 14 vols. (New York: D. Appleton & Co., 1862–75), 4:764–65.

42. I have identified more than fifty officers and enlisted men who were court-martialed or summarily dismissed for expressing opposition to emancipation; others were denied promotion. I plan to discuss these cases in a book-length study of how Union soldiers viewed emancipation. For a few examples, see Court-Martial Case files LL-1359, MM-0448, MM-3652, and NN-0856; Court-Martial Case of Newton B. Spencer, *Civil War Times Illustrated* Collection, MHI.

43. James O. Miller to Nellie McClellan, September 1, 1864, George B. McClellan Sr. Papers, LC; Stephen W. Sears, *George B. McClellan: The Young Napoleon* (New York: Ticknor & Fields, 1988), 363–64, 382–83.

44. Alanson Randol to Barlow, October 13, 1864, Barlow Papers.

45. John S. Collier and Bonnie B. Collier, eds., *Yours for the Union: The Civil War Letters of John W. Chase, First Massachusetts Light Artillery* (New York: Fordham University Press, 2004), 345, 363, 376. This soldier was unable to vote because Massachusetts never enfranchised its soldiers. See also John H. Rippetoe to Mary J. Rippetoe, September 18, 1864, Rippetoe Letters, Civil War Miscellaneous Collection, MHI.

46. Lewis G. Schmidt, *A Civil War History of the 147th Pennsylvania Regiment* (Allentown: Lewis G. Schmidt, 2000), 1000.

47. John D. Cottrell to Maggie, April 24, 1865, in Richard M. Trimble, ed., *Brothers 'Til Death: The Civil War Letters of William, Thomas, and Maggie Jones, 1861–1865* (Macon: Mercer University Press, 2000), 141.

48. Nevins, *Diary of Battle*, 476. This soldier refused to vote for Horatio Seymour's reelection in New York in 1864, but he did end up voting for George McClellan for president.

49. See, for example, the letters of Henry P. Hubbell in the Hubbell Family Papers, Special Collections, Firestone Library, Princeton University; James A. Bayard to Thomas F. Bayard, January 23, 1863, Thomas F. Bayard Papers, LC; Lewis Hanback to Hettie, October 8, 1864, Lewis Hanback Letters, Filson Historical Society; George D. Williams to Henry S. Jay, March 24, 1864, Henry S. Jay Papers, Civil War Miscellaneous Collection, MHI; Frank L. Klement, *Dark Lanterns: Secret Political Societies, Conspiracies, and Treason Trials in the Civil War* (Baton Rouge: Louisiana State University Press, 1984), 157–58.

50. See, for example, John Morton to Mother, January 13, 1863, Morton Letters; B. Theodore Parks to Col. Henry C. Eyer, January 31, 1863, Parks Letters; Benjamin F. Stalder to Parents, November 11, 1862, Benjamin F. Stalder Papers; and George G. Sinclair to Francis Sinclair, November 12, 1862, and January 6 and 27, 1863, George G. Sinclair Papers, all in Civil War Miscellaneous Collection, MHI; Benson Bobrick, *Testament: A Soldier's Story of the Civil War* (New York: Simon & Schuster, 2003), 226–27. See also Joan E. Cashin, "Deserters, Civilians, and Draft Resistance in the North," in Joan E. Cashin, ed., *The War Was You and Me: Civilians in the American Civil War* (Princeton: Princeton University Press, 2002), 262–85.

51. Court-Martial Case file MM-2213.

52. McClellan to Marble, September 17, 1864, Marble Papers.

New Perspectives in Civil War Ethnic History and Their Implications for Twenty-First-Century Scholarship
Christian B. Keller

1. Ella Lonn, *Foreigners in the Confederacy* (Chapel Hill: University of North Carolina Press, 1940); and *Foreigners in the Union Army and Navy* (Baton Rouge: Louisiana State University Press, 1950). Mirroring the academic awakening regarding ethnicity in the war, popular culture is also starting to realize that ethnic considerations, especially ethnic identity, may help the public understand the conflict better. It has been slow going, however, and television series and movies are a case in point. The 1939 motion picture *Gone with the Wind* starred Vivien Leigh as Scarlett O'Hara, the daughter of an Irish immigrant who settled in Georgia, made his fortune as a cotton planter, and still spoke with an Irish accent. Several decades passed until the 1980s miniseries *North and South* and *Love and War*, based on the John Jakes novels, likewise featured another daughter of an original Irish immigrant, played by Wendy Kilbourne, who married into the powerful Anglo-American Hazard family of Pennsylvania. The 1989 movie *Glory*, perhaps still the best Hollywood film on the war, offered a noticeable comment on Irish–black relations with the inclusion of Sergeant Major Mulcahy, who drilled the African American recruits of the 54th Massachusetts—including the characters portrayed by Morgan Freeman, Denzel Washington, and Jihmi Kennedy—to the breaking point. More recently, the movies *Gettysburg* and *Gods and Generals* featured Sergeant "Buster" Kilrain, the avuncular (and fictional) Irish-born confidant of Colonel Joshua Chamberlain of the 20th Maine, and the

film *Gangs of New York* gave screen time to the lives of Irish immigrants and their struggles against nativism in New York City directly before the war. Not surprisingly, the increasing popular interest in ethnic Civil War themes is strongly tilted toward the Irish. The only serious allusion to the Germans in the conflict appears to be limited to the character Jake Roedel in the 1999 film *Ride with the Devil*, in which actor Tobey Maguire ably conveys the personal dilemmas experienced by a second-generation German immigrant whose allegiances are split between his Unionist, German-born father and his pro-Confederate guerrilla friends in wartime Missouri.

2. Few popularly known Civil War historians in the last fifty years have spilled much ink on northern or southern ethnic Americans. For instance, Bruce Catton remarked in his *Never Call Retreat* (New York: Doubleday, 1965) about the "hard luck organization" that constituted the Federal Eleventh Corps and very briefly described its stand at Chancellorsville. He gave no credence to the Irish participation at Fredericksburg. James I. Robertson's *Soldiers Blue and Gray* (Columbia: University of South Carolina Press, 1988) offers two paragraphs on the Germans and a bit more for the Irish on p. 27, but nothing else in Robertson's vast amount of scholarship comments on ethnic soldiers. James M. McPherson's *Battle Cry of Freedom: The Civil War Era* (New York: Oxford University Press, 1988) is substantially better, but mentions ethnic soldiers and civilians only fleetingly throughout, and his *For Cause and Comrades: Why Men Fought in the Civil War* (New York: Oxford University Press, 1997) includes a paragraph on ethnic soldiers. Gary Gallagher's *The Union War* (Cambridge: Harvard University Press, 2011) incorporates some of the recent scholarship on northern ethnicity in a few strong sections analyzing voting and political behavior.

3. A sampling of the newer and better yet topically circumscribed scholarship might include Earl J. Hess, *A German in the Yankee Fatherland: The Civil War Letters of Henry A. Kircher* (Kent: Kent State University Press, 1983); Stephen D. Engle, *Yankee Dutchman: The Life of Franz Sigel* (Baton Rouge: Louisiana State University Press, 1993); James P. Gannon, *Irish Rebels, Confederate Tigers: The 6th Louisiana Volunteers, 1861–1865* (Campbell, CA: Savas Publishing Company, 1998); Christian G. Samito, ed., *Commanding Boston's Irish Ninth: The Civil War Letters of Colonel Patrick R. Guiney, Ninth Massachusetts Volunteer Infantry* (New York: Fordham University Press, 1998); Kelley O'Grady, *Clear the Confederate Way: The Irish in the Army of Northern Virginia* (Campbell, CA: Savas Publishing Company, 2000); Mark H. Dunkelman, "Hardtack and Sauerkraut Stew: Ethnic Tensions in the 154th New York Volunteers, Eleventh Corps, during the Civil War," *Yearbook of German-American Studies* 36 (2001): 69–90; Christian B. Keller, "Pennsylvania and Virginia Germans in the Civil War: A Brief History and Comparative Analysis," *Virginia Magazine of History and Biography* 190, no. 1 (2001): 37–86; Martin Oefele, *German-Speaking Officers in the U.S. Colored Troops, 1863–1867* (Gainesville: University Press of Florida, 2004); and Joseph R. Reinhart, ed. and trans., *Two Germans in the Civil War: The Diary of John Daeuble and the Letters of Gottfried Rentschler, 6th Kentucky Volunteer Infantry* (Knoxville: University of Tennessee Press, 2004). The best comprehensive studies include David T. Gleeson, *The Irish in the South, 1815–1877* (Chapel Hill: University of North Carolina Press, 2001); sections of Kerby A. Miller, *Emigrants and Exiles: Ireland and the Irish*

Exodus to North America (New York: Oxford University Press, 1988); Christian G. Samito, *Becoming American under Fire: Irish Americans, African Americans, and the Redefinition of Citizenship during the Civil War Era* (Ithaca: Cornell University Press, 2009); Robert N. Rosen, *The Jewish Confederates* (Columbia: University of South Carolina Press, 2000); Walter Kamphoefner and Wolfgang Helbich, eds., *Germans in the Civil War: The Letters They Wrote Home* (Chapel Hill: University of North Carolina Press, 2006); and Susannah Ural's *The Harp and the Eagle: Irish-American Volunteers and the Union Army, 1861–1865* (New York: Fordham University Press, 2006); and her edited anthology of essays, *Civil War Citizens: Race, Ethnicity, and Identity in America's Bloodiest Conflict* (New York: New York University Press, 2010). William Burton's *Melting Pot Soldiers: The Union's Ethnic Regiments*, 2nd ed. (New York: Fordham University Press, 1998), originally published in 1988, is at times insightful, but too often makes overarching generalizations that cannot be substantiated by the evidence he offers, which is often taken directly from Ella Lonn. The resulting analysis is uneven and incomplete. Dean Mahin's recent *The Blessed Place of Freedom: Europeans in Civil War America* (Washington, DC: Brassey's, 2002) is a compilation of selected previous authors' works on the subject, with little original analysis and some erroneous conclusions.

4. A certain dissertation adviser of mine, opining on what kind of Civil War study would be a guaranteed "best seller," claimed that one about Lincoln's doctor's dog, set in New York City, would be a smash hit.

5. As a general note, works and primary sources cited here that were written in the German language have been translated by the author. Any errors in translation are strictly my own.

6. Three works commend themselves regarding non-Irish or -German immigrants. William M. McKnight's *Blue Bonnets o'er the Border: The 79th New York Cameron Highlanders* (Shippensburg, PA: White Mane Books, 1998); and Michael Bacarella's *Lincoln's Foreign Legion: The 39th New York Infantry, the Garibaldi Guard* (Shippensburg, PA: White Mane Books, 1996), respectively examine regiments principally formed by Scots and Italians, although strong elements of other ethnicities were present in both. Ural's edited collection *Civil War Citizens* contains valuable commentary on non-Irish or -German immigrants, especially those of Jewish descent, as well as chapters regarding Native American and African American contributions. Mahin's *Blessed Place of Freedom* includes succinct chapters on some of these nationalities. It should be noted that the vast majority of Polish and Hungarian immigrants lived in predominantly German neighborhoods in the cities of the North and often enlisted in ethnically German regiments.

7. See Ural, *The Harp and the Eagle*; Lawrence Frederick Kohl, ed., *Irish Green and Union Blue: The Civil War Letters of Peter Welsh, Color Sergeant* (New York: Fordham University Press, 2002); Kohl's splendid introduction to D. P. Conyngham's classic work, *The Irish Brigade and Its Campaigns* (New York: Fordham University Press, 1994); Frank Boyle, *A Party of Mad Fellows: The Story of the Irish Regiments in the Army of the Potomac* (Dayton, Ohio: Morningside House, 1996); Paul Jones, *The Irish Brigade* (reprint, Gaithersburg, MD: Olde Soldier Books, n.d.), 124, 156–57, 167; William McCarter, *My Life in the Irish Brigade* (reprint, Campbell, CA: Savas Publishing Company, 1996), 183. Also see

Samito, *Becoming American under Fire*, especially chapter 5; and most of the chapters in Philip T. Tucker, *God Help the Irish! The History of the Irish Brigade* (Abilene, TX: State House Press, 2007).

8. Chauncey Herbert Cooke to Doe Cooke, 19 July 1863, reprinted in Chauncey H. Cooke, *Soldier Boy's Letters to His Father and Mother, 1861–1865* (News Office, 1915), 97; James S. Pula, *The Sigel Regiment: A History of the 26th Wisconsin Volunteer Infantry, 1862–1865* (Campbell, CA: Savas Publishing Company, 1998); Kamphoefner and Helbich, *Germans in the Civil War*; Martin Oefele, "German Americans and the War up to Gettysburg," in David L. Valuska and Christian B. Keller, *Damn Dutch: Pennsylvania Germans at Gettysburg* (Mechanicsburg, PA: Stackpole Books, 2004); Stephen D. Engle, "A Raised Consciousness: Franz Sigel and German Ethnic Identity in the Civil War," *Yearbook of German-American Studies* 34 (1999): 1–17; Engle, "Yankee Dutchmen: Germans, the Union, and the Construction of Wartime Identity," in Ural, *Civil War Citizens*, 28–30, 37–41; Christian B. Keller, *Chancellorsville and the Germans: Nativism, Ethnicity, and Civil War Memory* (New York: Fordham University Press, 2007); Uriah N. Parmeke to mother, 8 May 1863, in Samuel Spencer Parmeke and Uriah N. Parmeke Papers, Perkins Library, Duke University. The checkered reputation of northern German troops in the Civil War often brings to mind a natural comparison with an entirely different public conception regarding their participation in the Revolutionary War. Pennsylvania, Maryland, and Virginia aggregately sent several battalions composed exclusively of German-born troops into the Continental service, where, under the leaderships of men like Major General Peter Muhlenberg, they achieved wide notoriety as hard and loyal fighters in most of George Washington's campaigns. Frederick Muhlenberg, Peter's brother, served as first Speaker of the House of Representatives. The positive memory of German American participation in the Revolutionary War had all but worn away in the northern public's mind by 1861 thanks to the nativist movement of the 1850s.

9. Benjamin A. Gould, *Investigations in the Military and Anthropological Statistics of American Soldiers* (New York: U.S. Sanitary Commission, 1869), 37–38; for an example of an inflated number, see Wilhelm Kaufmann, *The Germans in the American Civil War*, trans. Steven Rowan (1911, reprint, Carlisle, PA: J. Kallman Publishers, 1999), 1, where he claims German-born Federals numbered 216,000; Lonn, *Foreigners in the Union Army and Navy*, 90; Bruce, *The Harp and the Eagle*, 2; Kamphoefner and Helbich, *Germans in the Civil War*, 9, 22; for a more detailed discussion of second-generation ethnic soldiers and their likely numbers, see Christian B. Keller, "Flying Dutchmen and Drunken Irishmen: The Myths and Realities of Ethnic Civil War Soldiers," *Journal of Military History* 73, no. 1 (2009): 117–45; rebel soldier "Fontaine," on northern "hirelings," quoted in Lonn, *Foreigners in the Confederacy*, 420.

10. Michael Holt, *Forging a Majority: The Formation of the Republican Party in Pittsburgh, 1848–1860* (New Haven: Yale University Press, 1969); Kathleen Neils Conzen, *Immigrant Milwaukee, 1836–1860: Accommodation and Community in a Frontier City* (Cambridge: Harvard University Press, 1976), particularly chapters 1 and 4; Bruce Levine, *The Spirit of 1848: German Immigrants, Labor Conflict, and the Coming of the Civil War* (Urbana: University of Illinois Press, 1992), especially chapters 4, 5, 8, and 9; Paul J. Kleppner, "Lincoln and the Immigrant Vote: A Case Study of Religious Polarization," in Frederick C.

Luebke, ed., *Ethnic Voters and the Election of Lincoln* (Lincoln; University of Nebraska Press, 1971). For examples of the revisionist ethnocultural school, see Lesley Ann Kawaguchi, "Diverging Political Affiliations and Ethnic Perspectives: Philadelphia Germans and Antebellum Politics," *Journal of American Ethnic History* 4, no. 1 (1984): 9–30; and Walter D. Kamphoefner, "German-Americans and Civil War Politics: A Reconsideration of the Ethnocultural Thesis," *Civil War History* 37, no. 3 (1991): 232–46. The leading Irish political studies include Kevin Kenny, ed., *New Directions in Irish-American History* (Madison: University of Wisconsin Press, 2003); Gleeson, *The Irish in the South*; Miller, *Emigrants and Exiles*; and Susannah Ural, *The Harp and the Eagle*. Leading recent works on German wartime loyalties include Joerg Nagler, *Fremont contra Lincoln: Die deutchamerikanische Opposition in der Republikanischen Partei waehrend des amerikanischen Buergerkrieges* (New York: Peter Lang, 1984); Martin Oefele, *True Sons of the Republic: European Immigrants in the Union Army* (New York: Praeger, 2008); Engle's *Yankee Dutchman* and "Raised Consciousness"; and Christian Keller, *Chancellorsville and the Germans*. *Boston Pilot* quoted in Francis R. Walsh, "The Boston Pilot Reports the Civil War," *Historical Journal of Massachusetts* 4 (June 1981): 14; Ural, *The Harp and the Eagle*, 1–4. The *Pilot* was well-known for switching its opinions, sometimes within the same issue.

11. Boyle, *Party of Mad Fellows*, 229–331; Ural, *The Harp and the Eagle*, 134–35; and her essay, "'Ye Sons of Green Erin Assemble': Northern Irish American Catholics and the Union War Effort, 1861–1865," in Ural, *Civil War Citizens*, 100, 107, 113–18; Iver Bernstein, *The New York City Draft Riots: Their Significance for American Society and Politics in the Age of the Civil War* (New York: Oxford University Press, 1990), 23–24, 112–13, 122–24. The removal of George B. McClellan from command of the Army of the Potomac in the fall of 1862 also disenchanted many Irishmen in the ranks.

12. Kawaguchi, "Diverging Political Affiliations and Ethnic Perspectives"; Stanley Nadel, *Little Germany: Ethnicity, Religion, and Class in New York City, 1845–1880* (Chicago: University of Illinois Press, 1990), 8; Kamphoefner and Helbich, *Germans in the Civil War*, 6–12; Joseph R. Reinhart, ed. and trans., *August Willich's Gallant Dutchmen: Civil War Letters from the 32nd Indiana Infantry* (Kent: Kent State University Press, 2006), 7–12; also see Reinhart's introduction to his *Two Germans in the Civil War*; Albert Krause to parents and siblings, 11 September 1862, reprinted in Kamphoefner and Helbich, *Germans in the Civil War*, 198; Stephen Engle, "Raised Consciousness," 5–7; Keller, *Chancellorsville and the Germans*, 21–23, 38.

13. *New York Times*, 5 May 1863; *New York Herald*, 5 May 1863; Ernst Damkoehler to Mathilde Damkoehler, 10 May 1863, quoted in Pula, *Sigel Regiment*, 141; Schimmelfennig's report is in the *Official Records of the Union and Confederate Armies in the War of the Rebellion*, 128 vols. (Washington, DC: Government Printing Office, 1901), ser. 1, vol. 25, pp. 662–63. For a complete analysis of the reportage of Chancellorsville and the Eleventh Corps in the Anglo-American press, see Keller, *Chancellorsville and the Germans*, 76–91; for German American reactions, including much coverage of the German-language press, see pp. 92–122.

14. Martin Seel, 74th Pennsylvania Infantry, to brother, 24 September 1863, translation and transcription at Archives, Fredericksburg–Spotsylvania National Military Park, Virginia; Engle, "Raised Consciousness," 11–13.

15. John Higham, *Strangers in the Land: Patterns in American Nativism* (New Brunswick: Rutgers University Press, 1955). Lonn clearly bought into the myth of the drunken Irishman. "Intemperance was one of their vices," she argued, "and when they were intoxicated, there was constant brawling and fighting among themselves and with other groups; indeed so contentious were they that inebriation was not necessary to start a fight." Lonn, *Foreigners in the Union Army and Navy*, 648. Burton overgeneralized even more: "Irish regiments did have a serious alcohol abuse problem." *Melting Pot Soldiers*, 153. Dean Mahin's work, *Blessed Place of Freedom*, fails to consider any foreign-language sources at all and simply repeats what authors from Lonn to those in the mid-1990s have offered in their research; Donald Allendorf's well-written but unanalytical book *Long Road to Liberty: The Odyssey of a German Regiment in the Yankee Army—the 15th Missouri Volunteer Infantry* (Kent: Kent State University Press, 2006) tries to make sweeping generalizations about primary and secondary source materials on German regiments in his introduction without, apparently, having completed a historiographic review of these sources. He concludes that the 15th Missouri was just like any other Missouri regiment in the end, even though he found that 74 percent of its soldiers had been born in Germany.

16. See Kamphoefner and Helbich, *Germans in the Civil War*; and Helbich, "German-Born Union Soldiers: Motivation, Ethnicity, and 'Americanization,'" in Wolfgang Helbich and Walter D. Kamphoefner, eds., *German-American Immigration and Ethnicity in Comparative Perspective* (Madison, WI: Max Kade Institute, 2004), 295–325; Engle, "Raised Consciousness"; Ural, *The Harp and the Eagle*, especially the last two chapters; Reinhart, *August Willich's Gallant Dutchmen*, 12–17; Keller, *Chancellorsville and the Germans*, chapters 6 and 7; Keller, "Flying Dutchmen and Drunken Irishmen," 140–45; and David Gleeson's forthcoming manuscript on the Irish in the Confederacy (which has a substantial section on the northern Irish), summarized at the Second Biennial Conference of the Society of Civil War Historians, Richmond, Virginia, 19 June 2010. Fitzgibbon quoted in Ural, *The Harp and the Eagle*, 213; Dr. Welsch, "Deutch-Amerikaner, aber keine amerikanisirte Deutsche," *Deutsch-Amerikanische Monatshefte* 4 (April 1867): 348–56; Conzen, *Immigrant Milwaukee*; and Conzen, "The Paradox of German-American Assimilation," *Yearbook of German-American Studies* 16 (1981): 153–60. Christian Samito's *Becoming American under Fire*, although not antiassimilationist, adopts a culturally pluralistic interpretation of Irish acculturation after the war. He argues, like Ural, that Irish blood on the battlefield paved the way for legitimate claims to Irish American citizenship following Appomattox, but agrees that dual loyalties likely motivated most Irish-born Union soldiers during the war itself.

17. See, for instance, Paul A. Cimbala and Randall M. Miller, eds., *An Uncommon Time: The Civil War and the Northern Home Front* (New York: Fordham University Press, 2002); Robert M. Sandow, *Deserter Country: Civil War Opposition in the Pennsylvania Appalachians* (New York: Fordham University Press, 2009); and J. Matthew Gallman, *Northerners at War: Reflections on the Civil War Home Front* (Kent: Kent State University Press, 2010) for studies utilizing ethnicity in their analyses. Recent leading works on nativism in the nineteenth-century United States include Tyler Anbinder, *Nativism and Slavery: The Northern Know-Nothings and the Politics of the 1850s* (New York: Oxford University Press, 1992); Dale T. Knobel, *"America for the Americans": The Nativist Movement in the United*

States (New York: Twayne Publishers, 1996); and Knobel, *Paddy and the Republic: Ethnicity and Nationality in Antebellum America* (Middletown: Wesleyan University Press, 1986). The classic, now dated, nonetheless remains Ray Allen Billington, *The Protestant Crusade, 1800–1860: A Study of the Origins of American Nativism* (1938, reprint, Gloucester, MA: Peter Smith, 1963).

18. James W. Vanderhoef to sister and family, 17 May 1863, Letters of Captain James W. Vanderhoef File, Brooklyn Public Library; Adolph Bregler to parents, 10 May 1863, Bregler Pension File, 27th Pennsylvania, App. 172.294, certif. 128.498, National Archives and Records Administration, Washington, DC; Otto Heusinger, *Amerikanische Kriegsbilder: Aufzeichnungen aus den Jahren 1861–1865* (1869, reprint, Wyk/Foehr, Germany: Verlag fuer Amerikanistik, 1998), 117; William Wheeler to Theodosia Davenport Wheeler, 14 May 1863, reprinted in William Wheeler, *Letters of William Wheeler of the Class of 1855, Y.C.* (Privately published, 1875), 387. For a comprehensive analysis of German American soldiers' letters regarding the fighting at Chancellorsville, see Keller, *Chancellorsville and the Germans*, chapter 3, and for Anglo-American soldiers' perspectives, chapter 4.

19. Philadelphia *Public Ledger*, 6 May 1863; Philadelphia *Inquirer*, 6 and 7 May 1863; Charles Parker to "dear friend Edgar," 15 May 1863, Parker Letters, William L. Clements Library, University of Michigan; James Miller to William Miller, 12 May 1863, William S. Schoff Collection, William L. Clements Library, University of Michigan; Daniel O. Macomber to "friend Eben," 15 May 1863, Lewis Leigh Collection, Book 6, Folder 14, United States Army Military History Institute, Carlisle Barracks, Pennsylvania. Stephen W. Sears, in his masterful work *Chancellorsville* (New York: Houghton Mifflin, 1996), 286, quotes from several eyewitness accounts that fleeing Eleventh Corps soldiers were shot by officers from other corps.

20. Carl Schurz to Joseph Hooker, 17 May 1863, Schurz Papers, Container 4, Library of Congress.

21. Highland, Illinois, *Highland Bote*, 8 and 22 May 1863; Pittsburgh *Freiheitsfreund und Courier*, 9 and 30 May 1863; *Pittsburger Demokrat*, 16 May 1863. Nearly all the prominent German American papers alternated between defending the German troops, attacking Anglo-American leaders, or lamenting the lost Sigel. For some more examples of good editorials covering these topics, see, for instance, the New York *Criminalzeitung und Bellestrisches Journal*, 15 and 22 May 1863; the Boston *Pionier*, 20 May 1863; and the Chicago *Illinois-Staats-zeitung*, 7 and 22 May 1863.

22. See John Keegan, *The Face of Battle: A Study of Agincourt, Waterloo, and the Somme* (New York: Vintage Books, 1977), 216–78; Paul Fussell, *Wartime: Understanding and Behavior in the Second World War* (New York: Oxford University Press, 1989), 129–43; Reid Mitchell, "From Volunteer to Soldier: The Psychology of Service," in Michael Barton and Larry M. Logue, eds., *The Civil War Soldier: A Historical Reader* (New York: New York University Press, 2002), 375–80; and James M. McPherson, "On the Altar of My Country," also in Barton and Logue, *Civil War Soldier*, 456–67. For post-Chancellorsville German American political activities, intra-regimental discrimination against Anglo-Americans, and feelings of alienation within primarily Anglo-American regiments, see Keller, *Chancellorsville and the Germans*, chapter 6. Ural and Samito also deal with this issue for the Irish in their books.

23. Friedrich Lexow, "Die Deutchen in Amerika," *Deutch-Amerikanische Monatshefte* 3 (January 1866): 149–54; and (March 1866): 255–61; Friedrich Kapp, "Rede, gehalten am 19. Juli 1865 in Jones Wood, in New York, zum Schluss des neunten deustchen Saengerfestes," reprinted in *Deutsch-Amerikanische Monatshefte* (August 1865): 182–88. Also affecting German Americans' conceptions of ethnic identity in the 1860s through the 1880s were Prussia's spectacular victories over Denmark, Austria, and France in a series of wars that led to German unification. That event was clearly celebrated in all the postwar German-language publications I researched, and raised German American pride immediately after the war, likely making a culturally pluralistic approach to assimilation even more appropriate in the eyes of most immigrants.

24. For an argument supporting the position that ethnic leaders generally spoke for their constituency or readership, see Keller, *Chancellorsville and the Germans*, 8.

The Black Flag and Confederate Soldiers:
Total War from the Bottom Up?
Michael J. Bennett

1. Daniel N. Rolph, *My Brother's Keeper: Union and Confederate Acts of Mercy during the Civil War* (Mechanicsburg, PA: Stackpole Books, 2002); "The Rebellion," *New York Times*, April 24, 1864; U.S. War Department, *The War of the Rebellion: A Compendium of the Official Records of the Union and Confederate Armies*, 128 vols., ser. 1 (Washington, DC: Government Printing Office, 1880–1901) (hereafter referred to as *OR*), 22 (1): 816–18; *OR*, 32 (1), 682; Helyn Tomlinson, ed., *Dear Friends: Civil War Letters and Diary of Charles Edwin Cort* (n.p., 1962), 136–37; Claire Sweedburg, ed., *Three Years with the 92nd Illinois: The Civil War Diary of John M. King* (Mechanicsburg, PA: Stackpole Books, 1999), 192–201; Richard B. Harwell, ed., *Kate: The Journal of a Confederate Nurse* (Baton Rouge: Louisiana State University Press, 1987), 321.

2. J. David Hacker, "A Census-Based Account of the Civil War Dead," *Civil War History* 57 (December 2011): 307–48; Joseph K. Barnes, ed., *The Medical and Surgical History of the War of the Rebellion (1861–66),* 6 vols. (Washington, DC: Government Printing Office, 1870–1888), 1:xxxvii–xxxviii.

3. The question begins with Mark E. Neely Jr., "Was the Civil War a Total War?" *Civil War History* 37 (March 1991): 5–28; James M. McPherson, *Drawn with the Sword: Reflections on the American Civil War* (New York: Oxford University Press, 1996), 66–86; Edward Hagerman, *The American Civil War and the Origins of Modern Warfare* (Bloomington: Indiana University Press, 1992), 169; Mark Grimsley, *The Hard Hand of War: Union Military Policy Toward Southern Civilians, 1861–1865* (Cambridge: Cambridge University Press, 1995); Charles Royster, *The Destructive War: William Tecumseh Sherman, Stonewall Jackson, and the Americans* (New York: Knopf, 1991), 108.

4. Niall Ferguson, "Prisoner Taking and Prisoner Killing in the Age of Total War: Towards a Political Economy of Military Defeat," *War in History* 11, no. 2 (2004): 150.

5. Mark E. Neely Jr., *The Civil War and the Limits of Destruction* (Cambridge: Harvard University Press, 2007), 199; Thomas Head, "The Development of the Peace of God in Aquitaine (970–1005)," *Speculum* 74, no. 3 (1999): 656–86.

6. Dave Grossman, *On Killing: The Psychological Cost of Learning to Kill* (New York: Basic Books, 1999), xxiii–xxiv.

7. Drew Gilpin Faust, *This Republic of Suffering: Death and the Civil War* (New York: Knopf, 2008), 33; Mark S. Schantz, *Awaiting the Heavenly Country: The Civil War and America's Culture of Death* (Ithaca: Cornell University Press, 2008); Earl J. Hess, *The Union Soldier in Battle: Enduring the Ordeal of Combat* (Lawrence: University Press of Kansas, 1997), 105–7.

8. Hess, *Union Soldier in Battle*, 107.

9. Joseph Glatthaar, *General Lee's Army: From Victory to Defeat* (New York: Free Press, 2007), 175, 181; Thomas L. Connelly, *The Marble Man: Robert E. Lee and His Image in American Society* (Baton Rouge: Louisiana State University Press, 1977), 94.

10. Glatthaar, *General Lee's Army*, 176–78; David Donald, "The Confederate as Fighting Man," *Journal of Southern History* 25 (1959): 193; Daniel E. Sutherland, *A Savage Conflict: The Decisive Role of Guerrillas in the American Civil War* (Chapel Hill: University of North Carolina Press, 2008); OR, 19 (1), 143, 1026; OR, 19 (2), 597, 617–18, 618–19, 629–30.

11. Carl Von Clausewitz, *On War* (New York: Penguin Classics, 1982), 102–3; Paul D. Escott, *After Secession Jefferson Davis and the Failure of Confederate Nationalism* (Baton Rouge: Louisiana State University Press, 1992), 46–47; Gregory J. W. Urwin, ed., *Black Flag over Dixie: Racial Atrocities and Reprisals in the Civil War* (Carbondale: Southern Illinois University Press, 2004), 7.

12. Harry Lewis to Mother, August 9, 1862, Harry Lewis Letters, 1861–64, Southern Historical Collection, University of North Carolina; T. W. Monfort to Wife, March 18, 1862, Typescript, Georgia Archives; Jeff Toalson, ed., *Send Me a Pair of Old Boats and Kiss My Little Girls: Civil War Letters of Richard and Mary Watkins* (New York: iUniverse.com, 2009), 44.

13. Oliver C. Bosbyshell, *The 48th in the War* (Philadelphia: Avil Printing Company, 1895), 100. In an odd episode, that same night Stonewall Jackson suggested that Lee's army mount a nighttime counterattack against demoralized Union forces. In order to avoid any confusion, Jackson suggested they strip "perfectly naked." See Arthur Fremantle, *Three Months in the Southern States: April–June 1863* (Edinburgh: William Blackwood & Son, 1863), 320.

14. James Painter to Brother, July 21, October 9 1861, James B. Painter Letters, Special Collection, University of Virginia; Edwin Fay to Sarah Fay, July 10, 1863, in Bell I. Wiley, ed., *This Infernal War: Confederate Letters of Sergeant Edwin H. Fay* (Austin: University of Texas Press, 1958), 292; Frank Shephard to Wife, November 21, 1861, Shephard Letters, Schoff Civil War Collection, Clements Library, University of Michigan.

15. OR, 1, 172.

16. "The Black Flag," *Richmond Daily Dispatch*, November 14, 1861.

17. OR, ser. 4, 3, 883; James McPherson, *The Battle Cry of Freedom: The Civil War Era* (New York: Oxford University Press, 1988), 429; John B. Jones, *A Rebel War Clerk's Diary at the Confederate States' Capitol*, 2 vols. (Philadelphia: J. B. Lippincott & Co., 1866), 2:392, 482; Frank E. Vandiver, ed., *The Civil War Diary of General Josiah Gorgas* (Tuscaloosa: University of Alabama Press, 1947), 123–24; Charles Harris, *Under the Black Flag* (Independence, MO: Two Trails Publishing, 2001).

18. "The Black Flag," *Richmond Daily Dispatch*, November 14, 1861; *Richmond Examiner*, September 24, 1861; Robert U. Johnson and Clarence C. Buel, eds., *Battles and Leaders of the Civil War* (New York: DeVinne Press, 1884–87), 336–37.

19. James B. Painter to Brother, October 5, 1862, Painter Letters; U.S. War Department, *The War of the Rebellion: A Compendium of the Official Records of the Union and Confederate Armies*, 128 vols., ser. 4 (Washington, DC: Government Printing Office, 1880–1901), 1:505–6; James Jordan to Wife, November 10, 1862, Letters Typescript, Georgia Department of Archives and History, 2:456; Elizabeth W. Roberson, ed., *Weep Not for Me, Dear Mother* (Gretna, LA: Pelican Publishing, 1998), 155; Unsigned Letter, March 12, 1864, Demetria Ann Hill Papers, University of Texas; McPherson, *Battle Cry of Freedom*, 457.

20. John W. Partin, ed., "Report of a Corporal of the Alabama First Infantry on Talk and Fighting along Mississippi, 1862–1863," *Alabama Historical Quarterly* 20, no. 4 (1958): 585; Richard B. Abell and Fay A. Gecik, eds., *Sojourns of a Patriot: The Field and Prison Papers of an Unreconstructed Confederate* (Murfreesboro, TN: Southern Heritage Press, 1998), 173; John G. Barrett, ed., *Yankee Rebel: The Civil War Journal of Edmund D. Patterson* (Knoxville: University of Tennessee Press, 2004), 350; Norman D. Brown, ed., *Journey to Pleasant Hill: Civil War Letters of Elijah P. Petty* (San Antonio: Institute of Texan Culture, 1982); Frederick Anspach to Robert Anspach, June 23, 1864, Anspach Papers, Special Collections, University of Virginia.

21. "From the West," *Richmond Daily Dispatch*, April 29, 1862.

22. *OR*, 32, 149; "Ominous for Lincoln," *Richmond Daily Dispatch*, June 28, 1861; "Bowling Green," *Richmond Daily Dispatch*, January 3, 1862; *OR*, 34, 658; "Letter from the Gulf Shore," *Richmond Daily Dispatch*, January 18, 1862.

23. Robert P. Broadwater, "Louisiana Native Guards," *America's Civil War* (March 2004): 17–32; *Shreveport Daily News*, March 2, 1861.

24. "Black Flag Riflemen," *Richmond Daily Dispatch*, December 9, 1861; *OR*, 16 (1), 805; Thomas Mandes, "Blacks, Jews Fight on Side of South," *Washington Times*, June 15, 2002.

25. "From New Orleans," *Richmond Daily Dispatch*, November 25, 1861; James Hallaburton, *Louisiana Native Guards* (Baton Rouge: Louisiana State University Press, 1995); *OR*, 15 (1), 551; Henry W. Howe, *Passages from the Life of Henry Warren Howe* (Lowell, MA: Courier-Citizen Co. Printers, 1899), 211; Richard Yates to Abraham Lincoln, July 11, 1862, Lincoln Studies Center, Knox College.

26. Robert Stiles, *Four Years under Marse Robert* (New York: Neale Publishing Company, 1910), 80–81; "About Finished," *Harper's Weekly*, June 7, 1862, 354; Charles L. Dufour, *Gentle Tiger: The Gallant Life of Roberdeau Wheat* (Baton Rouge: Louisiana State University Press, 1957), 80; Terry L. Jones, "Wharf-Rats, Cutthroats, and Thieves: The Louisiana Tigers, 1861–1862," *Louisiana History* 27(Spring 1986): 147–165; Terry L. Jones, *Lee's Tigers: The Louisiana Infantry in the Army of Northern Virginia* (Baton Rouge: Louisiana State University Press, 2002), 62.

27. "Bayoneting Our Wounded," *Harper's Weekly*, August 17, 1861, 522–523; "No Quarter at First Bull Run by Confederates," *New York Times*, July 25, 1861; U.S. Congress, *Report of the Joint Committee on the Conduct of the War, 1863,* 3 vols. (Washington, DC: Government Printing Office, 1863), 2:452, 463–64.

28. Joseph B. Sweigart to Cousin, July 24, 1862, Valley of the Shadow, University of Virginia; *OR*, 11 (1), 617; *OR*, 11 (1), 625; *OR*, 42 (1), 445–56; Horace Emerson to Ivey Emerson, July 26, 1861, Emerson Family Papers, Schoff Civil War Collection.

29. *Report of the Joint Committee*, 2:452, 467; Thomas L. Wilson, *A Brief History of the Cruelties and Atrocities of the Rebellion* (Washington, DC: n.p., 1864), 14–19; Richard Irbay, *Historical Sketch of the Nottoway Grays* (Richmond: J. W. Fergusson & Son, 1878), 12–13.

30. Francis Vinaca to Father, December 16, 1864, Vinaca Papers, Schoff Civil War Collection; Henry Tracey to Elsie Leake, Leake Family Papers, Schoff Civil War Collection; "Bayoneting Our Wounded," *Harper's Weekly*, August 17, 1861, 522–23; "No Quarter at First Bull Run by Confederates," *New York Times*, July 25, 1861; *OR*, 11 (1), 617, 625: *OR*, 42 (1), 445–56; *OR*, 44, 585–86, 601; *OR*, 5, 325: *OR*, 47 (2), 533; *Report of the Joint Committee*, 2:451, 453–54, 460–61, 475.

31. James Painter to Brother, July 21, October 9, 1861, Painter Letters; *Report of the Joint Committee*, 2:449, 450–53, 462–64, 472, 474; Jeremiah Williams to Susan Bigelow, March 20, 1862, Bigelow–Monk Papers, Schoff Civil War Collection.

32. "Report of the American Sanitary Commission," *British Medical News*, August 31, 1861.

33. George Biddle, *Artist at War* (New York: Viking Press, 1944), 177; Barnes, *Medical and Surgical History of the War of the Rebellion*, 1:xxxvii–xxxviii.

34. Robert K. Krick, *Conquering the Valley: Stonewall Jackson at Port Royal* (Baton Rouge: Louisiana State University Press, 2002), 412.

35. Fremantle, *Three Months in the Southern States*, 320; John Keegan, *Face of Battle* (New York: Viking Press, 1976), 322.

36. Michael Walzer, *Just and Unjust Wars* (New York: Basic Books, 1977), 151.

37. Rohloff Hacker to Phillip Hacker, August 2, 1861, Hacker Brothers Letters, Schoff Civil War Collection; Journal Entry, July 22, 1861, Charles Haydon Journal, Bentley Historical Library, University of Michigan; Horace Emerson to Brother, July 26, 1861, Emerson Family Papers, Schoff Civil War Collection; *Report of the Joint Committee*, 3:452, 463–64; "Murders of Defenseless Men," *Harper's Weekly*, February 7, 1863.

38. Harry Williams, "Benjamin F. Wade and the Atrocity Propaganda of the Civil War," *Ohio Archaeological and Historical Quarterly* 48 (January 1938): 33–43; William B. Hesseltine, "Atrocities: Then and Now," *Journal of Historical Review* 9, no. 1 (1945): 65–69; Transcript from NPR's *Fresh Air*, June 22, 2004 (interview with James McPherson).

39. Carl Hovey, *Stonewall Jackson* (New York: Small, Maynard, 1908), 41–42; Mary A. Jackson, ed., *The Life and Letters of General Thomas J. Jackson* (New York: Harper & Brothers, 1892), 310; Royster, *Destructive War*, 40.

40. *OR*, 12 (1), 15, 558–59, 616–17; William W. Goldsborough, *The Maryland Line in the Confederate Army, 1861–1865* (Baltimore: Guggenheimer, Weil & Co., 1900), 59–62; "Local News," *Baltimore Sun*, June 6, 1862.

41. *OR*, 12, 559, 616–18; *OR*, 15, 551–52; Goldsborough, *Maryland Line in the Confederate Army*, 63. See also Robert E. Bonner, *Flag Passions of the Confederate South* (Princeton: Princeton University Press, 2002), 149. Bonner contends that from time to time Confederate women brought out "their black silk to prepare for a new stage of combat."

42. Edward A. Pollard, *Life of Jefferson Davis with a Secret History of the Southern Confederacy* (London: National Publishing Company, 2005), 281–82.

43. Rohloff Hacker to William and Thomas Hacker, September 3, 1861, Hacker Brothers Letters; Joseph Field to Kate Field, May 21, 1864, Field Letters, Schoff Civil War Collection; Hugh Roden to George Roden, May 5, 1862, Roden Letters, Schoff Civil War Collection; Joseph Sharp to William Vandergrift, June 8, 1862, Vandergrift Letters, Schoff Civil War Collection; Sidney O. Little to Mother, June 17, 1863, Little Letters, Schoff Civil War Collection; Michael Miller to Lile Miller, July 9, 1862, Civil War Collection, Gilder Lehrman Institute; Lewis Martin to Folks, July 18, 1862, Martin Papers, Schoff Civil War Collection; George Trowbridge to Wife, July 31, 1864, Schoff Civil War Collection; Bruce Catton, *Terrible Swift Sword* (New York: Doubleday, 1963), 468.

44. *OR*, ser. 2, 5, 795–97; *Journal of the Confederate Congress of America, 1861–1865,* 7 vols. (Washington, DC: Government Printing Office, 1904–5), 3:11, 239, 469. See also General Order No. 60, August 21, 1862, whereby Davis ordered that black soldiers and their officers be executed as "outlaws." Eric T. Dean Jr., *Shook over Hell: Post-traumatic Stress, Vietnam, and the Civil War.* (Cambridge: Harvard University Press, 1997); Jason Phillips, "Battling Stereotypes: A Taxonomy of Common Soldiers in Civil War History," *History Compass* 6 (November 2008): 1407–25; "Order of Retaliation," July 30, 1863, in Roy P. Basler, ed., *Collected Works of Abraham Lincoln,* 9 vols. (New Brunswick: Rutgers University Press, 1953), 6:357.

45. B. F. Batchelor to Wife, December 19, 1861, in Helen J. H. Rugeley, ed., *Batchelor–Turner Letters, 1861–1864: Written by Two of Terry's Texas Rangers* (Austin: Steck Co., 1961), 3; George S. Burkhardt, *Confederate Wrath, Yankee Rage: No Quarter in the Civil War* (Carbondale: Southern Illinois University Press, 2007), 1; Jason Phillips, *Diehard Rebels: The Confederate Culture of Invincibility* (Athens: University of Georgia Press, 2007); Michael Barton and Larry M. Logue, eds., *The Civil War Soldier: A Historical Reader* (New York: NYU Press, 2002), 239; Benjamin Borton, *On the Parallels or Chapters of Inner History* (Woodstown, NJ: n.p., 1903), 39–40; William Lusk, *War Letters of William Thompson Lusk* (New York: n.p., 1911), 231–32; J. C. Williams, *Life in Camp: A History of the Nine Months Service of the 14th Vermont Regiment* (Claremont, NH: Claremont Manufacturing Co., 1864), 7; Andrew J. Boies, *Record of the 33rd Massachusetts Volunteer Infantry* (Fitchburg, MA: Sentinel Printing Company, 1880), 17; Francis A. Walker, *History of the Second Army Corps in the Army of the Potomac* (New York: Charles Scribner's Sons, 1887), 153; John L. Smith, *History of the Corn Exchange Regiment: 118th Pennsylvania Volunteers* (Philadelphia: J. L. Smith, 1888), 122; Bruce Catton, *The Army of the Potomac: Glory Road* (Garden City, NY: Doubleday, 1952), 65–69; Richard S. Hartigan, *Lieber's Code and the Law of War* (Chicago: Precedent Publishing, 1983), 124–25.

46. The Lieber Code of 1863, Section III, paragraphs 60, 61, 79, in U.S. War Department, *The War of the Rebellion: A Compendium of the Official Records of the Union and Confederate Armies,* 128 vols., ser. 3 (Washington, DC: Government Printing Office, 1880–1901), 3:155–56. Article 60 states that "it is against the usage of modern war to resolve, in hatred and revenge, to give no quarter. No body of troops has the right to declare that it will not give, and therefore will not expect, quarter; but a commander is permitted to direct his troops to give no quarter, in great straits, when his own salvation makes it

impossible to cumber himself with prisoners. Article 61 states that "troops that give no quarter have no right to kill enemies already disabled on the ground, or prisoners captured by other troops." Lawrence P. Cogswell Jr., ed., *Civil War Letters of Sgt. Patrick Henry Goodrich: A Soldier in the Connecticut Twentieth Regiment, Company D* (Glastonbury, CT: L. P. Cogswell, 2001), 43. Section 56 of the code stated that "a prisoner of war is subject to no punishment for being a public enemy, nor is any revenge wreaked upon him by the intentional infliction of any suffering, or disgrace, by cruel imprisonment, want of food, by mutilation, death, or any other barbarity."

47. Peter Mereness to Helen Arthur, November 1, 1863, Mereness Papers, Schoff Civil War Collection; Thomas Aplin to George Aplin, March 8, 1864, Aplin Papers, Schoff Civil War Collection; Brent Nosworthy, *Roll Call to Destiny: The Soldier's Eye View of Civil War Battles* (New York: Basic Books, 2008), 3; Thomas V. Wilson, "Treatment of Prisoners Captured at Chickamauga," 58–59; *OR*, 30 (4), 337–38; *OR*, 41 (2), 760–61; *Report of Judge Advocate Holt*, March 27, 1863; Grady McWhiney and Judith Lee Hallock, *Braxton Bragg and the Confederate Defeat* (Tuscaloosa: University of Alabama Press, 1991), 2:116.

48. E. C. Tillotson to Mary Tillotson, December 17, 1863, Tillotson Papers, Schoff Civil War Collection; John Bowers, *Chickamagua and Chattanooga* (New York: HarperCollins, 1994), 160; Susan C. Lawrence, "Beyond the Grave: The Use and Meaning of Human Body Parts: A Historical Introduction," in Robert F. Weir, ed., *Stored Tissue Samples: Ethical, Legal, and Public Policy Implications* (Iowa City: University of Iowa Press, 1998), 111–42

49. H. Christopher Kendrick to Father, June 6, 1863, Kendrick Papers, Southern Historical Collection, University of North Carolina; Diary Entry, December 16, 1862, Osmun Latrobe Diary, Maryland Historical Society; Gary Gallagher, *The Confederate War* (Cambridge: Harvard University Press, 1999), 105; Bell I. Wiley, *The Life of Johnny Reb: The Common Soldier of the Confederacy* (Indianapolis: Bobbs-Merrill Company, 1943), 16–17, 308–12; Urwin, *Black Flag over Dixie*, 5; James Painter to Brother, Painter Letters; Isaac Seymour to William Seymour, May 2, 1862, Seymour Collection, Schoff Civil War Collection.

50. Confederate States of America, *The Statutes at Large of the Confederate States of America, Passed at the First Session of the Second Congress, 1864* (Richmond, VA: R. M. Smith, 1864), 260.

51. John O. Collins to Wife, August 17, 1863, Collins Papers, Manuscripts, Virginia Historical Society; Michael DeGruccio, "Letting the War Slip through Our Hands: Material Culture and the Weakness of Words in the Civil War Era," in Stephen Berry, ed., *Weirding the War: Stories from the Civil War's Ragged Edges* (Athens: University of Georgia Press, 2011), 27–29.

52. Faust, *Republic of Suffering*, 33; Bertram Wyatt-Brown, *Southern Honor: Ethics and Behavior in the Old South* (New York: Oxford University Press, 1983); Franny Nudelman, *John Brown's Body: Slavery, Violence, and the Culture of War* (Chapel Hill: University of North Carolina Press, 2004), 6–7, 15, 177–78.

53. Brent Nosworthy, *Roll Call to Destiny: The Soldier's Eye View of Civil War Battles* (New York: Basic Books, 2008), 3; Wilson, "Treatment of Prisoners Captured at Chickamauga," 58–59; *OR*, 30 (4), 337–38; *OR*, 41 (2), 760–61; *Report of Judge Advocate Holt*, March 27, 1863; McWhiney and Hallock, *Braxton Bragg and the Confederate Defeat*, 2:116.

54. George Agassiz, ed., *Meade's Headquarters, 1863–1865: Letters of Colonel Theodore Lyman Trumbull from Wilderness to Appomattox* (Boston: Atlantic Monthly Press, 1922), 99–100; John Gibbon, *Personal Recollections of the Civil War* (New York: G. P. Putnam's Sons, 1928), 229; *OR*, 36 (1), 218–19.

55. Letter from Frank King, July 16, 1865, Frank R. King Papers, Alabama Department of Archives and History.

56. "The Rebellion," *New York Times*, April 24, 1864; *OR*, 22 (1), 816–18; *OR*, 32 (1), 470–71, 678–85; Tomlinson, *Dear Friends*, 136–37; Harwell, *Kate*, 321; *OR*, 47 (2), 546; *OR*, 32 (1), 684; Letter from Frank King, July 16, 1865, King Papers; Robert C. Wallace, *A Few Memories of a Long Life* (Fairfield, WA: YE Galleon Press, 1988), 50.

57. Michael Fellman, *Inside War: The Guerrilla Conflict in Missouri during the American Civil War* (New York: Oxford University Press, 1990).

58. "Massacre of the 5th Michigan," *New York Times*, August 25, 1864; James J. Williamson, *Mosby's Rangers: A Record of the Operations of the Forty-Third Battalion Virginia Cavalry* (New York: Time–Life Books, 1983), 213–15; John W. Munson, *Reminiscences of a Mosby Guerilla* (New York: Moffat, Yard and Co., 1906), 146–47; *OR*, 43 (1), 634.

59. *OR*, 43 (2), 909–10; John S. Mosby, "Retaliation: The Execution of Seven Prisoners of War by Col. John S. Mosby: A Self-Protective Necessity," in A. R. Brock, ed., *Southern Historical Society Papers* (Richmond: Virginia Historical Society, 1899), 314–22; Williamson, *Mosby's Rangers*, 288–91; Munson, *Reminiscences of a Mosby Guerilla*, 149–51. William B. Conway, "From the Wilderness to the Shenandoah Valley of Virginia 1864," *Atlanta Journal*, February 8, 1902.

60. George E. Deutsch, "Murder and Mayhem Ride the Rails: Union Soldiers on Rampage in Virginia," *Civil War Times* 48 (December 2009): 38–44.

61. Burkhardt, *Confederate Wrath, Yankee Rage*, 215; Hampton S. Thomas, *Some Personal Reminiscences of Service in the Cavalry of the Army of the Potomac* (Philadelphia: L. R. Hamersly & Co., 1889), 22; *OR*, 44, 585–86, 601.

62. Benjamin F. Oakes to J. S. Richardson, December 13, 1864, Civil War Letters and Diaries, Manuscript No. 0392, Virginia Military Institute, Preston Library; *OR*, 42, 447–49; *OR*, 32 (1), 682–83; *Memoirs of Ulysses S. Grant*, 646–48; George Kryder to Elizabeth Kryder, August 4, 1862, George Kryder Papers, Center for Archival Collections, Bowling Green State University.

63. *OR*, 43 (2), 480; *OR*, 43 (2), 587; *OR*, 43 (2), 606; U.S. Congress, House, *Murder of Union Soldiers in North Carolina*, 34th Cong., 2d sess., 1866, Ex. Doc. 98, serial 1263, 57, 62–63.

64. Joseph George Jr., "Black Flag Warfare: Lincoln and the Raids against Richmond and Jefferson Davis," *Pennsylvania Magazine of History and Biography* 115, no. 3 (1991): 292–318.

Liberia and the U.S. Civil War
Karen Fisher Younger

1. H. W. Dennis, Monrovia, to William McClain, Washington, DC, 24 June 1861, Letters from Liberia, American Colonization Records, Library of Congress, Washington, DC (hereafter ACS Records). Original spellings and grammar are used throughout the essay.

2. G. E. L. Patton, "A Woman's Work in Africa," *New York Age*, 1893, in William Dorsey Scrapbook Collection, Africa: Emigration, Colonization, Correspondence, 1874–1880, Cheyney University Archives and Special Collections, Lincoln, Pennsylvania.

3. Claude A. Clegg III, *The Price of Liberty: African Americans and the Making of Liberia* (Chapel Hill: University of North Carolina Press: 2004); Richard Hall, *On Africa's Shore: A History of Maryland in Liberia, 1834–1857* (Baltimore: Johns Hopkins University Press, 2003); Marie Tyler-McGraw, *An African Republic: Black and White Virginians in the Making of Liberia* (Chapel Hill: University of North Carolina Press, 2007). See also Alan Huffman, *Mississippi in Africa: The Saga of the Slaves of Prospect Hill Plantation and Their Legacy in Liberia* (New York: Gotham Books, 2003).

4. Kate Masur, "The African American Delegation to Abraham Lincoln," *Civil War History* 56 (June 2010): 117–44. See also James T. Campbell's *Songs of Zion: The African Methodist Episcopal Church in the United States and South Africa* (Chapel Hill: University of North Carolina Press, 1998).

5. Richard Newman, *The Transformation of American Abolitionism* (Chapel Hill: University of North Carolina Press, 2002); Randall Miller, *"Dear Master": Letters of a Slave Family* (1978; reprint, Athens: University of Georgia Press, 1990); G. J. Liebenow, *Liberia: The Quest for Democracy* (Bloomington: Indiana University Press, 1987); Amos Beyan, *The American Colonization Society and the Creation of the Liberian State: A Historical Perspective, 1822–1900* (Lanham, MD: University Press of America, 1991). See also T. W. Shick, *Behold the Promised Land: A History of Afro-American Settler Society in Nineteenth-Century Liberia* (Baltimore: John Hopkins University Press, 1980); Wilson J. Moses, *Alexander Crummell: A Study of Civilization and Discontent* (New York: Oxford University Press, 1989).

6. Kenneth Barnes, *Journey of Hope: The Back-to-Africa Movement in Arkansas in the Late 1800s* (Chapel Hill: University of North Carolina Press, 2004).

7. Eric Burin, *Slavery and the Peculiar Solution* (Gainesville: University Press of Florida, 2005).

8. See Mark E. Neely Jr., "Colonization," in *Lincoln's Proclamation: Emancipation Reconsidered*, ed. William Blair and Karen Fisher Younger (Chapel Hill: University of North Carolina Press, 2009), 45–74; Eric Foner, "Lincoln and Colonization," in *Our Lincoln: New Perspectives on Lincoln and His World*, ed. Eric Foner (New York: Norton, 2008), 135–66; Foner, *The Fiery Trial: Abraham Lincoln and American Slavery* (New York: Norton, 2010); Michael Vorenberg, "Abraham Lincoln and the Politics of Black Colonization," *Journal of the Abraham Lincoln Association* 14 (Summer 1993): 44.

9. In 1816, after decades of debate among black and white intellectuals on the merits of colonization, the country's prominent politicians, ministers, and philanthropists founded the ACS. The society's aim was the resettling of black Americans in Africa, but the motivations of its adherents varied. Some saw their efforts as a way to end slavery—reforming the United States by ending slavery, and Africa by sending black American Christians as missionary emigrants. Many members acted out of deep religious convictions, hoping to evangelize Africa and make amends for the injustices perpetrated by the United States. Others supported colonization because they believed free blacks were a threat and should be removed from the United States. P. J. Staudenraus's *The African Colonization Move-*

ment, 1816–1865 (New York: Columbia University Press, 1961) remains the most comprehensive, if dated, history of the movement.

10. *New-York Evening Post*, 7 February 1820, 2.

11. Independence in 1847 prompted some African Americans to reassess their opinion about colonization. Between 1847 and 1848, migration to Liberia grew tenfold. It continued to increase in the years that followed, as the passage of a series of devastating state and federal laws cast doubt on the future of black Americans in the United States.

12. From the beginning, free black leaders and most free blacks viewed the ACS as a racist organization, in partnership with white slave owners and white northerners who wanted to rid the United States of free blacks. In the 1850s, as prospects for any future in the United States looked grim, some black leaders still viewing the ACS as a racist organization looked to other locations for black emigration. Some considered Haiti or Central America. Martin Delany, a Pennsylvania native, tried to establish a colony in Yoruba, a region of present-day Nigeria. In the end, however, no black Americans actually emigrated under Delany's plan and only a few left for Haiti, but by the beginning of the Civil War, more than ten thousand black American settlers had come to Liberia.

13. Clay-Ashland was named after Henry Clay and his estate Ashland in Lexington, Kentucky, and was established in 1846 by immigrants primarily from Kentucky, under the auspices of the ACS. Tobias M. Oatland, Clay-Ashland, to William McClain, Washington, DC, 13 February 1861, Letters from Liberia, ACS Records.

14. Jacob Miller, "Speech of Mr. Miller, of N. Jersey, on the Expediency of Recognizing the Independence of Liberia," *Frederick Douglass Paper*, 25 March 1853.

15. "The Relations of Our Government to Liberia," *Frederick Douglass Paper*, 25 March 1853.

16. Some examples include *Senate Journal*, 31st Cong., 1st sess., 7 January 1850, 56; 18 February 1850, 160; 27 February 1850, 179; 8 April 1850, 216; *Senate Journal*, 32nd Cong., 1st sess., 17 February 1852, 210; *Senate Journal*, 32nd Cong., 2nd sess., 20 December 1853, 101; 17 January 1853, 48; *Senate Journal*, 33rd Cong., 1st sess., 417; *Senate Journal*, 34th Cong., 3rd sess., 18 December 1857, 49; 10 February 1857, 184; *House Journal*, 31st Cong., 1st sess., 30 January 1850, 433; 28 February, 619; *House Journal*, 31st Cong., 2nd sess., 11 March 1850, 653; *House Journal*, 32nd Cong., 1st sess., 6 April 1852, 562; *House Journal*, 33rd Cong., 1st sess., 3 August 1854, 1269; *House Journal*, 35th Cong., 1st sess., 9 March 1857, 388.

17. William McClain, Washington, DC, to Joseph J. Roberts, Monrovia, 22 April 1852, Letters from Liberia, ACS Records.

18. "Letter from President Joseph J. Roberts," *African Repository* 29, no. 8 (1853): 228.

19. William McClain, Savannah, to Joseph J. Roberts, Monrovia, 8 November 1853, Letters from Liberia, ACS Records.

20. Roy P. Basler, ed., *Collected Works of Abraham Lincoln*, 9 vols. (New Brunswick: Rutgers University Press, 1953–55), 5:48.

21. Bills and Resolutions, Senate, 37th Congress, 2nd Session.

22. *Congressional Globe*, 37th Cong., 2d sess., 2534.

23. Ibid., 2505.

24. Ibid., 2527.

25. C. L. Randamie, Monrovia, to William McClain, Washington, DC, 7 January 1862, Letters from Liberia, ACS Records.

26. William Douglas, Carysburg, to William McClain, Washington, DC, 16 August 1865; H. W. Dennis, Monrovia, to William McClain, Washington, DC, 24 June 1861; John Seys, Monrovia, to William McClain, Washington, DC, 1 July 1861; B. A. Payne, Greenville, Sinoe, to William McClain, Monrovia, 12 March 1862, all in Letters from Liberia, ACS Records.

27. Bell I. Wiley, ed., *Slaves No More: Letters from Liberia, 1833–1869* (Lexington: University of Kentucky Press, 1980), 211.

28. H. W. Dennis, Monrovia, to William McClain, Washington, DC, 24 June 1861, Letters from Liberia, ACS Records.

29. J. S. Smith, Buchanan, to William McClain, Washington, DC, 1 November 1862, Letters from Liberia, ACS Records.

30. H. M. Davis, Monrovia, to William Coppinger, Washington, DC, 20 August 1865, Letters from Liberia, ACS Records.

31. J. H. Deputie, Greenville, to William McClain, Washington, DC, 11 September 1862, Letters from Liberia, ACS Records.

32. "Letters from Liberia," *African Repository* 42, no. 1 (1866): 24.

33. *African Repository* 41, no. 4 (1865): 121.

34. Quoted in William E. Allen, "Sugar and Coffee: A History of Settler Agriculture in Nineteenth-Century Liberia," PhD diss., Florida International University, 2002, 120.

35. "Letters from Liberia," *African Repository* 30, no. 1 (1864): 5.

36. Allen, "Sugar and Coffee," 127.

37. "Annual Message of President Warner," *African Repository* 42, no. 2 (1866): 98.

38. A. E. Wilham, Alabama, to William Coppinger, Washington, DC, 1 April, 1868, Incoming Correspondence, ACS Records.

39. Edward Hill, North Stanton County, North Carolina, to William Coppinger, Washington, DC, 5 April 1868, Incoming Letters, ACS Records.

40. Charles Snyder, Halifax, North Carolina, to William Coppinger, Washington, DC, 12 April 1868, Domestic Letters, ACS Records.

41. A. E. Wilham, Alabama, to William Coppinger, Washington, DC, 1 April, 1868, Domestic Letters, ACS Records.

42. Edward Hill, North Stanton County, North Carolina, to William Coppinger, Washington, DC, 5 April 1868, Domestic Letters, ACS Records.

"No Regular Marriage": African American Veterans and Marriage Practices after Emancipation
Andrew L. Slap

Paul Christopher Anderson, Barbara Gannon, Michael Green, Anthony Kaye, Brian Miller, and LeeAnn Whites all read drafts of this essay and provided valuable comments.

1. Chaplain Chauncey P. Taylor to General Lorenzo Thomas, November 21, 1865, in Chauncey P. Taylor's Service Record, Record Group 94, Compiled Military Service Records, National Archives, Washington, DC (hereafter referred to as CMSR); Chaplain

Chauncey P. Taylor to General Lorenzo Thomas, July 31, 1865, in Keith P. Wilson, *Campfires of Freedom: The Camp Life of Black Soldiers during the Civil War* (Kent: Kent State University Press, 2002), 199–200.

2. Daniel Patrick Moynihan, *The Negro Family in America: The Case for National Action* (Washington, DC: U.S. Government Printing Office, 1965); John W. Blassingame, *The Slave Community: Plantation Life in the Antebellum South* (New York: Oxford University Press, 1972), 103; Herbert G. Gutman, *The Black Family in Slavery and Freedom, 1750–1925* (New York: Pantheon Books, 1976), 426, 431.

3. Leon F. Litwack, *Been in the Storm So Long: The Aftermath of Slavery* (New York: Vintage Books, 1979), 240; Eric Foner, *Reconstruction: America's Unfinished Revolution, 1863–1877* (New York: Harper & Row, 1988), 84; Peter Bardaglio, *Reconstructing the Household: Family, Sex, and the Law in the Nineteenth-Century South* (Chapel Hill: University of North Carolina Press, 1995), 132.

4. Keith P. Wilson, *Campfires of Freedom: The Camp Life of Black Soldiers during the Civil War* (Kent: Kent State University Press, 2002), 198; Elizabeth Regosin, *Freedom's Promise: Ex-slave Families and Citizenship in the Age of Emancipation* (Charlottesville: University of Virginia Press, 2002), 85; Tera Hunter, "Slave Marriages, Families Were Often Shattered by Auction Block," interview with Michael Martin on National Public Radio, February 11, 2010, http://www.npr.org/templates/story/story.php?storyId=123608207; Henry Louis Gates Jr., "John Lewis and Cory Booker," Finding your Roots, PBS (March 3, 2012). For some other examples of historians emphasizing the desire of African Americans to create legal marriages during and after the Civil War, see Leslie A. Schwalm, *A Hard Fight for We: Women's Transition from Slavery to Freedom in South Carolina* (Champaign: University of Illinois Press, 1997), 243; Amy Dru Stanley, *From Bondage to Contract: Wage Labor, Marriage, and the Market in the Age of Slave Emancipation* (New York: Cambridge University Press, 1998), 44–45; Ira Berlin, Joseph P. Reidy, and Leslie S. Rowland, eds., *Freedom's Soldiers: The Black Military Experience in the Civil War* (New York: Cambridge University Press, 1998), 154–55.

5. Brenda E. Stevenson, *Life in Black and White: Family and Community in the Slave South* (New York: Oxford University Press, 1996); Noralee Frankel, *Freedom's Women: Black Women and Families in Civil War Era Mississippi* (Bloomington: Indiana University Press, 1999), 80–81.

6. Anthony Kaye, *Joining Places: Slave Neighborhoods in the Old South* (Chapel Hill: University of North Carolina Press, 2009), 213–14.

7. Laura F. Edwards, *Gendered Strife and Confusion: The Political Culture of Reconstruction* (Champaign: University of Illinois Press, 1997), 45, 56; Nancy Bercaw, *Gendered Freedoms: Race, Rights, and the Politics of Household in the Delta, 1861–1875* (Gainesville: University Press of Florida, 2003), 106; Donald R. Shaffer, *After the Glory: The Struggles of Black Civil War Veterans* (Lawrence: University Press of Kansas, 2002), 109; Elizabeth Regosin and Donald Shaffer coedited a book in 2008 that blends their previous interpretations but is closer to Shaffer original position. For instance, "Widow's pension claims reveal the importance of marriage to slaves and ex-slaves. They also bear witness to a range of intimate relationships among them." *Voices of Emancipation: Understanding Slavery, the Civil War, and Reconstruction through the U.S. Pension Files* (New York: New York University Press, 2008), 114.

8. Edwards, *Gendered Strife and Confusion*, 47; Stevenson, *Life in Black and White*, 235; Bercaw, *Gendered Freedoms*, 102; Shaffer, *After the Glory*, 6.

9. Assistant Secretary M. W. Miller to the Commissioner of Pensions, undated, in Ann Horn, Civil War Pension File, Record Group 15, National Archives, Washington, DC (hereafter referred to as CWPF). Ann Horn had a number of different surnames during her life, so for consistency and clarity the name she filed for a pension with will be used throughout.

10. Ann Horn, Deposition, April 9, 1900, and E. J. Johnson and Rebecca Foust, General Affidavit, November 16, 1901, Ann Horn CWPF. Ann Horn estimated her age to be between sixty and seventy in 1900. The Federal Census Records for 1840 and 1850 support Horn's account of her life, even though as a slave she was not mentioned by name. The 1840 Census shows that a Banks M. Burrow lived in Carroll County, Tennessee, adjacent to Madison County, and owned sixty-eight slaves, ten of whom were females under the age of ten. The 1850 Slave Schedule shows that a Napoleon Burrow in Jefferson County, Arkansas, the location of Pine Bluff, owned thirty-seven slaves, several of which based on age and sex could have been Ann. United States of America, Bureau of the Census, *Sixth Census of the United States, 1840* (Washington, DC: National Archives, 1840), Carroll County, Tennessee; and United States of America, Bureau of the Census, *Seventh Census of the United States (Slave Schedule), 1850* (Washington, DC: National Archives, 1850), Jefferson County, Arkansas.

11. Manuel Horn, CMSR; Richard Browning, General Affidavit, November 15, 1897, and Ann Horn Deposition, September 17, 1900, Ann Horn CWPF.

12. Kaye, *Joining Places*, 213; Bercaw, *Gendered Freedoms*, 106.

13. Isaac Polk, Deposition, September 5, 1900, Thomas Gattrell, General Affidavit, April 20, 1897, Ann Horn, General Affidavit, July 20, 1901, Ann Horn CWPF.

14. Thomas Gattrell, General Affidavit, April 20, 1897, Ann Horn CWPF; Morgan Black and Clem Willis, Affidavit, May 16, 1891, Phillip Bellfield CWPF, in Regosin and Shaffer, *Voices of Emancipation*, 140. The 63 USCT shared many similarities with the 3 USCHA, having been partly raised in Memphis and even having two of its companies temporarily stationed at Fort Pickering in 1865. Phillip Bell was in Company E, while Companies B and K were sent to Fort Pickering.

15. Millie Davis, General Affidavits, August 6, 1906 and May 18, 1907, Millie Davis CWPF. Millie Davis had a number of different surnames during her life, so for consistency and clarity the name she filed for a pension with will be used throughout.

16. Millie Davis, General Affidavits, August 6, 1906 and May 18, 1907 Millie Davis CWPF; Regosin and Shaffer, *Voices of Emancipation*, 142; *State v. A. B. Rhodes*, Supreme Court of North Carolina, Raleigh 61 NC 453, 1868; Sisley Hunt, Deposition, July 11, 1908, and Russell Hines, General Affidavit October 27, 1906, Millie Davis CWPF. For more on the practice of quitting after emancipation, see Frankel, *Freedom's Women*, xii, 12, 104–9.

17. Millie Davis, Declaration of a Widow for Accrued Pension, June 7, 1906, and Deposition, May 18, 1907, Millie Davis CWPF; Owen Davis CMSR; Adell Miller, May 29, 1907, Millie Davis CWPF; Shaffer, *After the Glory*, 109.

18. Louisa Mathews, Depositions, July 12, 23, 1907, Charles Cowan, Deposition, July 15, 1907, and H. L. Elliot, Special Examiner, to V. Warner, Commissioner of Pensions, July 25, 1907, Millie Davis, CWPF.

19. Litwack, *Been in the Storm So Long*, 240; Frankel, *Freedom's Women*, 84–88.

20. Regosin and Shaffer, *Voices of Emancipation*, 137.

21. Ibid., 137.

22. Ibid., 135–45; Frankel, *Freedom's Women*, 90–91.

23. Bercaw, *Gendered Freedoms*, 110; Regosin, *Freedom's Promise*, 85; Stanley, *From Bondage to Contract*, 45; Edwards, *Gendered Strife and Confusion*, 45; Shaffer, *After the Glory*, 104. Stevenson, *Life in Black and White*, x–xi.

24. Shaffer, *After the Glory*, 230–31n44.

25. Frank Towers, "Partisans, New History, and Modernization: The Historiography of the Civil War's Causes, 1861–2011," *Journal of the Civil War Era* 1, no. 2 (2011): 252.

26. Sam Roberts, "51% of Women Are Now Living without a Spouse," New York Times, January 17, 2007; Mark Mather and Diana Lavery, "In U.S., Proportion Married at Lowest Recorded Levels," Population Reference Bureau, September 2010, http://www.prb.org/Articles/2010/usmarriagedecline.aspx; Paul Gilroy, *The Black Atlantic: Modernity and Double Consciousness* (Cambridge: Harvard University Press, 1993).

"She Is a Member of the 23rd": Lucy Nichols and the Community of the Civil War Regiment
Barbara A. Gannon

1. "The 23rd Spins Yarns," *Salem* (Indiana) *Democrat*, October 21, 1898; "Obituary Notes," *New York Times*, January 31, 1915. For the most recent and best-known interpretation of the relationship between Civil War reunions and Civil War memory at the end of the nineteenth and beginning of twentieth centuries, see David Blight, *Race and Reunion: The Civil War in American Memory* (Cambridge: Harvard University Press, 2001). Civil War memory, its uses and misuses, has been its own battleground for decades. Ironically the losers, and not the winners, successfully articulated what should be remembered about the causes, courses, and consequences of the Civil War—the so-called Lost Cause. See Gaines M. Foster, *Ghosts of the Confederacy* (New York: Oxford University Press, 1986); Charles Reagan Wilson, *Baptized in Blood* (Athens: University of Georgia, 1980); Thomas L. Connelly and Barbra L. Bellows, *God and General Longstreet* (Baton Rouge: Louisiana State University Press, 1995); and Gary W. Gallagher and Alan Nolan, eds., *The Myth of the Lost Cause and Civil War History* (Bloomington: Indiana University Press, 2000). Of particular note in this essay collection is Alan Nolan's contribution, "The Anatomy of a Myth," which includes an uncompromising assessment of the Lost Cause and its relationship to the facts of Civil War history. More recently, there has been more interest in northern Civil War memory. See John R. Neff, *Honoring the Civil War Dead: Commemoration and the Problem of Reconciliation* (Lawrence: University Press of Kansas, 2005); Robert Hunt, *The Good Men Who Won the War* (Tuscaloosa: University of Alabama Press, 2010); and Barbara A. Gannon, *The Won Cause: Black and White Comradeship in the Grand Army of the Republic* (Chapel Hill: University of North Carolina Press, 2011). For a study of women who worked in hospitals, including nurses, see Jane E. Schultz, *Women at the Front: Hospital Workers in Civil War America* (Chapel Hill: University of North Carolina Press, 2004).

2. For more on women disguising themselves as men and serving in Civil War regiments, see Elizabeth D. Leonard, *All the Daring of the Solider: Women of the Civil War Armies* (New York: Norton, 1994); and DeAnne Blanton and Lauren M. Cook, *They Fought Like Demons: Women Soldiers in the American Civil War* (Baton Rouge: Louisiana State University Press, 2002). A number of studies chronicle African American units in the Civil War. See Benjamin Quarles, *The Negro in the Civil War* (New York: Russell and Russell, 1953); Dudley Taylor Cornish, *The Sable Arm Negro Troops in the Union Army, 1861–1865* (Lawrence: University Press of Kansas, 1987); Ira Berlin et al., *The Black Military Experience*, 2nd ser., vol. 1, of *Freedom: A Documentary History of Emancipation, 1861–1867* (New York: Cambridge University Press, 1982); and *Freedom's Soldiers: The Black Military Experience in the Civil War* (New York: Cambridge University Press, 1998); Joseph Glatthaar, *Forged in Battle: The Civil War Alliance of Black Soldiers and White Officers* (New York: Meridian Books, 1991); and Noah Trudeau, *Like Men of War: Black Troops in the Civil War, 1862–1865* (New York: Little, Brown, 1998).

3. Shadrach Hooper, "A Historical Sketch of the 23rd Volunteer Infantry" (n.p., 1910), 1, available digitally at http://www.nafclibrary.org/Resources/Adults/Indiana/Service/23rd IndianaVolunteer.pdf. For more on localized recruiting, soldier motivation, and battlefield performance, see James McPherson, *For Cause and Comrades: Why Men Fought in the Civil War* (New York: Oxford University Press, 1998); and Dora L. Costa and Matthew E. Kahn, *Heroes and Cowards: The Social Face of War* (Princeton: Princeton University Press, 2008).

4. Margaret E. Wagner, Gary W. Gallagher, and Paul Finkleman, eds., *The Library of Congress Civil War Desk Reference* (New York: Simon and Schuster, 2009), 374–75. Regiments were more important to the average soldiers than any other organization; for example, brigades were composed of a number of regiments. There were some exceptions to this rule. Soldiers sometimes identified with elite brigades such as the Irish Brigade (USA) and the Stonewall Brigade (CSA); however, most Civil War soldiers were not in elite units and their service focused on their regiment. For studies of these brigades, see Phillip Thomas Tucker, *God Help the Irish: The History of the Irish Brigade* (Abilene, TX: McWhiney Foundation Press, 2007); and James I. Robertson, *The Stonewall Brigade* (Baton Rouge: Louisiana State University Press, 1978). For some of the best regimental studies, see John J. Puller, *The Twentieth Maine: The Story of Joshua Lawrence Chamberlain and His Volunteer Regiment* (Mechanicsburg, PA: Stackpole, 2008); and Scott Walker, *Hell Broke Loose in Georgia: Survival in a Civil War Regiment* (Athens: University of Georgia Press, 2007).

5. Hooper, "Historical Sketch of the 23rd Volunteer Infantry," 16; Records of the Department of Veterans Affairs, Granville Holtsclaw, Twenty-Third Indiana Infantry, *Case Files of Approved Pension Applications of Veterans Who Served in the Army and Navy Mainly in the Civil War and the War with Spain 1861–1934*, Record Group 15, National Archives Building, Washington, DC (hereafter *Civil War Pension File[s]*). All pension files cited in this essay, except for Lucy Nichols's records, document soldiers enlisted in the Twenty-Third Indiana Infantry. See also Frederick Dyer, *Compendium of the War of the Rebellion* (Dayton, OH: Morningside, 1978), 1128. Hooper's study has different figures on the casual-

ties of this unit; however, Dyer's *Compendium* is considered authoritative. For a creative use of pension records in a related historical study, see Donald Shaffer, *After the Glory: The Struggle of Black Civil War Veterans* (Lawrence: University Press of Kansas, 2004).

6. Yalobusha County Court, Mississippi, *Order of Judge, Wineford Amanda Higgs Property*, 1848. The judge's decision regarding Lucy was found by Floyd County, Indiana, residents who discovered Lucy Nichols's Civil War service as part of their study of the Underground Railroad in their county. For a summary of their findings, see Pamela R. Peters, Curtis H. Peters, and Victor C. Megenity, "Lucy Higgs Nichols: From Slave to Civil War Nurse," *Traces of Indiana and Midwestern History* 22, no. 1 (2010): 34–39. Lucy was not alone; creating and maintaining a family in slavery was difficult. For some of the best studies of family life in slavery, see Herbert G. Gutman, *The Black Family in Slavery and Freedom, 1750–1925* (New York: Vintage, 1976); Eugene D. Genovese, *Roll, Jordan, Roll: The World the Slaves Made* (New York: Vintage, 1976); and John Blassingame, *The Slave Community: Planation Life in the Antebellum South* (New York: Oxford University Press, 1979). Studies on northern soldiers and their view of emancipation has been the subject of a number of important studies; see McPherson, *For Cause and Comrades*; Chandra Manning, *What This Cruel War Is Over: Soldiers, Slavery, and the Civil War* (New York: Knopf, 2007); and Gary Gallagher, *The Union War* (Cambridge: Harvard University Press, 2011).

7. Lucy (née Higgs) Nichols, Army Nurse, *Civil War Pension File*. Jane E. Schultz documents the challenges of "regimental women" like Lucy Nichols. These women included laundresses, cooks, and nurses. Unlike Lucy, many of these women were paid. See Schultz, *Women at the Front*, 33, 34, 38–39, 40, 56–57, 59–60, 80. Magnus Brucker (1828–74) was born in Germany and studied medicine at the universities at Heidelberg and Strasburg. He fled his native land due to his involvement in the 1848 revolution. He was a Republican member of the state legislature. While the original letters he wrote during the war are in German, English translations are included in his papers. See Magnus Brucker, *Papers*, 1861–68, Indiana Historical Society, Indianapolis.

8. Nichols, *Civil War Pension File*. For a description of a regimental hospital, see John C. Thompson, *History of the Eleventh Rhode Island Volunteers in the War of the Rebellion* (Providence: Providence Press, 1881) 66; and Charles B. Johnson, *Muskets and Medicine: Or Army Life in the Sixties* (Philadelphia: F. A. Davis, 1917), 129–34.

9. Brucker, *Papers*, April–May 1862; and Hooper, "Historical Sketch of the 23rd Volunteer Infantry," 7, 10. For more on the type of medical care provided by Lucy Nichols and the other members of the regimental hospital, see Frank R. Freemon, *Gangrene and Glory: Medical Care during the American Civil War* (Champaign: University of Illinois Press, 2001).

10. William Fox, *Regimental Losses in the American Civil War* (1889; reprint, Gulf Breeze, FL: eBooksonDisk.com, 2002), 122.

11. The Twenty-Third Indiana was mustered into service on July 29, 1861, and mustered out July 23, 1865; the regiment served a few days short of four years, or just over 1,450 days. Using Dyer's *Compendium*, it appears that the Twenty-Third fought in a number of battles, including Shiloh (two days), Port Gibson (one), Raymond (one), Champions Hill (one),

assaults on Vicksburg on May 9 and 22 (two), an assault on Kennesaw (one), Atlanta (one), Jonesboro (two), and Bentonville (three)—or fourteen days of battle. The Twenty-Third also participated in a number of sieges: Corinth (thirty-one days), Vicksburg (forty-six), Atlanta (thirty-four), and Savannah (twelve)—or about 123 days, which is less than 10 percent of 1,400. See Dyer, *Compendium*, 1128.

12. Hooper, "Historical Sketch of the 23rd Volunteer Infantry," 1, 3, 6.

13. Brucker, *Papers*, March 1862; John S. McPheeters, *Correspondence and Records, 1863–1910*, March 1864, Indiana Historical Society, Indianapolis; and "The 23rd Spins Yarns." The importance of marching in soldiers' letters is illustrated by the title of a collection of Civil War letters, Wilbur Fisk's *Hard Marching Every Day: The Civil War Letters of Wilbur Fisk, 1861–1865*, ed. Ruth Rosenblatt and Emil Rosenblatt (Lawrence: University Press of Kansas, 1994).

14. Hooper, "Historical Sketch of the 23rd Volunteer Infantry," 5, 8; Decatur S. Jocelyn, *Civil War Pension File*.

15. McPheeters, *Correspondence and Records*, September–December 1863. For a description of a regimental hospital, see Johnson, *Muskets and Medicine*, 129–34.

16. Nichols, Pension *File*; W. H. H. Terrell, *Report of the Adjutant General of the State of Indiana, Volume 2, Roster of Officers, 1861–1865* (Indianapolis: W. R. Holloway State Printer, 1865), 221. For more on Sherman's March, see Joseph T. Glatthaar, *March to the Sea and Beyond: Sherman's Troops in the Savannah and Carolina Campaigns* (Baton Rouge: Louisiana State University Press, 1995); and Noah A. Trudeau, *Southern Storm: Sherman's March to the Sea* (New York: Harper Perennial, 2009).

17. H. H. Terrell, *Report of the Adjutant General of the State of Indiana, Volume 4, Roster of Enlisted Men, 1861–1865* (Indianapolis: Samuel L. Douglass, State Printer, 1866), 520, 522.

18. Hooper, 18; Nichols, *Civil War Pension File*.

19. Nichols, *Civil War Pension File*.

20. U.S. Department of the Interior, *Report of the Secretary of the Interior (Bureau of Pensions) Being Part of the Messages and Documents Communicated to the Two Houses of Congress at the Beginning of the Second Session of the Fiftieth Congress* (Washington, DC: Government Printing Office, 1888), 68–69. If you add up the reasons that soldiers received pensions, it is far greater than the number of Union soldiers who might have gotten these benefits. In a footnote, the commissioner explained this discrepancy. "Two or more disabilities exist in the same individual, as for example, a gunshot wound, hernia, and rheumatism." Most veterans in the files examined in this study had more than one illness. The Civil War pension had its critics. William H. Glasson argued in 1918 that "the most serious evils that have risen have been in connection with the [Civil War] service pension system." *Federal Military Pensions in the United States* (New York: Oxford University Press, 1918), 147.

21. Nichols, *Civil War Pension File*. Nichols's file includes a number of requests from the Pension Bureau to the War Department to explain her status. In response, they explained that she lacked official status because women could not serve in brigade or regimental hospitals.

22. Nichols, *Civil War Pension File*.

23. Nichols, Lorenzo D. Emory, Alexander S. Banks, Benjamin B. John, Jocelyn, *Civil War Pension Files*.

24. Charles H. Kepley, *Civil War Pension File*.

25. Holtsclaw, James S. Knowland, *Civil War Pension File*.

26. Nichols, *Civil War Pension File*.

Contributors

Michael J. Bennett is currently the Earhart Civil War Fellow at the University of Michigan, Clements Library. Before that he was Visiting Assistant Professor of History at High Point University (2008–11). He received his PhD from Saint Louis University. Prior to joining the faculty he was a Visiting Professor at Wake Forest University (2006–8) and Kent State University (2002–6). His research interest is the American Civil War in the areas of the relationship between war and society and the law. His book *Union Jacks: Yankee Sailors in the Civil War* (University of North Carolina Press, 2004) won numerous awards, including the Civil War Roundtable of New York City's Fletcher Pratt Literary Award for the Best Civil War Book of 2004 and the North American Society for Oceanic History's John Lyman Book Award as the Best Book in United States Naval History for 2004.

Barbara A. Gannon is an assistant professor of history at the University of Central Florida. She is the author of *"The Won Cause": Black and White Comradeship in the Grand Army of the Republic* (University of North Carolina Press, 2011), which received Honorable Mention for the 2012 Lincoln Prize. She has also published "Sites of Memory, Sites of Glory: African-American Grand Army of the Republic Posts in Pennsylvania," in *Making and Remaking Pennsylvania's Civil War* (Pennsylvania State University Press, 2001), and has presented papers at numerous conferences, including the Southern Historical Association and the Society of Military History.

Michael F. Holt is the Langbourne M. Williams Professor of American History (1974) at the University of Virginia. He is the author of seven books, including *The Rise and Fall of the American Whig Party: Jacksonian Politics and the Onset of the Civil War* (Oxford University Press, 1999), which was runner-up for the Lincoln Prize in 2000, and his most recent book is *Franklin Pierce* (Times Books, 2010). He has also coedited a book and is coauthor of one of the standard textbooks of the Civil War era, *The Civil War and Reconstruction*, 3rd edition, revised (Norton, 2001).

Harold Holzer is senior vice president of The Metropolitan Museum of Art and chairman of the Abraham Lincoln Bicentennial Foundation. He is the author, coauthor, or editor of forty-two books on Lincoln and the Civil War era.

Matthew Isham is managing director of the George and Ann Richards Civil War Era Center at the Pennsylvania State University and managing editor of the journal *Civil War History*. His dissertation, completed in 2010, is titled "'Breaking Over the Boundary': The Role of Party Newspapers in Democratic Factionalism in the Antebellum North, 1845–1852."

Christian B. Keller is Professor of History at the United States Army War College in Carlisle, Pennsylvania. Along with many scholarly articles focusing on the ethnic experience in the Civil War, he is author of *Chancellorsville and the Germans: Nativism, Ethnicity, and Civil War Memory* (Fordham, 2007) and coauthor of *Damn Dutch: Pennsylvania Germans at Gettysburg* (Stackpole, 2004). He is currently editing and translating the memoirs of a German American soldier in the 41st New York.

Timothy J. Orr is an assistant professor of history at Old Dominion University. His dissertation examined urban military mobilization in the North during the Civil War. He is the author of two essays, "'A Viler Enemy in Our Rear': Pennsylvania Soldiers Confront the North's Antiwar Movement," in *The View from the Ground: The Experiences of Civil War Soldiers* (University Press of Kentucky, 2006), and "'On Such Slender Threads Does the Fate of Nations Depend': The 2nd U.S. Sharpshooters at the Battle of Gettysburg," in *"The Most Shocking Battle I Ever Witnessed": The Second Day at Gettysburg* (Gettysburg National Military Park, 2008). He has edited *"Last to Leave the Field": The Life and Letters of First Sergeant Ambrose Henry Hayward, Company D, 28th Pennsylvania Volunteer Infantry* (University of Tennessee Press, 2011).

Robert M. Sandow is an associate professor of history at Lock Haven University of Pennsylvania. He is the author of *Deserter Country: Civil War Opposition in the Pennsylvania Appalachians* (Fordham University Press, 2009) and has presented numerous articles and conference papers. His recent work addresses issues of political dissent and rural protest on the northern home front.

Andrew L. Slap is an associate professor of history at East Tennessee State University. He is the author of *The Doom of Reconstruction: The Liberal Republicans in the Civil War Era* (Fordham University Press, 2006) and editor of *Reconstructing Appalachia: The Civil War's Aftermath* (University Press of Kentucky, 2010). His current project on African American communities around Memphis during the Civil War era is under contract with Cambridge University Press.

Michael Thomas Smith is an assistant professor of history at McNeese State University. He is the coeditor of *Letters from a North Carolina Unionist: John A. Hedrick to Benjamin S. Hedrick, 1862–1865* (North Carolina Division of Archives and History, 2001), and the author of *A Traitor and a Scoundrel: Benjamin Hedrick and the Cost of Dissent* (University of Delaware Press, 2003) and *The Enemy Within: Fears of Corruption in the Civil War North* (University of Virginia Press, 2011). His articles have appeared in *American Nineteenth Century History*, the *New England Quarterly*, and other journals.

Matthew Warshauer is a professor of history at Central Connecticut State University. He is the author of numerous books, including *Connecticut in the American Civil War: Slavery, Sacrifice, and Survival* (Wesleyan University Press, 2011) and *Andrew Jackson and the Politics of Martial Law: Nationalism, Civil Liberties, and Partisanship* (University of Tennessee Press, 2006). He has also published numerous articles and essays, and edits the journal *Connecticut History*.

Jonathan W. White is an assistant professor of American Studies at Christopher Newport University, in Newport News, Virginia. He is the author of *Abraham Lincoln and Treason in the Civil War: The Trials of John Merryman* (Louisiana State University Press, 2011), and has another book, titled *"To Aid Their Rebel Friends': Politics and Treason in the Civil War North,"* under contract with LSU Press. White has published *A Philadelphia Perspective: The Civil War Diary of Sidney George Fisher* (Fordham University Press, 2007) and articles in *Civil War History, American Nineteenth Century History, Ohio Valley History*, and the *Pennsylvania Magazine of History and Biography*.

Karen Fisher Younger is the former managing director of the George and Ann Richards Civil War Era Center at the Pennsylvania State University and managing editor of the journal *Civil War History*. She is coeditor of *Lincoln's Proclamation: Emancipation Reconsidered* (University of North Carolina Press, 2009).

Index

THE NORTH'S CIVIL WAR

Paul A. Cimbala, series editor

Anita Palladino, ed., *Diary of a Yankee Engineer: The Civil War Story of John H. Westervelt, Engineer, 1st New York Volunteer Engineer Corps.*

Herman Belz, *Abraham Lincoln, Constitutionalism, and Equal Rights in the Civil War Era.*

Earl J. Hess, *Liberty, Virtue, and Progress: Northerners and Their War for the Union.* Second revised edition, with a new introduction by the author.

William L. Burton, *Melting Pot Soldiers: The Union's Ethnic Regiments.*

Hans L. Trefousse, *Carl Schurz: A Biography.*

Stephen W. Sears, ed., *Mr. Dunn Browne's Experiences in the Army: The Civil War Letters of Samuel W. Fiske.*

Jean H. Baker, *Affairs of Party: The Political Culture of Northern Democrats in the Mid–Nineteenth Century.*

Frank L. Klement, *The Limits of Dissent: Clement L. Vallandigham and the Civil War.* With a new introduction by Steven K. Rogstad.

Lawrence N. Powell, *New Masters: Northern Planters during the Civil War and Reconstruction.*

John A. Carpenter, *Sword and Olive Branch: Oliver Otis Howard.*

Thomas F. Schwartz, ed., *"For a Vast Future Also": Essays from the* Journal of the Abraham Lincoln Association.

Mark De Wolfe Howe, ed., *Touched with Fire: Civil War Letters and Diary of Oliver Wendell Holmes, Jr.* With a new introduction by David Burton.

Harold Adams Small, ed., *The Road to Richmond: The Civil War Letters of Major Abner R. Small of the 16th Maine Volunteers.* With a new introduction by Earl J. Hess.

Eric A. Campbell, ed., *"A Grand Terrible Dramma": From Gettysburg to Petersburg: The Civil War Letters of Charles Wellington Reed.* Illustrated by Reed's Civil War sketches.

Herbert Mitgang, ed., *Abraham Lincoln: A Press Portrait.*

Harold Holzer, ed., *Prang's Civil War Pictures: The Complete Battle Chromos of Louis Prang.*

Harold Holzer, ed., *State of the Union: New York and the Civil War.*

Paul A. Cimbala and Randall M. Miller, eds., *Union Soldiers and the Northern Home Front: Wartime Experiences, Postwar Adjustments.*

Mark A. Snell, *From First to Last: The Life of Major General William B. Franklin.*

Paul A. Cimbala and Randall M. Miller, eds., *An Uncommon Time: The Civil War and the Northern Home Front.*

John Y. Simon and Harold Holzer, eds., *The Lincoln Forum: Rediscovering Abraham Lincoln.*

Thomas F. Curran, *Soldiers of Peace: Civil War Pacifism and the Postwar Radical Peace Movement.*

Kyle S. Sinisi, *Sacred Debts: State Civil War Claims and American Federalism, 1861–1880.*

Russell L. Johnson, *Warriors into Workers: The Civil War and the Formation of Urban-Industrial Society in a Northern City.*

Peter J. Parish, *The North and the Nation in the Era of the Civil War.* Edited by Adam L. P. Smith and Susan-Mary Grant.

Patricia Richard, *Busy Hands: Images of the Family in the Northern Civil War Effort.*

Michael S. Green, *Freedom, Union, and Power: The Mind of the Republican Party During the Civil War.*

Christian G. Samito, ed., *Fear Was Not In Him: The Civil War Letters of Major General Francis S. Barlow, U.S.A.*

John S. Collier and Bonnie B. Collier, eds., *Yours for the Union: The Civil War Letters of John W. Chase, First Massachusetts Light Artillery.*

Grace Palladino, *Another Civil War: Labor, Capital, and the State in the Anthracite Regions of Pennsylvania, 1840–1868.*

Christian B. Keller, *Chancellorsville and the Germans: Nativism, Ethnicity, and Civil War Memory.*

Robert M. Sandow, *Deserter Country: Civil War Opposition in the Pennsylvania Appalachians.*

Craig L. Symonds, ed., *Union Combined Operations in the Civil War.*

Harold Holzer, Craig L. Symonds, and Frank L. Williams, eds., *The Lincoln Assassination: Crime and Punishment, Myth and Memory.* A Lincoln Forum Book.

Earl F. Mulderink III, *New Bedford's Civil War.*

George Washington Williams, *A History of the Negro Troops in the War of the Rebellion, 1861–1865.* Introduction by John David Smith.

Randall M. Miller, ed., *Lincoln and Leadership: Military, Political, and Religious Decision Making.*

David G. Smith, *On the Edge of Freedom: The Fugitive Slave Issue in South Central Pennsylvania, 1820–1870.*

Andrew L. Slap and Michael Thomas Smith, eds., *This Distracted and Anarchical People: New Answers for Old Questions about the Civil War–Era North.*